Lecture Notes in Computer Science

T0237854

Commenced Publication in 1973
Founding and Former Series Editors:
Gerhard Goos, Juris Hartmanis, and Jan van Leeuwen

Editorial Board

Zhigeng Pan   Adrian David Cheok
Wolfgang Müller   Abdennour El Rhalibi (Eds.)

Transactions on Edutainment II

 Springer

Editors-in-Chief

Zhigeng Pan
Zhejiang University, State Key Lab of CAD&CG
Hangzhou,China,
E-mail: zhigengpan@gmail.com

Adrian David Cheok
National University of Singapore, Mixed Reality Lab
Singapore
E-mail: adriancheok@mixedrealitylab.org

Wolfgang Müller
University of Education, Media Education and Visualization Group
Weingarten, Germany
E-mail: mueller@md-phw.de

Guest Editor

Abdennour El Rhalibi
Liverpool John Moores University
School of Computing
Liverpool, UK

Library of Congress Control Number: 2008929516

CR Subject Classification (1998): K.3.1, K.3.2, H.5.1, H.5.2, I.3.7, I.2.6

ISSN	0302-9743 (Lecture Notes in Computer Science)
ISSN	1867-7207 (Transactions on Edutainment)
ISBN-10	3-642-03269-9 Springer Berlin Heidelberg New York
ISBN-13	978-3-642-03269-1 Springer Berlin Heidelberg New York

springer.com

© Springer-Verlag Berlin Heidelberg 2009
Printed in Germany

Typesetting: Camera-ready by author, data conversion by Scientific Publishing Services, Chennai, India
Printed on acid-free paper   SPIN: 12722549   06/3180   5 4 3 2 1 0

Preface

With great pleasure we present the second volume of the new journal *Transactions on Edutainment*. This journal, part of the Springer series *Lecture Notes in Computer Science*, is devoted to research and development in the field of edutainment. Edutainment, also known as educational entertainment or entertainment-education, denotes all forms of entertainment designed to educate as well as to provide fun. This approach is motivated by the increasing demands on individuals for life-long learning and the need to integrate effective learning opportunities throughout life. As such, edutainment has attracted increasing interest in the last few years.

The first five articles of this issue represent a selection of outstanding contributions from GDTW 2008, the 6th International Conference in Game Design and Technology held in the UK, in November 2008. The main aims of the workshop are: (1) To provide a forum to discuss state-of-the-art games design and current and future games technology with the specialists. (2) To enable academics and researchers in computer game technology and computer entertainment to present their work during the research sessions, and to seek opportunities for collaboration with industry and for academic research partners. (3) To facilitate relationships and collaboration between academics promoting computer games technology courses, the UK games industry and supporting organizations. These five papers cover mainly the topic of edutainment platforms or methodology: "Coordinating Heterogeneous Game-Based Learning Approaches in Online Learning Environments," "Networking Middleware and Online-Deployment Mechanisms for Java-Based Games," "A Testbed for P2P Gaming Using Time Warp, How to Steer Characters in Group Games," and "Time-Based Personalized Mobile Game Downloading."

The next six articles represent a selection of outstanding contributions from Cyberworlds 2008 held in Hangzhou, China, in September 2008. Some topics of this conference are related to those of this new journal. They include mobile games, E-learning, Web-based learning and edutainment, intelligent agents in cyberworlds, cyber fairs and digital museums, game engines, game algorithms, and multi-user Web games, VR/AR/MR for industrial design, digital heritage, shared virtual worlds, collaborative work using cyberworlds, human animation in cyberworlds, virtual reality, augmented reality, and mixed reality. These six papers cover topics on virtual avatars, game designing, educational systems etc. The paper titles are: "Adopting Virtual Characters in Virtual Systems from the Perspective of Communication Studies," "Teaching Me Softly: Experiences and Reflections on Informal Educational Game Design," Visual/Haptic-Based Biomolecular Docking and Its Application in E-Learning," "Exploring Movie Recommendation Systems Using Cultural Metadata," "Virtual and Augmented

Reality Tools for Teleportation: Improving Distant Immersion and Perception," and "HES-SPATO: An Online History Educational System Based on SCORM."

The following nine papers are regular papers. In "Proxy 2: An Audio Game Accessible to Visually Impaired People Playable Without Neither Visual nor Verbal Instructions," Thomas Gaudy et al. made a game, all the players managed to progress in the game but not all understood all the principles of the game. For this kind of game, they assume that players do not have to understand the game during the first contact but they have to be encouraged to continue interaction. "Design Tools for Online Educational Games: Concept and Application" is an invited paper. Louise Sauvhas developed a series of generic educational game design shells to enable teachers, trainers and community service workers to create educational games that provide effective learning conditions and are adapted to their distance learning needs. In "Earth and Planetary System Science Game Engine," Gloria J. Brown-Simmons et al. presented a game engine for using unconventional interaction and visualization techniques to experience geophysical environments. Players are provided with dynamic visualization "assets," which enable them to discover, interrogate and correlate scientific data in a game space. The spirit of exploration is to give players the impetus to truly understand how complex the Earth and planetary systems work and their intrinsic beauty, the impact of humans, and a sense of responsibility to serve as caretakers of those systems. In "An XML Tree–Based Leveled Filtering Method and Its Application," Jiming Chen et al. present a new XML tree-based leveled filtering method - LevelFilter. In "Fostering Students' Participation in Face-to-Face Interactions and Deepening Their Understanding by Integrating Personal and Shared Spaces," Etsuji Yamaguchi et al. introduced *CarettaKids* into the social context of a classroom environment to evaluate whether integration of personal and shared spaces can help promote students' participation in synchronous/co-located interactions in the classroom and deepen their understanding of subject matter.

In "Make Learning Fun with Programming Contests," Gines Garcia-Mateos et al. propose a new methodology based on two key ideas: (a) replacing the final exam with a series of activities in a continuous evaluation context; and (b) making those activities more appealing to the students. In "KEI-Time Traveler: A Virtual Time Machine with Mobile Phones for Learning Local History," Hiroyuki Tarumi et al. present the KEI-Time Traveler, a kind of "virtual time machine" that requires only commercially available mobile phones with no hardware attachment. In "A 3D Campus on the Internet—A Networked Mixed Reality Environment," Jiung-yao Huang et al. present a study of networking the mobile augmented reality system with the conventional networked virtual environment for implementing a virtual campus. In the final paper "Photo Realistic 3D Cartoon Face Modeling Based on Active Shape Model," the authors present a novel framework to automatically build 3D cartoon face models from a single frontal face image.

The papers in this issue present a large number of application examples of edutainment, which gives more evidence on the high potential and impact of edutainment approaches. We would like to express our thanks to all those people who contributed to this issue. They are the authors of all the papers of this issue, the reviewers for those regular papers, and the IPC of the two related conferences (GDTW 2008, and Cyberworlds 2008) for recommending high-quality articles for this new journal. Special thanks go to Yi Li, Ruwei Yun and Qiaoyun Chen from the Editorial Office of this journal in Nanjing Normal University; they put a lot of effort in contacting authors, managing the reviewing process, checking the format of all papers and collecting all the material.

April 2009

Adrian David Cheok
Zhigeng Pan
Abdennour El Rhalibi

LNCS Transactions on Edutainment

This journal subline aims to provide a highly visible dissemination channel for remarkable work that in one way or another addresses research and development on issues related to this field. It targets to serve as a forum for stimulating and disseminating innovative research ideas, theories, emerging technologies, empirical investigations, state-of-the-art methods, and tools in all the different genres of edutainment, such as game-based learning and serious games, interactive storytelling, virtual learning environments, VR-based education, and related fields. It will cover aspects of educational and game theories, human–computer interaction, computer graphics, artificial intelligence, and systems design.

Editorial Board

Abdennour El Rhalibi	JMU, UK
Daniel Thalmann	EPFL, Switzerland
Kok-Wai Wong	Murdoch University, Australia
Gangshan Wu	Nanjing University, China
Hyun Seung Yang	KAIST, Korea
Xiaopeng Zhang	IA-CAS, China

Editorial Assistants

| Ru-wei Yun | Nanjing Normal University, China |
| Qiao-yun Chen | Nanjing Normal University, China |

Editorial Office

Edu-Game Research Center, School of Education Science
Nanjing Normal University, Ninghai Road 122, Nanjing 210097, China
E-mail: edutainment@njnu.edu.cn;njnu.edutainment@gmail.com
Tel/Fax: 86-25-83598921

Table of Contents

Papers from GDTW 2008

Papers from Cyberworlds 2008

Regular Papers

Coordinating Heterogeneous Game-Based Learning Approaches in Online Learning Environments

Javier Torrente, Pablo Lavín Mera, Pablo Moreno-Ger,
and Baltasar Fernández-Manjón

<e-UCM> Research Group
Dpt. Software Engineering and Artificial Intelligence - Universidad Complutense de Madrid
C/ Profesor José García Santesmases sn. 28040 Madrid, Spain
(+34) 913947599
{jtorrente,plavin}@e-ucm.es, {pablom,balta}@fdi.ucm.es

Abstract. Game-based learning is quickly becoming a popular trend in Technology-Enhanced Learning. However, the field is very broad with many different initiatives being classified as game-based learning. On the other hand, instructors are demanding effective ways to track the interaction of the students with the games and to assess the learning process. The diversity is a major issue in this regard, requiring instructors to understand each game and to evaluate different kinds of games in different ways. In this work we present a unified mechanism to gather tracking and assessment information from different and varied games. All the information is stored in an online learning environment, where the instructor can consult it. The keystone of the approach is a tracking and assessment API that can be implemented by different games on the client-side and by diverse online learning environments on the server-side. This approach is illustrated with the <e-Adventure> family of educational platforms, which support this interoperable API.

Keywords: Game-based learning; adventure games; authoring tools; learning management systems; in-game assessment; adaptation; mobile learning.

1 Introduction

The notion of using videogames for education, although not new, is gaining momentum and becoming an established trend in the field of Technology-Enhanced Learning [3, 22, 36]. Even though a complete discussion of the educational benefits of game-based learning would be beyond the scope of this work, it is to be noted that the reasons behind this approach have evolved and matured, abandoning the initial position in which videogames were used in education just because kids enjoy them. Games have become an established entertainment industry, engaging people of all kinds of age, gender, race or social status [10], which makes them a good way to enhance the fun factor of the learning experiences, augmenting in this manner the motivation of all kind of learners. Besides, videogames (even entertainment-driven videogames) are built on principles related to constructivist learning [11], setting the player into an active and exploratory role instead of the passive "sit-and-listen" method. Additionally, games promote situated-learning, allow the players to explore the rules of the

Z. Pan et al. (Eds.): Transactions on Edutainment II, LNCS 5660, pp. 1–18, 2009.

game world by trial and error (with a very short and effective feedback cycle [18]) and, if set in an appropriate domain, they can be an effective tool to understand determined fields of knowledge [12, 37].

However, even if the academic community is beginning to accept the educational benefits of this paradigm [21, 36], not every game has educational value and there are a number of instructional aspects that must be taken into account when designing game-based learning experiences. One of the most important aspects is how to make sure that the students are actually learning while interacting with the game [20]. It is important to track the activity of the students, making sure that they are learning the right lessons, preventing them from making wrong assumptions, and promoting reflection about the contents and mechanics of the game.

A basic approach would be to organize play sessions in which the instructor is present, watching and guiding the students. However, this method is not scalable in traditional schooling, and mostly impossible in online learning environments. A more sophisticated alternative for these environments, as proposed in [24] would be to take advantage of the closed interaction between student and game to track the activity of the student and send the information to an online Learning Management System (LMS) where the instructor can check the tracking information gathered.

But the field of game-based learning is very wide [33] and still very young and mutable, just as the videogame industry itself. First, many approaches can be labelled as game-based learning [17]. From simple *edutainment* games for young children that sugar-coat educational content with popular cartoon characters, to high-end 3D massively multiplayer educational gaming for corporate environments, it becomes hard to define and measure the characteristics of the field.

Additionally, different situations may require different types of games. Firstly, not all the genres and types of games are adequate to learn in all the domains of study. Moreover, even in a single domain, diverse target audiences or educational contexts may also demand different types of games, even to the point of some cases requiring a non-game-based alternative [34]. Some students/domains may favour simpler 2D games which are simpler to use and have less technical requirements for their execution. Some other cases may require more advanced 3D games, either to increase the immersive factor or to grasp the attention of students with gaming habits (who are probably used to state-of-the-art commercial games). In some situations it may even be possible to explore the possibilities of mobile gaming for Just-In-Time learning situations or to really achieve the learning anywhere and anytime motto of traditional e-learning approaches [14].

Thus, in a mainly game-based online learning environment, we may find that a unique type of videogame could be insufficient. This would lead to complex heterogeneous game-based learning systems with diverse (game-based and/or traditional) learning materials in which students choose (or are assigned) the approach that is more appropriate according to their profile.

This diversity represents a challenge when it comes to tracking the activity of the students and controlling whether they are learning the appropriate concepts (i.e. the learning goals are being successfully accomplished). With different game-based learning approaches being put into practice at the same time on the same environment, there is a need of an entity able to coordinate all of them and register the results of the games for assessment purposes without involving an extra burden for the instructor.

In this work we show our approach for the management of this complex scenario. This approach is exemplified through the <e-Adventure> family of educational game platforms, which put this principle into practice. It is a set of educational game platforms supporting the production of multiple types of games for diverse learning scenarios, including 2D and 3D adventure games for either desktop or mobile devices (Pocket PCs, PDAs, mobile phones, etc.). All these platforms implement a common tracking and assessment API that gathers information from the interaction with the learner and connects them to an online Learning Management System (LMS). This common gateway allows the integration of different heterogeneous games in the same learning environment, which is coordinated and controlled by a "central entity" (the LMS) that can be managed by the instructor. Thanks to this structure the scheme is not limited to games of the <e-Adventure> family, as any game implementing the Assessment API could interoperate with the LMS.

Thus, the document is structured as follows: in section 2 the diverse field of game-based learning is analyzed in terms of the possible approaches and situations covered in the field. Then, in section 3 some issues regarding the integration of game-based learning in on-line environments are discussed. The <e-Adventure> family with a description of the common tracking and assessment API is presented in section 4. In section 5, a case of application is given, in which a course with four different learning approaches (game-based and web-based) ruled by a LMS was developed. Finally, in section 6, we discuss some conclusions and outline future lines of work.

2 The Diversity of Game-Based Learning

As previously mentioned, Game-Based Learning is a broad term that would include any initiative in which any kind of computer or videogame is part of a learning process. This section provides an informal classification of the initiatives found in academic discussions in terms of their complexity, target audience and situations of applicability in order to give a general scope of the field.

2.1 Edutainment

In spite of its etymology (combining the words education and entertainment), the term *edutainment* is often used in the literature to describe those products in which play, fun and game design take a secondary role [32]. These products are often interactive multimedia presentations of the regular school content, targeting young children and using popular cartoon characters as a motivating aspect.

The *edutainment* market has been (and still is) very profitable, with hundreds of titles published yearly. However, its peak was mostly in the 90s, along with the popularization of multimedia computers, and was motivated mainly by the engagement of parents and tutors who thought these approaches could help their children to improve their school results. However, many of these products had a relatively low quality as they do not get a proper balance between fun and learning value (in many cases, the outcome has the learning value of a bad learning experience and the fun factor of a bad game), loading the term *edutainment* with a negative value [22].

2.2   2D Educational Games: Low Costs and Low Technical Requirements

One of the key challenges preventing the application of game-based learning approaches is their cost. Michael & Chen, during a session on *serious games* in the 2005 Game Developers Conference ran a survey to estimate the average development cost of a serious games project [22]. The result was that more than 52% of the projects had a cost above $100.000. Similarly, [3] estimates the development cost for a next-generation simulation between 15 and 30 persons-year.

These numbers are far beyond the budget of most educational projects. For this reason, many educational game proponents advocate for simpler games that can be developed at a more reasonable cost [20]. In this case, game authoring platforms such as the *Game Maker¹*, or genre-focused tools such as *Adventure Maker²* and *Adventure Studio³* are often mentioned in the literature [1] as an effective method to reduce the development costs of the games.

These games also have other advantages. First, their technical requirements are far lower than those of modern commercial games. This facilitates the distribution of game-based contents to broader audiences without demanding a constantly updated (and expensive) computer. Additionally, their simpler interfaces may be more comfortable for mature students who are not always used to the more dynamic and complex commercial games.

Indeed, in the last few years it has become obvious that simpler games appeal to broader audiences. The boom of the Internet-based casual gaming market, or the huge success harvested by Nintendo in both the DS™ (platform in which learning products such as *Brain Age*™ or *English Training*™ are at the top of the best-selling games) and the Wii™ consoles should be enough proof of that.

However, these games always run a risk of being perceived by certain student populations as dated and excessively simplified, loosing the motivation and immersion characteristics of game-based learning [28].

2.3   3D and Multiplayer Games: Catering for Discerning Students

The commercial game industry is in a process of constant and extremely fast technological innovation, always trying to capture the attention of the players with more impressive graphics, physics and other aspects that enhance the realism. This adds a great pressure to the educational gaming field. Will these hard-core gamer populations accept simpler educational games as real games?

Of course, modern technology comes at a cost, and this requires special considerations: Is the target audience big enough so as to justify the investment? In some cases, the best approach might be to seek relatively modern 3D games, but one or two generations behind the current state-of-the-art and with the support of specialized easy-to-use authoring tools such as *The 3D Game Maker*™⁴ or the *Homura IDE* to keep the development costs at reasonable levels [7].

---

¹ http://www.yoyogames.com/gamemaker
² http://www.adventuremaker.com/
³ http://www.adventuregamestudio.co.uk/
⁴ http://t3dgm.thegamecreators.com/

However, the perception of avid gamers is not the only reason why some educational games must innovate technologically. Some domains may require a higher level of immersion and/or realism than the offered by 2D games, making 3D games a better alternative. In this line, when realism is an important factor in the learning process, state-of-the-art graphics may also be required.

Other modern aspects, such as multiplayer (or massively multiplayer) features may also be required in determined circumstances. This is the case, for example, in the ongoing efforts to train emergency services that employ realistic 3D multiplayer environments to rehearse emergency planning including interaction among the players [16]. In such scenarios, the stakes are sufficiently high so as to justify the increased development cost.

2.4 Mobile Games: Learning Anytime and Anywhere

Now the number of mobile devices (PDAs, cell phones, portable game consoles, pocket PCs, etc) available in the market is increasing exponentially with a special success among teenagers. The use of mobile devices opens a wide range of possibilities, reaching even the educational field, in what has been called m-Learning [19]. The main characteristic of m-Learning is the mobility factor which makes possible the improvement of the learning experience in different ways. As the simplest approach mobile devices can be used as reference tools, allowing the user to interact in the real world with the elements he or she is learning about, improving in this way the "in field" work (e.g. think about a botanic course where students could access the web-based documentation of the plants while they see them during a visit to a botanical garden or a natural place). Some other studies show the advantages of using this kind of devices in disfavoured locations or wherever computers can not be accessed [14].

One of the main possibilities offered by the inclusion of mobile devices in educative experiences is the so called Just-in-Time learning. This is the possibility of accessing the knowledge at the moment and the place where it is necessary. This characteristic, for example, might allow a professional to learn how to use a lorry without the chance of causing any damage with a wrong action. Arguing in the same line m-Learning can be useful for students which wanted to improve their skills when they are travelling, waiting for someone, or just in their spare time (this can be particularly relevant when the learning content is game-based).

Moreover, modern mobile phones and PDAs usually include extra features typical of other kind of devices, such as GPS receptors or Bluetooth connections. The use of these features offers new possibilities for educational experiences. Among these, the possibility of developing location-based applications deserves to be highlighted. In these systems the movement or the position of the user is another input for the system, improving in this way the user's feeling of immersion [25, 31]. Besides, some other devices (which use is very extended in some cases) such as digital cameras have yielded a number of initiatives for the development of mobile augmented reality systems (also known as Mobile AR) [8]. These systems merge the physical and the virtual worlds, enhancing the environment which surrounds the user with computer-made virtual elements.

In spite of the advantages offered by m-Learning, this approach on its own would be insufficient in some situations and should be complemented with other approaches.

For example, students could get tired rapidly playing long videogames on a mobile device. A desktop version of the game would be desirable in order to alternate playing with the computer and the mobile device. Besides m-Learning educational experiences must be designed specifically with the particularities of these devices in mind, which affect both the contents and the interface. This is a complex but relevant process in order to reduce the negative effects due to the reduced display and the computational limitations so the advantages offered by these systems are not dimmed [6, 27].

3 Game-Based Learning and E-Learning

Another key issue in game-based learning is how to distribute the content to the students. In this sense, a possible approach is to use online learning platforms for this distribution [34], allowing the students to play the games at home (or, in the case of the mobile versions, on the move) and at their own pace.

E-learning applications have evolved from the passive content repositories in the 90's into comprehensive web-applications that manage all aspects of the learning experience. The new Learning Management Systems (LMS) offer communication mechanisms, provide student tracking and evaluation tools for the instructors and keep a profile with the progress of each individual student. Additionally, they are no longer reduced to distance education, with many educational institutions (including almost all the universities) deploying these systems as an extra support for their traditional teaching models.

Additionally, there is an important line of research in adaptive online learning environments that tries to adapt or select the content that is more appropriate for a particular student (taking into account the student's profile) [5, 15, 26]

This approach would be especially suited for dealing with heterogeneous game-based learning approaches. The same system can host different courses with different types of educational games. Indeed, even the same course could include several alternative types of games for different types of students or contexts. Moreover, the same LMS can also host the contents in traditional (web-based) formats for those students that do not like educational games and prefer to follow a more traditional approach [34].

Having alternative web-based content is important not only for those students that do not like games. In some cases, due to time or environment constraints, playing a game may not be an appropriate learning activity. More importantly, games are probably one of the media forms posing more accessibility challenges [13]. On the other hand, web-based content has been the subject of accessibility studies for many years. Therefore, in game-based learning, a web version of the content can serve as a more accessible alternative for people with special needs or functional diversity.

We can thus find complex heterogeneous learning systems in which game-based and traditional approaches coexist. The adaptation layer decides which is the more adequate depending on the profile of the student, the learning context, the situation, etc.

But simply delivering all the games through the LMS does not solve the main problem of how to integrate and coordinate all the alternative learning paths and how to verify that the learning goals are being accomplished in each case. This integration is a key problem to be addressed in a manner that at the same time the system scalability and interoperability issues are also guaranteed.

4 The <e-Adventure> Family

The <e-Adventure> family is a set of platforms devised for the production and execution of educational videogames. Those platforms are specifically focused on the low cost production of games of the adventure genre (games like those in the Monkey Island™ series), due to the good educational traits of this kind of games, which have been broadly identified and analyzed in the literature [4, 37].

The objective is to provide diverse solutions to cover the needs and requirements of the widest possible range of students and situations. Therefore, the family is compounded of 3 platforms, which are described in the next three subsections: the <e-Adventure> platform, devoted for the creation of common point-and-click adventure games using 2D world representations (section 4.1); the <e-Adventure3D> platform, which follows the same idea but focused on 3D worlds (section 4.2); and finally a mobile version of <e-Adventure> specially devised for mobile learning (section 4.3).

However, what makes this family of products especially relevant to cover the issues previously highlighted, is that they all implement a common in-game Tracking and Assessment API which connects all of the platforms to a centralized Learning Management System where the instructors can consult the gathered data (section 4.4).

4.1 The <e-Adventure> Platform

The original <e-Adventure> platform is compounded by two applications: a game editor and a game engine. The game editor is instructor-oriented so a typical instructor with neither programming background nor game-making skills can produce their own educational point-and-click adventure games [35].

The low development costs of these games, along with the narrative-centric nature of the adventure genre make the <e-Adventure> platform adequate for a wide range of contexts and situations (e.g. procedural simulation). For instance, <e-Adventure> is adequate for game-like training simulations. Firstly, work environments (such as labs) can be represented in <e-Adventure> with little effort by taking photos of the real location (Figure 1), which helps students to get used to the machines and tools they will find there. Secondly, the activity of the students can be tracked while they play thanks to the assessment engine, checking in this manner if the stages of the simulation are completed correctly and in the right order (especially useful when the simulation is about a complex procedure with many stages to be completed in a certain order).

Actually the effectiveness of the <e-Adventure> games has been proved in several applications, among which we can highlight some medical procedure simulations [23].

Moreover, it is possible to take advantage of the importance that the narration (i.e. the storyboard) has in these games for the teaching of long pieces of theory or facts sequences through a good story (as the case of study in section 5 depicts).

Fig. 1. Screenshot of the edition of a medical procedure game-based simulation with the <e-Adventure> game editor

4.2   The <e-Adventure3D> Platform

In spite of the promising results obtained with <e-Adventure>, we cannot ignore that there is a public that may find the genre of point-and-click adventure games as dated and uninteresting. As it is discussed in section 2.3, some students with gaming habits find these games too "old-fashioned" and therefore not attractive. For that reason we developed a platform for the creation of more modern-looking 3D adventure games following the same principles as in the original <e-Adventure> platform (i.e. instructor-oriented, education-specific traits, etc.). It is true that the development cost of these games is higher due in part to the high cost of the 3D resources, but it is a good approach to capture the interest and attention of a public which is expecting from a game more than a simple 2D world. Besides, the interaction with a 3D world seems to be more appropriate for simulations requiring an extra dose of realism and precision.

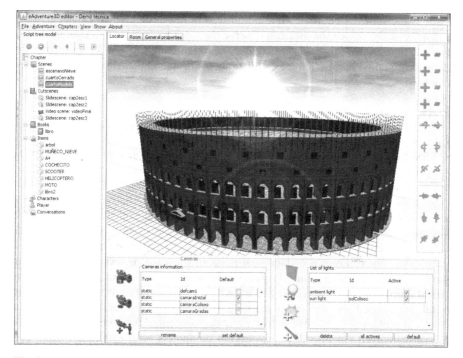

Fig. 2. Screenshot of the edition of a 3d adventure game for the teaching the history of Rome

As seen in Figure 2, the creation of a 3D adventure game with the <e-Adventure3D> editor is similar to the creation of a 2D point-and-click adventure game, once the artistic resources are provided.

4.3   The <m-Adventure> Platform

Due to the increasing success of the mobile gaming platforms and the possibilities offered by the new mobile devices, we also decided to extend <e-Adventure> platform with a new mobile engine, called <m-Adventure>.

The main idea is that the <m-Adventure> engine can use the same videogames generated by the original <e-Adventure> game editor. However, before the games are executed on the mobile device, some necessary modifications need to be carried out to get it running under the restriction of the device (e.g. resizing of the images, removing of any resources not allowed by the device, etc). Despite the special needs of these devices, the use of this platform allows the users to access the content at the moment they desire.

As the videogames developed by the <e-Adventure> editor do not require a critical response speed, those are especially suitable for mobile devices with low performance speed and limited resources (e.g. mobile phones). On the other hand, the <e-Adventure> platform has been proved to be very useful for the learning of complex procedures, as it has been previously described. Bringing this platform to mobile devices gives users the possibility of accessing the game content during these procedures and to practice certain actions in a safe system (e.g. lab sessions). In such situations it can be a great reviewing tool instead of consulting a heavy manual, as on the display of the device the user can observe the same tools or even locations than in the real action. In this sense we can say that the <m-Adventure> platform provides the user with a quality Just-In-Time Learning, accessing the contents exactly when they are needed.

4.4 The Tracking and Assessment API

As it has been described in the previous three subsections, the <e-Adventure> family provides diverse solutions for game-based learning. Instructors will choose the more appropriate option according to the needs and preferences of the students and the learning context.

Using all these tools, it is possible to create diverse game-based materials for the same course, providing a scenario with various "learning paths". However, those paths are disconnected, which brings some disadvantages to the instructors. It is not only the extra effort required to create the content of the different paths, but also how to coordinate them. From a pedagogical point of view instructors must check that, regardless of the learning path followed by the student, the learning goals are being attained successfully, a task which gets even harder when you have to pay attention to several game-based and web-based learning paths. Besides, instructors need to find a solution to problems such as the delivery and deployment of the games to the assorted platforms involved (mobile devices, desktop computers with different system features, etc.).

In <e-Adventure> these issues are addressed by providing a common API for assessment and tracking purposes. The API works as a middleware between the games and a LMS. In this manner, the game engine can be used to gather the results of the game; produce a detailed assessment report with partial or final grade according to a set of assessment rules defined by the instructor; and, finally, send a machine-readable version of the report to the LMS to be attached to the profile of the student.

As it can be observed in Figure 3, the API manages the communication between a game being executed in the student's computer and the LMS. This means that the API needs to be implemented in both the server-side and the client side.

Some LMS already support the SCORM (*Sharable Content Object Reference Model*) set of specifications [2], promoted by the U.S. Department of Defense in order to unify how the educational contents are packaged, distributed and executed. In particular, SCORM defines a mechanism for the communication between active content and the server, allowing the content to submit information to the server such as the completion status of the content.

The API proposed in <e-Adventure> is based on SCORM's communication specifications. This means that, in those cases in which the server supports SCORM, there is no need of implementing the server-side of the API. On the other hand, if the target LMS is not SCORM-compliant, the server-side API must be implemented and connected to the LMS.

Regarding the client-side, all the products in the <e-Adventure> family implement the API. However, it should not be restricted to these platforms. The API is open and based on SCORM's communication specifications: the *IEEE Data Model for Content to Learning Management System Communication* [29] and the *IEEE ECMAScript API*

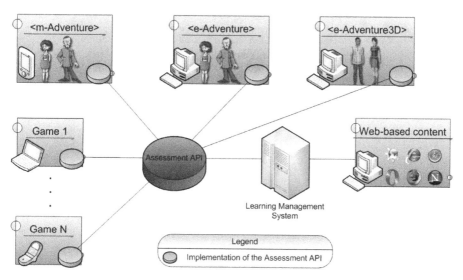

Fig. 3. Scheme of the communication between the elements of a heterogeneous game-based learning system through an assessment and tracking common API

for Content to Runtime Services Communication [30]. This means that an educational game developer can implement this API in other game engines, yielding a truly scalable approach that allows multiple kinds of games to be integrated in the same system.

5 1492: Case of Study of a Heterogeneous Game-Based Learning System

In order to evaluate the Tracking and Assessment API and its educational advantages, we created a heterogeneous on-line game-based course, as it is described in this section. It must be noted that this case study focuses on testing and validating the flexibility and LMS compatibility of the tracking and assessment API. It is not our intent to compare the performance of the different game-based learning approaches, or to validate the very concept of game-based learning. As a consequence of the same arguments, the games implemented are just introduced in this section but the design and implementation details (usability, instructional design, development costs, etc.) are not in-depth analyzed; however, a brief explanation of the learning context is given to exemplify a possible scenario where the ideas presented in this paper could be applied.

5.1 Application Context and Target Audience

Due to the narrative orientation of the <e-Adventure> games (which are really adequate for story-telling) we decided to focus the course on the Spanish History subject, present in almost all the years of the pre-higher Spanish educational system. Besides,

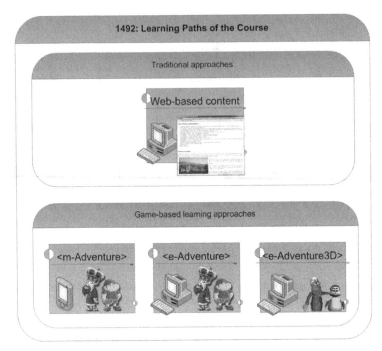

Fig. 4. Different materials (i.e. learning paths) of the heterogeneous game-based learning system

the broad target audience was a solid reason in favour of a heterogeneous system with different learning approaches in order to satisfy the prospects of most of the audience.

The contents of the course are diverse episodes of the Spanish History. In particular, one of the topics focuses on the events that happened in the year 1492, one of the most active and influential years in the beginnings of the Spanish Kingdom. Among the numerous events and changes experienced by the country in that year, two are considered to be especially important. First, 1492 is the year in which the alliance of northern kingdoms finished the conquest of the south regions they started centuries ago thanks to the capture of Granada. As a result, the Spanish Kingdom closed their main front of war and concentrated its attention in exploration, financing Columbus' expedition to America and starting the Imperialistic era of Spanish History. These events make this year a compulsory topic of discussion and study in all the Spanish History courses for students in primary and secondary school, making it an interesting topic for the game-based learning portion of the course.

5.2 General Structure and Materials of the Learning System

The game-based portion of the course is implemented as three distinct games covering the same topic: The Conquest of Granada in 1492. The story is set around a boy, Cristobalín, who is told by his history teacher to write an essay about the year 1492 to improve his knowledge of the subject. When the student starts reading for his essay he falls asleep, immersing in a dream where he relives the events leading to the Conquest of Granada.

Fig. 5. Screenshots of the <e-Adventure> (left) and <e-Adventure3D> (right) versions of the 1492 game

Using all the products of the <e-Adventure> family, three different games were created: The original game –a 2D adventure game-, an improved and more appealing 3D adventure game and a simplified version for execution in mobile devices. In addition, a web-based (more traditional) approach is also available for those students for which a game is not desirable.

The course was deployed in a LMS based on the open source tool Moodle [9]. In order to better illustrate that the approach is not restricted to SCORM-compliant environments (and given that SCORM support in Moodle is still an open issue), we extended the environment with a server-side implementation of the tracking and assessment API.

5.3   Description of the Learning Paths

The first learning path is based on a *point-and-click* adventure game developed with <e-Adventure> (Figure 5 left). The simplicity of these games and low technical requirements make it a good choice for most of the students trying to complement their knowledge of the subject at home with any or few guidance of the teacher.

The second alternative in the system is a 3D version of the first game developed with the <e-Adventure3D> platform (Figure 5 right). Basically the storyboard of the game is the same (the boy Cristobalín is told to produce a research essay about the year 1492), but enhanced with the possibilities offered by a 3D-based in-game world. This game could attract the attention of those students expecting something next to current commercial approaches. Probably this will be the choice for teenagers, which in many cases are used to play videogames more often in they free time.

The third game-based approach is basically a mobile version of the <e-Adventure> platform. The purpose of this approach was to attract some young students who use their mobile phones frequently and not only for making and receiving calls and messages, but for gaming as well (Figure 6 left).

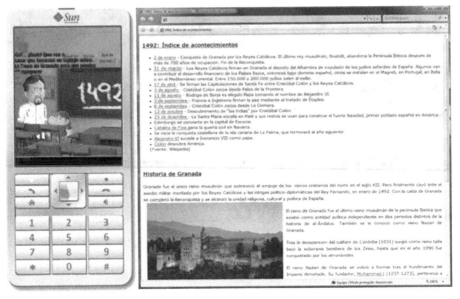

Fig. 6. <m-Adventure> version of 1492 (left) and a fragment of the web-based content of the course (right)

Finally, the last learning path is a web-based alternative (Figure 6 right); more adequate for those students presenting difficulties in self-study and which perhaps would require further guidance instead of the freedom of interaction that a videogame provides. This last approach is basically a compilation of all the facts occurred on 1492 in Spain, gathered from diverse sources such as Wikipedia.

5.4   Assessing the Performance of the Students

The learning process in any of the four available paths is evaluated with a different test, adapted to the characteristics of each format.

The 2D version and the mobile version of the game include a final scene in which the student interacts with a virtual teacher, who asks a number of test questions about the content. The student answers using the multiple-response mechanism supported by the in-game conversations and the grade is computed. The 3D version uses a more sophisticated approach, computing a grade as the student plays the game. All the game versions, in addition to the grade, prepare a tracking report as indicated using the tracking features offered by the tracking mechanisms offered by the <e-Adventure> platforms as described in [24].

On the other hand, the traditional (web-based) version includes a typical multiple-choice test (with an additional free-text question) to be answered by the student within the system.

The grades computed through any of the three version of the game are processed by the Tracking and Assessment API, normalized, and submitted to the LMS.

The grades are stored in the LMS along with the traditional grades obtained by the students following the web-based path. When the instructor accesses the LMS to

Fig. 7. Assessment record of the course in a Moodle LMS

check the grades, all the student-grades are stored together (see Figure 7). The detailed tracking reports from the game versions are stored in the free-form text question from the traditional exam. This gives the instructors a unified interface to follow the progress of their students, regardless of the type of game they used to follow the content.

6 Conclusions and Future Work

Game-based learning is a very active and diverse field with promising educational benefits. However, due to the wide range of approaches, systems and target audiences there are some issues that need to be addressed.

In this paper we propose to deal with these inconveniences through an LMS. To connect the games with the LMS those need to implement a common Assessment API. In this manner games can track and evaluate the activity of the students according to the rules determined by the instructor, and produce an assessment report which is sent to the LMS. On its side, the LMS processes the report and attaches it to the profile of the student. In addition, this principle has been exemplified with the

<e-Adventure> family of platforms for the production of educational adventure games for diverse contexts and target audiences.

This approach guarantees the interoperability and scalability of the system, as any game or platform implementing the API could be introduced.

The SCORM-oriented approach taken when creating the Tracking and Assessment API means that several LMS will be almost automatically compliant with these games, although more research is required to systematize a process to widen the spectrum of different LMS which can communicate with the assessment API. We also intend to provide implementations of the client-side API for different popular game engines and platforms. According to this idea, a future line of research will be to develop a more refined communication layer not only for assessment but also for adaptation purposes, allowing in this manner that any standard LMS can communicate with any videogame implementing the common API in both directions.

The final objective of this line of research is to rationalize the use of games in education by providing a solid ground that allows these games to be introduced in pre-existing educational environments. In our view, the modern LMS can be the foundation on which to build game-based learning experiences. But the diversity of game-based learning approaches and the variety of competing LMS implementations requires unification efforts. Our work tries to facilitate the interoperability, trying to allow any educational game to communicate with any LMS.

Acknowledgements. The Spanish Committee of Science and Technology (projects TIN2005-08788-C04-01, TSI-020301-2008-19 and TIN2007-68125-C02-01) has partially supported this work, as well as the Complutense University of Madrid (research group 921340) and the EU Alfa project CID (II-0511-A). Special thanks to Roberto Tornero Santamarina, Manuel J. Miguel García and César Liras Álvarez for the great design and implementation of the game 1492.

References

1. Academic ADL Co-Lab., Outbreak Quest: A 90-day Game Development initiative (2004), http://www.academiccolab.org/resources/documents/OutbreakQuest.pdf (retrieved, September 2008)
2. Advanced Distributed Learning (ADL), Sharable Content Object Reference Model, ADL-SCORM (2005), http://www.adlnet.org/ (retrieved, September 2008)
3. Aldrich, C.: Learning by Doing: A Comprehensive Guide to Simulations. In: Computer Games, and Pedagogy in e-Learning and Other Educational Experiences. Pfeiffer, San Francisco (2005)
4. Amory, A.: Building an Educational Adventure Game: Theory, Design and Lessons. Journal of Interactive Learning Research 12(2/3), 249–263 (2001)
5. Brusilovsky, P.: Adaptive Educational Systems on the World-Wide-Web: A Review of Available Technologies. In: Proceedings of the WWW-Based Tutoring Workshop at 4th International Conference on Intelligent Tutoring Systems (ITS 1998) (1998)
6. Churchill, D., Hedberg, J.: Learning Object Design Considerations for Small-Screen Handheld Devices. Computers & Education 50(3), 881–893 (2008)

7. Dennett, C., Cooper, S., Ariff Sabri, M., Carter, C., El Rhalibi, A., Merabti, M., Fergus, P., Price, M.: 3D Java Game Development with Homura. In: Proceedings of the Game Design and Technology Workshop and Conference (GDTW 2008), pp. 104–107 (2008)
8. Doswell, J., Harmeyer, K.: Extending the 'Serious Game' Boundary: Virtual Instructors in Mobile Mixed Reality Learning Games. Paper presented at the Digital Games Research Association International Conference (DiGRA 2007) (2007)
9. Dougiamas, M., Taylor, P.: Moodle: Using Learning Communities to Create an Open Source Course Management System. In: Proceedings of the World Conference on Educational Multimedia, Hypermedia and Telecommunications 2003, pp. 171–178 (2003)
10. Entertainment Software Association (ESA). Essential Facts about the Computer and Videogame Industry (2007),
http://www.theesa.com/facts/pdfs/ESA_EF_2007.pdf
(retrieved September 2008)
11. Gee, J.P.: What video games have to teach us about learning and literacy. Palgrave Macmillan, Basingstoke (2003)
12. Gee, J.P.: Good videogames and good learning: collected essays on video games. Peter Lang Publishing, New York (2007)
13. International Game Developers Association (IGDA). White paper on Accessibility in games: Motivations and approaches (2004)
14. Kam, M., Rudraraju, V., Tewari, A., Canny, J.: Mobile Gaming with Children in Rural India: Contextual Factors in the Use of Game Design Patterns. In: Proceedings of the 3rd Digital Games Research Association International Conference (2007)
15. Karampiperis, P., Sampson, D.: Adaptive learning resources sequencing in educational hypermedia systems. Educational Technology & Society 8(4), 128–147 (2005)
16. Kaufman, M., Dev, P., Youngblood, P.: Application of multiplayer game technology to team based training of medical first responders. Paper presented at the Interservice/Industry Training, Simulation & Education Conference (I/ITSEC) (2005)
17. Kirriemur, J., McFarlane, A.: Literature review in games and learning. NESTA Futurelab., Bristol (2004)
18. Koster, R.: Theory of Fun for Game Design: Paraglyph (2004)
19. Litchfield, A., Dyson, L., Lawrence, E., Zmijewska, A.: Directions for m-learning research to enhance active learning. In: Proceedings of the ASCILITE - ICT: Providing choices for learners and learning, pp. 587–596 (2007)
20. Mayo, M.: Games for science and engineering education. Communications of the ACM 50(7), 30–35 (2007)
21. McFarlane, A., Sparrowhawk, A., Heald, Y.: Report on the educational use of games: TEEM: Teachers Evaluating Educational Multimedia (2002),
http://www.teem.org.uk/publications/teem_gamesined_full.pdf
(retrieved, September 2008)
22. Michael, D., Chen, S.: Serious Games: Games that Educate, Train, and Inform. Thomson, Boston (2006)
23. Moreno-Ger, P., Blesius, C.R., Currier, P., Sierra, J.L., Fernández-Manjón, B.: Rapid Development of Game-like Interactive Simulations for Learning Clinical Procedures. In: Proceedings of the Game Design and Technology Workshop and Conference (GDTW 2007), pp. 17–25 (2007)
24. Moreno-Ger, P., Burgos, D., Sierra, J.L., Fernández-Manjón, B.: Educational Game Design for Online Education. Computers in Human Behavior 24(6), 2530–2540 (2008),
http://dx.doi.org/10.1016/j.chb.2008.03.012

25. Natkin, S., Yan, C., Jumpertz, S., Market, B.: Creating Multiplayer Ubiquitous Fames Using an Adaptive Narration Model Based on a User's Model. Paper presented at the Digital Games Research Association International Conference (DiGRA 2007) (2007)
26. Paramythis, A., Loidl-Reisinger, S.: Adaptive Learning Environments and eLearning Standards. Electronic Journal of eLearning 2(1), 181–194 (2004)
27. Parsons, D., Ryu, H., Cranshaw, M.: A Study of Design Requirements for Mobile Learning Environments. In: Proceedings of the Sixth IEEE international Conference on Advanced Learning Technologies (ICALT 2006), pp. 96–100. IEEE Computer Society, Los Alamitos (2006)
28. Prensky, M.: Digital Game Based Learning. McGraw-Hill, New York (2001)
29. Richards, T.: IEEE Standard for Learning Technology - Data Model for Content to Learning Management System Communication (2003)
30. Richards, T.: IEEE Standard for Learning Technology - ECMAScript API for Content to Runtime Services Communication (2004)
31. Schrier, K.L.: Revolutionizing history education: Using augmented reality games to teach histories. Master Thesis, Massachusetts Institute of Technology, Cambridge, MA (2005), http://hdl.handle.net/1721.1/39186 (retrieved, September 2008)
32. Sim, G., MacFarlane, S., Read, J.: All work and no play: Measuring fun, usability, and learning in software for children. Computers & Education 46(3), 235–248 (2006)
33. Tang, S., Hanneghan, M., El Rhalibi, A.: Describing Games for Learning: Terms, Scope and Learning Approaches. In: Proceedings of the Game Design and Technology Workshop and Conference (GDTW 2007), pp. 98–102 (2007)
34. Torrente, J., Moreno-Ger, P., Fernández-Manjón, B.: Learning Models for the Integration of Adaptive Educational Games in Virtual Learning Environments. In: Pan, Z., Zhang, X., El Rhalibi, A., Woo, W., Li, Y. (eds.) Edutainment 2008. LNCS, vol. 5093, pp. 463–474. Springer, Heidelberg (2008)
35. Torrente, J., Moreno-Ger, P., Fernández-Manjón, B., Sierra, J.L.: Instructor-oriented Authoring Tools for Educational Videogames. In: Proceedings of the 8th International Conference on Advanced Learning Technologies (ICALT 2008), pp. 516–518. IEEE Computer Society, Los Alamitos (2008)
36. Van Eck, R.: Digital game-based learning: It's not just the digital natives who are restless. EDUCAUSE Review 41(2), 16–30 (2006)
37. Van Eck, R.: Building Artificially Intelligent Learning Games. In: Gibson, D., Aldrich, C., Prensky, M. (eds.) Games and Simulations in Online Learning: Research and Development Frameworks. Information Science Publishing, Hershey (2007)

Networking Middleware and Online-Deployment Mechanisms for Java-Based Games

Chris Carter[1], Abdennour El Rhalibi[1], Madjid Merabti[1], and Marc Price[2]

[1] School of Computing & Mathematical Sciences, Liverpool John Moores University,
Byrom Street, Liverpool, L3 3AF, UK
C.J.Carter@2007.ljmu.ac.uk, a.elrhalibi@ljmu.ac.uk,
m.merabti@ljmu.ac.uk
[2] BBC Research and Development. Kingswood Warren, Tadworth, Surrey, KT20 6NP, UK
Marc.Price@bbc.co.uk

Abstract. Currently, web-based online gaming applications are predominately utilising Adobe Flash or Java Applets as their core technologies. These games are often casual, two-dimensional games and do not utilise the specialist graphics hardware which has proliferated across modern PCs and Consoles. Multi-user online game play in these titles is often either non-existent or extremely limited. Computer games applications which grace the current generation of consoles and personal computers are designed to utilise the increasingly impressive hardware power at their disposal. However, these are commonly distributed using a physical medium or deployed through custom, proprietary networking mechanisms and rely upon platform-specific networking APIs to facilitate multi-user online game play. In order to unify the concepts of these disparate styles of gaming, this paper presents two interconnected systems which are implemented using Java Web Start and JXTA P2P technologies, providing a platform-independent framework capable of deploying hardware accelerated cross-platform, cross-browser online-enabled Java games, as part of the Homura Project.

Keywords: Web Technologies, Distributed Systems, Java, Homura, NetHomura, Java Monkey Engine, jME, Java Web Start, Deployment, JXTA, Peer to Peer Networking, P2P Games.

1 Introduction

The Homura games project [1] investigated the development of a cross-platform games engine and Integrated Development Environment (IDE) for the development of hardware-accelerated 3D Java games using open-source technologies. This project aims to extend the functionality provided by the Homura Engine, adding systems catering for both the deployment and networking of games built upon the platform, via existing web technologies. Homura is implemented using Java, with the Eclipse IDE and Java Monkey Engine (jME) proving the base for the editor and engine respectively. The deployment platform provides a game portal web application, which facilitates authenticated access to the Homura-based games and securely and robustly deploys the games to the client computers via the Internet. The portal offers features

Z. Pan et al. (Eds.): Transactions on Edutainment II, LNCS 5660, pp. 19–32, 2009.

such as automatic updates and the ability to easily enhance existing deployment through additional game content. In addition to the distribution mechanism, the portal also provides an interface which allows users to search for other games, create friendships with other members and instantaneously receive communications regarding the release of new titles on the portal. The system manages game data from in-game experiences such as high-scores and game specific statistics. The networking middleware platform allow developers to easily create Homura-based games which can offer multiplayer, online gameplay in a cost-effective manner leveraging the resource sharing capabilities of the P2P networking topology, whilst still retaining centralised control over access rights and the maintaining the integrity of persistent game data. This paper describes the motivations for the project, the initial design and analysis phase and the architectural structure of the resulting prototype, named NetHomura. The paper concludes by illustrating a test case of the deployment of a hardware accelerated puzzle game built using the Homura framework in a cross platform manner.

2 Existing Technologies

Online Games portals (such as EA's Pogo [2]) principally use the proprietary Adobe Flash technology to distribute web-based and downloadable game titles through web browsers. These titles commonly offer casual, single player or AI-controlled multiplayer gameplay and utilise the omnipresent Flash Player. Whilst the latest version of Flash supports the development of networked online multiplayer games such as Habbo Hotel [3] through its ActionScript language bindings, networking with Flash often requires additional proprietary systems in order to host the system, such as the ElectroServer Flash Socket Server.

Another available proprietary technology is the Unity game engine [4]. This provides browser based play for Windows and Mac OS X via its custom plug-in for Internet Explorer, Firefox and Safari (implemented as a 3MB ActiveX control for

Fig. 1. Tropical Paradise - Unity Demo [4]

Internet Explorer). In comparison to Flash, Unity provides a much more powerful framework for online games, enabling hardware-accelerated 3D games using DirectX and Open GL to embed within a web page and execute directly within the browser window, or in full screen mode. A similar proprietary technology is being developed by the creators of the Torque Game Engine, Garage Games, called Instant Action [5].

Figure 1 illustrates the potential power of the Unity platform and its Tropical Paradise technical demo. Currently however, there is minimal utilization of open-source technologies to provide this level of gaming performance and aesthetic via the Internet.

3   Key Design Decisions

Prior to implementing the deployment system and networking middleware for the Homura system, the method of deployment was chosen, and a base network API was selected. As the project is to be integrated into the Homura framework, it was crucial to understand the platform and underlying technologies. This section provides a high-level overview of the Homura Engine, and the reasons behind the choices of networking and deployment support.

3.1   Homura and Homura IDE

As stated before, Homura provides both a games engine API and IDE. The engine builds upon the open-source Java Monkey Engine (jME) [6] whilst the open-source Eclipse IDE as base of the games editing facilities. jME was conceived by Mark Powell in 2003 and has developed into a large community based project. Programmed entirely in Java, jME uses the LightWeight Java Games Library (LWJGL) as its low-level OpenGL-based rendering sub-system. It provides a high performance scenegraph based graphics API, which allows for organization of the games entities into a tree structure, where a parent node can contain any number of children nodes, but a child node must contains a single parent. The nodes are organized spatially so that whole branches of the graph can be culled. This allows for complex scenes to be rendered quickly, as typically, most of the scene is not visible at any one time. The scenegraph's leaf nodes consist of the geometry that will be rendered to the display.

jME Features. Whilst jME is an open-source technology, over the last five years it has matured into a feature rich system which is one of the most performant graphical implementation in Java. Key Features that are provided with the Java Monkey Engine are: [7]

- **Bounding System** - All geometry can be enclosed in a bounding system. Boxes, Capsules and Spheres.
- **Collision and Picking** - Efficient bounding volume and triangle accurate picking and collision.
- **Curves** - Bezier curves can be utilised for node control.
- **Effects** - GLSL Shader Support, Vertex and Fragment Program Support (ARB Shaders), Extensible Particle System, Lens Flare, Cloth Simulation, Screen tinting.

- **FastMath Library** – Provides an approximation system for linear algebra using look-up tables.
- **Level of Detail** - Discrete Level of Detail using a switching mechanism for fast model switching. Continuous Level of Detail dynamically collapses triangles of a single model.
- **Lighting System** - Handles up to eight lights at a time with utilities for optimal light selection. jME supports directional light, spot light and point light.
- **Model Loading** - COLLADA, 3DS, OBJ, MD2, MD3, Milkshape, ASE and MD5 support. Supports skin and bones and weighted skeletal animation.
- **Multi-Format Imaging-** Support for BMP, uncompressed TGA, JPG, PNG, GIF and DDS image formats.
- **Shadow System** – Support for Z-Pass Shadow Volumes.
- **State System** - Minimizes OpenGL state changes by tracking and managing the status of the OpenGL machine. Allows for the merging of Texture and Light states within the tree.
- **Terrain** - Terrain blocks act as singular geometry. Terrain Pages implements a Quad tree of Terrain blocks.
- **Texture System** - Supports mip-mapping, environmental mapping, multi-texturing.

3.2 Java Deployment

As the games will be integrated into the Homura Engine and thus jME, they will be developed using Java. Currently, there are two methods of deploying Java-based applications via the internet, Applets and Java Web Start. The Java Web Start technology [8] was chosen as the base platform for the deployment system as it offers several key advantages over using Applets, detailed later in this paper. Java Web Start (JWS) is a standard component of the Java Standard Edition Development Kit (Java SE JDK) and is distributed as a part of the Runtime Environment (JRE). The JRE is required by users in order to execute Java Applications and provides a browser plug-in called the Java Plugin. The Java Plugin is freely available for all major operating systems and browser environments, making the technology ubiquitous amongst desktop PC users. JWS utilises the Java Network Launching Protocol (JNLP) [9] to configure exactly how an application is deployed from a server location to the clients' machines. The protocol uses a simple, standardised XML schema to define several key aspects of the deployment process.

- The appearance of the download window presented to the client upon deployment initiation.
- The creation of desktop and system shortcuts.
- The off-line availability of the application.
- References to any external Java Archive (JAR) files required
- Support for Operating System and architecture specific (e.g. x86/x64/PPC) libraries.
- Dynamic Properties passed as arguments to the application.
- The permissions and security access provisioning of the application.

- Specification of the entry point of the application.
- The configuration of resource updates from the initial deployment location.

Web Start Features and Advantages. An Applet is a specialised Java application, which is embedded directly into the HTML of a web page, and transferred and executed directly on the client machine, within the context of the browser. The browser integration of Applets inherently limits the ability to run full-screen applications, and also restricts the resolutions at which games can operate. With Applets, the Java Virtual Machine is invoked directly as a process within the browser, and multiple applets must share a JVM instance, which carries a performance and resource overhead. Applets enforce memory restraints that can only be customised by the end user, and are heavily reliant on the security model of the browser for their operation.

JWS applications are executed completely independent of the browser, and each instance is executed within a separate Java process with performance equal to that of standard Java applications. The browser independence means that the application can be adjusted to a variety of resolutions and can run in windowed or full-screen mode with no overheads. An application can be configured by the developer or system administrator to consume additional resources by adjusting the JVM's start-up configuration through the JNLP specification. JWS applications can be easily integrated into HTML pages via a link to the JNLP file, which when executed, invokes the cross-platform Java plug-in, subsequently handling the execution of the application. As a result, JWS exhibits excellent cross platform, cross-browser support. In comparison, the inconsistencies found with the implementation of Applets across browsers and Operating Systems makes the creation of a consistent user experience a difficult task.

Applets require that the game applications base class must inherit from the Java Applet API, which has a defined manner in the way it executes and has to interact smoothly with the containing browser, handling a variety of events, many of which are completely irrelevant to the underlying application. Because applications deployed using JWS are essentially standard Java Applications, far fewer restrictions are imposed on the developer. It is an undemanding task to develop an application which can be distributed as both a standard Java Application and a Web Start. The JNLP protocol also allows for greater freedom in JVM choice, offering the ability to provide automatic upgrades to the user's Java Run-time Environment (JRE), whilst supporting side-by-side installation of multiple JVM versions.

With JWS, the installation of native libraries onto the end user's machine is seamless and eliminates the complexities which can be encountered when attempting the same process using Applets. This is a crucial factor, as LWJGL and consequently jME and Homura rely on native libraries for supporting OpenGL, non-standard input devices such as gamepads and joysticks and also for hardware accelerated audio capabilities provided by libraries such as OpenAL and FMOD.

3.3 Networking for Java-Based Games

Java features an extensive networking API incorporated into the JDK, which many additional networking solutions APIs are built upon, including those designed for Java games. Two such examples of these are Sun's Project Darkstar [10] and the jME-affiliated Java Game Networking (JGN) [11] which are both open source. Both of these libraries provide game-specific Client-Server APIs, and can be integrated with jME, and therefore Homura. Darkstar provides a shardless Client-Server architecture for MMOG titles using Java, and is capable of supporting thousands of players by utilising the Sun Games Server (SGS) technology as the backbone.

However, as stated in the introduction, the ethos of this project is to create a system that allows a Java-based game to be created with minimal costs, by utilising open-source technologies. Client-Server architectures are popular in game networking, because they are relatively simple to implement, allow the developer to maintain absolute control over the state of game and the use of a centralized authority makes cheat-detection and user access control a simple task. However, scalability is an issue, as it is often inflexible and also extremely costly due to the amount of dedicated hardware required to sustain such design. The network has to be over-provisioned to handle peak loads and limits the deployment of user-generated content [12]. Client-Server games may also have limited life-spans, as they will only remain active whilst the server infrastructure is still supported. The issue of hardware costs means that using Client-Server architecture to support many games is infeasible for small-scale developers, and would create a barrier of entry for using this platform. A Peer-to-Peer (P2P) solution would allow the system to utilize the resources of the connected users (CPU, Memory and Network Bandwidth), creating an easily scalable system and one that is in keeping with the aforementioned ethos. Therefore, the Java version of the JXTA [13] P2P platform (JXSE 2.5) was selected as the underlying networking library for the middleware solution. JXTA is an open source initiative created by Sun Microsystems in 2001 to standardise and provide a set of P2P protocols. JXTA comprises of a set of six protocols that support common P2P networking tasks, such as peer discovery, organization of peers, peer identification and verification and messaging. The JXTA protocols [14] uses the open standards of XML schemas to define their semantics and subsequently allow JXTA to operate independent of language, operating system, network topology and even the underlying transport protocol. The Java JXSE version is the reference implementation of the JXTA standards. JXTA does not preclude the usage of Client-Server topologies, and persistent peers can be utilized to great effect. It neither excludes nor inherently depends on centralized control points. JXTA has been used as the basis for many recent P2P studies, and its feasibility for use within game-related network programming (even large scale applications, e.g. MMOGs) is proven [15].

4 System Overview

The NetHomura deployment platform and networking middleware is still evolving. This paper presents the work completed during the preliminary phase of the project. This first stage includes the implementation of the deployment platform, and the initial API for the creation of multiplayer online Homura-Based games. The Future Developments section of this paper documents the expectations and upcoming direction of this project, and how it can be further improved and refined in the next phases of development. In this section: we present the combined architecture of the two technologies and the interactions which exist between them; we explain the deployment process, how it can be used to rapidly and securely deliver feature and content rich games via standard web technologies; and we discuss the infrastructure of the network overlay which the client applications will form during the course of a networked game session.

4.1 Deployment Platform and Networking Middleware

Deployment Platform Overview. The deployment solution provides a web application which provides a portal for access to games built using the Homura platform. The deployment portal provides the following features to the user and developer:

User Accounts/Authenticated Access: Users have their own profile, and are authenticated into the system via an encrypted username/password mechanism. The user's views within the system are customized based on their account details, providing them with an in-game identity, age-restricted access to the games, the ability to create friends with other users, and associates them with an in-game Avatar.

Game Catalogue Facilities: The System catalogues the available games, based on their genre, multiplayer and online facilities, and allows users to easily search and download new games based on their preferences. Previously downloaded games are stored so they can easily start their favourite games, or re-download them to another machine.

Game Statistics Storage: The system stores and displays game statistics, such as the number of times a game has been played, and game high-scores, based on all users across a single game, or all a particular user's score across all games.

Caching and Update Facilities: Once a user has downloaded the game, it is cached so that subsequent executions are instantaneous, and allows updates to be delivered to the user automatically, when they are available.

Logging and Access Control - The System features a logging engine which stores the IP address of the users, any data modifications to the database and allows the system administrator to ban or temporarily disable accounts, add new games to the system as well a system wide configuration which allows the application to be gracefully taken offline for maintenance.

Networking Middleware Overview. The networking middleware provides a high-level implementation of the JXTA networking facilities, allowing the game developer to incorporate networking easily into their application. The middleware currently provides the following features:

- 8-16 Concurrent Players within a single game instance.
- Creation of a network connection from a peer.
- Creation and joining of Peer Groups.
- Sending and Receiving Game-Related Messages.
- Communication of Shared Data to the data repository.
- Representations of users and game session as Java Objects.
- Monitoring of peer latency and bandwidth across the session.

4.2 System Architecture

NetHomura utilises two physical servers to host the solution: a SUSE Linux, Apache
2.0 combined web and application server running PHP 5.2.6 and a Database Server
running MySQL 5.0.1. This forms a LAMP (Linux-Apache-MySQL-PHP) configuration, which is commonly used for standard web applications. The application is extremely portable and would work equally well on a Windows-based machine using
either Apache 2.0 or IIS. The use of two servers is due to the internal infrastructure
available and could easily be combined into a single server. Figure 2 provides an
overview of the architecture, illustrating the physical and logical layout of the application and the communications permitted between the server and the game clients.

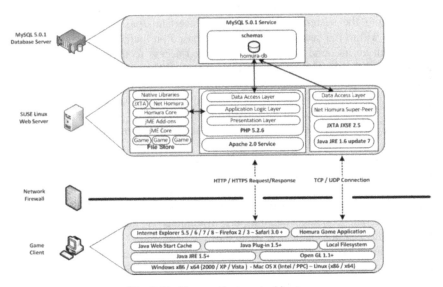

Fig. 2. NetHomura System Architecture

The deployment solution is programmed using a blend of Object-Oriented and
Page-Oriented PHP, and is separated into a three-tiered architecture:

Data Access Layer – The solution uses MySQL for its persistent storage. A PHP
Data Access layer has been implemented, which abstracts the database from the application, allowing the system to retrieve application class instances representing the
database objects, and handles the insertion or modification of data within the database
based on the current state of the application class. This abstraction also means the
database can be replaced with another RDBMS (e.g. Postgres), or use another solution, such as XML files to store the data.

Application Layer – The Application layer provides classes which represent the
data in the database and encapsulates the application logic. The system current features implementations of users, games, online game modes; game scores etc. The
class instance data is modified by actions carried out by the user via the application
interface, using a simple getter/setter pattern.

Presentation Layer – The solution programmatically constructs the HTML and JavaScript-based page template and displays dynamic views of the system to the user, using the classes of the Application Layer. This abstraction means that the entire look and feel of the application can be replaced without affecting the application logic and allows the system to incorporate AJAX/DHTML libraries to enhance the user experience.

The games and supporting libraries (Homura, jME, Native DLLs/SOs) are stored on the server's local file system and are not directly accessible from outside of the server. The files are stored as JAR files and are compressed using the g-zip compression system. This minimizes the size of the game distribution. The partitioning of the JARs means that, once a client has downloaded their first game the Homura framework is installed, and that any future game installation will only require the game JAR to be distributed, further reducing installation times.   The JARs are signed using digital signatures so their integrity and authenticity can be verified, combating binary modification (commonly used for online cheats). This also means that the application does not have to run within the standard Java sandbox, providing additional permissions to the application, such as running Native Libraries (e.g. OpenGL), storing data locally on the user's machine, and creating outbound network connections (used by the middleware). The Server also hosts a persistent JXTA Super Peer, which can be accessed by any of the Clients running NetHomura based games. This Peer is used to advertise the location of other games users, to insert/modify any persistent data (scores, logging information, user-identifiers). This peer is used to allocate network functionality to connected peer applications, delegating more and more power to the peers, and acts as a proxy, so that peers cannot directly access the database. Both the deployment and middleware provide multi-platform support. A game client can currently use Windows, Linux, or Mac OS X Operating Systems and Internet Explorer, Firefox or Safari browsers and requires OpenGL to be installed on the system. The users need at least version 1.5 of the Java JRE (which can be automatically installed by the deployment application). Games are placed in the Java Web Start cache within the local file system.

4.3 Deployment Process

Java Web Start applications are usually deployed using a static JNLP file with a reference link embedded within an HTML page. However, this method is unsecure, and means that anyone with knowledge of the location of the JNLP file can access and deploy the game. Thus, the deployment architecture dynamically creates the JNLP file to protect the games from unrestricted access. Figure 3 illustrates this process for a Windows machine running either Firefox or Internet Explorer.

A user who is authenticated into the deployment portal can locate a game via the search mechanism, and view the games details (download size, multiplayer modes, online support, screenshots etc.). The application provides a 'Launch' button, which then invokes the deployment of the game. The game's unique identifier is passed to the JNLPFactory class of the deployment application layer. This class queries the database via the data access layer to retrieve the required resources of the game, JVM settings, properties (used to pass user-specific data to the applications) and dynamically constructs the JNLP file, which is returned to the client via an HTTP response.

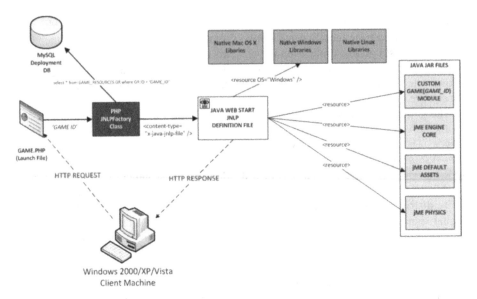

Fig. 3. Deployment Process using Windows

The browser then passes the JNLP file to the Client's Java Plugin which parses the JNLP file and downloads the game application and resources associated with the application. The Client's architecture and Operating System is established by the Plugin so that only the Native Libraries relevant to the client are downloaded. Once the game is cached, it is then executed using the Client's JVM. The process is similar for subsequent executions. When the JNLP is sent, the contents of the JWS cache on the client's machine is analysed and differentiated against the server copies. If new versions of any of the associated JARs, or any new JARs added to the application (e.g. new level packs, assets) then these are downloaded and returned to the client.

4.4 Peer-to-Peer Networking

The networking middleware of NetHomura utilises the key concepts of the JXTA framework, and builds upon them for the purposes of gaming, with the resulting network created by the framework is a hybrid P2P topology, as illustrated by Figure 4, which details both the network structure and the software architecture of the peers within the system.

Middleware Overview. The NetHomura middleware integrates with the Homura Engine to create a *GameStateManager* to control the game. This manages an internal stack of *HomuraGameState* instances. *HomuraGameState* is an abstract class which implements the game loop of each state, providing methods for initialisation of content, handling user input and updating the state of the game world (members of the scenegraph), and a rendering the scenegraph to screen. The NetHomura games are comprised of concrete implementations of this class (e.g. *MainMenuState*, *Loading-State*, *PuzzleGameState*, etc.). The middleware provides an additional implementation, *NetState*, which encompasses the additional interactions of a network game, by

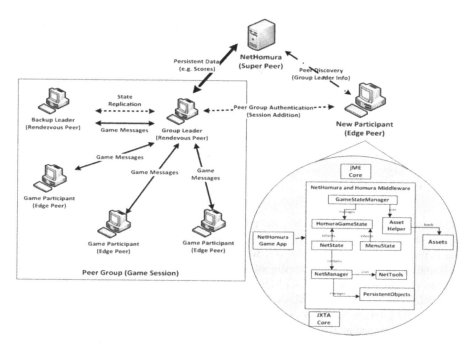

Fig. 4. Sample P2P Game Interactions via NetHomura

adding methods to receive messages, send messages, join and leave games. The *Net-State* class uses an instance of the middleware's *NetManager* class, which handles peer-management facilities such as discovering available game sessions, creation of new game session, tracking and modifying persistent, shared data objects used within the game, managing references to connected peers, sending messages to particular peers and retrieving messages that are received from peers. The *NetManager* also handles session control, such as disconnecting and joining into both the entire network and game sessions. The role of the game developer using the middleware is to create game-specific messages which inherit from the base *NetHomuraMessage* class. This class encapsulates the in-game messages sent between peers, and using the *Net-Tools* class to construct efficient managements using the functions to efficiently serialise Java object into messages. These messages can then be broadcast using the *NetManager*. The middleware also provides the concept of *GameSessionAdvertisments*, which are used to create and communicate the details of a particular game session to other peers so that they can participate in a session.

Network Topology. Games built using the NetHomura framework construct a hybrid P2P topology. Initially, the NetHomura *Super Peer* on the deployment server forms a Client-Server network, which acts as the gateway to the P2P game sessions, authenticating the user based on their deployment credentials and transmitting the location of any sessions available for the user's game. A game session is organised as a *Peer group*. The Peer group is assigned a group leader, which becomes a JXTA *Rendezvous Peer*.(initially the creator of the group).The Rendezvous peer is responsible for broadcasting the services offered by the group (e.g. the game session) using JXTA's advertisement framework. The rendezvous peer is also responsible for propagating messages received from other peers within the peer group to all other members [14], who are connected as *Edge Peers*. Edge Peers have a single responsibility, to communicate their current game state to the group leader. A replica of this peer is also created to provide redundancy. If the group leader disconnects, then leadership is switched. Peers are connected using *JXTA Socket* connections, communicating via TCP/UDP. A secure connection using TLS is created between the group leader and the Super Peer to securely transmit persistent data, for entry into the deployment database.

5 Preliminary Analysis

As stressed throughout this paper, the project is in its infancy, and many additional features require implementation and testing in order to construct the final solution. The deployment system's capabilities were tested on a variety of Virtual Machines, each implementing a different configuration of OS and browser from a clean installation (no previous games) and Java JRE 6 installed. The test machine is a 2.4GHz Intel Core 2 Duo, with 4GB of RAM, an Nvidia 8600GT 256MB graphics card, and connected to the internet via a 2Mb standard broadband connection. The Elemental Puzzle game (developed as part of the Homura Project) is used as the test case. Figure 5 illustrates the Windows Vista deployment of this game using Internet Explorer 7.

Table 1 illustrates the results of the installation averaged across 10 clean installations of the test machines. The measurement records the time from deployment launch until the game window appears (including JVM invocation time).

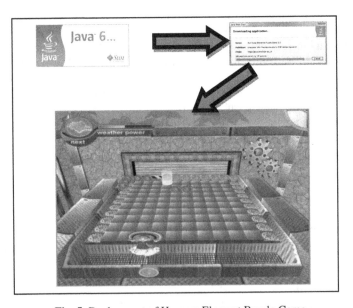

Fig. 5. Deployment of Homura Element Puzzle Game

Table 1. Homura Game Deployment Tests

Operating System	Browser Tested	Avg. Download Time
Windows Vista	Internet Explorer 7	2m 14s
Windows XP	Internet Explorer 6	1m 57s
Ubuntu 8.04	Firefox 3.02	2m 28s
Fedora Core 7	Firefox 2.04	2m 25s

The game was successfully deployed and executed on each of the test machines. The download also includes the deployment of the entire Homura framework, including jME, so subsequent game installation times will be dramatically reduced. Whilst the raw source of the game is 35MB, the JWS version is 10MB, including the Homura Framework and jME.

Whilst the core of the networking middleware has been created, it is yet to be complete integrated with Homura-based games, and thus cannot be illustrated in use.

6 Future Developments

There are several enhancements and future directions that can be taken in the future development phases in order to fully realize the potential of the proposed solution. Currently, the content of the system is directly added to the database via a set of scripts and stored procedures. The deployment system can be further developed to provide a set of back-end tools which allow the management of games, users, and application configuration through a web interface. This should be a relatively trivial implementation, using the existing data-access and application tiers. The Digital Signature signing process of the game and engine JARs is currently completed manually using the key signing tools distributed with the Java 5 SE JDK. This could be incorporate into either the administration tools of the deployment or the build process of the Homura IDE. The middleware component requires the completion of the test games in order to evaluate its performance and scalability properly. The first phase is to support between 8-16 concurrent players during a game session. The next phase will involve the incorporation of networking algorithms such as dead-reckoning, Area of Interest Management, cheat-detection to increase the scalability of the system by an order of magnitude [16].

7 Conclusion

In this paper, we have presented a novel architecture and prototype system, which aims to unify the deployment of hardware-accelerated Java-based 3D games applications with online capabilities. NetHomura provides a multi-tiered deployment platform that is secure, robust, and easily portable to a wide range of web servers. The networking middleware provided allows developers to built content and feature rich online-games in conjunction with the Homura Engine and IDE. Due to nature of the technologies used within the NetHomura framework, and combined with the Homura engine and IDE, it is possible to enable the creation of a game which, from development through to hosting, deployment and networking, can be created with little or no financial outlay for the developer. This would enable small-scale developers to distribute modern games applications to users worldwide. The games can incorporating online, multi-player game-play utilising the processing and networking resources of the game's users to construct a scalable network providing a smooth consistent and responsive experience. With the future development of this project, it is hoped this goal can be obtained.

References

1. LJMU Homura Sites - Homura Engine and Homura IDE. Liverpool John Moores University, http://java.cms.livjm.ac.uk/homura (cited December 20, 2008)
2. Pogo Online Game Portal. EA Pogo.com, http://www.pogo.com/home/home.do (cited December 20, 2008)
3. Flash Based MMOG. Habbo Hotel, http://www.habbo.co.uk/ (cited December 20, 2008)
4. Unity Game Engine. Unity Game Engine - Official Site, http://unity3d.com/ (cited December 20, 2008)
5. Instant Action - Garage Games. InstantAction.com, http://www.instantaction.com/ (cited December 20, 2008)
6. Official Site - Home. Java Monkey Engine (jME), http://www.jmonkeyengine.com/ (cited December 20, 2008)
7. jME Starter Guide - jME 1.0. Java Monkey Engine, http://www.jmonkeyengine.com/wiki/doku.php?id=user_s_guide (cited December 20, 2008)
8. Official Java Web Start User's Guide. Sun Microsystems - Java, http://java.sun.com/javase/6/docs/technotes/guides/javaws/developersguide/contents.html (cited December 20, 2008)
9. Java Launching Protocol - JSR Specification Documentation. Sun Microsystems - Java, http://jcp.org/en/jsr/detail?id=56 (cited December 20, 2008)
10. Community Web Site. Project Darkstar, http://www.projectdarkstar.com/ (cited December 20, 2008)
11. JGN - Java Game Networking API - Official Site. Java Game Networking, http://javagn.org/ (cited December 20, 2008)
12. Knutsson, B., Lu, H., Xu, W., Hopkins, B.: Peer-to-Peer Support for Massively Multiplayer Online Games. In: INFOCOM, vol.1 (2004)
13. Official JXTA Development Site. Java Development Community - JXTA (cited December 20, 2008), https://jxta.dev.java.net/
14. Verstrynge, J.: Practical JXTA. Lulu Enterprises (2008)
15. El Saddik, A., Dufour, A.: Peer-to-Peer Suitability for Collaborative Multiplayer Games. In: Proceedings of the Seventh IEEE International Symposium on Distributed Simulation and Real-Time Applications (2003)
16. Smed, J., Hakonen, H., Koukoranta, T.: A Review on Networking and Multiplayer Computer Games. Technical Report, Turku Centre For Computer Science (2004)

A Testbed for P2P Gaming Using Time Warp

Stefan Tolic and Helmut Hlavacs

University of Vienna, Dept. of Distributed and Multimedia Systems
Lenaug. 2/8, Vienna, Austria
getraktna@gmail.com, helmut.hlavacs@univie.ac.at

Abstract. Peer-to-peer based gaming is a new paradigm for distributed multiplayer online gaming that has attracted attention in the last years. It is known that P2P based topologies offer good scaling properties and mitigate unfairness otherwise observed for peers being far away and thus having large network lags. However, removing inconsistencies for high paced action games like FPS or tank battle games requires the implementation of a Time Warp-like mechanism, which itself may hinder gameplay for high lags. In this paper we present a tank battle game named Panzer Battalion. Created from scratch, this game follows the P2P approach and implements Time Warp for removing inconsistencies. Panzer Battalion is meant as a testbed for creating rollbacks and understanding, how Time Warp rollbacks depend on network lag, and how gameplay is altered by them.

1 Introduction

Multiplayer online games nowadays connect players from all over the world. Often players from different continents play together the same game. Due to the spatial distance, network packet delivery might require a substantial amount of time when sent from one player to another or to a central server. Depending on the *game type*, this inherent *network lag* (aka network latency) may then cause unfair conditions [1,2], or different views and game states which might even contradict each other [3]. Contradicting game states are also called *inconsistencies*. However, in case of low interactivity, for instance for RTS or MMORPG games, network lag does not necessarily have a strong effect on the outcome [4,5].

In this paper we introduce a testbed for observing the occurrence of inconsistencies and their removal when applying Time Warp, which is described below. The testbed is a fast paced tank battle game that was developed solely for this purpose.

2 Related Work

Basically there are three types of topologies for multiplayer online games [6]. The simplest topology uses one central server that solely simulates the game environment and stores all game states.

Z. Pan et al. (Eds.): Transactions on Edutainment II, LNCS 5660, pp. 33–47, 2009.

Though being simplistic, this approach offers several drawbacks. First, a centralized environment is likely to run into performance problems, and scaling to hundreds or even thousands of clients taking part in the same game is difficult. Second and even more important, some players being far away from the server will observe a high lag, and usually their game input will arrive at the server much later than the one of their opponents. Especially for highly interactive games this means a considerable disadvantage, rendering the resulting game to be unfair, even though schemes for selecting the optimal hoster exist [7].

A more sophisticated approach would use $N > 1$ *mirrored game servers* in order to divide the load implied by all clients amongst the servers, and to move the replicated and locationally dispersed servers as close to the clients as possible [8,9,10]. Of course, being fixed in nature, servers remain in their locations and cannot dynamically move closer to their clients.

Finally, no dedicated server provider may exist and hosting the game is solely left to the clients. Especially in the recent years this new *peer-to-peer* paradigm has been researched extensively [11]. In a P2P topology, $N > 1$ clients, in this case called *peers*, participate in a game and no dedicated server exists. Scalability is provided by a principle called *locality of interest* [12] or *area of interest* [13,14]. Players are located in a certain area in the virtual world and the player's peer only needs to communicate with peers having players in the same area [15]. Splitting the virtual world in this way results in so-called *zones* [16]. A general problem of P2P based systems is the difficult prevention of cheating [17].

Both mirrored servers and P2P approach, however, require that $N > 1$ computers store parts of the game state in parallel. One way of doing this is to define that each zone is simulated by one server or peer only, acting as the central server of this zone. This again yields the problem of lag differences for different clients of the same zone. Another approach is to fully *replicate* the game state amongst N servers/peers. For the P2P topology this means that parts or all peers of a zone hold a full copy of the whole game state concerning their zone, and game state updates must be communicated to all other peers in the same zone. Since state updates are delayed by the network, inconsistencies may occur and may give rise to incorrect decisions [3].

In this paper we assume a P2P architecture with full replication for each zone, i.e., each peer of a zone simulates the whole zone itself. We focus on fighting games like FPS or tank battle games, with high interactivity and actions that cause instant game state changes (like shooting). In such fighting games, network lags may for instance lead to the effect that on one peer a playing character is shot (because the message making this player move was delayed by the network), while on another peer the player is moved in time and hence is not shot [18].

Basically there are three techniques to fight or at least mitigate the occurrence of inconsistencies. First, a technique called *Dead Reckoning* applies prediction of object movements, based on last known position and speed [19,20]. In the above example, the predictor would estimate the network lag between the two peers and would estimate the position of each player at a given time. Dead Reckoning based on synchronized clocks is then called Globally Synchronized

Dead Reckoning [20]. Although Dead Reckoning is able to reduce the number of occurring inconsistencies, it is not able to remove them in case they actually occur. Since prediction is never 100% accurate, and relies on suitable models, inconsistencies still may occur and lead to unwanted paradoxes.

Second, a technique called *Local Lag* puts each incoming packet into a queue and delays it for a fixed pre-defined time [21]. This way, packets arriving out-of-order may be put in-order in the local buffer, and inconsistencies may be removed. Local Lag only works efficiently in case the local delay is larger than the largest network lag. Since packets are always delayed, this technique is not usable for fast paced action games with high interactivity, e.g., FPS games, which are considered to be unplayable for latencies higher than 100 ms. However, Local Lag can actually be combined with Dead Reckoning to achieve better results [22].

Finally, the only option to actually remove inconsistencies in case they occur is given by a technique called Time Warp [23]. Time Warp is a technique well known in the area of parallel and distributed discrete event simulation (PDES) [24]. In Time Warp, the virtual world is split between logical processes (LPs), a generalization of peers simulating a distributed game. Each LP periodically stores a snapshot of its entire (game) state. In case a peer observes an inconsistency (because it received a *straggler* message from another peer), it performs a *rollback* and restores the game state that was observed right before the inconsistency time. In a way, the time is rolled back into the past. A peer rolling back may also decide that it sent messages to other peers in the past that were based on wrong assumptions, and thus caused inconsistencies there. In such a case the peer then sends so-called *null-messages* (void-messages), causing rollbacks on other peers. This may result in waves of null-messages flooding the whole P2P system, and undoing lots of work that was previously computed. Since peers by default simulate independently from each other, assuming that no inconsistencies occur, Time Warp is also often called to be an *optimistic* approach. In contrast, since Local Lag assumes that always inconsistencies occur and thus delays every single message, such approaches are also known as *pessimistic* techniques.

In our work we focus on Time Warp like systems, and ask how rollbacks and null-messages depend on network lag. Time Warp has been studied extensively in PDES, and is usually applied to a fully simulated system without real user interaction. In the gaming domain, in [25] the authors built a testbed based on Quake III, which was adapted to run Time Warp. The authors used bots only, and relate the influence of network lag and the usage of different Local Lag settings onto bot performance and Time Warp frequencies. In [26] the authors adapted a well known tank battle game called BZFlag[1] in order to evaluate a newly proposed hybrid architecture between client-server and P2P, using a central arbiter. They actually carried out experiments with real users, as we did, but did not focus on Time Warp. In [27] the authors adapted a simple third person capture-the-flag game, and a Quake 2 clone to combine Local Lag and Time Warp in a mirrored server setting.

---

[1] http://bzflag.org/

The contribution of our work is as follows. We developed a tank battle game called "Panzer Battalion" from scratch, implementing high-quality graphics and control in order to provide a realistic game feeling. The game is meant to be a testbed for evaluating how rollbacks are created, depending on network lag, number of players, and other parameters. We explicitly focus on running experiments with real users, here also deriving their subjective opinion on how rollbacks influence the gaming experience.

3   Panzer Battalion

The game "Panzer Battalion" was written for assessing Time Warp for P2P type decentralized, fast paced games. It is a surreal third person shooter, written in C++ under Linux. Players control a tank, collect power-ups and fight other players. The implementation relies on OpenGL for rendering, SDL for threads, window management, input handling and sound, DevIL[2] for image loading, arabica[3] for XML parsing, and BSD sockets for network communication. The graphics engine makes use of depth-fail stencil shadows, cartoon shading, normal mapping and other various shader effects. Running it requires the availability of an NVIDIA GForce 6xxx or higher, or any other graphics card that supports Fragment Shader 3.0 or higher.

Figure 1 shows a screen shot of "Panzer Battalion". Players steer their own tank and roam through a plane. The tanks can shoot at each other, and in contrast to BZFlag, shots hit instantaneously, i.e., the velocity of a shell is infinite. Additionally, the plane is full of obstacles that block the view, and players

Fig. 1. "Panzer Battalion" screenshot

---

[2] http://openil.sourceforge.net/
[3] http://www.jezuk.co.uk/cgi-bin/view/arabica

can hide behind them. Figure 1 also shows some power-ups that can be collected in order to up-level the power of each tank. Power-ups include armor strengthening, increasing the gun fire rate, the gun's effectiveness, the engine speed, and additional shields. On the other side there are also booby-traps destroying a tank's armor. Indeed each power-up looks the same, and consuming them thus introduces a momentum of surprise.

Tank movement, graphics, and the game physics have been designed to be as realistic as possible in order to maximize the gaming fun. We think that real experiments with real human subjects need a game that maximizes the gaming experience.

3.1   Message Handling

"Panzer Battalion" implements a fully decentralized network topology based on the P2P paradigm. Each peer actually simulates its own version of the entire virtual game world. This means that the entire game logic is being interpreted on every instance of the game, for the whole game. Another important point is that every instance communicates with every other instance directly instead of using a central server. Since each peer computes its own game version, no player is having disadvantages because of high network lags. On the other hand, as was pointed out previously, inconsistencies may occur and may cause different, contradicting game states on different peers. The advantages of such a system are, for one, a complete removal of a single point of failure, meaning there is no game instance without which the game would fail. Additionally, as instances interact directly, we avoid the situation that certain players "far away" (large round trip time) from the server cannot play the game due to high lag. In "Panzer Battalion" however, while the interaction with players "near" to an instance would be smooth, the interaction with far away players will suffer from high lags. Because of this a situation might occur where different instances of the game would have different game states. In order to further discuss the problem in the next section the design of "Panzer Battalion" is described.

3.2   Game Engine Design

The entire game logic is based on two message queues: the *inner* and *outer* queue (see Figure 2).

The inner queue is responsible for all the events relevant to the game play itself. For example a message containing the data for the move of a particular object is processed in the inner queue. The outer message queue handles all network based tasks, such as connecting, transmitting messages, clock synchronization, etc. The meaning of "MQ" is to emulate network latency (see Section 3.4). Every message has a time stamp, and messages are ordered in ascending order in the inner queue. The only messages that are sent over the network are those containing the action of the *tank* controlled by the player playing that particular instance of the game. In case a tank does something, for instance move or shoot, a message is put into the inner queue of the tank's game instance, and in case

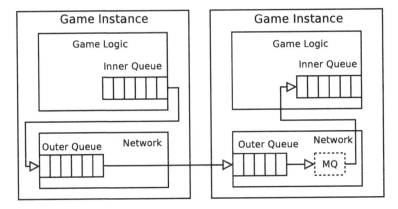

Fig. 2. Flow of messages through the inner and outer queues

Table 1. Messages sent between peers

Message	Interpretation
Move to location	A tank appears a certain location
Change angles	Viewing direction of a tank
Shoot	A tank shoots
Dead	A tank broadcasts that it has died
Damage	A tank receives damage
Respawn	A dead tank comes back to life

it is relevant to others, it is put into the outer queue as well (and subsequently sent to every other game instance). Upon receiving a message from another peer, the message is first put into the outer queue. From there it is passed on to the inner queue, where it is finally executed. The game logic, the rendering and input handling is asynchronous with the inner queue and synchronous with the outer queue. Table 1 shows the messages that are sent between the different game instances (peers).

In order to be able to determine inconsistencies, we synchronize the computer clocks of the peers as accurately as possible. This is done by using a protocol similar to the network time protocol (NTP) [28]. Before sending a message, the system time of a peer is determined by calling SDL GetTime(). This time stamp is then added to the message and sent to other peers.

3.3 States, Inconsistencies and Rollbacks

We define an inconsistency as an occurrence of the following situation: Assume that $N > 1$ peers send a number of messages to each other, and that each message determines an event that is applied a certain time stamp. Further assume that time stamps are all different due to high resolution clocks. Due to this time stamp, all messages can be ordered. At one particular peer the messages arrive at its inner queue and are executed. Due to network latencies, this execution of messages might not be done in the same order, as imposed by the message time stamps. This out-of-order execution leads then to a game state S_1. Now assume that executing the messages in-order would actually lead to a game state S_2. We say that an inconsistency has occurred if $S_1 \neq S_2$.

In order to remove inconsistencies, we implemented Time Warp. "Panzer Battalion" records its entire game state every 100 ms. Figure 3 a) shows the inner queue of any game instance. The execution pointer points to the next message to be executed. The messages left to this pointer have already been executed, the messages to the right are yet to be executed. At periodic time instances, the states are saved.

Figure 3 b) shows the reception of a late message in the inner queue. At this time point it is not known whether this message would actually cause an inconsistency. The game instance then decides to rollback to the saved state before this straggler, in this case state S_{i-1} (see Figure 3 c)). The execution pointer is set to the message right after S_{i-1} and all messages after S_{i-1} are actually re-executed. An example for a rollback and its possible consequences are shown in Figures 4 and 5. First a tank A shoots another tank B, destroying it as a result. However, shortly after a rollback is carried out since the game instance of tank A did not get a shoot message from B in time, stating that actually B shot first. Upon arrival of this straggler, A is forced to rollback, and tank A is destroyed by B's shot.

A well-known problem of Time Warp is given by inconsistencies on one peer causing inconsistencies on other peers. Suppose that peer A sends a message m,

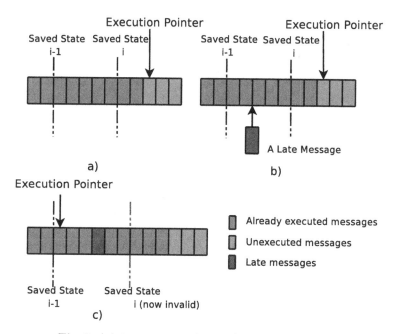

Fig. 3. A late message arrives and triggers a rollback

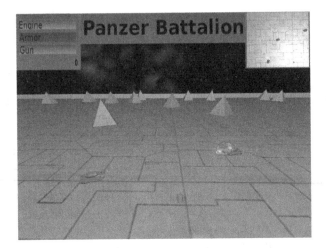

Fig. 4. Before a rollback: a tank A (left) shoots a tank B (right)

Fig. 5. After the rollback: Tank B shoots tank A

and then later receives a late message m' which contains an event that happened before that of m, and because of which m should *not have been sent*. Peer A is now aware of this fact and carries out a rollback, but since it already has sent m to all other peers (and m should not have been sent), the other peers already have received and executed m, leading to further inconsistencies (see Figure 6 a)). The game instance that received this late message now knows of this fact, but of course other peers do not. The message m should never have been transmitted. This problem is solved through implementation of *null-messages*. These are messages saying that a certain message should not have existed and was false. In our previous example, after receiving m', A transmits $\bar{m}$ which voids the already sent message m. Any other instance upon receiving of $\bar{m}$ (see

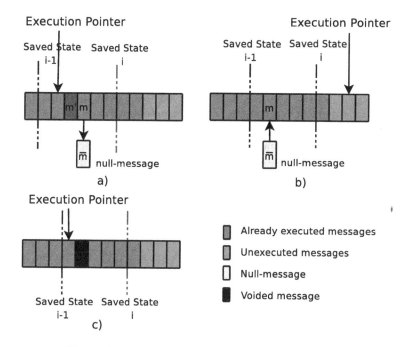

Fig. 6. A null-message arrives and triggers a rollback

Figure 3 b)) does a rollback, and skips the execution on the message m that was voided, thus synchronizing its state with the other instances (see Figure 3 c)).

However rollbacks are rather expensive and should be avoided as much as possible. Messages lagging only several milliseconds need not cause a time warp. In addition, a full time warp may not always be desirable, even if it prevents a situation that should not have happened. As an example imagine a situation, where a player A kills player B. However a rollback occurring a few seconds later shows that B actually was supposed to survive the shot. A looses the frag and B is warped back, most likely in the middle of the battle, only to die again, which ends up being unpleasant for all players.

Even with rollbacks and null-messages it is hard to be certain that the states in all instances are the same. An additional measure used is that all messages are *self-sufficient*. This means that every message contains all the data required to make the change in the game state without depending on information not contained in the message. As an example, a message bearing date of object translation should not be implemented as: "translate object A by a vector V", as the end result depends on the current state of the object A. Instead the movement should be done as such: "move object A to position P". Another example would be shooting. Instead of "the object A shot" a message looking like "an object A positioned at P with rotation angle R shot" is more appropriate. This ensures that if there was an inconsistency in, say, a position of an object, after receiving the next move message the inconsistency would be corrected.

3.4 Network Latency Emulation

In order to assess the effect of network latency in a decentralized gaming scenario, "Panzer Battalion" implements an artificial latency unit. Messages are delayed in a queue between the outer and inner queue, called *middle queue* (see "MQ" in Figure 2). A message that should be moved from outer to inner queue is temporarily stored in the middle queue for some predefined time dt. This artificial lag can be adjusted per game instance during gameplay. It must be noted that the resulting behavior is actually different from Local Lag, since during its stay in the middle queue, the message is not seen by the inner queue, and hence not taken into account when executing other messages.

It is interesting to note that the render loop consumes most of the computing performance of the game, and itself introduces a Local Lag. As a result, even if the emulated network lag of the middle queue is set to $dt = 0$, several messages are often passed from the middle queue to the inner queue at once or in short successions, making them executed in the same pass in the inner queue, and the inconsistencies caused by them are fixed in a single rollback.

4 Experimental Results

The experiments were carried out in our laboratory, consisting of several Linux PCs interconnected by FastEthernet. In these first experiments we aimed at finding general dependencies of Time Warp rollbacks on network latency. Second, we wanted to examine the behavior of human players in a networked game with high latency in a decentralized P2P system using Time Warp. Both issues are treated in the next two sections.

4.1 Rollbacks

In a first set of experiments, in each experiment two persons played against each other for five minutes. The network lag in the middle queue was set to $dt = 0, 200, 400$ and 600 ms. Each experiment was run two times, resulting in a total of eight experiments. The games were run at 60 frames per second on average. We recorded the number of rollbacks that occurred within these 5 minutes, and the maximum time a message had been late for each rollback.

Table 2 shows the average number of rollbacks that occurred at each peer, depending on the emulated network lag. It can be seen that this number first rises sharply, but decreases after 200 ms. An explanation for this is provided below.

In our experiments for each rollback we computed how late each message causing the rollback was (a rollback can be caused by more than one message), and for each rollback recorded the maximum value of these times. Figures 7, 8, and 9 show the histograms of these lateness values.

The first game shown in Figure 7 was recorded without any artificial lag and caused on average 285 rollbacks per player. Even if the artificial lag created by

Table 2. Average number of rollbacks for different lags

Lag (ms)	Average number of rollbacks
0	285
200	630
400	462
600	301

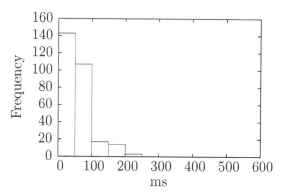

Fig. 7. Number of rollbacks depending on how late a message was (no lag)

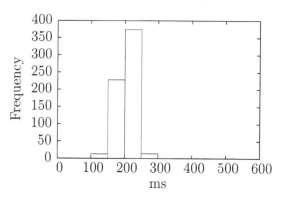

Fig. 8. Number of rollbacks depending on how late a message was (200 ms lag)

the middle queue was set to $dt = 0$, inconsistencies occurred, for once due to the render loop, and second, due to small offsets of the peer clocks. As a result, over 50% of those rollbacks were caused by messages late less then 50 ms, and nearly 90% less then 100 ms. It is interesting to note that in these experiments the effects of rollbacks were not visible to the players.

Figure 8 shows the rollback lateness distribution of the same game with a 200 ms lag. In five minutes there were 630 rollbacks per player on average. The players noted the game at this point was somewhat irritating, and the effects of the rollbacks were often visible. However, the game still was acknowledged as being playable.

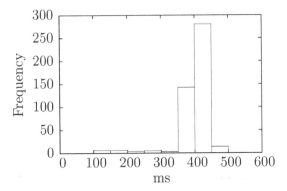

Fig. 9. Number of rollbacks depending on how late a message was (400 ms lag)

Finally, Figure 9 shows the rollback lateness distribution in the case of a 400 ms lag. There were 462 recorded rollbacks per player on average, which is about 27% less than in the 200 ms case. This is due to having many late messages executed in single a rollback, and also, as will be pointed out in the next section, due to a change of tactics by the players, shifting from a dynamic to a more static gameplay. The effects of rollbacks here were very annoying. Players stated that the game in effect was no more playable.

In the 600 ms case players were no more able to control their gameplay. Rollbacks were actually clearly visible as such. The gaming experience was disastrous, even though the number of rollbacks decreased to the order of magnitude of the zero lag case (see next section).

4.2   Player Behavior

Another set of games were played in which the playing *behavior* was monitored. In each experiment three players were involved. The player input was recorded, and categorized into two categories: *dynamic* and *static*. Dynamic includes moving the tank, evading being shot, racing for power-ups etc. Static input includes aiming and shooting enemies. The games started with 0 ms lag, and during the game the lag was constantly increased to the values 200, 400 and 600 ms. Table 3 shows the percentage of dynamic vs. static input.

The experiment shows that with the lag increase, tactics started being more static. In the end when the lag was around 600 ms, for most cases the game

Table 3. Dynamic vs. static

Lag (ms)	Dynamic (%)	Static (%)
0	59.3	40.67
200	48.9	51.0
400	26.4	73.5
600	21.0	78.9

could be broken down to the following: a player would respawn, rush to the killing ground, where the battles were fought over and over again. Then he/she would stop and spend the rest of that life aiming at and shooting other players, with minimal evasion tactics. When asked about why this tactic was chosen, players replied that it was getting hard to earn the frag, and thus the general tactic was to prefer to be able to shoot someone, and increase the risk of being shot yourself. Aiming and assessing where the opponent actually is was more difficult when moving, and thus movements were stopped.

In addition the players replied that it was getting hard to guess the intentions of other players, and often realizing too late that they were in danger. While this is partially due to the lag itself, players said that introducing a clearly visible rollback often created confusion, for example it was harder to keep track of one's relative position to other players in short distance battles. This was more visible with the local lag being greater. Players first noticed this with the lag being about 400 ms, and in games with artificial lag of 600 ms, they tried to avoid fights at short distance altogether.

5   Conclusions

In this paper we introduce "Panzer Battalion", a testbed for assessing the effects of rollbacks on gameplay in a tank battle game, and how these rollbacks depend on network conditions. We put considerable efforts into the development of "Panzer Battalion", in order to generate a realistic positive gaming experience. Due to the development from scratch, we were able to make important design decisions for our testbed without being forced to alter third party source code.

In a first set of experiments we evaluated the effect of network lag and rollbacks. We showed that for increasing network lag, after reaching a maximum, the number of rollbacks drops again, due to the fact that more and more messages cause only one rollback.

We also showed how gamers change their behavior, away from a dynamic to a more static behavior in case the network lag grows too large. In general for large lags, Time Warp still may provide consistency, but this comes with a price. The game gets increasingly unplayable, and when using Time Warp rollbacks too far into the past must be avoided.

References

1. Beigbeder, T., Coughlan, R., Lusher, C., Plunkett, J., Agu, E., Claypool, M.: The effects of loss and latency on user performance in unreal tournament. In: NetGames 2004 (2004), http://www.sigcomm.org/sigcomm2004/netgames.html
2. Dick, M., Wellnitz, O., Wolf, L.: Analysis of factors affecting players' performance and perception in multiplayer games. In: NetGames 2005 (2005), http://www.research.ibm.com/netgames2005/

3. Yasui, T., Ishibashi, Y., Ikedo, T.: Influences of network latency and packet loss on consistency in networked racing games. In: NetGames 2005 (2005), http://www.research.ibm.com/netgames2005/
4. Claypool, M.: The effect of latency on user performance in real-time strategy games. Computer Networks 49(1), 52–70 (2005); Special issue: Networking issues in entertainment computing
5. Fritsch, T., Ritter, H., Schiller, J.: The effect of latency and network limitations on mmorpgs (a field study of everquest2). In: NetGames 2005 (2005)
6. Cronin, E., Filstrup, B., Kurc, A.R., Jamin, S.: An efficient synchronization mechanism for mirrored game architectures. In: NetGames 2002 (2002)
7. Gargolinski, S., Pierre, C.S., Claypool, M.: Game server selection for multiple players. In: NetGames 2005 (2005), http://www.research.ibm.com/netgames2005/
8. Lee, K.W., Ko, B.J., Calo, S.: Adaptive server selection for large scale interactive online games. Computer Networks 49(1), 84–102 (2005); Special issue: Networking issues in entertainment computing
9. Brun, J., Safaei, F., Boustead, P.: Server topology considerations in online games. In: NetGames 2006 (2006)
10. Webb, S.D., Soh, S., Lau, W.: Enhanced mirrored servers for network games. In: NetGames 2007 (2007)
11. Schiele, G., Suselbeck, R., Wacker, A., Hahner, J., Becker, C., Weis, T.: Requirements of peer-to-peer-based massively multiplayer online gaming. In: Proceedings of the Seventh IEEE International Symposium on Cluster Computing and the Grid (CCGRID 2007), pp. 773–782 (2007)
12. Morse, K.L., Bic, L., Dillencourt, M.: Interest management in large-scale virtual environments. Presence: Teleoperators and Virtual Environments 9(1), 52–68 (2000)
13. Rhalibi, A.E., Merabti, M., Shen, Y.: AoIM in peer-to-peer multiplayer online games. In: Proceedings of the 2006 ACM SIGCHI international conference on Advances in computer entertainment technology (2006)
14. Hu, S.Y., Chen, J.F., Chen, T.H.: Von: A scalable peer-to-peer network for virtual environments. IEEE Network 20(4), 22–31 (2006)
15. Knutsson, B., Lu, H., Xu, W., Hopkins, B.: Peer-to-peer support for massively multiplayer games. In: IEEE Infocom 2004 (2004)
16. Iimura, T., Hazeyama, H., Kadobayashi, Y.: Zoned federation of game servers: a peer-to-peer approach to scalable multiplayer online games. In: NetGames 2004 (2004)
17. Kabus, P., Terpstra, W.W., Cilia, M., Buchmann, A.P.: Addressing cheating in distributed mmogs. In: NetGames 2005 (2005), http://www.research.ibm.com/netgames2005/
18. Palant, W., Griwodz, C., Halvorsen, P.: Consistency requirements in multiplayer online games. In: NetGames 2006 (2006)
19. Pantel, L., Wolf, L.C.: On the suitability of dead reckoning schemes for games. In: NetGames 2002 (2002)
20. Aggarwal, S., Banavar, H., Khandelwal, A., Mukherjee, S., Rangarajan, S.: Accuracy in dead-reckoning based distributed multi-player games. In: NetGames 2004 (2004)
21. Mauve, M., Vogel, J., Hilt, V., Effelsberg, W.: Local-lag and timewarp: Providing consistency for replicated continuous applications. IEEE transactions on Multimedia 6(1), 47–57 (2004)
22. Zhang, Y., Chen, L., Chen, G.: Globally synchronized dead-reckoning with local lag for continuous distributed multiplayer games. In: NetGames 2006 (2006)

23. Mauve, M.: How to keep a dead man from shooting. In: Proc. of the 7th International Workshop on Interactive Distributed Multimedia Systems and Telecommunication Services (IDMS 2000) (2000)
24. Jefferson, D.R.: Virtual time. ACM Transactions on Programming Languages and Systems (TOPLAS) 7(3), 404–425 (1985)
25. Liang, D., Boustead, P.: Using local lag and timewarp to improve performance for real life multi-player online games. In: NetGames 2006 (2006)
26. Pellegrino, J.D., Dovrolis, C.: Bandwidth requirement and consistency resolution latency in multiplayer games. In: NetGames 2003 (2003)
27. Müller, J., Gössling, A., Gorlatch, S.: On correctness of scalable multi-server state replication in online games. In: NetGames 2006 (2006)
28. Mills, D.L.: Network time protocol (version 3). RFC 1305 (March 1992)

How to Steer Characters in Group Games

I. Abiyasa Suhardi[1] and Jörn Loviscach[2]

[1] Universität Bremen, Bibliotheksstr. 1, 28359 Bremen, Germany
abiyasa@abiamy.com
[2] Fachhochschule Bielefeld, Wilhelm-Bertelsmann-Straße 10, 33602 Bielefeld,
Germany
joern.loviscach@fh-bielefeld.de

Abstract. Video games played by several persons using the same screen require specific user interfaces. In this work, we look at options to let players steer a number of on-screen characters. To this end, we have built a prototype system that employs a number of Nintendo Wii Remote devices for input. We have devised three types of control that are based on different sensors available in these devices. In addition, we propose a mode to enable teams of players to collaboratively control a single character. This paper closes with a preliminary evaluation based on a prototypical game.

1 Introduction

A vital reason why people play games is to have a social experience with friends or family [1]. Group games in front of a single shared video screen become particularly simple through the ubiquity of the Nintendo Wii Remote game control device: Every player can bring his or her controller. In theory, the size of such a group may range from two persons to an audience filling a movie theater. For manageable experiments, however, this study limits its scope to a range of 4 to 16 players.

This work addresses three main questions: How can a system support a large number of Wii Remote devices? Which kinds of interaction methods are feasible with the Wii Remote in group gaming? How do users perform with those interaction methods and which do they enjoy? – To answer these questions, a group game prototype has been developed and evaluated. The system consists of a game server and several input clients to which the Wii Remote devices connect.

This paper is structured as follows: Section 2 surveys related work. Section 3 introduces the design of the underlying game, the implementation of which is described in Section 4. The different options for control are described in Section 5. Section 6 reports about the tests conducted; Section 7 concludes this work.

2 Related Work

Some games sold for the Nintendo Wii console such as the racing game Mario Kart Wii offer a multiplayer mode in which each of up to four players can control

Z. Pan et al. (Eds.): Transactions on Edutainment II, LNCS 5660, pp. 48–58, 2009.

his or her own on-screen character in parallel to the others. Games such as Wii Sports support only two players at the same time. Wii Play and WarioWare admit four players, who, however, have to take turns. To the authors' knowledge, the only Wii game which possesses a cooperative mode so far is Super Mario Galaxy. Its cooperative mode is called "Co-Star mode" and has an asymmetric nature: The character Mario is mainly controlled by the first player; a second player can join or leave the game at any time and can support the first player for instance by collecting game items.

WiiArts [2] is a collaborative and expressive art project that employs Wii Remote devices. Up to three users can interact to create an auditory or a visual performance; the latter is projected onto one single large screen. Even though the setup is related to ours, the control functions of WiiArts such as painting and a flashlight mode are rather different.

To handle theater-sized audiences, several researchers developed inexpensive but relatively limited interaction devices. The interaction happens in analogy to majority vote; none of these approaches is intended to grant each single member of the audience full control over one specific item on the screen. Carpenter's Cinematrix system [3,4] is based on a bi-color paddle. The players present their paddles to a camera; the number of paddles and the displayed colors are determined by image processing. Maynes-Aminzade et al. [5] track the overall lateral motion of the audience; the players lean their body to the left or right to control the game. Another option presented in the same work is to hand a laser pointer to every member of the audience. Through image processing one can count how many laser pointers are directed toward a specific region of the screen. Feldmeier and Paradiso [6] employ a small device that emits a radio frequency signal every time the player shakes it.

3   Game Design

The game prototype presented here is inspired by real-world fruit harvest festivals or mushroom picking. It is designed to be simple, along the line of existing Wii games, which also facilitates evaluation. The objective of all players is to steer their character to collect as many as possible items from the screen in a fixed time frame, see Figure 1.

This game belongs to the fast-action genre. The player has to quickly decide about the character movement while competing with other players. The main target group of the game is that of casual gamers.

Sticking to the game's casual type, the players are represented on screen by human-like but cartoonish characters with tiny bodies and large heads of different colors and shapes. At any time, ten to twenty game items are available in the playing field. A character collects an item simply by moving across it. A collected item disappears immediately; ten points are added to the character's score. (The number of ten allows using finer increments for specific rewards in a future version.) Less than half a second later, the system will add another item at a random position of the playing field. This is done to maintain an approximately constant number of items inside the game area.

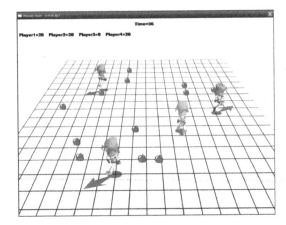

Fig. 1. In the game prototype, a number of players compete in collecting items (shown: four players, each controlling a single character through tilting)

An arrow beneath each character indicates its current direction and speed. To facilitate identification, the arrow possesses the color of the character. When one character is about to collide with another character, it stops moving.

4   System Overview

The Wii Remote incorporates both a triaxial accelerometer and an infrared-sensitive camera [7]. Whereas the former can be used without further devices, the latter requires setting up infrared light beacons, such as Nintendo's Sensor Bar that at its two ends contains clusters of diodes emitting infrared light. The intelligent light sensor inside the Wii Remote can track up to four beacons; the sensor reports their positions in its 2D camera coordinate frame. The field of view of the infrared sensor is about 36 degrees wide [8]; hence, the standard Sensor Bar confines the usable range to two to four meters distance from it.

The Wii Remote uses Bluetooth to establish a wireless connection. However, due to a limitation in the standard, a single Bluetooth adapter can only connect to a maximum of seven other devices at the same time [9]. In practice, a PC can only connect to six Wii Remotes simultaneously; the communication with the fifth and the sixth Wii Remote is not stable enough, so effectively only four Wii Remotes can be used [10]. Coincidentally or not, this is also the maximum number the Nintendo Wii console can connect to simultaneously.

To work with larger groups of players, we set up a client-server system so that up to 16 Wii Remotes can be used in parallel, see Figure 2. The input clients are responsible for handling the Wii Remotes using Bluetooth connections and forwarding the input data to the game server, which handles the game engine and the display. The clients and the server communicate through UDP messages over Ethernet or wireless LAN. Using client PCs distributed in the audience also facilitates covering a larger area, as the communication range of the Wii Remote

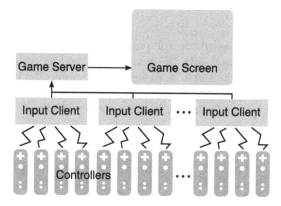

Fig. 2. Several client PCs, each with up to four connected Wii Remotes, are linked to the game server via an IP-based network

Fig. 3. 64 sprite images are used to animate the characters. A selection is shown here.

is limited to a radius of approximately ten meters. The four assignable LEDs available on each Wii Remote are used to indicate an ID number, so that every player knows which device is his or hers.

For the communication with the Wii Remote, the prototype employs Brian Peek's library (http://www.brianpeek.com/) in version 1.5.2. It is not only simple to use and supports C#, the main programming language for the prototype, but can also connect to up to four Wii Remotes. The latter feature is still uncommon with other libraries.

The game server animates and renders the game characters, the playing field, and the game objects in 3D using the game engine IrrlichtNET CP 0.8, a version of the Irrlicht Engine (http://irrlicht.sourceforge.net) adapted to the .NET framework. The game server also handles collision detection and records the scores, the position, and the speeds of all game characters for later analysis.

The game characters and the game objects are rendered as billboards showing animated sprites of 128×128 pixels. Per character, 64 sprites are available, see Figure 3. The maximum speed of a character is set to 600 units per second; the playing field has a size of 1600×1400 units.

5 Control

We have devised three types of control: pointing, tilting, and gamepad. Each one is based on a different sensor, with the gamepad method reflecting classical input devices. All players use the same input method; it cannot be changed during a round of the game. In addition, we experimented with a "team mode," in which several players can control a single character cooperatively.

5.1 Pointing

With the pointing method, the player directs the Wii Remote toward the screen to control a cursor through the infrared-sensing camera. The character moves as if it chases the cursor, see Figure 4. It stops running once it reaches the cursor. In order to make the character running all the time, the player has to move the cursor and keep a distance between the cursor and the game character. The character moves only when the Wii Remote's button "A" is pressed so that the users do not have to point all of the time.

Fig. 4. The character's speed and direction are determined by the difference vector between the positions of the game character and the cursor

The two xy positions of the beacons reported by the camera are averaged to compute an xy midpoint. This is mirrored about the center of the screen and then used as cursor position. The character's speed and direction are determined by the distance vector between the game character and the cursor. If the distance is below 56 units, the speed is set to zero. Above that, the speed scales linearly with the distance. The speed attains its maximum and is clamped there when the distance exceeds 400 units.

5.2 Tilting

To steer a character by tilting, the player holds the Wii Remote in an upright orientation and leans it sideways, similar to a joystick. For doing so, the Wii Remote can be held with one hand or both hands, see Figure 5.

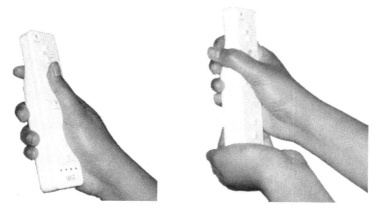

Fig. 5. The Wii Remote may be held in two different ways to control the game character by tilting

Fig. 6. The game character's speed and direction are determined by how far and in which direction the user tilts the controller

The tilting can be sensed through the forces that gravity exerts onto the two axes of the accelerometer that point in horizontal directions when it is held upright. The angle values measured along these axes determine the direction of the character's motion and are mapped linearly to its velocity, see Figure 6, again with a threshold from below (6 degrees) and clamping from above. The maximum speed is reached when tilting the device by 64 degrees. In contrast to the pointing method, the tilting method does not require the user to press any button to make the character run.

5.3 Gamepad

With the gamepad input method, the user controls the character through the cursor buttons, see Figure 7. This method mimics the standard game control to

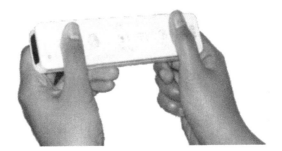

Fig. 7. The Wii Remote may be held like a gamepad

which video gamers have gotten used. A similar approach is optionally employed by Nintendo's Super Smash Bros game. The left thumb rests on the directional buttons; the right thumb can push the buttons "1" and "2," which may be employed in future versions of the game. Two adjacent cursor buttons may be pressed simultaneously so that the game character can move in eight different directions. The longer the user keeps the button pressed, the faster the character runs. It reaches its maximum speed when the player holds the cursor button(s) for 1.5 seconds.

5.4 Team Mode

The number of displayed game characters is limited due to the resolution of the screen and the visual capabilities of the users. An additional team mode helps to reduce the number of game characters on the screen while still admitting a large number of players. Here, a single game character is collectively controlled by a team of two to four players. This requires more cooperation and social activity between the players and may enhance the game experience. Cinematrix [4] comprises a game in which the members of the audience have to cooperate to fly a plane. People start to shout to suggest the best course. Similar effects are known from the Aminzade system [5].

The team mode can be played using any of the three interaction methods which have been explained before: pointing, tilting, or gamepad. A game character's running speed and direction is determined by averaging the velocity vectors resulting from the input of all players controlling this character. Each game character possesses arrow indicators for all its players, see Figure 8. Thus, every player sees his or her input being represented. Otherwise, there may be a tendency to produce some deviant input in order to check that one's actions have any effect at all [4,5].

6 Testing and Evaluation

The system and the interaction methods were subjected to both a technical test and an evaluation by prospective users.

6.1   Setting

In a preliminary evaluation we sought answers to the following questions: How well do the players control the character by pointing, tilting, or using the gamepad? How well do the players control the character in the team mode? Which input method is preferred? How do team mates communicate with each other and coordinate their actions?

We invited six test users (five male, one female; age 22 to 29). Four of them are students; the other two have full-time jobs in IT or graphic design. All possess a Wii game console at home and use it to play for one to three hours per week. A 20-inch LCD monitor was installed as game screen. The participants sat in a line about two meters away from the screen.

Fig. 8. In the team mode, the character is controlled by the average input of several players

The subjects were instructed to do several input sequences (pushing buttons, tilting, and moving the cursor) to familiarize themselves with the different interaction methods. This also was an ultimate check the system had to pass to validate the collection and processing of input data.

The subjects played the game using the three input methods (tilt, point, and gamepad) and three game modes (single players; three teams with two players each; and two teams with three players each). For each combination of input method and game mode, three game rounds of 40 seconds each were played, amounting to 27 rounds in total. After three rounds in the same configuration, the subjects were asked to complete a brief questionnaire about their likings. At the end, a concluding questionnaire was administered.

6.2   Results

With six Wii Remote devices at hand, the technical setup has been successfully tested with two input clients (each with three devices or one with four and the other with two devices) and three input clients (each with two devices). To not confuse devices, the Bluetooth pairing process works only sequentially. This turned out to become a headache for larger numbers of devices.

Figure 9 shows the overall results, where the scores of the three rounds for each configuration have been summed for simplicity. Within-subject t-tests on the underlying data demonstrated for single players and teams of two and three players that the pairwise differences between pointing, tilting, and gamepad are statistically significant with error probabilities well below the five-percent level.

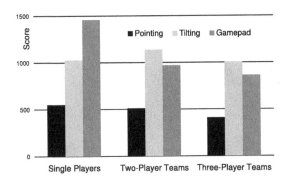

Fig. 9. The performance differences of the input methods also show up in this plot of averaged scores of different subjects and teams

On average, the player scores are lowest with the pointing method. All players commented that they found the character hard to control using the cursor pointer and they did not like this method. Two players felt that pointing the cursor while holding the "A" button was not easy.

Unsteady or jumpy cursor motion is also known from commercial Wii games, as reported in forums such as GameSpot (http://www.gamespot.com). The sensor is prone to errors introduced through wrong placement of the beacons as well as interfering IR sources like direct sunlight, light bulbs, or even reflections off shiny tables. A better algorithm needs to cope with additional or lost IR sources. One may even try to predict the cursor motion from former data. GlovePIE [11] provides several scripts for this purpose.

With tilting, the players scored much better than with pointing. All six subjects liked this input method. They felt that the control was more natural, easy to understand, and more precise than pointing. The highest scores in the single-player mode were achieved, however, with the gamepad. All subjects agreed that it is much easier to control the character using this method. Nonetheless, five out of six players preferred tilting over using the gamepad. They felt uncomfortable holding the controller in the sideway position. Other than in the single mode, in the team mode the control by tilting yielded the highest scores. All subjects agreed that this kind of team mode is the most enjoyable. The players coordinated with their team mates for instance through shouting suggestions for a direction to take.

One reason for the better control by tilting over gamepad input in team mode is the following: With teams of two persons we often saw the characters not moving at all because the players invoke opposite motion directions, which canceled in the sum. This is more likely to happen with the gamepad because the users are limited to eight directions and – even worse – clearly prefer the four cardinal ones.

The game feedback through the score display and the game timer turned out to be a neglected issue: The players were too busy with the game character and the game objects. Several times the subjects were surprised that a round was "suddenly" over or that they just had won the game. A solution may be to use non-visual means such as a beep ten seconds before a round of the game ends.

7   Conclusion and Outlook

We presented and compared several methods to steer characters in group games. The most prominent finding may be that the most effective control of the game – as exemplified by the gamepad input – may not be preferred by the players. A similar phenomenon was visible in the team mode: Even though the performance drops in comparison to the single-player mode, the subjects remark that it is more fun to play in a team, especially when they are allowed to shout.

This study examined only single sensors in isolation; future research could look into combining different ones. On top of that, other sensors such as gyroscopes may be added. Concerning gameplay, one may research into variations such as introducing a character's ability to jump, to attack or stun others, or to steal from them. Teams comprising several on-screen characters may be formed. To better visualize the team mode, the human-like characters may be replaced with objects known to be slow to steer such as tanker ships.

References

1. Rouse, R.: Game Design: Theory and Practice. Wordware Publishing (2001)
2. Lee, H.J., Kim, H., Gupta, G., Mazalek, A.: WiiArts: creating collaborative art experience with WiiRemote interaction. In: TEI 2008: Proceedings of the 2nd international conference on tangible and embedded interaction, pp. 33–36 (2008)
3. Carpenter, L.: Cinematrix, video imaging method and apparatus for audience participation. U.S. Patents #5210604 and #5365266 (1994)
4. Carpenter, L., Carpenter, R.: Cinematrix interactive entertainment system (2001), http://www.cinematrix.com
5. Maynes-Aminzade, D., Pausch, R., Seitz, S.: Techniques for interactive audience participation. In: SIGGRAPH 2002: ACM SIGGRAPH 2002 conference abstracts and applications, p. 257 (2002)

6. Feldmeier, M., Paradiso, J.A.: Giveaway wireless sensors for large-group interaction. In: CHI 2004 extended abstracts on human factors in computing systems, pp. 1291–1292 (2004)
7. WiiLi: Wiimote (2007), http://www.wiili.org/index.php/Wiimote
8. Shirai, A., Geslin, E., Richir, S.: WiiMedia: motion analysis methods and applications using a consumer video game controller. In: Sandbox 2007: Proceedings of the 2007 ACM SIGGRAPH symposium on video games, pp. 133–140 (2007)
9. Bhagwat, P.: Bluetooth: Technology for short-range wireless apps. IEEE Internet Computing 5(3), 96–103 (2001)
10. Kharitonova, Y.: CRA DMP student work in computing research (2007), http://www.cra.org/Activities/craw/dmp/awards/2007/Kharitonova/week2.html
11. Kenner, C.: GlovePIE (2007), http://carl.kenner.googlepages.com/glovepie

Time-Based Personalised Mobile Game Downloading

Worapat Paireekreng, Kowit Rapeepisarn, and Kok Wai Wong

School of Information Technology
Murdoch University
South street, Murdoch, 6150
Perth, WA, Australia
{w.paireekreng,k.rapeepisarn,k.wong}@murdoch.edu.au

Abstract. Mobile device is an important gadget for many people today, regardless whether it is used for communication, entertainment or keeping up to date. With the advancement of mobile Internet, mobile devices are also used for many conventional PC based Internet applications. One such example is downloading games. Downloading mobile games via mobile device seems to be one of the more favorite activities for many mobile devices today. However, users may have different preferences in what genres of games they will be more interested in at different time of the day. In this paper, a personalised mobile game recommendation system which takes into consideration the time-of-day and time-of-week is used to provide a more personalised experience. From the data collected, it can be seen that at different time periods users may download different games and from different game genres.

Keywords: Mobile Personalisation, Time-based, Recommendation System, Games, Game theme, Mobile game.

1 Introduction

There is a rising trend of mobile games developed for a huge range of mobile devices over the past few years. During different time of the day, mobile device can also be used as an entertainment device for relaxation. Computer game has been viewed as an interactive media that is played most often when people have free time. Therefore it is easy to realize the impact by combining mobile phone culture and entertainment games. This leads to the popular trend in developing mobile games. Many mobile games have been developed in recent years. Some even transform popular console or PC games in the past to mobile platform. However, there could be too many games for mobile users to select. Additionally, users may prefer different mobile games at different time of the day. When users download games, too much time can be spent browsing content. The time use for browsing will be charged depending on the package data usage or time consumption according to network provider. Furthermore, many users have to pay for the game. Although some mobile games provide demo or trial version, the users still need to spend time browsing for something they like.

In this paper, we look at a recommendation system, which considered the downloaded games as well as user's expected playing period. The genre or theme of the game should also be taken into consideration. Eventually, the recommendation

Z. Pan et al. (Eds.): Transactions on Edutainment II, LNCS 5660, pp. 59–69, 2009.

system will configure the game downloading menu via mobile internet. In addition, time and theme of game can be used primarily to predict user's needs. This will greatly reduce the browsing time the user spends searching for the type of games he/she prefers. In order to solve this problem, personalisation concept can be applied to the mobile game downloading menu. This paper presents the personalised mobile game recommendation system by using context information like time-of-day, day-of-week and the theme of the game. The system uses the context information to cluster and display appropriate menu to enhance the downloading speed. This paper also tries to reduce the need for the user to browse through several levels of menu in order to find what they want. Whenever user downloads the game, the menu that is able to meet the user's needs according to the context information will be displayed on the top of the menu. User can easily click to download or play the most desired game. The system can also identify the period used during weekend and time-of-day. In this paper, we have used a simple and straightforward technique which does not require a lot computation in the mobile device to present the most suitable games for the users. We work on a simple algorithm with the knowledge that the computing power on a mobile is always limited.

2 Literature Reviews

2.1 Game Theme

Game Genre. There are many kinds of games that people like to play. They may play for different reasons such as relaxation, quick escape from real world or as a challenge. Some may like one game genre while some like another. Game genre or game theme seems to be the important factor in determining the user's needs. It is also suggested that some game themes are more appropriate for different time and location when putting in the mobile game context. The game genre can be divided into several kinds such as action, RPG, casual or adventure games. Each genre has its unique characteristics. For example in action games, the goals are to move and involve in the game at all times. There are many levels and it needs skillful hand-eye coordination and quick reflexes without much strategy. In contrast, RPG or Role-playing games take a long time to finish and its character can grow and improve in skill. The other interesting game genre is casual game. This kind of game is easy to learn and not difficult to master. Importantly, it is often played in short bursts. The purpose of these games is for quick fun. Players want to get in and out quickly. In addition, puzzle games can also be challenging as well. It involves working on solving a puzzle without much storytelling. This genre of game is normally confined to just one screen. These two game genres seem to be suitable for mobile device.

Game Genre and Characteristic of the Players. There is a relationship between the characteristic of each person and game genre, suggesting that different people may play different game genre. As a result, the mobile game provider should recommend the right game to the right people at the right time. There are researches related to this area such as Prensky's research [10]. The author claims that different game genres have different impact on the content of activities. The research also proposed several variables when selecting a game style including target group based on their age and gender. [6,7] studied the relationship of personal characteristic and game genres as well. It investigated the relationship of the appropriate game genre to learning theory and analysed the characteristics of game theme. The research found that game genre appeals to different people with distinct personal characteristic.

2.2 Personalisation

Overview. Due to an overload of information, personalisation seems to be the recommended solution in order to refine the problem of too much information. It can be used both on the web as well as the mobile internet. Jorstad et. al defined personalization [18] as a service and mechanism to allow user to adjust and adapt services to meet their needs. Additionally, other researchers found from the surveys that mobile users are keen to personalise their mobile phone [16]. The personalisation system can be referred in several ways. For example, in [9], the authors focused on devices personalisation where hardware and software capabilities such as display size, fonts, graphic, input device, language and time have been discussed.

Mobile Personalisation. When focusing on mobile personalisation, it can be divided into 2 main types; content presentation and content visualisation. Firstly, content presentation is related to how the relevant information is gathered when presenting to the user. Factors related to user profile and other information such as ambience information which will be discussed in the latter section is also included in this area of study [21, 2]. Secondly, content visualisation is concerned with semantic zoom and drill down information on the chart for displaying on the screen [12, 1].

However, this paper is trying to solve the problem in terms of content presentation on downloading the game from the mobile menu.

2.3 Ambience Information

This research is exploring the relevant factors in order to improve the accuracy of user navigation prediction and facilitate adaptive WAP menu for user. This can help user to reduce the clicks on their mobile device and reach the more interested content quickly. One important information which is related to content presentation is time. It can be classified by weekday or weekend with the information of the time-of-day. For example, context was described as a description of a situation similar to case-base reasoning when used in mobile [14,15]. The research suggested that system adaption is required for the change in the environment. Contextual information played an important role towards information retrieval in successive search. From [4], it can be seen that using time-framed information can improve the performance in the prediction of future browsing patterns. This research used time-framed separation of week and semester information using association rules. They also suggested that user would prefer different kind of information during different time of the day. This suggested that the displayed information on the mobile device should vary from time to time in order to match the users' need during different time of the day [2]. In [19], this research also used time-of-day as a factor to develop the personalisation system for mobile content presentation. It tried to re-arrange the main WAP menu for mobile customers in order to predict what the users would like during different time of the day.

2.4 User Navigation Prediction

User session means the time that user connects through the mobile internet for a specific time continuously. This is the time from the user starts the connection till the time it is disconnected from the server. The user session is normally shorter than web browsing on a desktop. It is mainly due to the reason that it is not so convenience when using mobile device for browsing. Therefore, if there is some mechanism to predict which contents or pages user will use in the session, it will facilitate user efficiency and reduce content access time. This can lead to higher user satisfaction.

The feature of hyperlink on mobile internet is often displayed as a menu lists or options on the mobile device. The user has to click the option or menu item of interest to go to the desired content. These options or menus are known as user navigation. As can be seen from the content presentation or content filtering on mobile internet, personalisation can be achieved by predicting user navigation.

The aim of the research in this area is to reduce the click distance of the mobile internet usage session between the first page menu and the desired option menu. It tries to display relevant topics which may be needed by the user in the shortest time [17,3,20]. Nonetheless most research focused on WAP portals and personalised levels of menu while our research is trying to propose the level-free content personalisation. In addition many works also implemented techniques such as Markov model, Bayesian network and Naïve Bayes to predict the user navigation using profiling data [11,13,5].

However, some complex computation may not be appropriate for small content providers that have insufficient information relating to user profile and user preference. With this reason, case-base reasoning technique seems be common to provide mobile content personalisation.

3 Research Methodology

3.1 Experimental Design

The data of the research was conducted and gathered from the server log file of a mobile game provider in Thailand. The data in the log file was recorded in terms of mobile internet usage per session from the organisation's customer database. In addition, the log file also recorded the content name and content category of the company's file server and there were date and time usage information as well.

There were 25,699 records of users' sessions in the log file. This consists of 7,485 unique users. The user of the company can be divided into two types, specifically member and non-member. The member type customers can download unlimited content including Java games by monthly subscription. Therefore, this type of members is not too concerned about the number of downloaded games. However, they may be concerned with the difficulty in finding the interested game at the shortest time due to data charges. In contrast, non-members would be concerned about both the connection fee and finding the interested games fast. In Thailand, there are more pre-paid customers than post-paid customers. The pre-paid customers seem to be more restrictive with their budget than the post-paid customers as well.

The experiment was designed by adding the three main factors on the data in the log file which are day-of-week, time and game's theme. Firstly, the day-of-week data was separated into 2 types - weekday and weekend. For example, if the user downloads the games on Saturday and Sunday, these sessions would belong to weekend. Secondly, time-of-day would be inserted in the record. This can be divided into 4 periods - morning, afternoon, evening and night respectively. Finally, the content category was divided by game's theme. The overall process of the experiment will be discussed in the next section.

3.2 Process

Pre-processing phase is first carried out by gathering the log file. Then, the data was transferred to a database for the convenience of issuing queries. The data cleaning process is also an important process in this phase. There could be much irrelevant information in the log file and this process will eliminate those unwanted information. For example, users who are unable to download the game were removed from the database. Data conversion and formatting were performed as well. In the main process, classification of data based on the context information was implemented. Each important factor was used to classify the data in each group. The results were managed and sent to the user as a personalised downloadable game menu, which will be corresponding to the user's needs based on time information.

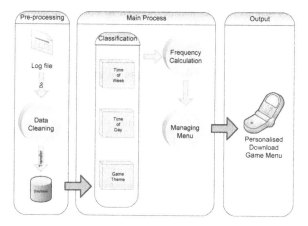

Fig. 1. The downloading game menu process overview

4   Results

4.1   Classification Factors

Three main results related to the factors are tabulated in the tables. The first table (Table 1) shows that action game is the favorite game theme based on the

Table 1. Time-of-week and game theme factors

Game Theme	Weekend		Weekday	
	Frequency	Percentage	Frequency	Percentage
Action	5162	72.53%	7789	70.52%
Adventure	377	5.30%	619	5.60%
Casual	782	10.99%	1181	10.69%
Others	9	0.13%	36	0.33%
Puzzle	500	7.03%	872	7.89%
RPG	14	0.20%	16	0.14%
Strategy	95	1.33%	180	1.63%
Sports	178	2.50%	352	3.19%
Total	7117	100.00%	11045	100.00%

time-of-week factor, topping at around 70% when compared with other themes. This is followed by casual, puzzle and adventure games at 10.99%, 7.03% and 5.30% respectively. The rank seems to be the same when compared across the weekday results except puzzle and adventure games, which have higher percentages. It can be seen that the RPG game is not a popular game theme for mobile game due to longer storytelling and time needed to complete the game. Therefore, in the downloading game menu during weekday, more games on puzzle theme may be added.

The next result used time-of-day factor which was also separated by time-of-week to rank the most downloaded game theme. It can be seen from Table 2 that there are different proportion of downloaded game theme in each period or time-of-day and in the time-of-week as well. The results are shown in the table below.

After the time-of-week, time-of-day and game theme factors are calculated and sorted, we obtained the result of the proportion of downloaded games via mobile phone. The most popular game themes are action, casual, puzzle and adventure games. Importantly, if the menu uses the result from action game only, the other game theme would have less chance of being downloaded by the customers. Thus, to obtain well distributed opportunity, the proportion of the favorite games will be used as a guide in preparing the download menu. The menu items on mobile screen will be adapted according to time-of-week and time-of-day as well. Each game theme contains its own rank, and only those favorite game themes that are above a selected threshold will be displayed on the main downloading menu. It is worth noting that there is a quota for the providers to offer their games in each game theme to the customers. For example, action games will be given top 7 games in its container, while casual, puzzle and adventure games could have one game for their quota. This is done in a way that the service providers can manipulate the games available in the main downloading menu to increase profit.

Table 2. Time-of-day and time-of-week factors

Time	Weekend							
	1		2		3		4	
Game Theme	Freq.	%	Freq.	%	Freq.	%	Freq.	%
Action	779	75.63	1532	75.17	1344	68.61	1507	72.11
Adventure	66	6.41	84	4.12	131	6.69	96	4.59
Casual	90	8.74	220	10.79	244	12.46	228	10.91
Others	4	0.39	1	0.05	1	0.05	3	0.14
Puzzle	51	4.95	133	6.53	151	7.71	165	7.89
RPG	4	0.39	6	0.29	3	0.15	1	0.05
Strategy	27	2.62	42	2.06	55	2.81	54	2.58
Sports	9	0.87	20	0.98	30	1.53	36	1.72
Total	1030	100.00	2038	100.00	1959	100.00	2090	100.00
Time	Weekday							
	1		2		3		4	
Game Theme	Freq.	%	Freq.	%	Freq.	%	Freq.	%
Action	1281	72.50	1862	71.64	2435	71.81	2211	67.24
Adventure	100	5.66	156	6.00	190	5.60	173	5.26
Casual	150	8.49	268	10.31	339	10.00	424	12.90
Others	6	0.34	6	0.23	8	0.24	16	0.49
Puzzle	118	6.68	196	7.54	261	7.70	297	9.03
RPG	3	0.17	0	0.00	8	0.24	5	0.15
Strategy	79	4.47	80	3.08	89	2.62	104	3.16
Sports	30	1.70	31	1.19	61	1.80	58	1.76
Total	1767	100.00	2599	100.00	3391	100.00	3288	100.00

4.2 Proposed Downloading Game Menu

Proposed Menu According to Time-of-week. From the results obtained using time-of-week for clustering, we found that it is similar to using only time-of-week to re-arrange the menu. The results also show that it can increase the chance of downloading by giving the quota to bring the top rank in each category to the main downloading menu. On the other hand, if we use only frequently downloaded games, the games in other game genres will not be downloaded at all. Furthermore, the proposed menu system can be used and implemented for the personalised downloading mobile game system. It also facilitate user to download the more in-terested game according to their needs. Due to confidentiality, the actual game names cannot be disclosed in this paper. Therefore, game-ids will be used in this paper instead of the game names.

Table 3. Proposed menu using time-of-week factors

Weekend / Weekday	
Game-id	**Game Type**
Game-041	Action
Game-160	Casual
Game-310	Action
Game-253	Action
Game-155	Action
Game-311	Action
Game-252	Action
Game-067	Adventure
Game-048	Puzzle
Game-245	Action

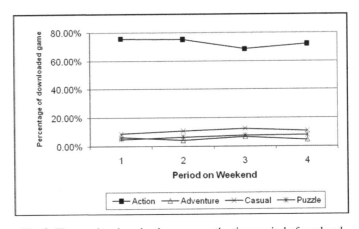

Fig. 2. The trend to download game over the time period of weekend

Proposed menu according to time-of-day combined with time-of-week. As can be seen from figure 2, the graph shows that action games in period 3 of weekend tends to decrease. However, the percentage of casual game increases with puzzle game. The percentage on the adventure games fluctuated within the periods. As a result the weekend downloading game menu on the third period can be altered from the normal menu using time-of-week factors. When the quota of action game is decreased, the competition among other game theme will occur. The most frequently downloaded games at that time will have the place to show the downloading items or its name on the game menu. For the example, in the experiment, action game gains 6 places out of 10 while the other gain 1 place. Therefore, the second ranked games in each remained category are compared to find the maximum frequency in order to gain that place. The result shows that the second ranked game has the most frequency is in the puzzle game category. It can be seen from Table 3 in period 3 of weekend that at least 5 out of 10 ranking downloading game menu is different from the proposed menu using time-of-week factors. Compared to period 4 of weekend, the menu order is different from the period 3 and slightly different from using only time-of-week factor. Nevertheless, this can facilitate the user to download the more interested game to their mobile phone according to time-of-week and time-of-day. This can reduce the click distance to find the desired game and the scroll down levels to find the desire games.

On the weekday, it can be observed that the percentage of downloading action game has declined in the fourth period. In contrast, the percentages of downloading casual and puzzle games have increased.

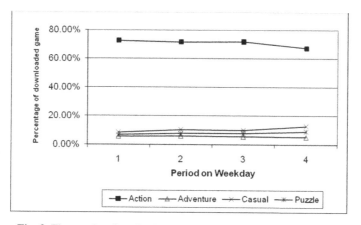

Fig. 3. The trend to download game over the time period of weekday

Table 4. Proposed menu using combination factors on weekend

Weekend Period 3 Menu		Weekend Period 4 Menu	
Game-id	**Game Type**	**Game-id**	**Game Type**
Game-041	Action	Game-041	Action
Game-160	Casual	Game-160	Casual
Game-310	Action	Game-310	Action
Game-253	Action	Game-253	Action
Game-067	Adventure	Game-155	Action
Game-155	Action	Game-311	Action
Game-311	Action	Game-252	Action
Game-252	Action	Game-048	Puzzle
Game-048	Puzzle	Game-067	Adventure
Game-068	Puzzle	Game-245	Action

Table 5. The proposed menu using combination factors on weekday

Weekday Period 4 Menu	
Game-id	**Game Type**
Game-041	Action
Game-160	Casual
Game-310	Action
Game-253	Action
Game-067	Adventure
Game-155	Action
Game-311	Action
Game-252	Action
Game-048	Puzzle
Game-068	Puzzle

5 Conclusions

This paper proposed a simple method to facilitate the user on mobile game download-ing. The proposed method introduces a personalisation mobile game recommendation system using time-of-week and time-of-day information. Due to the increase number of mobile games being downloaded via mobile internet, it is getting more important to provide personalised experience. It can be observed that there are game genres prefer-ences during different time depending on the context. In order to provide faster and personalised service, re-arranging the game downloading menu seems to be important for users. The simulation results are based on server logs collected from a mobile game provider in Thailand. As reported from the results, it is concluded that our as-sumption of the factors are valid. It is important to consider those context factors when creating personalization mobile game recommendation systems.

References

1. Burigat, S., Chittaro, L., Gabrielli, S.: Navigation Techiniques for Small-screen Devices: An Evaluation on Maps and Web Pages. International Journal of Human-Computer Stud-ies 66, 78–97 (2008)
2. Paireekreng, W., Wong, K.W.: The Empirical Study of the Factors Relating to Mobile Content Personalization. International Journal of Computer Science and System Analy-sis 2, 173–178 (2008)
3. Quah, J.T.S., Seet, V.L.H.: Adaptive WAP Portals. Electronic Commerce Research and Applications 7(4), 377–385 (2009)
4. Wang, F., Shao, H.: Effective Personalized Recommendation Based on Time-Framed Navigation Clustering and Association Mining. Expert Systems with Applications 27, 365–377 (2004)

5. Xu, D.J., Liao, S.S., Li, Q.: Combining Empirical Experimentation and Modeling Techniques: A Design Research Approach for Personalized Mobile Advertising Applications. Decision Support Systems 44, 710–724 (2008)
6. Rapeepisarn, K., Wong, K.W., Fung, C.C., Khine, M.S.: The relationship between Game Genres, Learning Techniques and Learning Styles in Educational Computer Games. In: Pan, Z., Zhang, X., El Rhalibi, A., Woo, W., Li, Y. (eds.) Edutainment 2008. LNCS, vol. 5093, pp. 497–508. Springer, Heidelberg (2008)
7. Rapeepisarn, K., Wong, K.W., Fung, C.C., Khine, M.S.: Creating Effective Educational Computer Games for Undergraduate Classroom Learning: A Conceptual Model. i-manager's Journal of Educational Technology (2008)
8. Bates, B.: Game Design. Thomson, Boston (2004)
9. Hillborg, M.: Wireless XML Developer's Guide. McGraw-Hill, New York (2002)
10. Prensky, M.: Computer Games and Learning: Digital Game-Based Learning. In: Raessens, J., Goldstein, J. (eds.) Handbook of Computer Game Studies, pp. 97–122. The MIT Press, Cambridge (2005)
11. Anderson, C.R., Domingos, P., Weld, D.S.: Adaptive Web Navigation for Wireless Devices. In: 7th International Joint Conference on Artificial Intelligence, Seattle, Washington (2001)
12. Borodin, Y., Mahmud, J., Ramakrishnan, I.V.: Context Browsing with Mobiles - When Less is More. In: MobiSys 2007, San Juan, Puerto Rico, pp. 3–5 (2007)
13. Ghorbani, A.A., Xu, X.: A Fuzzy Markov Model Approach for Predicting User Navigation. In: IEEE/WIC/ACM International Conference on Web Intelligence, pp. 307–311 (2007)
14. Goker, A., Myrhaug, H.I.: User context and Personalisation. In: Proceeding for the 6th European Conference on Case Based Reasoning, Aberdeen, Scotland (2002)
15. Goker, A., Watt, S., Myrhaug, H.I., Whitehead, N., Yakici, M., Bierig, R., Nuti, S.K., Cumming, H.: An Ambient, Personalised, and Context-Sensitive Information System for Mobile Users. In: 2nd European Symposium on Ambient Intelligence, pp. 19–24. Eindhoven, The Netherlands (2004)
16. Hakkila, J., Chatfield, C.: Personal Customisation of Mobile Phones - A Case Study. In: NordiCHI 2006:Changing Roles, Oslo, Norway, pp. 409–412 (2006)
17. Halvey, M., Keane, M.T., Smyth, B.: Predicting Navigation Patterns on the Mobile-Internet Using Time of the Week. In: WWW 2005, Chiba, Japan, pp. 958–959 (2005)
18. Jorstad, I., Thanh, D.V., Dustdar, S.: Personalisation of Future Mobile Services. In: 9th International Conference on Intelligence in Service Delivery Networks, Bordeaux, France (2004)
19. Paireekreng, W., Wong, K.W.: Adaptive Mobile Content Personalisation Using Time-of-day. In: 7th International Conference on e-Business, Bangkok, Thailand (2008)
20. Smyth, B., Cotter, P.: Intelligent Navigation for Mobile Internet Portals. In: Workshop on Artificial Intelligence, Information Access and Mobile Computing. 18th International Joint Conference on Artificial Intelligence, Acapulco, Mexico (2003)
21. Wagner, M., Balke, W., Hirschfeld, R., Kellerer, W.: A Roadmap to Advanced Personalization of Mobile Services. In: ODBASE, Irvine, California (2002)
22. Wong, K.W.: Player Adaptive Entertainment Computing. In: Proceedings of Computer Games & Allied Technology 2008, Singapore, pp. 32–37 (2008)

Adopting Virtual Characters in Virtual Systems from the Perspective of Communication Studies*

Peiren Shao[1], Weimin Liao[1], and Zhigeng Pan[2,3]

[1] Communication Studies Institute, Zhejiang University, Hangzhou, Zhejiang, 310028
[2] State Key Lab of CAD&CG, Zhejiang University, Hangzhou, Zhejiang, 310027
[3] Edu-game Center, Nanjing Normal University, Nanjing, 210008
speiren@vip.sina.com, liao_weimin@sina.com,
zgpan@cad.zju.edu.cn

Abstract. Virtual characters can play important role in virtual systems because it can enhance mass communication effects via manners of interpersonal communication by well representing the information as well as improving the general publicity. This paper examines the categories of virtual characters by studying the story genres and identifies the potential resources for creating new virtual characters: the traditional and contemporary cultural resources. Creating successful virtual characters not only relates with the cultural identity, which is rooted in the rich cultural heritage resources, but also relies on the advanced technological realization. As a practical example in this project, the discussion about body modeling method shows the technical complexity and feasibility. For future research, better understanding the mechanism of human communication and learning from humanistic disciplines will fundamentally improve the quality of designing virtual characters.

Keywords: virtual characters, virtual systems, digital museum, communication studies.

1 Introduction

The virtual characters or virtual humans adopted in virtual systems are widely studied by many researchers in many aspects, for example, G.Stefan et al. provide "backend of the virtual system" to integrate the application design and narrative structure [1], H.Frank et al. present "the full process for creation of a life-like virtual human" from modeling and texturing to animation [2], M. Nadia and E. Arjan present their working on "improving the expressive capabilities" of interactive virtual humans [3].The virtual characters attracts lots of researchers, because it represent a leading direction in the field of virtue reality research and it also demand comprehensive studies from other disciplines, even in humanistic areas. This paper will discuss the adoption of virtual characters in virtual systems by using some practical cases in many circumstances, specifically in digital museum, which is a new practical area in the world, from the perspective of communication studies.

---

* Note: This paper is a revised version of a paper published on Cyberworlds 2008.

Z. Pan et al. (Eds.): Transactions on Edutainment II, LNCS 5660, pp. 70–89, 2009.

The use of virtual characters in digital museum to improve the public understanding about the knowledge, cultural meaning of the museum's collections is a new phenomenon, and a typical case for this study. In fact, the adoption of virtual characters in human learning has a long history, for example, the cartoon figures used in some publications and the mascots used in some festivals are all virtual characters instead of real persons; they represent lots of meanings and fulfill the suitable functions, which may provide comparative examples for us to understand the functions of virtual characters in digital museums. The reality about "virtual characters" or "virtual humans" often get critiques by the audience, simply because that the behaviors of the characters can look "wooden", "exhibiting perhaps, a lack of variety in response, a lack of emotional range or a lack of adaptation to the users' attitude towards the character"[4]. Some researches try to solve such problems by integrate the social context into technological foundations[5,6,7], for example, a study for improving man-machine communication by constructing multimodal recognition of human input and behavior[5], another study for computing three different affects type to simulate and control the facial expressions and other non-verbal communication of the virtual characters[7]. In spite of many critiques, the virtual characters still have potential wide usages in the future under the ongoing research improvement by many researchers and scientists.

The ideal virtual characters not only can express meanings by their verbal systems, but also can communicate with people by a series of nonverbal subsystems, such as facial expressions, head and body movements and postures, gestures, and eye gazes, etc. We consider that the virtual characters should share lots of similarities as the real human being in terms of human communication, because the technological development of virtual reality and other related information technology can make it fulfilled eventually. Therefore, an ideal virtual character adopted in a digital museum should have fundamental differences with any cartoon figure in printing media, because it can bring the audience to the real situation.

Under this condition and premise, we will mainly discuss the functions, categories, and potential resources of an ideal virtual character adopted in an ideal virtual tour for its digital museum, since we find that most of virtual characters adopted in the websites of their digital museums still have huge gap with real humans, especially in the nonverbal communication subsystems. In this study, the virtual characters we referred to are more advanced and should be adopted in digital museums; however, we might also use some virtual characters with primary technical level or in other virtual systems as examples to convey our points of view.

Before go to the detailed discussion, we will present some research results in our group in the past few years. We have been engaged in applying virtual characters (or we called avatars) in virtual environments we developed. In 2003, with the cooperation with some universities in Europe (under the framework of EU-Asia link project called ELVIS), we co-developed an authoring tool for storytelling. In such a system, we use the technology of 2.5D avatars, creating a set of virtual characters with Chinese cultures, or some characters adopted from some Chinese cartoon programs (Fig. 1 shows an example for adopting Big-head son, a popular virtual character in China). The second application of virtual characters is our virtual learning environment for computer graphics course. In such a system, each user has an avatar, and avatars can visit our classroom together, having discussion et al. (see Figure 2). The third application of virtual characters is our virtual shopping mall for buying products on Internet.

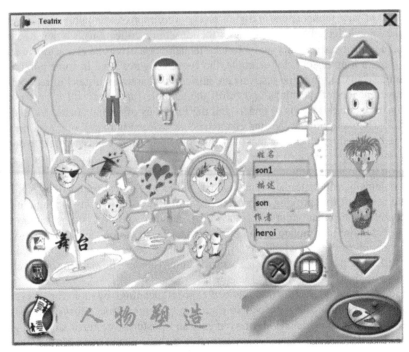

(a) Different characters with different behaviors (including emotion)

(b) Avatar (Big-head son) in specific virtual environment

Fig. 1. Virtual characters in ELVIS project

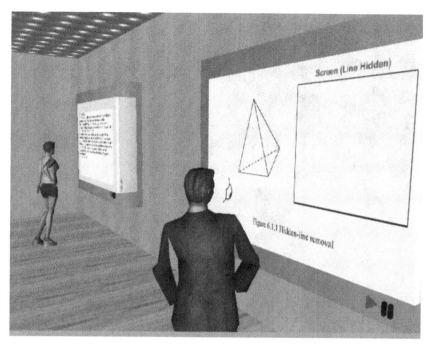

Fig. 2. Two virtual characters in virtual learning environment for CG course

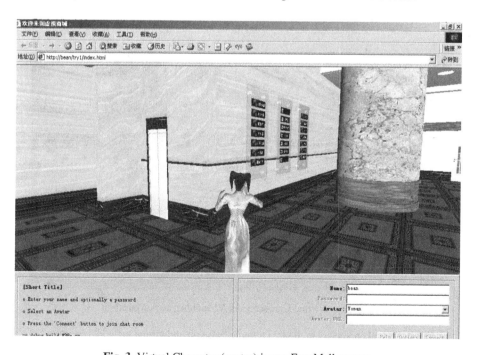

Fig. 3. Virtual Character (avatar) in our EasyMall system

(a) Virtual Characters in Digital Olympic Museum

(b) Virtual Characters in Virtual Network Marathon

Fig. 4. Virtual characters in digital Olympic museum and virtual network marathon

In such a system, each user has an avatar, and avatars can visit our different buying area, and talk to the virtual sellers (see Figure 3).

Another typical application is our Virtual network marathon (VNM), where users do physical exercise and competition in a distributed virtual environment. When users run on the elliptical machine, their body motions are captured by sensors. They can observe their actions and current environment real-time rendered through output screen, and control their actions by multimodal interactions or interactive with other users by network. There are three game modes, training, exercising and competing. Also users are able to choose the appropriate distance to run. Figure 4 shows the exercise (run through in digital Olympic museum) and competition modes of VNM.

2 Functions of Virtual Characters

2.1 The Comparison of Virtual Museum without and with Virtual Characters

First, let us examine some characteristics of the typical experiences of visiting a physical museum, a virtual museum (typically on-line museum, or a virtual tour area in the website) and a virtual museum with a virtual character guiding. Since J. Cooper [8] has done the comparison between the first two circumstances, we simply modify and add some facts in his original discussions.

Applying the concept and theory of "social presence" [9], which was one of the first theoretical frameworks to be applied to Computer-Mediated Communication, we analyze the differences among the three circumstances. Under this theory, the more cues of communication existed (no matters text or non-text, verbal or nonverbal); the higher sense of social presence can be received by the communicators. For the

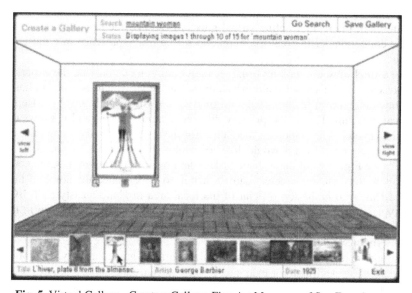

Fig. 5. Virtual Gallery - Create a Gallery, Fine Art Museums of San Francisco

Table 1. A comparison of physical and virtual (without and with virtual characters) museum experiences

Visiting Physical Museum	Visiting Virtual Museum	Virtual Museum Guiding by Virtual Character
Social presence in the real museum (may be in the historic site, not in the authentic situation)	Actually in front a computer and tele-presence in the real museum	Actually in front a computer, and tele-presence in the virtual reality (may be similar as the authentic situation)
Objects are physical, usually well preserved or protected (perhaps behind glass)	'Objects' are virtual, usually displayed in ideal artificial conditions	'Objects' are virtual, may be displayed in the authentic situation in virtual reality
Visitors browse objects in present	Visitors browse objects via a computer	Guiding by virtual character (via a computer)
Visitors see objects arranged and selected; Objects are fixed in their positions; Each object can only be in one location at a time; Only a fraction of the collection is ever on public display.	'Objects' are normally not pre-arranged, but stored in a database, ready to be retrieved by searching; Visitors may take efforts to understand the objects in a researching manner	'Objects' are normally pre-arranged; Visitors may see objects in a virtual situation guided by virtual characters; Visitors may feel the virtual reality of historical events in a storytelling manner
Other aids to interpretation are available, if desired (e.g. catalogues, text panels, extended labels, tours, lectures and other public programs)	Other aids to interpretation are normally not available immediately, but can usually be searched with search engines	Some explaining information might be provided or pop up when visitors take virtual tours; Speeches, music, subtitles or interactive questions might be delivered
Visiting can be a social experience (or a solitary experience)	Visiting is generally a solitary experience only	Visiting is actually an interaction, communication with the virtual character

visitors, the physical museum can provide the experience of real social presence in a real museum; the regular online virtual museum can provide the database for searching the collections of the real museum, and set up a tele-presence in a museum (see Figure 5).

The virtual museum with a virtual character guiding can provide the experience of tele-presence in the virtual reality (usually not muse t), which may be similar as the authentic situation in history or the original scene which might not be set up in the physical museum. This is the primary difference among them; and it shows that the virtual character is an important mediation for the audience to understand the content which the digital museum would like to exhibit. For example, in the 3D "Virtual Scene" (see Figure 6) of the website of Human Provincial Museum in China, a visitor can follow the virtual character, Lady Xinzhui, to look around the home of the Marquis of Dai, who is the top official of the local area in Han Dynasty (206 BC-220). This typical virtual scene is recovered from the archaeological discovery in the cultural historic site in Mawangdui Han Tombs, in the suburban area of Changsha City, Hunan Province, China.

Visiting the digital museums with a virtual character guided usually is involved in a procedure of storytelling. For example, a study at National Gallery of Art [10] shows that the teachers and students participated in the process can "find their own meanings

Fig. 6. Virtual Scene - Walking into the home of the Marquis of Dai, guided by Lady Xinzhui

in museum objects" by digital storytelling approach, which "personalizes and human-izes historical events, making them more appealing to students". In another word, the virtual characters provide the visitors another vehicle to understand and interpret the collections with much more learning funs.

At last, the visiting experiences are also different. In many physical museums, visi-tors should walk around the displayed areas sections by sections to learn the informa-tion under the aids of catalogues, text panels, extended labels, etc. Their visiting can be a social experience, if they are participated in a group. In online museums, visitors are generally expected to do their own exploration using browsers or search engines; and it is generally a solitary experience. If the visitors explore the virtual museum guided by virtual characters, they should interact and communicate with the virtual characters. The experience is a social experience, but it is also a computer-mediated communication simulated as face to face communication.

2.2 On Two Main Functions of Virtual Characters

From the perspective of communication studies [11], it is easy to understand the key point that the virtual characters for the digital museums actually exert mass communi-cation functions via manners of interpersonal communication, which is similar as the TV anchor for TV stations.

The adoption of virtual characters usually has two main aspects of functions: first, the virtual characters can gain the publicity effect because the lovely virtual charac-ters can draw huge attractions from the audience and bring a public recognizing to the museum; second, the virtual characters can make the visitor gain authentic experience about the situations which might not be existed any more. For example, exploring many historical events and communicate with all sorts of historical figures. The first is in macro level, and the second is in micro level. The first is external function, which is similar as the blossom; and the second is internal as the root; the first function should rely on the second. Both of the functions are related with the communication effects that the virtual characters created.

It is important to notice that the good reputation is rooted in the basic experience which the audience can communicate with the virtual characters. If the second function fulfilled is a shabby work, no matter how wonderful it began, it will eventually cause a fiasco or failure in the end, and give a final hurt to the publicity. Vinayagamoorthy, V. et al. in their STAR study [4] show a couple of cases that the "highly photo-realistic virtual humans" do not get the good feedbacks because they have "no or limited interactive ability", while other "expressive virtual characters" can make it successfully.

Let's examine a quintessential example of virtual character "Ananova" (see Figure 7) adopted in creative industry as the first virtual anchor in online TV broadcasting. When the "Ananova" was first introduced to all over the world in 2001, she made a huge sensation and drew great attentions from the public. The audience rushed to visit the website to look the beautiful virtual anchor, finally they find that she can only mimic a few nonverbal expressions and cannot respond to them adequately and appropriately. The appearance of "Ananova" just like a flower blossomed in a short period and cannot last consistently as a real human anchor, that is why we only can find the short message left in its website that "Please note: Ananova video is currently under development" (http://www.ananova.com/video).The case of "Ananova" give us insight about the virtual characters that the communication abilities with people (the audience) are fundamental and essentially important.

Fig. 7. Ananova: the first virtual anchor for TV

2.3 On the Communication Effects of Virtual Characters

In general, the virtual characters can generate positive communication effects via the manner of interpersonal communication by representing the information of the museum's collections. From the perspective of communication studies, the following effects are salient.

- Make many collections arranged in a virtual space and interpreted by a storyteller, usually the virtual character
- Create interpersonal communication channel in a virtual scene
- Create dialogue opportunity for the visitor to "talk with" virtual character

- Improve or ignite the visitors' curiosity and attention
- Give the visitors deep impression about the museum
- Create lots of fun for the visitors.

3 Genres of Virtual Characters

3.1 General Discussing about the Classification of Virtual Characters

Discussing the categories of virtual characters will benefit for us to further understand the functions of virtual characters. Usually, the criteria of classification will determine the classes. We can classify the virtual characters into 2 categories as 3D and non-3D according to the numbers of dimensions to present the figures. Based on the features of the virtual characters, we can also classify the virtual characters into 4 categories as the following:

- Historical virtual characters; For example, Abraham Lincoln (see Figure 9) is used as a virtual character.

- Contemporary virtual characters; For example, the TV anchor "Ananova" (see Figure 7). The designer can use the celebrity as the prototype to create new virtual characters.

- User-defined virtual characters; For example, at any avatar of 3D virtual chat room, the user can pick up and self-defined a new virtual character to explore the experience to dialogue with other virtual characters. According to a study [12], avatar-mediated networking can increase social presence and interpersonal trust among communicators in the process of collaborations leading by virtual characters.

- Impersonated animal virtual characters; For example, the mascots of Olympic Games can be developed as a virtual character for guiding people to visit the digital Olympic Memory Museum, for example a virtual reality program was conducted before the opening of 29th Olympic Games to show the sites and buildings for Qingdao Olympic Sailing Center by 5 lovely mascots called "Fuwa" with 5 nicknames as "Beibei", "Jingjing", "Huanhuan", "Yingying", "Nini" (see Figure 8). These five virtual characters were originated from different animals except for "Huanhuan", which is come from the image of fire.

There are also some other criteria for classification. Next, we will introduce the terminology of "genres" from literary theory to study thoroughly about the classification of virtual characters, because that a virtual tour in a digital museum is similar as reading a literature work from the perspective of communication studies.

3.2 Concept of "Genre" and Analytical Framework for Describing Virtual Characters

The word genre comes from the French (and originally Latin) word for "kind" or "class". The term is widely used in rhetoric, literary theory, media theory, and linguistics. A genre

Fig. 8. Fuwa Guiding Your Tour to Qingdao Olympic Sailing Center

is originally considered as a loose set of criteria for a category of composition; the term is often used to categorize literature and speech, but is also used for any other form of art or utterance. For example, literature is divided into three basic kinds of forms, which are the classic genres of Ancient Greece: poetry, drama, and prose.

As for the virtual characters, the concept of "genres" was introduced in a research for an edutainment program "Abraham Lincoln's Crossroads" [9].This project adopt a famous historic figure, the president of America, Abraham Lincoln, as the virtual character to teach student through a digital museum (see Figure 9). To generate "teachable moments", this study also introduces the concept "storytelling" and "story genre", and builds a framework for analysis. Since the "teachable moments" (actually the interactive communication opportunity with virtual character and visitors) are hard to captured, the study firstly try to match learning objectives to story elements at the abstract level from the instructional perspective.

Secondly, the study considers whether the obstacles that the learner will encounter have primarily to do with the principal character(s) in conflict with:

- Self
- Society
- Nature
- Another individual

Finally, the study considers the mood or manner of the story the designer have in mind. The author argued: "Will it be comic or fanciful? Will it be realistic instead? Or will it be gravely serious? Establishing the type of principal conflict and the

Fig. 9. Abraham Lincoln's Crossroads

perspective from which the protagonist's trials will be presented will point you in the direction of distinct story type – the story genre" [13]. Under this Analytical framework, the genres are classified as roughly 3×4 sub-genres (see Table 2), which are: self-parody; diary or journal; confession; satire or allegory; novel; epic; lampoon or romance; mystery; drama; adventure or fantasy; travelogue; myth.

Table 2. Examples of Genres Mapped to Learning Obstacles via Manner   (Modified from Reference [9])

Obstacles/Manner	Comic	Realistic	Serious
Self	self-parody	diary or journal	confession
Society	satire or allegory	novel	epic
Nature	lampoon or romance	mystery	drama
Another individual	adventure or fantasy	travelogue	myth

3.3   On the Functions of Genres or Sub-genres

Understanding the story genres have significant meaning to the story writing, hence the genres of virtual characters will enlighten the designer to create new lovely virtual characters for the audience. Different genres specify different connection to be demonstrated between the text and the reader; different genres of virtual characters will also determine the communication manner between the visitors and the virtual characters.

In the previous example in a historical scene to demonstrate the daily life of the Marquis of Dai's family (see Figure 6) in Hunan Provincial Museum, the hostess Lady Xinzhui is one of good choice as the virtual character to narrate her daily life in a genre of "diary or journal". The audience can watch the cartoon story in the same website to know the luxury of the elegant women in Han Dynasty and understand the civilization of that time in that region in China. Using the technology of "Flash", the designer pick up three typical scenes in different time periods (morning, noon and evening), and virtually show the luxurious life of Xinzhui to the public again: wearing silk gowns, eating delicious food, appreciating endless songs and dances. The story can also be presented through a 3D virtual character in a virtual scene.

If the genre adopted is different, the narrative and communication manner will be different. For example, in "Abraham Lincoln's Crossroads" case, the story genre is epic and the virtual character is chosen as a hero in history to make very important decisions. Thus, the designer of virtual characters can borrow the researching results from the genres studies and communication studies to broaden the resources and imaginations about the categories of virtual characters.

On the other hand, the interaction between the virtual character and the audience can also lead to different models and choices of virtual characters, similar as in case of text-reader relationship argued by Livingstone: "if different genres result in different modes of text-reader interaction, these latter may result in different types of involvement... critical or accepting, resisting or validating, casual or concentrated, apathetic or motivated" [14].

4 Methods and Potential Resources of Creating a New Virtual Character

Creating successful virtual characters not only relies on the advanced technological realization on appearance as well as the verbal and non-verbal communication systems, but also firmly relates with the cultural identity, which is rooted in the rich cultural heritage resources.

4.1 Methods for Creating New Virtual Characters

For technological realization in this project, we will mainly focus on the discussion about body modeling methods as examples. Basically, a variety of body modeling methods for virtual characters exist [15]. They fall into 4 major categories: authoring, capturing, interpolating, and modeling fitting.

For authoring methods, authors create a model from scratch by interacting with low-level building primitives such as vertices and edges. They often resort to commercial modeling software such as Maya for this purpose. Although these methods give maximal control to the author, they require high artistic talents and good proficiency of the underlying software.

Recently capturing methods became more popular. They use special equipments ranged from stereos [16] to 3D scanners. The resulting model often has holes in it and is over complex. More importantly, it must go through a hard and tedious rigging procedure to be animated. Then there are data-driven methods, which generate new model by interpolating [17] or segmenting then re-compositing [18] existing sets of example models.

The last category is model-fitting methods [19], which derive a new model by using information extracted from pictures to modify the generic one. The resulting model is visually appealing and animatable. The methods in the last category best suit to our need. There are two typical kinds of model fitting methods. The first one is presented by Hilton et al. [19] uses four orthogonal pictures to capture shape details of an individual. The core of the method was to project the generic model to the image space, make modification in 2D, then project back to 3D.

Lee et al. [20] argue that Hilton's method can cause visible seam in the result model and propose an enhanced method to solve this problem. Their method first computed the 3D position of a set of manually specified feature points. Main processing is composed of three steps: skeleton modification, rough skin modification based on feature points, and fine skin modification based on silhouette. The second step addressed the connection problems. But her method required that the generic model have strict grid topology linkage not found in almost all existing model.

Model fitting methods have three key points: identifying and extracting personal shape feature, deforming the generic model accordingly, preserving connectivity in the generic model. No doubt, better knowledge of nature of the human body will be helpful. In other research fields such as human animation, researchers also consider the nature of human body. Magnenat-Thalmann et al. use joint-local deformation [21] to deform the shape of animated hand. Others use similar mechanism to deform animated human body. All these algorithms made use of the cross-section structures of human body parts.

4.2 Two Aspects for Creating a New Virtual Character

For the designer, the prominent task is creating more lovely and suitable virtual characters. However, whether a virtual character is attractive and well-recognized by the audience or not, depends on two basic factors:

- From technical aspect, the virtual character has realistic appearance (face, clothes, facial expression, etc.) and internal communication skills (via verbal and non-verbal systems).

- From social aspect, the virtual character contains content of social meaning, cultural identification, and aesthetic values. The virtual character is a cultural icon to build a bridge to communicate with people each other. This aspect is easy to be ignored by the engineers who usually keen on the computing software or other computer programs.

This two factors usually are correlated each other, and the latter one have determinable power for creating a successful virtual character, because the virtual character is basically part of culture. It should be rooted in the rich cultural heritage resources, and the basic elements of virtual characters should come from the resources of cultural heritages; other wise the character would not have vibrate living force and it would be hard to be accepted by the audience.

4.3 Traditional Cultural Resources of Creating a New Virtual Character

Where are the potential resources of creating a new virtual character? In general, the history, literature, art and all the traditional civilized resources would be the right choices. As specified in different genres of virtual characters, the potential resources might have different inclinations for creating a new character. For example, if the genre is specified as epic and the story is about a historical hero for the digital museum, the nationwide historical figures would be the potential resources to study. The designer can find the appropriate one that the audience is familiar with his or her personality or story. Once the virtual character is created, it is easy to gain publicity and become popular. "Abraham Lincoln's Crossroads" is this kind of typical case.

Another interesting example of creating a virtual character is Mulan, which is originated from a Chinese poem, "Ballad of Mulan" ("MulanShi" in Chinese). In this poem, Mulan disguised herself as a man to take her elderly father's place in the army. She was later offered a government post by the emperor himself after her service was up. However, unwilling to commit anymore to the forces, she turned down the position so she could return to her family immediately. When her former colleagues visited her at home, they were shocked to see her dressed as a woman. Based on this literature work, the Walt Disney Pictures make an animated movie named after the heroine, Mulan. We can find that this virtual character is well-designed as a lovely girl with smiling similar as western girls and brave as ancient warriors. The cultural meanings are mixed and melted in a plot and adapt for the favor of contemporary audience. It is easy to identify that the digging into Chinese cultural heritage is one of the factors to make it successful. This example sheds light to the application in any digital museum projects; a designer can dig into the traditional heritage resources to create the appropriate virtual character.

Fig. 10. The Disney virtual character Mulan is originated from "Ballad of Mulan", a Chinese poem

4.4   Contemporary Resources of Creating a New Virtual Character

Not only the traditional cultural resources can be developed as the resources of virtual characters, the contemporary celebrities and public figures are also good resources of creating new characters. Making up a new virtual character is not easy, however simulating a celebrity can revoke the audience' enthusiasm and interests, and make the mimic virtual character becoming popular quickly. The difficulty is grasping the proper degree between similarity and variety. For example, an anonymous designer created some virtual characters (see Figure 11) in a video clip[1] of dancing performance in seashore. We can find that the leading virtual character in this video has almost exactly same gestures and facial expression as the photo of a popular Chinese TV game show anchor Li Yong (see Figure 12) posted in CCTV.com, the official website of Chinese Central Television Station. Ignoring the controversial issues (e.g. copy right and other legal right) of the work, some Chinese netizens (a term to describe the users of Internet who have basic right of expression and "free of speech") praise this piece of work, because it demonstrate the funny moment of an entertainment program and reveal the personality of a celebrity vividly.

Another example is also about the virtual TV anchor, named as Xiao Long (see Figure 13). Someone points out that the hair of Xiao Long is similar as one famous CCTV anchor Cui Yongyuan and the eyeglass is similar as another well-known PhoenixTV anchor Dou Wentao. Xiaolong is actually a combination of the two celebrities in contemporary China. These two anchors have their own personalities with humor expressions and have great popularity among Chinese audience, the designer get the shortcut way to win the popularity but also face the challenge to capture the humor elements in verbal and non-verbal communication systems to make this virtual character lovely as his two prototypes.

Fig. 11. A virtual character designed by an anonymous designer, is identified as Li Yong by Chinese Netizens

---

[1] The video clip can be watched at the URL: http://you.video.sina.com.cn/ b/4028946-1198371231.html

Fig. 12. Photo of Li Yong in the official website of CCTV (Resources: www.cctv.com)

Fig. 13. A new TV virtual character, Xiao Long, is designed as a combination of two famous Chinese TV anchors: Cui Yongyuan (Up left) and Dou Wentao (Down left)

Fig. 14. A virtual character to show martial art

We use TV anchor as examples, only because it is well-known and easy to convey the points. Actually any interesting humans and daily life can be the designing resources to create a good virtual character. An anonymous designer uses a martial art athlete as a model to create a virtual character (see Figure 14), which can be used to demonstrate the martial art (or Kong fu) in a digital museum or any edutainment for teaching students martial art.

5 Summary

For undertaking this study, we visit more than 30 Chinese provincial-level museums' websites; we find that only a few museums have set up online virtual tour for visitors and very rare digital museums have databases supported or with virtual characters guided. The case we selected is Hunan Provincial Museum; and its designing of virtual character is still in primary level and lacking of verbal and non-verbal interactive communication systems supported. Since the cases of adoption virtual characters in digital museums are rare, we use other virtual characters in animated movies and online TV as examples to convey our viewpoints. Because fundamentally the underlying principles are consistent, the conclusions are reliable.

In general, creating a successful virtual character not only relies on the advanced technological realization, but also firmly relates with the cultural identity and social recognition, which is rooted in the rich cultural heritage resources. On technological level, a good virtual character should have a good appearance firstly, but most important points rely on the verbal communication designing and nonverbal communication designing, even the emotion and personality designing. On the social level, a successful virtual character should gain the cultural identity from the society, either from the traditional or contemporary cultural resources. The classification of virtual characters as genres for storytelling may give the designers hint to create a wonderful cultural icon for digital museums or other virtual systems.

Since this paper is modified and extended from our previous work by examining the "functions, genres, resources" of virtual characters adopted in digital museum [15], the research findings and conclusions actually can be extended to other virtual systems. We outlines the most important points for creating a life-like virtual character from the perspective of communication studies, and emphasize the underlying cultural meaning of the virtual characters, which might provide another direction of thinking to reflect technology and computing algorithm. However, the details about the social meaning still need to be explained and studied in the future study, especially, the connections between the social and cultural context with the virtual character's inner communication skills, and the technological realizations, need to be father studied. For better revealing the social aspects of creating a new successful virtual character, it should rely on introducing new ideas and knowledge from anthropology, ethnography, sociology, history, and cultural studies and so on; for bridging the gap between the social aspects and technological aspects, the new methods from artificial intelligence might be introduced in the process, and this will leave for future study.

Acknowledgements

This research work is funded by Key NSF Project (Grant No. 60533080) and 863 Project (2006AA01Z303), on-line Expo in Shanghai on Intelligent Interaction and Navigation in VE (Grant No. 8dz0580208). We would like to express our thanks to all our colleagues in these projects.

References

1. Gobel, S., Iurgel, I.A., Rossler, M., Hulsken, F., Eckes, C.: Design and Narrative Structure for the Virtual Human Scenarios. The International Journal of Virtual Reality 6(4), 1–10 (2007)
2. Hulsken, F., Eckes, C., Kuck, R., Unterberg, J., Jorg, S.: Modeling and Animating Virtual Humans for Real-Time Applications. The International Journal of Virtual Reality 6(4), 11–20 (2007)
3. Magnenat-Thalmann, N., Egges, A.: Interactive Virtual Humans in Real-time Virtual Environment. The International Journal of Virtual Reality 5(2), 15–24 (2006)
4. Vinayagamoorthy, V., Gillies, M., Steed, A., Tanguy, E., Pan, X., Loscos, C., Slater, M.: Building Expression into Virtual Characters. In: Eurographics Conference State of the Art Report 2006 (2006)
5. Eckes, C., Biatov, K., Hulsken, F., Kohler, J., Breuer, P., Branco, P., Encarnacao, L.M.: Towards Sociable Virtual Humans: Multimodal Recognition of Human input and Behavior. The International Journal of Virtual Reality 6(4), 21–30 (2007)
6. Lockelt, M., Pfleger, N., Reithinger, N.: Multi-party Conversation for Mixed Reality. The International Journal of Virtual Reality 6(4), 31–42 (2007)
7. Kelsen, M., Gebhard, P.: Affective Multimodal Control of Virtual Characters. The International Journal of Virtual Reality 6(4), 43–54 (2007)
8. Cooper, J.: Beyond the On-line Museum: Participatory Virtual Exhibitions. In: Trant, J., Bearman, D. (eds.) Proceedings of Museums and the Web 2006. Archives & Museum Informatics, Toronto (2006)
9. Short, J., Williams, E., Christie, B.: The Social Psychology of Telecommunication. John Willey & Sons, Ltd., London (1976)

10. Springer, J., Kajder, S., et al.: Digital Storytelling at the National Gallery of Art. In: Bearman, D., Trant, J. (eds.) Proceedings of Museums and the Web 2004. Archives & Museum Informatics, Toronto (2004)
11. Shao, P.: Communication Studies, 2nd edn. Higher Education Press, Beijing (Chuanbo Xue. Beijing: Gaodeng Jiaoyu Chuban She in Chinese Pinyin format) (2007)
12. Bente, G., Rüggenberg, S., Krämer, N.C., Eschenburg, F.: Avatar-Mediated Networking: Increasing Social Presence and Interpersonal Trust in Net-Based Collaborations. Human Communication Research 34(2), 287–318 (2008)
13. Leon, J., Fisher, M.: The Use of Virtual Characters to Generate Teachable Moments. In: Trant, J., Bearman, D. (eds.) Proceedings of Museums and the Web 2006. Archives & Museum Informatics, Toronto (2006)
14. Livingstone, S.: The rise and fall of audience research: an old story with a new ending. In: Levy, M.R., Gurevitch, M. (eds.) Defining Media Studies: Reflections on the Future of the Field, pp. 247–254. Oxford University Press, New York (1994)
15. Magnenat-Thalmann, N., Seo, H., Cordier, F.: Automatic modeling of virtual humans and body clothing. Journal of Computer Science and Technology 19(5), 575–584 (2004)
16. Devernay, F., Faugeras, O.D.: Computing differential properties of 3-d shapes from stereoscopic images without 3-d models. In: Proc. of Computer Vision and Pattern Recognition, pp. 208–213 (1994)
17. Sloan, P.P., Rose, C., Cohen, M.: Shape by example. In: Symposium on Interactive 3D Graphics, pp. 135–143 (2001)
18. Funkhouser, T., Kazhdan, M., Shilane, P., Min, P., Kiefer, W., Tal, A., Rusinkiewicz, S., Dobkin, D.: Modeling by example. In: ACM SIGGRAPH 2004, pp. 652–663 (2004)
19. Hilton, A., Beresford, D., Gentils, T., Smith, R., Sun, W.: Virtual people: Capturing human models to populate virtual worlds. In: IEEE Computer Animation, pp. 174–185 (1999)
20. Lee, W., Gu, J., Magnenat-Thalmann, N.: Generating animatable 3d virtual humans from photographs. Computer Graphics Forum 10(3), 1–10 (2000)
21. Magnenat-Thalmann, N., Laperrière, R., Thalmann, D.: Joint-dependent local deformations for hand animation and object grasping. In: Proc. Graphics Interface, pp. 26–33 (1988)
22. Shao, P., Liao, W.: Functions, Genres, Resources: Discussing the Adoption of Virtual Characters in Digital Museum from the Perspective of Communication Studies. In: Proceedings of Cyberworlds 2008, pp. 621–626. IEEE Publisher, Los Alamitos (2008)

Teaching Me Softly:
Experiences and Reflections on Informal
Educational Game Design

Ulrich Wechselberger

University of Koblenz-Landau,
Institute For Computational Visualistics,
Universitaetsstr. 1, 56070 Koblenz, Germany
`wberger@uni-koblenz.de`

Abstract. Video games are highly engaging environments. Therefore, there is a growing interest in harnessing their motivational potential via game-based learning. However, putting curricular content into digital games is not trivial. Many educational games fail to combine teaching and gameplay in a subtle way, thereby suffer from low-grade design and fail to utilise the motivational potential of video games.

This article explicates some main issues of educational games and reflects on an approach to a more informal and harmonic design for educational games. Furthermore, it describes the *"Eduventure II"*, a research project investigating and testing these methods. The game developed in this prototype links the curriculum to narrative, simulation and game play layers. The here presented text describes the theoretical background, issues, concept and implementation of the prototype, as well as the lessons learnt from a pedagogical perspective.

Keywords: Game-Based Learning, Educational Game Design.

1 Introduction

Game-based learning has become an important issue for economy, society and research. The demand of lifelong learning increases the need for effective, motivating learning tools. Meanwhile, computer graphics and game technology made a quantum leap. Moreover, computer games have become common and popular among young people. As a result, scientists, educators and pedagogues consider computer games as an educational tool. However, this subject still has issues. This article addresses one of them – inferior integration of the learning content into the game – and reflects some theoretical thoughts and practical experiences regarding a more elegant and *"subtle"* educational game design.

At first, this article distinguishes play, games and computer games, as well as several uses of game-based learning. Part two discusses the potential of game-based learning from a pedagogical perspective, stressing on motivational and didactical benefits of digital games. The following sections describe a way to combine educational content with video games and its practical application within the Eduventure

Z. Pan et al. (Eds.): Transactions on Edutainment II, LNCS 5660, pp. 90–104, 2009.

II, a learning adventure targeting historical knowledge. Last, but not least, some conclusions regarding the used approach and further research are drawn.

2   From Play to Game-Based Learning

This article will be prefaced with a short paragraph on terminology. *Play* takes place within a frame often regarded as the *"magic circle"* [1, p. 94]. Within this frame, the player does not encounter negative consequences or functional pressures, which thereby supports *"lusory behaviour"* [2]. The world within the magic circle is not only risk-free, but also imaginary. Players overcome the borders of reality and apply new meanings to objects: During play, a matchbox can become a train, a car, a house or whatever the player wants it to be. Fabricatore refers to this circumstance as the concept of *"as if"* [2].

Salen and Zimmerman define a *game* as *"a system in which players engage in an artificial conflict, defined by rules, that results in a quantifiable outcome"* [1, p. 80]. By mentioning the artificial character of game worlds, this definition adapts the concept of *"as if"*. To simplify matters, this paper uses the terms *digital game, video game and computer game* synonymously, following Juul's definition: A video or computer game is, *"generally speaking, a game played using computer power and a video display"* [3, p. 36].

The terminology on game-based learning, however, still seems to be somewhat fuzzy and vague. Nevertheless, one could distinguish two forms of learning games. *Serious games* focus on the technical potential of video games for training and simulation, stressing authenticity and realism of the educational content. In contrast, *educational games* try to preserve a balance of fun and education, imparting the educational content in an entertaining and playful manner [4]. Both serious games and educational games (and even regular video games when applied in an educational context) can be used for several purposes, which I suggest to break down into four different ideal types. First, learning games can take over the role of a *teacher*, imparting knowledge and information. Secondly, they can be designed in order to *train* specific capabilities and skills. They can also be used for *overlearning and recapitulating* (as in the *"Triple A Game Show"* [5]). Last, but not least, pedagogues can use them as some sort of *"bait"*, which makes it much easier for them to get in touch with their clients and build a relationship. However, this article does not cover all possible forms and purposes of learning games. It focuses (a) on educational games that are (b) used for teaching.

3   Pedagogical Potential of Game-Based Learning

Computer games can be powerful educational tools mainly for two reasons: First, they incorporate well-established learning principles and provide resources for authentic simulation. Secondly, computer games are fun to play and therefore engaging. However, this does not automatically mean that educational games benefit from these factors as well. The following section provides background information and research findings concerning these issues.

3.1   Computer Games and Learning

Playing is often connected to learning processes. Fabricatore for instance connects the process of playing video games with several learning occasions (cf. figure 1), such as training of analytic, strategic and psychomotor skills as well as acquisition of game-relevant knowledge [2]. Moreover, scientists have indicated several learning principles embodied in computer games. For instance, Gentile and Gentile found seven factors beneficial for learning, including adaptation to player skills, interactivity, practice and overlearning [6]. Van Eck states that learning in computer games "*takes place within a meaningful (to the game) context*" [7, p. 18] and emphasises the role of a relevant context for learning principles (such as situated cognition and viability). Gee even elaborated 36 educational values of computer games, including motivation to start and keep on learning, customisation, possibility to test hypotheses and others [8]. Also, due to the increasing performance of state of the art hardware, video games can simulate graphics, physics and even artificial intelligence (e.g. in the game "*facade*" [9]). This enables the player to interact with systems that (for different reasons) can not be examined in real life (e.g. historical societies, hazardous environments, biological microsystems). Thereupon, one could consider computer games as effective learning environments.

On the other hand, research findings about learning in video games are unsatisfying. On the one hand, there is evidence of computer games very effectively supporting a narrow scope of psychomotor skills. They also train cognitive capabilities such as visual attention skills, spatial visualisation, problem solving,

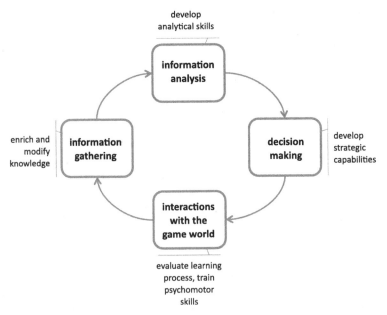

Fig. 1. Learning occasions within computer game play regarding to Fabricatore [2]

creative and critical thought [10]. However, research findings about knowledge acquisition through video games are rare and contradictous. This also applies to the internalisation of norms and moral values. Both values and information seem to be bound within the magic circle, which may in many cases block learning transfer into real life. This may be due to certain theoretical problems which arise when dealing with complex issues such as knowledge construction. Section 4.2 will deal with this issue in detail.

3.2 Motivational Effects of Computer Games

Playing games is fun. Play and games have been used to enhance the interest of adolescents in useful, yet somewhat unexciting matters (for example curricular contents) for decades. Thus, the most important hidden agenda regarding game-based learning is to utilise the motivational power of play and games for educational purposes. But where does this motivational potential come from? Many scientists believe that the power a player can wield over his environment while still challenged is a very important source of intrinsic motivation [11]. Computer games provide instant feedback and thereby deliver instant gratification. They also come up with other motivating features such as aesthetic graphical representation, a wide variation of options and scenarios, and others [12, pp. 128–129]. Accordingly, computer games appear to have great motivational potential.

However, although video games are very entertaining, learning games are not necessarily fun as well. Two main problems may come up when trying to benefit from the motivational potential by using learning games in an educational context: As mentioned earlier in this article, play is free of functional pressures and does not have negative consequences. Thus, a teacher cannot impose playing a game on a pupil without running the risk of disrupting the nature of play (and thereby corrupting part of its motivational source). Video games may become "*teacherised*" in an educational context [4], leading to the loss of their engaging potential. This is a constitutive problem with play and games used for teaching: By being exploited for purposes outside of the magic circle, play and games become serious, which is somehow paradox. This *constitutive issue* may not be fixable by game design. It is, however, more of a hypothetical nature. The second problem is more of a practical nature and concerns game design. Curricular objectives and game goals are often incongruent [11,13], and, as a result, educational games are often of *inferior quality*. Seymour Papert criticised the low-grade design of most edutainment products and educational games: "*Shavian reversals – offspring that keep the bad features of each parent and lose the good ones – are visible in most software products that claim to come from a mating of education and entertainment*" [14, p. 88]. Indeed, in most educational games there seems to be little cohesion between educational content and game structure [2]. Integration of the curricular content is stilted and artificial, thus gameplay, fun and entertainment are corrupted.

The here presented article concentrates on the second issue.

4   Theoretical Reflections on Video Game Semiotics

In order to overcome the obstacle of inferior educational game design, one has to find subtle, elegant ways to connect video game structure and educational content. Fabricatore proposed that educational game designers should embed knowledge *"naturally"* and with contextual relevance into gameplay [2], and curricular tasks should become elements of the gameplay. He exemplifies his thoughts by describing a Super Mario game. In this game, collectable coins are replaced by educational content (e.g. numbers). This approach can be taken even one step further. First, the connection between learning tasks and gameplay could be strengthened by creating a functional, semantic relation between them (this thought will be elaborated in the *"game player"* section later in this article (cf. section 4.1)). Secondly, it might not be possible to connect any kind of information to gameplay. For these contents one has to identify and elaborate further *"information carriers"* within digital games. In order to achieve this, one has to understand the semiotic structure of video games.

4.1   Semiotic Structure of Video Games

A useful semiotic framework, suitable both for game analysis and design, was introduced by Lindley [15]. He refers to video games as ludic systems involving three layers of encoding, each having different tradition, language and methodology: game play, narrative and simulation. Various game genres may focus on different layers (cf. figure 2).

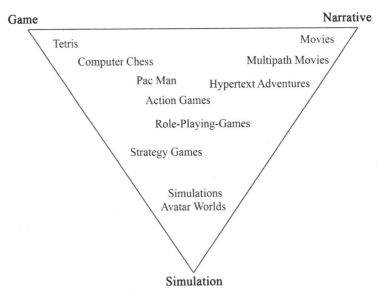

Fig. 2. Semiotic layers within computer games regarding to Lindley [15]

Game Layer. The most obvious semiotic level of video games is the game layer. Many abstract games like Pong [16] take place primarily on this layer. Lindley describes it as a *"framework of agreed rules"* [15]. These rules define the possibilities and boundaries of what a player can legally do while playing a game. They also specify the consequences of player actions. According to the more practical definition by Adams and Rollings [17, pp. 12–14], gameplay is constituted by the challenges a player faces during the game as well as the actions he addresses them with. Adams and Rollings describe numerous common challenges, for example:

- logical and mathematical challenges,
- factual knowledge challenges,
- exploration challenges (such as spatial awareness, mazes, etc.),
- conflict (stressing strategy, stealth etc.),
- economic challenges (e.g. achieving balance between several elements in a system),
- and others (for a complete list cf. [17, pp. 289–302].

In the course of subtle educational game design, these challenges could be semantically connected to the cognitive tasks postulated by the curriculum. Imagine a game that is supposed to teach the volumetric mass density of certain materials. A common, yet stilted and artificial approach would be to create, for example, an adventure game that just lets you collect materials, providing information regarding their mass density separately. In contrast, an elegant educational game design would, for instance, connect the mass density of the materials to an economic challenge and design a system (e.g. a large construction of teeter-tooters) where the player has to position the materials while maintaining the physical balance of the whole structure. This way, the educational content would be semantically connected to the gameplay. The computer would simulate the physics in realtime and thereby provide instant feedback regarding the effect on the balance. Also, this way the learning content would prove useful for achieving the goal of the game, thereby creating viability (cf. section 3.1). This game might be both more fun to play and more didactically effective, for the educational content is not only connected to gameplay, but also to the learning principles used in computer games.

Narrative Layer. The second game layer described by Lindley is the narrative layer. Games like hypertext adventures and game books take place mainly on this layer. Lindley defines narrative as *"a representation of the causally interconnected events of a story"* [15]. According to Lindley, a common narrative structure of computer games consists of three acts: establishment of the conflict, playing out its implication and finally solving it. In a much more detailed attempt, Glassner [18, pp. 35–123] breaks down narrative structures into three different parts:

- characters (consisting of several nested masks),
- plot (following common structures and containing typical elements)
- and story technique (providing a wide variety of narrative devices).

These parts may provide many *"information carriers"* for curricular content. For instance, designers of an educational game could bring back historical celebrities to a new virtual life in the form of non-player-characters. Information on the background of these celebrities could be connected to character masks and behaviour. Common plot structures and story techniques may be used to add connotations which may also encode curricular information (just imagine the semantic difference it makes if you connect a renowned, historical president not to the role of a hero, but to the role of a villain instead).

Simulation Level. Simulation games like Civilization [19] focus on the simulation level. According to Lindley, the simulation level addresses basic features and functions of the game world: It is *"the level at which the authored logic and parameters of a game system together with the specific interactive choices of the player determine an (implied) diegetic (i.e. represented) world"* [15]. Logic and parameters include, but are not limited to animation, physics, non-player character behaviour (and others). Moreover, this layer of semiotic encoding is based on an underlying set of rules, functions and constraints, developed by the game designers. Modern computers and game engines are capable of simulating these sets quite realistically and convincing. Interdependencies within complex systems (for instance ecosystems) can be rendered in realtime, thus creating authentic interactive simulation environments. In addition, modern computer technology simulate physics and photorealistic graphics. For educational games, these simulations may be directly connected to curricular content.

Conclusion. Lindley's framework provides three useful semiotic levels and thereby reveals adequate information carriers. Embedding knowledge deeply into these semiotic layers could lead to a harmonic and subtle educational game design, preserving game structure and thereby fun and entertainment. However, there may be a downside of a suchlike approach, which I would like to touch in the following section.

4.2   A Potential Downside of Subtle Educational Game Design

Hypothetically, the didactical potential of the above-mentioned approach may be reduced by mental structures referred to as frames or schemata [20]. These cognitive structures organise the perception of all kinds of data (e.g. signs, objects, situations) by applying meaning to them. During this process, an individual generates information and finally constructs and modifies its knowledge. This process is highly dependent on the situational context where the information is gathered. Cues help to identify the context and to select a respective cognitive frame for interpretation and evaluation of the information within. In brief, cues have an effect on the framing processes, thereby affecting perception and knowledge acquisition. A work by Robinson et. al. [21] demonstrates the impact of cues-affected, cognitive frames on perception: During an experiment, children had to rate foods that were served in both branded and unbranded wrappings.

Although all bags contained identical foods, the test subjects stated that the ones in the branded wrapper tasted better than the others. Robinson and his colleagues traced this result back to the impact of branding on the children's perception. This research may be connected to cognitive frames (*"branded foods are generally better than unbranded foods"*) which are activated by cues and context (branded wrappers) and produce (subjective) meaning and information (*"I like this food better than that one"*).

The concept of schemata and frames can also be applied to the reception of educational games. Imagine adolescents, playing a leisure game (or an educational game, subtly combining curricular content and gameplay) they believe to have no didactical purposes. Regarding the definition of play and games, the players stay within the magic circle, an artificial world mentally separated from the real word, following the concept of *"as if"* (cf. section 2). In principle, this magic circle is nothing but cognitive frame, separating meanings of the game world from the ones in the real world and organising the players' perceptions. Thus, if there is no *"wrapping"* branding the game elements as educational content, the players may only activate their *"play and games"* schemata. Because without any curricular cues, how should they know that they are dealing with authentic pieces of information that are supposed to be used in the real world? As a result, when it comes to knowledge acquisition through game-based learning, educational content may theoretically be overlooked. This hypothesis might apply mostly to (a) games that teach information (whose content is especially context-specific) and (b) educational games and regular video games (because, contrary to serious games, they usually miss the *"this is educational content"* cues). This hypothesis might explain the research findings mentioned above, which primarily document the training of skills and capabilities rather than the teaching knowledge in computer games.

Both this issue and the approach of an informal educational game design as described earlier have been researched within a project that was carried out by the Institute For Computational Visualistics at the University of Koblenz-Landau in Germany. This project will be introduced in the following section.

5   The Eduventure-II-Project

5.1   Research Questions and Project Procedure

The Eduventure-II-project attends to the following questions:

1. How can curricular content be embedded into an educational game without spoiling the structure of the game and the coherence of the subject matter?
2. Can a game following such a design approach engange players more effectively? How do the players perceive the educational content within the game?
3. What practical experience can be gathered that could be useful for similar projects?

In order to address these issues, an educational game prototype was designed within the project, which was supposed to serve as a test subject. At first, the curricular content was defined. In the meantime, video game semiotics as well as the combination of learning content and game structure was investigated. Based on these two steps an educational game was designed. After that, the game prototype was implemented, which was meant to be followed by the evaluation of the design approach and prototype. However, due to a cut of funding, the project was discontinued during the implementation phase. Nevertheless, our project team was able to design a game concept and implement a working, yet reduced prototype. The next section deals with the details of the concept.

5.2 Educational Content

For many pupils, history is a dry subject, and they are not particularly engaged by history lessons. The potential motivational and didactical benefits of video games may be of great value when addressing this issue. For this reason, the project focused on German cultural heritage and history. The curriculum consisted primarily of the following learning contents:

- After years of democracy under occupying forces from France, the city of Koblenz got under Prussian rule due to the Congress of Vienna in 1814/1815 and was subjected to the nationalistic authority of Prussia.
- After obtaining the city of Koblenz, the Prussian occupiers built a huge fortification system, designed in conformance with the most recent findings in fortification technology, protecting the city.
- This fortification system was said to be impregnable by force. It could only be compromised by either treason or espionage.
- There were plenty of disagreements between the citizens of Koblenz and the Prussian forces, based on ideological and organisational issues.
- Life was hard for the Prussian soldiers, for the fortress was not very comfortable and daily routines were exhausting.
- In 1848, the civilian population in the German states rebelled against the authorities, demanding freedom, democracy and national unity.

Fig. 3. A photograph of the Prussian fortress from the year 1900

– As a result, the military forces armed the fortresses in Koblenz in order to awe the citizens of Koblenz, keeping them from joining the rebellion. This arming consisted of several strategic measures.

The next section describes how this educational content was connected to the semiotic layers of the game.

5.3   Game Description

Game Concept. The Eduventure-II-prototype is a classic role playing / adventure game. We chose this game type because its structure is evenly distributed among the three semiotic layers mentioned above (cf. figure 2).

Within the game, the player assumes the role of a thief. He is hired by an éminence grise to infiltrate the Prussian fortress during the Revolutions of 1848 in the German states. His objectives are to gather as much information about the Prussian forces as possible, to capture the contents of a mysterious box brought to the headquarters of the fortress and to find vulnerabilities in the Prussian system of defence. To accomplish this, the player character joins a group of workers that are arming the fortress. Next, he waits for the night in a hiding place. After sunset, he sneaks into the fortress, searching for an adequate uniform he could wear during the day. Having found a uniform, he is able to enter the core of the fortress and finally fulfil his remaining objective.

This gameplay experience was connected to the educational content that was described above. On the *simulation layer*, we encoded information about uniforms, equipment, architectural structures and tasks regarding the arming. For example, virtual uniforms and models are authentic. Also, we paid much attention to a high recognition value of the architecture. Additionally, we resorted to the game engines capability of importing heightmaps for terrain rendering. This way we were able to use real geoinformation (acquired by the local land surveying office) for the simulation of the fortresses environment (cf. figure 4).

Furthermore, we encoded information on the *narrative level*. Story and virtual characters were connected to information about the background of the revolutions, the conflict between civilians and Prussian forces, and what life was like for a soldier working at the fortress. For instance, dialogues with labourers and soldiers reveal details about the differences between the civilians and military forces. Also, some archetypical virtual characters demonstrate the rough mentality of the Prussian occupying forces. In addition, the recruitment of the player character as a secret agent (and therefore the initial point of the story) is linked directly to the political background in 1848. In order to accentuate the tremendous obstacle the fortresses walls posed for potential attackers (cf. figure 5), we connected the task of conquering it to the common plot element *"crossing the threshold"* (cf. [18, pp. 61-62].

Last but not least, we connected some educational elements to the *gameplay layer*. Knowledge encoded on this layer includes Prussian fortification strategy, the tasks arming consisted of, as well as Prussian uniforms and equipment. For example, the player has to disguise himself as a Prussian soldier. Addressing factual knowledge challenge (cf. section 4.1), this task would result in getting caught

Fig. 4. The Eduventure's terrain rendering is based on real geoinformation

Fig. 5. The fortresses main wall (on the left) is connected to the common narrative element *"crossing the threshold"*

if the player chose the wrong uniform. Furthermore, the player has to perform authentic tasks coming up as the Prussians arm the fortress. Last, but not least he has to investigate and exploit authentic weaknesses within the fortification system in order to advance to the fortresses headquarters.

Game Technology. The Eduventure-II-prototype is a modification of the role-playing-game *"The Elder Scrolls IV: Oblivion"* [22]. Oblivion seemed like a fair choice because of its freely available construction set (used for creating modifications) and its progressive technology (e.g. graphics rendering, facial animation of NPCs, support of heightmaps and so forth). Customised virtual models were built and textured using 3ds Max [23]. The virtual fortress was created on the basis of real ground plans and satellite images (for the structure) and photographs (for the textures).

5.4   Player Reactions

Due to cut of funding, our findings on player reactions rest upon occasional, informal observations with only a handful of individuals instead of the originally intended, methodologically elaborated evaluation. Although this may have led to a lack of validity (considering statistical standards), our first experiences seem to confirm both assumptions regarding perception and reduced knowledge acquisition and increased motivation due to coherent game design (cf. section 4).

Regarding *motivational effects*, the game engines aesthetics seemed to attract young players. An early version of the Eduventure's prototype was presented at the computer expo *"Cebit"* in 2007 and seemed to be quite an eye-catcher. Young visitors enjoyed the aesthetics of the virtual fortress and characters. These players did not know about the educational purpose of the Eduventure. They just moved around the virtual territory and interacted with the game for the sheer fun of it. Unfortunately, it is an open question if they recognised any of the curricular contents of the game. However, they clearly had fun playing the game and were not *"scared away"* by stilted and artificial game design. Thus, the approach to educational game design as described above seems to preserve game structure and entertainment.

Older players provided some insights on the *perception of the educational content*. They had been told about the didactical intentions of the game. As a result, they expected a distinct presentation of educational content, pointed out by cues (cf. section 4.2), which they could not find due to the *"subtle"* design approach.

Fig. 6. A virtual Prussian Soldier in front of the fortress

One player even played several parts of the prototype and finally asked: "*Okay, but where is the educational content?*" Concerning our goal to overcome the gap between educational content and gameplay in order to preserve entertainment and motivation, this could be considered as a positive result. Subtle educational game design prevents the game from becoming "*teacherised*", thereby supporting motivation and entertainment. However, when it comes to instructional potential, the informal game design and absence of "*educational framing clues*" (cf. section 4.2) may cause players to overlook educational content. It is still unclear if this leads to reduced knowledge acquisition.

6   Lessons Learnt

In conclusion, subtle educational game design, which connects curricular elements to gameplay, story and simulation, preserves game structure. This has a positive effect on the players' engagement and motivation. However, compared to conventional educational game design, this approach apparently leads to framing processes which make the players mentally remain within the magic circle (cf. section 2). As a consequence, one might suggest to add more curricular cues to the gameplay and its social context in order to conduct the players away from the magic circle back to reality. But this could possibly amplify the constitutional conflict of play vs. seriousness mentioned above (cf. section 3.2). This issue is currently treated by a new project of our working group (cf. section 7).

Within the scope of the Eduventure-II-project, we experienced that in practice theoretical thoughts may lose some of their discriminatory power. Lindley's framework of semiotic levels within video games is a great tool for analysing games. However, in practice, borders between semiotic layers may become blurred. For instance, within a role-playing game, gameplay and narrative usually interdepend: The plot produces game objectives, which, in return, affect the story. Therefore, the distinction between two layers of semiotic encoding is sometimes more of a theoretical nature, as the practical game experience seems to take place on several blended semiotic layers. This does not only affect game design, but also its evaluation (for instance when one tries to find out if it makes any difference if curricular information is connected to the gameplay layer instead to the narrative). Therefore, for evaluation purposes it is important to keep these layers apart from each other in practical gameplay. Otherwise, one would produce measurement artefacts, thereby reducing the significance of his research results.

Apart from that, there are other factors influencing the impact of educational games. Scientists point out that not only the content, but also the amount of video game play, as well as interaction mechanics, may significantly affect learning outcomes [24]. Furthermore, some curricular contents may receive more attention than others (especially when connected to different semiotic layers or even different game tasks). These effects may be hard to foresee in advance.

Investigating the instructional and motivational potential of a game design approach as described above requires a functional, well designed game with high discriminatory power. Complex games and game engines (like the

Eduventure-II-prototype) may not be ideal for this purpose, for they can sustain exceptionally many technical pitfalls. Therefore, one might consider to concentrate on less complex game types like casual games, implemented within a less complex framework (e.g. Adobe Flash). Moreover we would encourage interdisciplinary projects, bundling resources and competencies of academics (from both educational and computer science) as well as professional game designers. This way, scientists could concentrate on their research and leave the practical design tasks to the experience and creativity of game designers.

7   Future Work

Framing processes and knowledge acquisition within computer games are highly complex, theoretical concepts, which have not yet been entirely investigated. For example, not only the game design and method of knowledge encoding may function as clues used during the framing process. The social and situational context in which the player encounters the game may play an important role as well. As a result, the issue of player perception within *"subtle"* educational games needs further research.

This also applies to the issue of motivational aspects. Connecting educational content to the semiotic structure of the video game might solve the problem of inferior and therefore unexciting educational game design. However, it is still unclear if the hypothetical constitutional conflict of play vs. seriousness (cf. section 3.2) has any impact on the players' engagement.

Both didactical and motivational issues are addressed by a research project currently carried out by the Institute For Computational Visualistics at the University of Koblenz-Landau, Germany. The objectives of this project are

- to develop and evaluate a theoretical framework specifying the impact of context and clues on cognitive framing
- and to measure potential effects of framing processes on both motivation and information.

Primarily, the computer games required for these tasks will be small and uncomplicated casual games based on Adobe Flash. In the meantime, our team is establishing contact to prospective game designers that might support us in designing the games.

References

1. Salen, K., Zimmerman, E.: Rules of Play. In: Game Design Fundamentals. MIT Press, Cambridge (2004)
2. Fabricatore, C.: Learning and videogames: An unexploited synergy. In: 2000 AECT National Convention, Long Beach (2000), http://www.learndev.org/dl/FabricatoreAECT2000.PDF (retrieved March 29, 2009)
3. Juul, J.: Half-real. In: Video Games between Real Rules and Fictional Worlds. The MIT Press, Cambridge (2005)

4. Royle, K.: Game-Based Learning: A Different Perspective. Innovate 4(4) (2008), http://innovateonline.info/?view=article&id=433 (retrieved March 29, 2009)
5. CAT2 Lab: Triple A Game Show (n.d.), http://scil.stanford.edu/news/game4-06.htm (retrieved March 29, 2009)
6. Gentile, D.A., Gentile, J.R.: Violent Video Games as Exemplary Teachers: A Conceptual Analysis. Journal of Youth and Adolescence 37(2), 127–141 (2008), http://www.springerlink.com/content/7706114365625653/ (retrieved March 29, 2009)
7. van Eck, R.: Digital Game-Based Learning. It's Not Just the Digital Natives Who Are Restless. Educause review, (March/April 2006), http://www.educause.edu/ir/library/pdf/erm0620.pdf (retrieved March 29, 2009)
8. Gee, J.G.: What video games have to teach us about learning and literacy. Palgrave Macmillan, New York (2003)
9. Procedural Arts: Facade (2005), http://www.interactivestory.net (retrieved March 29, 2009)
10. Mitchell, A., Savill-Smith, C.: The use of computer and video games for learning. A review of the literature. Learning and Skills Development Agency (2004), http://www.lsda.org.uk/files/PDF/1529.pdf (retrieved March 29, 2009)
11. Becta: Computer Games in Education project: Aspects (2001), http://snipurl.com/becta2001 (retrieved March 29, 2009)
12. Prensky, M.: Digital game-based learning. McGraw-Hill, New York (2001)
13. Squire, K.: Changing the Game: What Happens When Video Games Enter the Classroom? Innovate, 1(6) (2005), http://innovateonline.info/index.php?view=article&id=82 (retrieved March 29, 2009)
14. Papert, S.: Does easy do it? Children, Games and Learning. Game developer magazine (June 1998), http://www.papert.org/articles/Doeseasydoit.html (retrieved March 29, 2009)
15. Lindley, C.A.: The Semiotics of Time Structure in Ludic Space As a Foundation for Analysis and Design. Game Studies 5(1) (October 2005), http://www.gamestudies.org/0501/lindley/ (retrieved March 29, 2009)
16. Atari: Pong (1972)
17. Adams, E., Rollings, A.: Fundamentals of Game Design. Prentice Hall, Upper Saddle River (2006)
18. Glassner, A.: Interactive Storytelling. Techniques for 21st Century Fiction. A K Peter, Natick (2004)
19. Firaxis: Civilization IV (2005), http://www.civilization.com (retrieved March 29, 2009)
20. Anderson, J.: Cognitive Psychology and its Implications. Worth Publishers, New York (2005)
21. Robinson, T.N., Borzekowski, D.L.G., Matheson, D.M., Kraemer, H.C.: Effects of Fast Food Branding on Young Childrens Taste Preferences. Archives of Pediatrics and Adolescent Medicine 161(8), 792–797 (2007)
22. Bethesda Softworks: The Elder Scrolls IV: Oblivion (2006), http://www.elderscrolls.com/games/oblivion_overview.htm (retrieved March 29, 2009)
23. Autodesk: 3ds Max (n.d.), http://www.autodesk.com/3dsmax (retrieved March 29, 2009)
24. Rosser, J.C., Lynch, P.J., Haskamp, L., Gentile, D.A., Yalif, A.: The impact of video games in surgical training. Archives of surgery 142(2), 181–186 (2007), http://archsurg.ama-assn.org/cgi/reprint/142/2/181 (retrieved March 29, 2009)

Visual Haptic-Based Biomolecular Docking and Its Applications in E-Learning

Olga Sourina, Jaume Torres, and Jing Wang

Nanyang Technological University, Singapore
eosourina@ntu.edu.sg

Abstract. Visual haptic-based biomolecular docking systems could be used for both research and e-learning in research intensive disciplines such as biology, physical chemistry, molecular medicine, biophysics, structural biology, bioinformatics, etc. The assembly of molecules in a three-dimensional space or molecular docking is used for rational drug design where a ligand docks onto a receptor. The computer-aided design systems allow a real-time interactive visualization and manipulation of molecules in virtual environment. These techniques help the user to understand molecular interactions. In recent years, besides the visualization techniques, there has been increasing interest in using haptic interfaces to facilitate the exploration and analysis of molecular docking. Haptic device enables the users to manipulate the molecules and feel its interaction during the docking process in virtual experiment on computer. In this paper, we describe a visual haptic-based biomolecular docking system that we developed for research in helix-helix docking and propose its application in e-learning. We also describe haptic-based collaborative e-learning scenarios.

Keywords: Haptic interfaces, molecular visualization, biomolecular docking, virtual environments, e-learning.

1 Introduction

Cyberworlds can integrate tools both for research and e-learning. With advancement in computer graphics and virtual reality, e-learning benefits from visual analysis tools and virtual interfaces. For life science related disciplines, the modern molecular visualization systems allow visualization and analysis of complex biological structures. Haptic-based visual biomolecular docking is a new area of research that allows developing the interactive systems that could be used in rational drug design. Biomolecular docking is 3D assembling of molecular structures to predict the preferred complimentary molecular shapes when they are bound to each other to form a stable complex. In this paper, we describe a visual haptic-based biomolecular docking system that we developed for research in helix-helix docking and propose its application in e-learning.

It is a growing realization that digital technologies, and specifically virtual laboratories using simulated immersive environments [1-3], have the potential to enhance education at all levels. In some cases, it is more economical than the manipulation of expensive equipment such as X-ray, electronic microscopes, or high safety virus-manipulation installations. In other cases, it is simply more effective, as students cannot

Z. Pan et al. (Eds.): Transactions on Edutainment II, LNCS 5660, pp. 105–118, 2009.
© Springer-Verlag Berlin Heidelberg 2009

use their intuition and every day experience to grasp certain concepts or their inter-connection. This would be the case in disciplines that use molecular representations, where conventional tools such as graphics or videos are of limited applicability. For example, traditional learning in biology and chemistry is usually complemented by visualization tools to aid in the understanding of molecular structures [4-8]. A recent study has shown, however, that a combination of visual and tactile experience has the potential to dramatically accelerate understanding and assimilate concepts [9-11].

Another important positive aspect of immersive virtual environments with haptic feedback is to create positive students contacts with science and technology at an early age. This can have a long-lasting impact in the student and help reduce the decline in interest in science at pre-university age. Clearly, the possibility to actively manipulate molecular systems is particularly empowering, and acts as an extra motivation for the student. This active engagement can potentially increase attention to learning, in con-trast to the passive learning obtained when watching a video demonstration.

Haptic technology provides interactivity through forces transmitted by the haptic device. This makes possible to manipulate atoms and molecules, and transform bio-molecular interactions into sensory experiences during a virtual experiment. Based on our research in biomolecular docking for drug design we developed a prototype of visual haptic-based biomolecular docking system that could be applied both in re-search and e-learning.

The paper is organized as follows. Section 2 describes examples of molecular visu-alization systems, haptic-based molecular docking systems, and introduces the re-search background in helix-helix docking. Section 3 describes basic concepts of our visual haptic-based biomolecular docking system and gives an example of helix-helix docking. In Section 4, applications in e-learning are proposed. In Section 5, conclu-sion is given and future works on e-learning collaborative applications are discussed.

2   Research Background

2.1   Molecular Visualization and Haptic-Based Systems for Education

Modern molecular visualization systems allow visualization and analysis of complex biological structures and could be used as e-learning tools. There are popular molecu-lar visualization systems such as RasMol [5], PyMol [6], JMol [12] that can be used for visualization of 3D molecular structures, animating molecules, exporting geome-try, etc. The systems could be used both in education and research but they should be downloaded on the PC. There are web-based molecular visualization systems that are even more suitable for e-learning. Currently, the most popular web-based systems are WebMO [13], WebMol[14], FirstGlance [15], etc. The systems provide simple build-ing, calculating and viewing of the molecular structures. In such systems, visualiza-tion results can be easily shared in the class with the Internet access. Most of the modern systems also allow visualization of electron density, electrostatic potential, and Connolly or van der Waal surfaces and can be integrated with other visualization and analysis programs. On the other hands, such systems lack of haptic interface.

Haptic-based molecular docking is a very new topic. There are no available haptic-based molecular visualization systems or molecular docking systems for download.

Recently available in the market new haptic devices with cost around US\$ 250 make possible to use them in education for simple simulations. Thus, the research on using haptic devices in e-learning systems especially for teaching of life science disciplines is becoming very important.

In [10], Davies et al developed a prototype Molecular Visualiser (MV) application based on Web3D standards with extension for support of the haptic interaction. MV provides the user with visualizations of molecular systems, potential energy surfaces, and wave packet dynamics. These can be displayed in a web browser using VRML, or be delivered to a virtual environment in which haptic properties are assigned based on the molecular dynamics of the system. The use of MV for both research and teaching is discussed. The prototype uses PHANTOM device. The authors mainly focused on the visualization of the molecular models in the paper but do not study molecular docking problem. Lai-Yuen and Lee [16] developed computer-aided design system for molecular docking and nanoscale assembly. The authors use their own lab-built 5DOF haptic device. The paper discusses the docking of ligand to protein. During this docking process, the force feedback is calculated according to van der Waals forces. The system is implemented as a standalone system. Liu and Sourin [17] proposed a functional approach for modeling the geometry objects. The function-based objects were added in VRML. The users are able to define an implicitly defined function of any shape. Later, Wei et al [18-19] extended [17] by incorporating haptic based feature to the new FVRML nodes. A new density node was proposed for the haptic implementation and discussed in the paper. In [20], we described haptic-based visual molecular docking targeting research on helix-helix docking. In this paper, we focus on e-learning applications.

2.4 Helix-helix Docking

During the past decade, efforts have been made to predict complex structures from the structures of individual proteins. Membrane protein structure determination is till the Wild West of Structural Biology. Structural determination using classical techniques such as X-ray diffraction or Nuclear Magnetic Resonance (NMR) is hindered because of the experimental problems associated with lipid-embedded domains. Given the experimental difficulties in membrane protein structure determination, there is a pressing need for prediction methods. Prediction of membrane protein structure consists of two parts: one is topology, the other one is helix-helix interaction. Prediction of location of TM helices and topology has been in general successful. It is often possible to develop a limited set of topological models from the sequence. The total success of membrane protein structure prediction, however, depends largely on the second challenge, which is to correctly pack topologically arranged helices. In this respect, the fact that the main contribution to transmembrane interhelical packing is van der Waals interactions converts the problem into a docking one. Of course, there are a number of programs that attempt to solve the molecular docking problem, which entails finding the optimum interaction between two molecules by using a scoring function. These programs normally use a conformational search algorithm to explore the conformational space, which is exceptionally time-consuming. In those studies, drug-receptor or protein-protein interactions are the preferred subject of study.

We proposed and developed visual haptic-based molecular docking system to explore the conformational space of helix-helix interaction manually in the hope to find an optimal conformation with the minimum amount of time. Docking the transmembrane helices is a difficult task for automatic conformational search algorithms when polytopic membrane protein structure is explored because of the exponential increase in conformations as the number of α-helices is increased. Given the difficulties in exploring the whole conformational space available in polytopic membrane proteins, our strategy for docking TM helical domains is to use a manual approach in a virtual reality environment. This manual approach greatly simplifies the searching task, as changes in helix register, tilt and rotational orientation of the helices around their long axis are accomplished by hand. Feedback is provided as attraction or repulsion forces felt by the user, which has been generated after calculating bonding and nonbonding interactions.

3 Basic Concept

We developed a prototype of Transmembrane α-helices Docking System HMolDock (Haptic-based **Mol**ecular **Dock**ing), using the haptic device PHANTOM 1.5/6DOF (6 degrees of freedom) [20].

The molecular structure file format in the Protein Data Bank .pdb [21] is chosen as an input, although there are wide variety of file formats based on standard Cartesian (x, y, z) coordinates (e.g., .mpl, .car, .pdb) for which conversion programs could be used. For now, molecular visualization and van der Waals interaction are accomplished. Atom coordinates are got from input PDB files. Atom radius and correspondent color are determined based on atom type and its belonging residue which are extracted from PDB data. Two molecules or one molecule and the probe are visualized on the screen. The user can assign a haptic mouse to the probe or to one of the molecules and move the probe/molecule towards/around to another molecule. An interaction force is calculated at each position, and the resulting attraction/repulsion force is felt by the user through the haptic device. The force direction and its magnitude are visualized as a vector. Thus, a probe/molecule can be selected by the haptic mouse and moved around to let the user 'feel' the force changing.

The rough binding region can be decided interactively by the user based on complimentary shapes. The surface and sphere models are implemented in the system. The key requirement in simulating of the ligand binding process is to have a good model of the interaction between ligand and receptor. During binding, the ligand is moving in the potential field created by the receptor's atoms, and the system is searching for a stable low potential configuration. While moving one of the molecules around binding site based on complimentary shapes, the potential energy at each position is calculated and compared, the minimum value of potential energy is recorded together with the position of the ligand molecule.

The possible docking orientations between molecular systems are sampled with input from force calculations that is fed back to the user through the haptic device. The molecular systems are visualized with their van der Waals surfaces. The force feedback requires a high refresh rate (at least 1 kHz); therefore interaction energy calculations should be simplified. In future, the interactive forces could be calculated in advance and stored in a volumetric grid. During the manipulation, the Cartesian coordinates corresponding to interactions with local energy minima are dynamically stored on the volumetric grid.

When only forces in rigid docking are required, we use the Lennard-Jones (L-J) potential as the main scoring function, as it has been found to be the most important in transmemebrane α-helix interaction [22].

The essential features are approximated quite well by a Lennard-Jones potential (also referred to as the L-J potential, 6-12 potential or, less commonly, 12-6 potential), which can be expressed as:

$$V(r) = 4\varepsilon \left[(\sigma / r)^{12} - (\sigma / r)^{6} \right],$$ (1)

where ε is the depth of the potential well, σ is the (finite) distance at which the inter-particle potential is zero and r is the distance between two particles. The $(1/r)^{12}$ term describes repulsion, and the $(1/r)^{6}$ term describes attraction. The LJ potential changes relatively to the distance between molecules.

The force function is the negative of the gradient of the above potential:

$$F(r) = -\nabla V(r) = -d(V(r)\tilde{r}) / dr$$
$$= 24\varepsilon \left[2(\sigma^{12} / r^{13}) - (\sigma^{6} / r^{7}) \right] \tilde{r}$$ (2)

where ε is the depth of the potential well between hetero-atomic particle pairs, σ is the (finite) distance at which the inter-particle potential is zero and r is the distance between one particle in receptor and the other in ligand.

The interactions between two large molecules (assume M atoms in receptor and N atoms in ligand) are represented by the potential energy created between them. The LJ potential and force formulas are shown below:

$$V(r) = \sum_{i=1}^{M} \sum_{j=1}^{N} 4\varepsilon_{ij} \left[\left(\sigma_{ij} / r_{ij} \right)^{12} - \left(\sigma_{ij} / r_{ij} \right)^{6} \right]$$ (3)

$$F(r) = \sum_{i=1}^{M} \sum_{j=1}^{N} 24\varepsilon_{ij} [2(\sigma_{ij}^{12} / r_{ij}^{13}) - (\sigma_{ij}^{6} / r_{ij}^{7})] \tilde{r}$$

where σ_{ij} and ε_{ij} are LJ parameters for particle i in receptor and j in ligand; r_{ij} is the distance between the particle pair; $\tilde{r}$ is the distance unit vector.

There are many different force field models that can be used to simulate proteins and other molecules implemented in AMBER [23], CHARMM [24], MM3 [25], MM4 [26] and MMFF94 [27]. If each force field is normally developed for a particular type of molecule, they rather well adapt to different structures in atomic types. The one we use and which is described below is called OPLS-aa [28] [29] [30]. It was parameterized for use in protein simulations, and also for small organic molecules, and has functional groups for all 20 common amino acids.

For the homo-atomic pairs, there are published LJ parameters available (i.e. [31] for OPLS-aa). For the homo-atomic pairs, the interaction of hetero-atomic pairs, the effective values of σ and ε are calculated from those for the homo-atomic pairs. The way of calculation is called a mixing rule. OPLS-aa uses the same non-bonded functional forms as AMBER, and the Lennard-Jones terms between unlike atoms are computed using the mixing rule [32].

$$\sigma_{ij} = \sqrt{\sigma_{ii}\sigma_{jj}}$$

(4)

$$\varepsilon_{ij} = \sqrt{\varepsilon_{ii}\varepsilon_{jj}}$$

In future, for educational purposes, we would give the user a choice of forces simulating the behavior of molecular systems depending on the case of study.

Molecular visualization is very important for the finding of complementary shapes. The presentation of molecular with smooth surface allows make docking process more intuitive. In molecular docking systems, three types of molecular surfaces are used: van der Waals, Solvent Accessible Surface (SAS), and Connolly surface. In Figure 1, an example of surfaces relation is shown.

There are different implementations of molecular surface visualization. The LSMS method introduced in [33] is claimed to be able to calculate and display a molecular surface about 1.5-3.14 times faster on average than Swiss-PDBViewer, PyMol and Chimera, which are three of the most widely used molecular visualization tools.

In our system, we implemented a van der Waals surface as a union of sphere surfaces, and for the visualization of SAS and Connolly surface we implemented Marching Cube algorithm [34]. In Figure 2, van der Waals surfaces of two helices are visualized. To differentiate the helices, two color schemes are used.

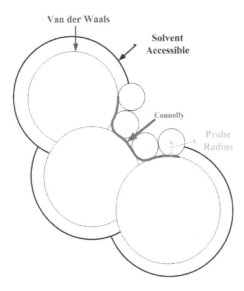

Fig. 1. Van der Waals (VdW), Solvent Accessible Surface (SAS) and Connolly Molecular Surfaces

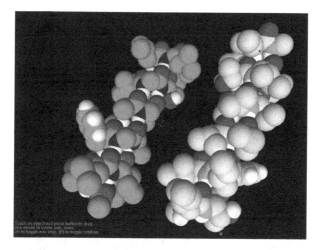

Fig. 2. Van der Waals surface model of a homodimer with two different color schemes

In Figure 3 and 4, the SAS and Connolly surfaces of two helices visualized by our system are shown.

In Figure 5, the screen captures of our system to study docking of two α-helices are pictured. The figures show as they move closely the attraction/repulsion force is visualized with vector and can be felt through the haptic device. The attraction/repulsion force in this case is mostly due to van der Waals force interactions, as no charged residues are present.

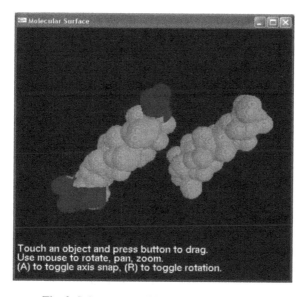

Fig. 3. Solvent-accessible surface visualization

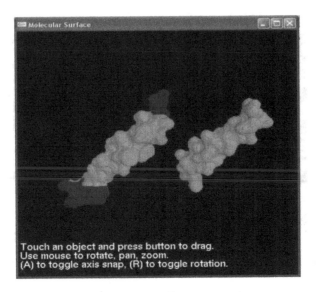

Fig. 4. Connolly surface visualization

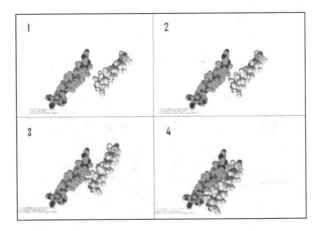

Fig. 5. Demonstration of docking process of αIIb integrin transmembrane helix and a designed antibody-like complementary peptide anti-αIIb

4 Applications in E-Learning

As it was described in Section 3, we are developing the prototype system HMolDock for transmembrane α-helices docking in rational drug design. On the other hands, the system could be widely applied in e-learning. E-learning is a computer based learning that generally includes learning using any stand alone software systems, any web-based learning, and learning in collaborative environments through the Internet. It includes face-to-face instructions and/or distance learning. We are developing two systems: one is haptic based stand alone application that could be used in face-to-face instructions environment, and another one is web-based system that can be implemented in collaborative virtual environment. Such system could be used for both face-to face and distance learning. PC with haptic device PHANTOM 1.5/6DOF is shown in Figure 6(a). Students using the HMolDock system prototype are pictured in Figure 6(b).

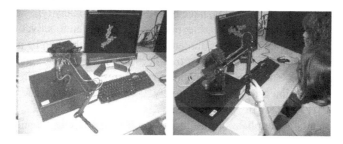

Fig. 6. (a) PC with haptic device (b) Students using HDockMol

Our tools could be used as a first introduction to physics and chemistry in secondary or even primary school. For example, van der Waals forces are responsible for the gecko's unique ability to cling to smooth surfaces. In chemistry and physics, this is one of the most important types of forces. However, its effects are not obvious in macroscopic interactions. This is probably the reason why the students find it difficult to grasp. While the use of graphs and formulas are a common way of teaching this molecular interaction, with our approach the students could move the molecules and feel the attraction or repulsion force. The clinging effect observed in the gecko can thus be understood through the haptic device. This force can also be visualized as a vector that changes its length (force magnitude) and direction.

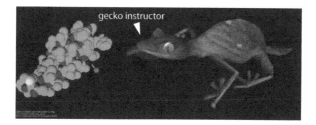

Fig. 7. Study of van der Waal forces in the presence of a gecko instructor

Our approach assumes a future development of haptic-rendering plugins with force simulation that is implemented in VRML and X3D browsers. The virtual labs should include classrooms/lab settings and intelligent agents for teaching life science subjects at school level. Haptic-enable docking experiments for study of intermolecular forces could be simulated in familiar to children environment like 3D classroom/lab and even with a gecko avatar (Fig. 7) giving instructions and explaining the basic concepts.

Although van der Waals forces can be represented using simple atoms, we show here a more complex example that would be suitable for university undergraduate students. The example in Figure 8 is especially pertinent to molecular medicine, where an important strategy is to achieve function regulation by modulation of protein-protein interactions. In membrane proteins, a recent approach targets the transmembrane region with certain peptides [35]. The rationale is that transmembrane mutations, for example in receptor tyrosine kinases, have been associated to many types of cancer and developmental deficiencies, which are explained by unregulated activation. Inactivation of the receptor is thus crucial for targeted treatment, and this can be achieved with synthetic α-helices that target the native α-helices of the receptor. Figure 8(a) shows the two transmembrane domains, target and probe, corresponding to αIIb intregrin and a designed anti-αIIb integrin [35], respectively. The helices move close and they become in contact (Figure 8(b)).

Thus, an educational application of our approach is to study in a realistic environment the effects of mutations on helix-helix interactions, and therefore in the protein's activity.

With our system, the university students would able to study protein-protein or ligand-protein interactions by downloading molecular structures and working in the

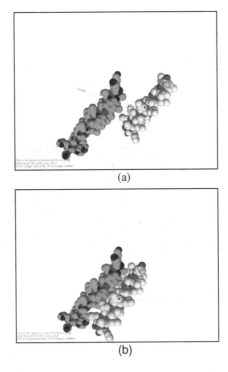

(a)

(b)

Fig. 8. Interaction of αIIb integrin transmembrane helix and a designed antibody-like complementary peptide anti-αIIb

developed immersive virtual environment from any personal computer connected to the Internet. Force-feedback desktop haptic devices will provide tactile feedback to feel and understand interaction forces in molecular systems giving the students the sense of holding the ligand molecule at their fingertips [11].

5 Conclusion and Future Work

In this paper, we introduced visual haptic-based biomolecular docking system to study helix-helix interaction and proposed applications of the system in e-learning. We are going to make further improvements on visualization techniques and are planning to develop the docking navigation algorithms to make the docking more efficient and intuitive to the user. Our system is implemented as a standalone application that can be used individually on PC and as web-based application that can be integrated into collaborative user environment. The pdb files can be chosen and automatically downloaded from Protein Bank website. Web-based application with VRML uses haptic device to enhance the user experience in virtual 3D environment. For now, the implementation of molecular docking in immersive virtual environment has limitations in number of atoms participating in force calculations and visual rendering. Therefore, research on the methods for fast visual rendering in immersive virtual environments (IVE) is very important.

Another important novel component of our application in biomolecular education is an implementation of the system as virtual lab in collaborative virtual environments [35-36]. Current technology allows one to connect to the world very quickly with the Internet. There are a lot of virtual environments for gaming which attract million of users. For example, video game "World of Warcraft" has about 10 million subscribers. Real life virtual collaborative environment like "Second Life" has about 1 million subscribers. In those environments, people can chat and play together as a team no

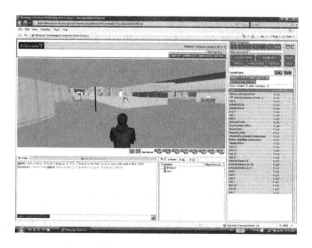

Fig. 9. NTU's Virtual Campus Snapshot

matter where they are. In Nanyang Technological University (NTU), a Virtual Campus was developed [36-37]. The screenshot of the NTU's virtual campus is shown in Figure 9. We are going to put our virtual biomolecular lab into the Virtual Campus environment.

Web-integrated tools are cost effective and can be easily used and shared. In works [18-19], we did the preliminary study on using a force-feedback device in collaborative environment with VRML. In work [38], we described visual immersive haptic-based mathematics study in collaborative virtual environment. We are going to perform web-based haptic collaboration with virtual objects using FVRML plugin described in [18-19]. Since VRML and X3D do not natively support collaboration, a third party communication platform has to be used or developed. Examples of such platforms are open-source DeepMatrix (*http://www.deepmatrix.org*), blaxxun Communication Platform (*http://www.blaxxun.com*), and Bitmanagement Collaborate (*http://www.bitmanagement.com*). The Virtual Campus of NTU is built using VRML and the blaxxun Communication Platform. NTU Virtual Campus is a photo-realistic collaborative virtual world. It includes virtual models of the land, buildings, interiors, avatars, and texture images resembling the real campus of NTU. There are also interiors of the main places, tutorial rooms, lecture theaters, and student hostels.

The virtual laboratories could be added to Virtual Campus. The users can type text messages and communicate with other users within the same session. During the class session, molecular models will be displayed on demand, and discussion of biological content with other students or instructor will be further facilitated by haptic-based collaborative access to 3D molecular system. We design and develop a collaborative framework in immersive virtual environment for application in biomolecular education. We propose collaborative student-to-student, instructor-to-student, and student-to-instructor scenarios. In the instructor-to-student scenario, an instructor moves probe/atom around molecular system with the use of his/her haptic device on the desktop, then the students in the virtual lab can feel repulsion and attraction force between the probe and molecular system through their own haptic device. Student-to-student scenario is used in student's team projects. Student-to-instruction scenarios are used for student feedback and result submissions. In future, we are also planning to do experiments on the student's learning process and evaluation of effectiveness of collaborative haptic-based education. Application of these virtual reality tools would improve students understanding of concepts related to intermolecular interaction.

We would like also to conclude that Cyberworlds should be a general platform for integration of research and e-learning in science.

Acknowledgements

This project is supported by MOE NTU grant RG10/06 "Visual and Force Feedback Simulation in Nanoengineering and Application to Docking of Transmembrane α-Helices".

References

1. Martinez-Jimenez, P., Pontes-Pedrajas, A., Polo, J., Climent-Bellido, M.S.: Learning in Chemistry with Virtual Laboratories. J. Chemical Education 80(3), 346–352 (2003)
2. Morozov, M., Tanakov, A., Gerasimov, A., Bystrov, D., Cvirco, E.: Virtual Chemistry Laboratory for School Education. In: Fourth IEEE International Conference on Advanced Learning Technologies (ICALT 2004), pp. 605–608 (2004)
3. Riganelli, A., Gervasi, O., Laganana, A., Alberti, M.: A Multiscale virtual reality approach to the chemical experiments. In: Sloot, P.M.A., Abramson, D., Bogdanov, A.V., Gorbachev, Y.E., Dongarra, J., Zomaya, A.Y. (eds.) ICCS 2003. LNCS, vol. 2658, pp. 324–330. Springer, Heidelberg (2003)
4. Luo, Y., Guo, P., Hasegawa, S., Sato, M.: An Interactive Molecular Visualization System for Education in Immersive Multi-projection Virtual Environment. In: Third International Conference on Image and Graphics, Hong Kong, pp. 485–488. IEEE Computer Society Press, Los Alamitos (2004)
5. Sayle, R.A., Milner-White, E.J.: Rasmol: Biomolecular graphics for all. Trends in Biochemical Sciences (TIBS) 20(9), 374 (1995)
6. DeLano, W.L.: The pymol molecular graphics system (2002),
   http://www.pymol.org
7. Sourina, O., Korolev, N.: Geometric querying of time-dependent data for data mining in molecular dynamics. In: Proc. of Cyberworlds 2004, pp. 351–355. IEEE Press, Los Alamitos (2004)
8. Sourina, O., Korolev, N.: Visual Mining and Spatio-Temporal Querying in Molecular Dynamics. The Journal of Computational and Theoretical Nanoscience 2(4), 492–498 (2005)
9. Sankaranarayanan, G., Weghorst, S., Sanner, M., Gillet, A., Olson, A.: Role of haptics in teaching structural molecular biology. In: 11th Symposium on Haptic Interfaces for virtual Environments and Teleoperator Systems, pp. 363–366 (2003)
10. Davies, R.A., John, N.W., MacDonald, J.N., Hughes, K.H.: Visualization: Visualization of molecular quantum dynamics: a molecular visualization tools with integrated Web3D and haptics. In: 10th International Conf. on Web Technology Web3D 2005, pp. 143–150 (2005)
11. Persson, P.B., Cooper, M.D., Tibell, L.A.E., Ainsworth, S., Ynnerman, A., Jonsson, B.-H.: Designing and Evaluating a Haptic System for Biomolecular Education. In: IEEE Virtual Reality Conference, pp. 171–178 (2007)
12. JMol: an open-source Java viewer for chemical structures in 3D,
    http://jmol.sourceforge.net
13. WebMO: free World Wide Web-based interface to computational chemistry packages with features for chemicals, crystals, materials and biomolecules, http://www.webmo.net
14. WebMol: Java PDB Viewer,
    http://www.cmpharm.ucsf.edu/~walther/webmol.html
15. FirstGlance in Jmol; A simple tool for macromolecular visualization,
    http://molvis.sdsc.edu/fgij/index.htm
16. Lai-Yuen, S.K., Lee, Y.-S.: Interactive Computer-Aided Design for Molecular Docking and Assembly. Computer-Aided Design & Applications 3(6), 701–709 (2006)
17. Liu, Q., Sourin, A.: Function-defined Shape Metamorphoses in Visual Cyberworlds. The Visual Computer 22(12), 977–990 (2006)
18. Wei, L., Sourin, A., Sourina, O.: Function-based Haptic Interaction in Cyberworlds. In: 2007 International Conference on Cyberworlds, pp. 225–232. IEEE Press, Los Alamitos (2007)

19. Wei, L., Sourin, A., Sourina, O.: Function-based visualization and haptic rendering in shared virtual spaces. The Visual Computer 24(10), 871–880 (2008)
20. Sourina, O., Torres, J., Wang, J.: Visual Haptic-based Biomolecular Docking. In: 2008 International Conference on Cyberworlds, pp. 240–250. IEEE Press, Los Alamitos (2008)
21. PDB - Protein Data Bank, Brookhaven National Laboratory,
    http://www.rcsb.org/pdb
22. Bowie, J.U.: Helix packing in membrane proteins. J. Mol. Biol. 272(5), 780–789 (1997)
23. Weiner, S.J., Kollman, P.A., Case, D.A., Singh, U.C., Ghio, A.C.G., Profeta Jr., S., Weiner, P.K.: A new force field for molecular mechanical simulation of nucleic acids and proteins. J. Am. Chem. Soc. 106, 765–784 (1984)
24. Brooks, B.R., Bruccoleri, R.E., Olafson, B.D., States, D.J., Swaminathan, S., Karplus, M.: CHARMM: A program for macromolecular energy, minimization, and dynamics calculations. J. Com. Chem. 4, 187–217 (1983)
25. Lii, J.-H., Allinger, N.L.: The MM3 force field for amides, polypeptides and proteins. J. Comp. Chem. 12, 186–199 (1991)
26. Allinger, N.L., Chen, K., Lii, J.-H.: An improved force field (MM4) for saturated hydrocarbons. J. Comp. Chem. 17, 642–668 (1996)
27. Halgren, T.A.: Merck molecular force field. IV. Conformational energies and geometries. J. Comp. Chem. 17, 587–615 (1996)
28. Jorgensen, W.L., Maxwell, D.S., Tirado-Rives, J.: Development and testing of the OPLS all-atom force field on conformational energetics and properties of organic liquids. J. Am. Chem. Soc. 118, 11225–11236 (1996)
29. Damm, W., Frontera, A., Tirado-Rives, J., Jorgensen, W.L.: OPLS all-atom force field for carbohydrates. J. Comp. Chem. 18, 1955–1970 (1997)
30. Rizzo, R.C., Jorgensen, W.L.: OPLS all-atom model for amines: resolution of the amine hydration problem. J. Am. Chem. Soc. 121, 4827–4836 (1999)
31. OPLS-aa force field parameter,
    http://egad.berkeley.edu/EGAD_manual/EGAD/examples/
    energy_function/ligands/oplsaa.txt (August 28, 2007)
32. Martin, M.G.: Comparison of the AMBER, CHARMM, COMPASS, GROMOS, OPLS, TraPPE and UFF force fields for Prediction of vapor-liquid coexistence curves and liquid densities. Fluid Phase Equilib. 248, 50–55 (2006)
33. Can, T., Chen, C.-I., Wang, Y.-F.: Efficient molecular surface generation using level-set methods. Journal of Molecular Graphics and Modelling 25(4), 442–454 (2006)
34. Lorensen, W.E., Cline, H.E.: Marching Cubes: A high resolution 3D surface construction algorithm. Computer Graphics 21(4), 163–169 (1987)
35. Yin, H., Slusky, J.S., Berger, B.W., Walters, R.S., Vilaire, G., Litvinov, R.I., Lear, J.D., Caputo, G.A., Bennett, J.S., DeGrado, W.F.: Computational Design of Peptides That Target Transmembrane Helices. Science 315, 1817–1822 (2007)
36. Prasolova-Førland, E., Sourin, A., Sourina, O.: Place Metaphors in Educational Cyberworlds: a Virtual Campus Case Study. The Visual Computer 22(12), 1015–1028 (2006)
37. Sourin, A., Sourina, O., Prasolova-Førland, E.: Cyber-learning in Cyberworlds. Journal of Cases on Information Technology 8(4), 55–70 (2006)
38. Sourin, A., Sourina, O., Wei, L., Gagnon, P.: Visual Immersive Haptic Mathematics in Shared Virtual Spaces. In: Gavrilova, M.L., Tan, C.J.K. (eds.) Transactions on Computational Science III. LNCS, vol. 5300, pp. 1–19. Springer, Heidelberg (2009)

Exploring Movie Recommendation System Using Cultural Metadata

Shinhyun Ahn[1] and Chung-Kon Shi[2]

[1] Graduate School of Culture Technology, KAIST,
Yuseong-gu, Daejeon, 305-701, Republic of Korea
[2] School of Humanities & Social Sciences, KAIST,
Yuseong-gu, Daejeon, 305-701, Republic of Korea
{demiahn,chungkon}@kaist.ac.kr

Abstract. With the advent of the World Wide Web, it has captured and accumulated 'Word-of-Mouth (WoM)' such as reviews, comments, user ratings, and etc., about cultural contents including movies. We paid attention to WoM's role as cultural metadata. 'Recommendation systems' are services which recommend users new items such as news articles, books, music, and movies they would like. We developed a simple and low-cost movie recommendation system harnessing vast cultural metadata, about movies, existing on the Web. Then we evaluated the system, and analyzed its strength. As a result, we could be aware of the potential of cultural metadata.

Keywords: Movie Recommendation, Movie Reviews, Cultural Metadata.

1 Introduction

'Recommendation systems' are services which recommend users new items such as news articles, books, music, and movies they would like. Recommendation Systems based on AI technology have been explored especially around 1990s, when the WWW and internet services grew explosively all around the world. As the WWW evolved and the number of items with which were provided for users augmented considerably, it was getting more difficult for users to make choices of 'good' items. On the other hand, the evolution of the WWW has led various researches on information retrieval techniques including NLP (natural language processing). Both ask for solutions which facilitate choices and technical conditions for implementation have made recommendation systems researched and developed actively.

People talk almost every day. They depict thoughts and feelings about something through their word-of-mouth. However these talks are temporal and vanishing, and fly away. The WWW has a characteristic to transform these temporal 'parols' into spatial 'texts'. Texts are lasting and preserved in the Web. Indeed, the WWW is a mine of numerous thoughts and impressions.

A part of parols on the Web is about cultural contents like music, soap operas, books, and movies. Reviews and comments on cultural contents are published on user blogs. Qualitative discourses such as ratings, reviews, and comments have been accumulated on cultural contents DB sites. These parols about cultural contents have been aggregated by numerous users spontaneously and culturally, and formed colorful qualitative discourses and reputations. They are indeed 'cultural metadata' with a great potential.

Z. Pan et al. (Eds.): Transactions on Edutainment II, LNCS 5660, pp. 119–134, 2009.

We developed a simple and low-cost movie recommendation system harnessing vast cultural metadata, about movies, on the Web and analyzed the strength of the system. As a result, we could be aware of the potential of cultural metadata.

2 Recommendation System

Recommendation systems (1) predict the user preferences for new items compared with user's preferences for already experienced items and (2) recommend him/her items predicted having high preferences within some constraints. This process is formulated like below.

$$f(<user, item>) = user\ preference \tag{1}$$

$$g(<user, items, [constraints]>) = list\ of\ recommendation \tag{2}$$

Although many recommendation systems have been developed, there are two main streams of approaches to recommendation system research, CBR (Content-Based Recommendation) and CF (Collaborative Filtering).

2.1 CBR (Content-Based Recommendation)

CBR (Content-Based Recommendation) analyzes the contents of new items and recommends those which are the most similar to a user preference profile that is an aggregate of the contents of items the user has liked. CBR has its roots in the IR (Information Retrieval) techniques and, therefore, has the advantage in dealing with text-based items like news articles, books, URL, and so on ([1, 2]). Recently, as text-based metadata for audio/visual/video items such as music, pictures, drawings, or movies are created and provided widely, it's possible for CBR to deal with a variety of items.

The simplest way of CBR is to provide the most similar items to the target item regardless of users' individual preferences. To give an example, a similar albums and artists list serviced by 'yahoo music!' falls into this category. Baumann and Hummel developed the music recommendation system by comparing between the reviews of artists existing on the Web ([3]).

However, as each user has an individual taste, a user preference profile is devised. A user preference profile is extracted mainly from the contents of items the user liked in the past. Sometimes, users are asked for their ratings for sample items. Using user preference profiles opened a door to the personalized recommendation services.

CBR has a few strengths. First of all, as the idea of algorithm is simple to understand, it's easy to explain a process of making recommendations to users. This is important in that users provide their preference information more willingly when appreciating the system. The more users understand the system, the more they trust it. Moreover, CBR is practical and serviceable. It requires not many resources for a computation process, although the total number of items managed in the system is huge. Also, non-personalized services are possible without user preference profiles. Above all, its coverage is wide, because there is no constraint except item analysis techniques.

However, CBR has several shortcomings like below ([4]). The modalities of data with which CBR can deal are limited. Only a very shallow analysis of certain kinds of content can be supplied. For example, it's difficult to extract features from the beauty

Table 1. Characteristics of two approaches to recommendation system

	Content-Based Recommendation	Collaborative Filtering
comparison between	item & item, item & user	user & user
strength	· Easy: It is easy to understand. · High Reliability: Appreciating a recommendation process facilitates eliciting user feedback. · Cheap: Resource consumption for computation is low. · Light: Non-personalized service is possible without the user preference information. · High Coverage: A range of items available for recommendation is wide.	· Diversity: It can deal with any kind of content. · Serendipity: It provides items with dissimilar content with those experienced in the past.
weakness	· Shallow: Only a very shallow analysis of certain kinds of content can be supplied. · Over-specialization: the user is restricted to seeing items similar to those already experienced.	· Sparsity: The lack of user preference data causes a performance decline, and makes it difficult to find nearest-neighbors for users with peculiar taste. · Scalability: Increase of user preference data leads to a performance improvement, but much more resources are consumed.

of movie scenes, the tone colors of music, and the flavors of. The value of design, multimedia information, and loading times of web pages are also easy to be ignored. Metadata about items can be a key to this problem, because they are mostly textual and easy to deal with.

Secondly, recommended items are apt to be over-specialized. When the system can only recommend items scoring highly against a user's profile, the user is restricted to seeing items similar to those already experienced. This problem is often addressed by injecting a note of randomness, or mutation operations ([5]).

Finally, there is a problem in eliciting user feedback, that is, ratings for items the user experienced already. Rating items is a bothering task for users. This problem is not a problem just in CBR, and common to most recommendation systems.

2.2 CF (Collaborative Filtering)

CF (Collaborative Filtering, Collaborative Recommendation, or Social Filtering) systems are somewhat different from CBR in that rather than recommend items similar to the items the user liked in the past, they recommends items other similar users have liked. For each user a set of "nearest neighbor" users are found with whose past ratings there is the strongest correlation. Preferences for new items are predicted based on a combination of the preferences known from the nearest-neighbors. This approach to recommendation assumes that people's tastes are not randomly distributed, and there are general trends and patterns within the tastes of a person and between groups of people. Actually, experiences and opinions of friends, or other users serve as a good reference when making a choice of new items. CF automates a process of recommendations through "WOM (Word-Of-Mouth)" ([6]). The following is a general algorithm of CF.

1) User preference profiles are extracted from the users ratings for items the users have experienced already.
2) Similarity scores between the user and other users are computed by comparing user preference profiles. Especially nearest-neighbor users with whose past ratings there is the strongest correlation are found.
3) The user preference for a new item is inferred from the preferences of nearest-neighbors for it.
4) A list of items with highly predicted preferences is recommended to the user.

Ringo [6], one of the first CF systems, recommended music artists according to the above process. GroupLens [7] is a news articles recommendation service, and Bell-core Video Recommender [8] provides a movie recommendation when users send their ratings for movies they have seen through e-mail. MovieLens [9] also provides a movie recommendation on the Web.

CF solves all of the shortcomings given for CBR. CF can deal with any kind of content, because the contents difficult to be analyzed like audio, video, idea, emotions, and others are converted to user ratings, the numerical data easy to be dealt with. Moreover there is a serendipity in CF, because it provides items with dissimilar content to those experienced in the past.

CF also has a few shortcomings. First of all, new items without user ratings cannot be recommended. If the number of items without user ratings is large, the coverage of recommendation becomes narrow. Secondly, when the number of users is small, it's so difficult to find nearest-neighbors that the recommendation performance is dropped considerably. It's also hard to expect good recommendation to users with peculiar taste because of sparsity of nearest-neighbors for them. On the other hand, if a scale of users and items data increases, recommendation performance also improves. However, larger resources are required for computing, which results in lowering practicality.

CBR and CF are not contrary to each other; they can complement each other to improve recommendation performance ([4, 10]). Chen and Aickelin [11] have developed movie recommendation system using AIS (Artificial Immune Systems), and O'Connor and Herlocker [12] have applied CF algorithms after clustering items based on user ratings distribution. FilmTrust [13, 14] is a website that integrates Semantic Web-based social networks, augmented with users' trust preferences. FilmTrust has assumed that people rely more upon those whom they trust, and used trust ratings as weights.

There are recommendation systems using semantic and Web information. MOV-IES2GO have considered genres, actors/actresses, and directors all together to recommend movies by using the voting theory. They have provided various kinds of services utilizing semantic information like movie synopses. Good et al. [16] have combined a Web information retrieval agent with CF system and resulted in providing more precise recommendations. Music recommendation system using artists' reviews on the Web also have been devised ([3]).

3 Cultural Metadata

Cultural metadata is defined as 'the information that is implicitly present in huge amounts of data and needs to be extracted with techniques for information retrieval.'([3]) With the advent of the World Wide Web, it has captured and accumulated 'Word-of-Mouth(WoM)' such as reviews, comments, userratings, and etc., about cultural contents including movies. We paid attention to WoM's role as cultural metadata.   Especially,   the   IMDb   (The   Internet   Movie   Database, http://www.imdb.com), which is the biggest internet movie database, provides a few kinds of reliable cultural metadata.

Table 2. Metadata Type and Similarity Measure Methods

Metadata Type		Similarity Measure	
User Comments Plot Outlines Synopsis	Text-type	Document Vector Mood Vector	Cosine Measure
Plot Keywords Genres	Keyword-type	Document Vector	

Cosine Measure was used to compute similarities between movies. To do this, document vectors were created for all metadata and mood vectors were created for 3 text-type metadata.

Our system used 5 types of cultural metadata - user comments, plot outline, synopsis, plot keywords, and genres provided by the IMDb for movie recommendation.

1) User Comments: People write reviews about movies they've seen to share their impressions and opinions with other people. The important thing is that people who haven't seen that movie yet consult the comments to find out whether the movie deserves to be appreciated, because user comments represent the quality of movies implicitly. There are thousands of User comments for each movie on the IMDb at present. User comments are indeed the rich cultural metadata.

2) Plot Outlines: These are 5-10 line brief plot summaries created by users without judging the quality of the movie, because it is guided that plot outline should not include any analysis of the movie e.g. "This film is one of Hitchcock's finest" on the IMDb. Therefore, it is expected that plot outlines represent movie plots exclusively. However, plot outlines are sparse metadata in spite of their potential.

3) Synopsis: Synopsis is a longer summary of plot than plot outlines, but sparser than plot outlines (Table 3).

4) Plot Keywords: Plot keywords are controlled keywords relating to a movie plot. For example, plot keywords for Star Wars (1997) include 'Galactic War', 'Honor', 'Sabotage', and so on. Plot keywords are managed and controlled by the IMDb, so concrete and reliable cultural metadata.

5) Genres: Genres are also controlled metadata provided by the IMDB. Each movie is represented as a few genre categories as 'Action / Adventure / Family / Fantasy / Sci-Fi' for Star Wars.

At present, there is information for about 1,000,000 titles of movies, TV episodes, TV movies, TV series, miniseries, and video games on the IMDb. About 50% of them have genre descriptions; 30% have plot keywords; 12% have plot outlines; the

Table 3. Percentages of movies having metadata

metadata	number of movies having metadata	percentage
User comments	1,271	98.5%
Plot outlines	1,186	91.9%
Synopsis	447	34.6%
Plot keywords	1,263	97.8%
Genres	1,282	99.3%

Total number of sample movies: 1291 titles.

percentage of titles having user comments is supposed to be about 40%. However a half of 1,000,000 titles have very few influence actually. This means that most of recognized movies have at least genre description or user comments, and cultural metadata have potential to be utilized widely.

Above 5 of metadata are divided into two types, text-type and keyword-type. The former includes user comments, plot outlines, and synopsis, which fit into natural language, and the latter does plot keywords and genres, which are controlled vocabularies. There is a slight difference in dealing with those two types of metadata to compute similarities between movies.

4 Movie Recommendation Based on Cultural Metadata

Fig. 1 shows an overall process of our system. Basically, we computed similarities between movies with the above 5 types of metadata to make a recommendation list. To do this, we created a vector space for cultural metadata, and used a cosine measure method from information retrieval domain, and ConceptNet 2.1 ([18]), the commonsense reasoning toolkit developed by MIT Commonsense Computing Initiative.

First of all, we have selected 1291 of movies from the IMDb considering their ratings and box-office records. Then 5 types of metadata for each movie were collected automatically. Details of a process are as follows. The percentage of movies having each metadata is like Table 3. As expected, all but synopsis are rich enough to be used.

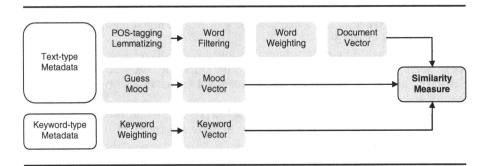

Fig. 1. Overall process of the system

4.1 Text-Type Metadata

Text-type metadata such as user comments, plot outlines, and synopses for 1291 movies are collected by web crawling. We aimed at exploring various potential of cultural metadata. Therefore we created mood vectors by using ConceptNet 2.1 ([17]), the commonsense reasoning toolkit of MIT, while extracted traditional document vectors for text-type metadata.

Using Document Vectors. We have analyzed text-type metadata morphologically. At first it was needed to remove some 'language noises' to create document vectors for each text-type metadata which are natural languages. We have regulated words of metadata by Part-Of-Speech tagging and lemmatizing by using the MontyLingua module of ConceptNet 2.1. Plural nouns were changed into singulars. Then words out of interest were filtered out. We chose nouns or modifying words, or both. This is based on our empirical commonsense that nouns and modifying words represent best the impressions of movies.

Filtered words form a term pool for each movie, which represents the attributes of the movie. From a term pool, we have created a document vector for each movie by using a TFIDF (Term Frequency Inverse Document Frequency) term weighting strategy.

$$TFIDF = TF \times \frac{1}{DF}$$

$$TF : term\ frequency\ in\ a\ document \tag{3}$$

$$DF : term\ frequency\ in\ the\ entire\ documents$$

When recommendation for similar movies to a target movie is requested, similarities of the movie to other movies are computed by using a cosine measure method like (4). Then the most similar movies above the threshold were provided as recommended movies for the target movie.

$$\frac{U \bullet V}{\|U\| \times \|V\|} \tag{4}$$

$$\cos ine\ measure\ of\ vector\ U\ and\ V$$

Using Mood Vectors. ConceptNet 2.1 is a commonsense reasoning toolkit and provides a vast commonsense DB and several reasoning functions, one of which is a 'GuessMood' function that outputs a mood vector for input text. Each mood vector has 6 components, (angry, surprised, disgusted, happy, sad, fearful), which represent the degree of emotions. The degree of each emotion is quantified as a value from 0 to 1 ([17]). Therefore, each text-type metadata for a movie can be transformed into a movie vector. The rest process of recommendation is identical to that using document vectors.

4.2 Keyword-Type Metadata

Keyword-type metadata including plot keywords and genres are controlled vocabularies, therefore keyword vectors were created through TFIDF term weighting without an additional regulation. Similarities computation and recommendation processes are same as the preceding.

5 Evaluation

Eight of test sets are used for evaluation (Table 4). We excluded a test set which uses mood vectors for recommendation, because its performance was prominently low. We guess the cause of low performance is due to the lack of sentences pertaining to movies in commonsense DB rather than the performance of commonsense reasoning. Each test set had the identical 23 movies for target movies. We made a selection having regard to the popularity, influence of movies, and genre balance.

Two judges have evaluated the performance of the system. Judges were not only movie researchers, but also experts in the movie industry. One of them was a film cutter, and the other was a scenario writer. This was because evaluators have to have seen most of subject movies, or be able to grasp the attributes of them quickly.

They have scored the degree of similarity like (5) between a target movie and recommended movies according to 5 types of evaluation criteria (Table 5). The scores range from 0 to 1.

$$precision = \frac{HM}{RM} \qquad (5)$$

HM : the number of similar movies to a target movie in a recommendation list
RM : the total number of recommended movies

Table 4. Test sets

Test Set	Metadata	Types of Selected Words
TS1	User Comments	Nouns
TS2	User Comments	Nouns & Modifiers
TS3	Plot Outlines	Nouns
TS4	Plot Outlines	Nouns & Modifiers
TS5	Synopsis	Nouns
TS6	Synopsis	Nouns & Modifiers
TS7	Genres	-
TS8	Plot Keywords	-

Table 5. Evaluation criteria

Criteria	Explanation
G (genre)	similarity of genres between the target movie and recommended movies
PL (plot)	similarity of plot
M (mood)	similarity of mood
A (actor/actress or staff)	overlap of actors/actresses or staffs
PR (preference)	predicted preference of users who liked the target movie for recommended movies

Table 6. Pearson correlation coefficients between judges

Criteria	G	PL	M	A	PR
Coefficient	0.84	0.81	0.83	0.97	0.70

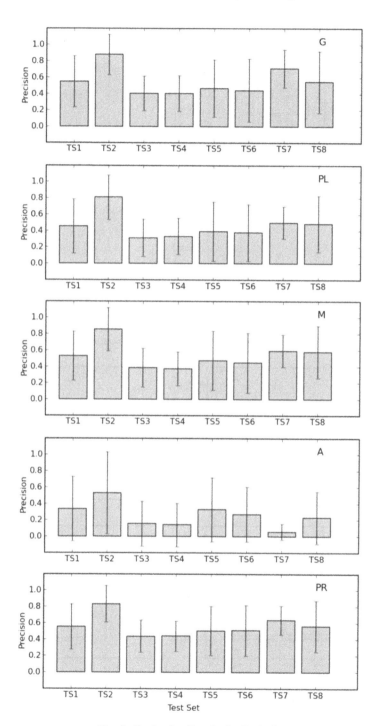

Fig. 2. Evaluation Results for Each Criterion

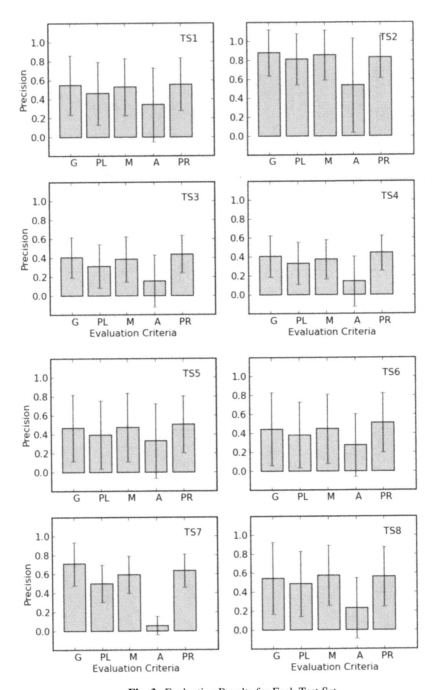

Fig. 3. Evaluation Results for Each Test Set

Table 7. Evaluation results

Test Set	G	PL	M	A	PR
TS1	0.55	0.46	0.53	0.34	0.56
TS2	0.88	0.81	0.85	0.53	0.83
TS3	0.41	0.32	0.39	0.16	0.44
TS4	0.40	0.33	0.37	0.14	0.44
TS5	0.47	0.39	0.47	0.33	0.51
TS6	0.44	0.38	0.45	0.27	0.51
TS7	0.71	0.50	0.60	0.06	0.64
TS8	0.55	0.49	0.58	0.23	0.56

Table 8. Difference of statistical significance in performance for each criterion (the number in parentheses is the performance rank among test sets)

Criteria	Difference of statistical significance in performance
G	TS2(1)>{TS1(3), TS4(7), TS3(8)}, TS7(2)>{TS4(7), TS3(8)}, TS1(3)>TS3(8)
PL	TS2(1)>{TS7(2), TS1(4), TS4(7), TS3(8)}
M	TS2(1)>{TS3(7), TS4(8)}, TS7(2)>TS4(8)
A	-
PR	TS2(1)>{TS4(7), TS3(3)}, TS7(2)>{TS4(7), TS3(8)}

Table 9. Number of recommended movies

Test Set	Average Number of Recommended Movies
TS1	2.26087
TS2	1.043478
TS3	5.347826
TS4	4.73913
TS5	1.565217
TS6	1.086957
TS7	10
TS8	1.478261

We checked out the correlation between their scores for the fair evaluation. Table 6 shows Pearson correlation coefficients between scores from two judges. All coefficients have high values above 0.5, which means that two judges agree with each other and the reliability of evaluation is high. In case of preference, the coefficient is slightly smaller than others, because estimation of preference is more subjective than other criteria.

We actually decided the threshold values to cut off a recommendation list empirically and, therefore the precision is not that exact. However, as a unique threshold was used for each test set, it's reasonable to accept the evaluation result to compare performance scores of 8 evaluation criteria for an identical test set.

Evaluation results are shown in Table 7, Fig. 2, and Fig. 3. Considering the type of test sets, TS2 which used nouns and modifiers from user comments had the highest precision for all criteria. This implies that user comments represent the various attributes of movies implicitly and richly. As you see in Table 9, for criterion G (genre), TS2 has shown higher precision than TS1, TS4, and TS3 significantly, which means that user comments are more appropriate than plot outlines to represent the movie contents, and that when using nouns and modifiers together the performance is better than when using nouns only. TS7, which used genre keywords, is also superior to TS4, and TS3 statistically significantly. For criterion PL (plot), TS2 also has the best performance, especially statistically better than TS7, TS1, TS4, and TS3. For criterion M (mood), TS2 has shown significantly better performance than TS3, and TS4, and TS7 does than TS4. In case of criterion A (actor/actress or staff), there is no statistically significant meaning in the result. Fianlly, TS2 is also superior to TS4, and TS3. TS7 again has shown the better precision than TS4, and TS3. Considering the gist of the result, TS2 outperformed all of others.

When comparing TS1 and TS2, we can see that modifiers play an important role in representing the impression of movies. TS7 which used genres has shown the better performance for all criteria. As we said earlier, genres are keyword-type metadata and composed of controlled vocabularies by experts. Therefore, it's easier to deal with genres than other types of metadata. Moreover there are conventional plots, moods, and user preferences within a movie genre. When using genres, precision is high and the number of recommended movies is much larger than other metadata as Table 8. However the coverage is limited to specific genres, so there is no possibility to recommend movies categorized as other genres. Maybe qualitative metadata like user comments can complement genres metadata.

Plot outlines (TS3, TS4) and synopsis (TS5, TS6) did not show the good performance maybe because of the sparsity of data. These represent semantic content of movies, so there are limits in dealing with them merely morphologically. In order to harness the potential of those metadata most, semantic analysis may be helpful.

Among evaluation criteria, precisions for G (genres), PR (preference) and M (mood) were high, while that for PL (plot) was slightly lower than G or PR (Table 10). Certainly morphological approach has limits in grasping the semantic content like plot fully. In case of A (actor/actress or staff), the precision was significantly low for all test sets. Because the names of actors/actresses or staffs is explicit information, while cultural metadata are implicit information. In spite of that, TS2 shows a slightly higher performance even for A. This reconfirms the intuition that user comments have a wide spectrum of movie information, and shows the potential of user comments as metadata about movies.

One of interesting things from Table 10 is that genre and preference, and genre and mood are correlated each other strongly, and there is no significant differences in their performances. This maybe show there is a commonsense in the relationships between genre and preference, and genre and mood.

Another interesting thing in the results is that recommendation for the series movies like Star Wars, Harry Potter, or The Lord of the Rings were highly evaluated. It seems that this is because the titles or the character names are mentioned in cultural metadata explicitly. This fact implies that a key to utilizing cultural metadata fully is to extract implicit semantic information and transform it into manageable data.

Table 10. Results of pearson correlation test, and paired T-test at 5% significance level

Criteria	G	PL	M	A
PR	= (**)	≠ (**)	≠ (**)	≠ (**)
A	≠ (**)	≠ (**)	≠ (**)	
M	= (**)	≠ (**)		
PL	≠ (**)			

** : Pearson correlation test shows that correlation is significant at 1% significance level (2-tailed).
≠ : Paired T-test shows that difference is significant at 5% significance level.
= : Paired T-test shows that difference is not significant at 5% significance level.

6 Discussion

We utilized 5 types of cultural metadata about movies for movie recommendation, and groped the potential of cultural metadata. As a result, user comments which represent a wide spectrum of implicit information, and genres metadata which are controlled and precise showed their high potential. However even for other types of metadata, it's expected that more delicate analysis techniques could improve their values.

For example, the results from morphological or semantic analysis of vocabulary in each cultural metadata did not be reflected in the process of recommendation. Zipf found long time ago that the distribution of word frequencies in English, if the words are aligned according to their ranks, is an inverse power law with the exponent very close 1. This means that the probability of attaining a certain size x is proportional to $x^{-\tau}$, where τ is greater than or equal to 1. A power law gives a finite probability to very large elements, whereas the exponential tail in a Gaussian distribution makes elements much larger than the mean extremely unlikely.

Fig. 4 is Zipf's ranked distribution of verbs in user comments. Li [19] has shown that the distribution of word frequencies for randomly generated texts is very similar to Zipf's law observed in natural languages such as English. Ideal Zipf's ranked distribution is linear in log scale like Fig. 4.

On the other hand, Fig. 5 is the distribution of modifiers in user comments. As seen in Figure, the curve shows a greater repetitiveness in the range of moderate frequencies than ideal line, which means modifiers in user comments has a more restricted vocabulary than others, and user comments have a common modifying words than represent the users' sentiments for movies. In the future, by classifying and clustering these sentimental modifiers it will be possible to compute the similarity between the thoughts and feelings for two movies more efficiently and accurately.

The approach described in this article has the strength as a recommendation system, in that its conceptual process is simple and intuitive, and low-cost. Also it can recommend movies without user preference profiles, and moreover provides serendipities by using a few cultural metadata which represent a variety of emotional, factual, qualitative attributes of movies. Recommendation systems not considering user

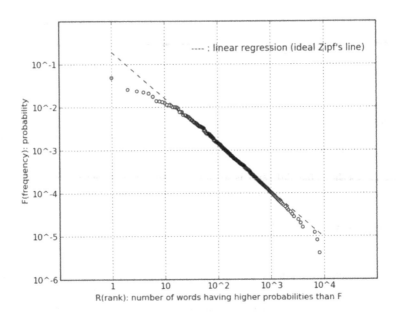

Fig. 4. Zipf's ranked distribution of VERB type words in user comments

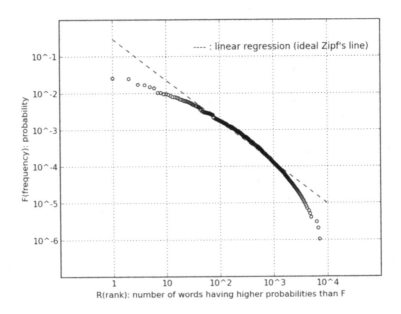

Fig. 5. Zipf's ranked distribution of modifiers in user comments

preferences are criticized as lowering the recommendation performance, but this is from the underestimation of users' navigation abilities. Internet does not only provide information in one way. Users navigate autonomously in the sea of paradigmatic information, evaluate the quality of information, and customize the information by themselves. Practical CBR is not inferior to CF which needs a few of prerequisites for the practical recommendation.

Moreover as this system harnessed the user comments for movies created by users, it expand a range of the concept of Folksonomies from keyword-type tags [20] to text-type qualitative discourse.

7 Conclusion

We utilized 5 types of cultural metadata about movies for movie recommendation, and groped the potential of cultural metadata. As a result, user comments which represent a wide spectrum of implicit information, and genres metadata which are controlled and precise showed their high potential.

We are planning deeper analysis of various cultural metadata for future work to improve the system and understand their potential fully. Also there are many possibilities on the Web to utilize cultural metadata beside the recommendation system. Interdisciplinary approach to analysis of cultural metadata as talks and parols may be one of keys to that goal.

References

1. Krulwich, B., Burkey, C.: Learning User Information Interests through Extraction of Semantically Significant Phrases. In: Proceedings of the AAAI Spring Symposium on Machine Learning in Information Access, pp. 110–112 (1996)
2. Lang, K.: Newsweeder: Learning to filter netnews. In: Proceedings of the 12th International Conference on Machine Learning (1995)
3. Baumann, S., Hummel, O.: Enhancing Music Recommendation Algorithms Using Cultural Metadata. Journal of New Music Research 34(2), 161–172 (2005)
4. Balabanovic, M., Shoham, Y.: Fab: Content-Based, Collaborative Recommendation. Communications of the Association for Computing Machinery 40(3), 66–72 (1997)
5. Sheth, B., Maes, P.: Evolving agents for personalized information filtering. In: Proceedings of the 9th IEEE Conference on Artificial Intelligence for Applications (1993)
6. Shardanand, U., Maes, P.: Social Information Filtering: Algorithms for Automating 'Word of Mouth'. In: Proceedings of the SIGCHI Conference on Human Factors in Computing Systems, pp. 201–217 (1995)
7. Konstan, J.A., Miller, B.N., Maltz, D., Herlocker, J.L., Gordon, L.R., Riedl, J.: GroupLens: Applying Collaborative Filtering to Usenet News. Communications of the Association for Computing Machinery 40(3), 77–87 (1997)
8. Hill, W., Stead, L., Rosenstein, M., Furnas, G.: Recommending and Evaluating Choices in a Virtual Community of Use. In: Proceedings of the SIGCHI Conference on Human Factors in Computing Systems, pp. 194–201 (1995)

9. Miller, B.N., Albert, I., Lam, S.K., Konstan, J.A., Riedl, J.: MovieLens Unplugged: Experiences with an Occasionally Connected Recommender System. In: Proceedings of the 8th International Conference on Intelligent User Interfaces, pp. 263–266 (2003)

10. Basu, C., Hirsh, H., Cohen, W.: Recommendation as Classification: Using Social and Content-Based Information in Recommendation. In: Proceedings of the fifteenth national/tenth conference on Artificial intelligence/Innovative applications of artificial intelligence, pp. 714–720 (1998)

11. Chen, Q., Aickelin, U.: Movie Recommendation Systems using an Artificial Immune System. Poster Proceedings of ACDM (2004)

12. O'Connor, M., Herlocker, J.: Clustering Items for Collaborative Filtering. In: Proceedings of SIGIR 2001 Workshop on Recommender Systems (2001)

13. Golbeck, J., Hendler, J.: FilmTrust: Movie Recommendations using Trust in Web-based Social Networks. In: Proceedings of IEEE CCNC 2006 (2006)

14. Golbeck, J.: Generating Predictive Movie Recommendations from Trust in Social Networks. In: Stølen, K., Winsborough, W.H., Martinelli, F., Massacci, F. (eds.) iTrust 2006. LNCS, vol. 3986, pp. 93–104. Springer, Heidelberg (2006)

15. Mukherjee, R., Dutta, P.S., Jonsdottir, G., Sen, S.: MOVIES2GO - An Online Voting Based Movie Recommender System. In: Proceedings of the Fifth International Conference on Autonomous Agents, pp. 114–115 (2001)

16. Good, N., Schafer, J.B., Konstan, J.A., Borchers, A., Sarwar, B., Herlocker, J., Riedl, J.: Combining Collaborative Filtering with Personal Agents for Better Recommendations. In: Proceedings of American Association for Artificial Intelligence (1999)

17. Liu, H., Singh, P.: ConceptNet - a Practical Commonsense Reasoning Tool-kit. BT Technology Journal 22(4), 211–226 (2004)

18. Adamic, L., Huberman, B.A.: Zip'f Law and the Internet. Glottometrics 3, 143–150 (2002)

19. Li, W.: Random Texts Exhibit Zipf's-Law-Like Word Frequnecy Distribution. IEEE Transactions on Information Theory 38(6), 1842–1845 (1992)

20. Wu, H., Zubair, M., Maly, K.: Harvesting Social Knowledge from Folksonomies. In: Proceedings of the seventeenth conference on Hypertext and hypermedia, pp. 111–114 (2006)

21. Lebart, L., Salem, A., Berry, L.: Exploring Textual Data. Springer, Heidelberg (1997)

Virtual and Augmented Reality Tools for Teleoperation: Improving Distant Immersion and Perception

Nicolas Mollet, Ryad Chellali, and Luca Brayda

TEleRobotics and Applications dept.
Italian Institute of Technology
Via Morego, 30 16163 Genoa, Italy
{luca.brayda,nicolas.mollet,ryad.chellali}@iit.it

Abstract. This paper reports on the development of a collaborative system enabling to tele-operate groups of robots. The general aim is to allow a group of tele-operators to share the control of robots. This system enables the joint team of operators and robots to achieve complex tasks such as inspecting an area or exploring unknown parts of an unknown environment.

Thanks to virtual and augmented reality techniques, a Virtual and Augmented Collaborative Environment (VACE) is built. This last supports a $N * M * K$ scheme: $N_{1;N}$ tele-operators control $M_{1;M}$ robots at $K_{1;K}$ abstraction levels. Indeed, our VACE allows to N people to control any robot at different abstraction's levels (from individual actuator's control $K = 1$ to final status specification $K = 3$). On the other hand, the VACE enables to build synthetic representations of the robots and their world. Robots may appear to tele-operators as individuals or reduced to a single virtual entity.

We present in this paper an overview of this system and an application, namely a museum visit. We show how visitors can control robots and improve their immersion using a head-tracking system combined with a VR helmet to control the active vision systems on the remote mobile robots. We also introduce the ability to control the remote robots configuration, at a *group* level. We finally show how Augmented and Virtual Reality add-ons are included to ease the execution of remote tasks.

1 Introduction

Tele-operation is dealing with controlling robots to remotely intervene in unknown and/or hazardous environments. This topic is addressed since the 40's as a peer to peer (P2P) system: a single human or tele-operator controls distantly a single robot. From information exchanges point of view, classical tele-operation systems are one to one-based information streams: the human sends commands to a single robot while this last sends sensory feedbacks to a single user. The forward stream is constructed by capturing human commands and translated into robot's controls. The backward stream is derived from the robot's status

Z. Pan et al. (Eds.): Transactions on Edutainment II, LNCS 5660, pp. 135–159, 2009.

and its sensing data to be displayed to the tele-operator. This scheme, e.g. one to one tele-operation, has evolved this last decade thanks to the advances and achievements in robotics, sensing and virtual-augmented realities technologies: these last ones allow to create interfaces that manipulate information streams to synthesize artificial representations or stimulus to be displayed to users or to derive adapted controls to be sent to the robots. Following these new abilities, more complex systems having more combinations and configurations became possible. Mainly, systems supporting N tele-operators for M robots has been built to intervene after disasters or within hazardous environments. Needless to say that the consequent complexity in both interface design and interactions handling between the two groups and/or intra-groups has dramatically increased. Thus and as a fundamental consequence the "one to one" or "old fashion" tele-operation scheme must be reconsidered from both control and sensory feedback point of views: instead of having a unique bidirectional stream, we have to manage $N * M$ bidirectional streams. One user may be able to control a set of robots, or, a group of users may share the control of a single robot or more generally, N users co-operate and share the control of M co-operating robots. To support the previous configurations, the N to M system must have strong capabilities enabling co-ordination and co-operation within three subsets:

- Humans
- Robots
- Human(s) and Robot(s)

The previous subdivision follows a homogeneity-based criteria: one use or develop the same tools to handle the aimed relationships and to carry out modern tele-operation. For instance, humans use verbal, gesture and written language to co-operate and to develop strategies and planning. This problem was largely addressed through collaborative environments (CE).

Likely, robots use computational and numerical-based exchanges to co-operate and to co-ordinate their activities to achieve physical interactions within the remote world. Known as swarm robotics, robots' groups behavior is a very active field and we will not consider it within this paper.

For human(s)-robot(s) relationships, the problem is different: humans and robots belong to two separate sensory-motor spaces: humans issue commands in their motor space that robots must interpret and execute the corresponding motor actions through actuators. Conversely, robots inform humans about their status, namely they produce sensing data sets to be displayed to users' sensory channels. Human-Machine Interfaces (HMI) could be seen here as spaces converters: from robot space to human space and vice versa. The key issue thus is to guarantee the bijection between the two spaces. This problem is expressed as a direct mapping for the one-to-one $(1 * 1)$ systems. For the $N * M$ systems, the direct mapping is inherently impossible. Indeed, when considering a $1 * M$ system for instance, any aim of the single user must be dispatched to the M robots. Likely, one needs to construct an understandable representation of M robots to be displayed to the single user. We can also think about the $N * 1$

systems: how to combine the aims of the N users to derive actions the single robot must perform?

This paper reports on developments we are conducting in our Lab to study bijective Human-Robot interfaces design. First, we present the platform and its capabilities to integrate and abstract any robots into Virtual and Augmented worlds. We give the general framework of the platform and some associated tools, such as scenario languages, to manage Robots' organization, Augmented Reality (tracked head-mounted display) system to improve teleoperators' immersion through the control of an active vision system on a remote mobile robot. We finally present an example of the actual deployment of the platform: remote artwork perception within a museum.

2   State of the Art

Robots are entities being used more and more to both extend the human senses and to perform particular tasks involving repetition, manipulation, precision. Particularly in the first case, the wide range of sensors available today allows a robot to collect several kind of environmental data (images and sound at almost any spectral band, temperature, pressure...). Depending on the application, such data can be internally processed for achieving complete autonomy [1,2] or, in case a human intervention is required, the observed data can be analyzed off-line (robots for medical imaging, [3]) or in real time (robots for surgical manipulations such as the Da Vinci Surgical System by Intuitive Surgical Inc., or [4]). An interesting characteristic of robots with real-time access is to be remotely managed by operators (Teleoperation), thus leading to the concept of *Telerobotics* [5,6] anytime it is impossible or undesirable for the user to be where the robot is: this is the case when unaccessible or dangerous sites are to be explored, to avoid life threatening situations for humans (subterranean, submarine or space sites, buildings with excessive temperature or concentration of gas).

Research in Robotics, particularly in Teleoperation, is now considering cognitive approaches for the design of an *intelligent* interface between men and machines. This is because interacting with a robot or a (inherently complex) multi-robot system in a potentially unknown environment is a very high skill demanding and high concentration task. Moreover, the increasing ability of robots to be equipped with many small - though useful - sensors, is demanding an effort to avoid any data flood towards a teleoperators, which would dramatically drawn the pertinent information. Clearly, sharing the tasks in a collaborative and cooperative way between *all* the $N * M$ participants (humans, machines) is preferable to a classical $1 * 1$ model.

Any teleoperation task is as much effective as an acceptable degree of immersion is achieved: if not, operators have distorted perception of distant world, potentially compromising the task with artifacts, such as the well know tunneling effect [7]. Research has focused in making Teleoperation evolve into Telepresence [8,9], where the user feels the distant environment as it would be local, up to Telexistence [10], where the user is no more aware of the local environment and he is entirely projected in the distant location. For this projection to be feasible, immersion is the key feature. VR is used in a variety of disciplines and applications: its main advantage consists in providing immersive solutions to a given Human-Machine Interface (HMI): the use of 3D vision can be coupled with multi-dimensional audio and tactile or haptic feedback, thus fully exploiting the available external human senses.

A long history of common developments, where VR offers new tools for teleoperation, can be found in [11][9][12][8]. These works address techniques for better simulations, immersions, controls, simplifications, additional information, force feedbacks, abstractions and metaphors, etc. The use of VR has been strongly facilitated during the last ten years: techniques are mature, costs have been strongly reduced and computers and devices are powerful enough for real-time interactions with realistic environments. Collaborative teleoperation is also possible [13], because through VR more users can interact in Real-Time with the remote robots and between them. The relatively easy access to such interaction tool (generally no specific hardware/software knowledge are required), the possibility of integrating physics laws in the virtual model of objects and the interesting properties of abstracting reality make VR the optimal form of exploring imaginary or distant worlds. A proof is represented by the design of highly interactive computer games, involving more and more a VR-like interface and by VR-based simulation tools used for training in various professional fields (production, medical, military [14]).

Furthermore, in this multi-robots teleoperation context, complex tasks have to be *specified*, involving several actors with time and resource constraints, with synchronizations problems and potential dynamic modifications according to teleoperators' actions. In the literature, first solutions used in Virtual Environments to describe tasks were based on low-level languages (state-machine, parallel, hierarchical, etc.). As those languages could describe complex behaviors, they could be used to describe complex tasks involving several behaviors [15]. Quickly, the need of abstraction became a priority, in order to simplify scenario authoring and their separation with low-level languages for future usages. Many studies have been conducted to create new dedicated *scenario languages*, allowing elegant descriptions of complex situations, involving complex actors. Applications have been made in many fields: tutoring systems [16], fire-fighting simulation and training for collaborative actions [17], interactive museum with virtual actors [18], huge military training environments on maintenance operations [19]. To the best of our knowledge, such an advanced approach about Scenario Languages has not been directly applied in the field of Robotics.

3   Contributions

We firstly describe an overview of our framework. Then we present the abstraction layers proposed to teleoperators. Finally, we give an overview of the interactions process within our system.

3.1   Overview of the System

In our framework we first use a VACE for abstracting and standardizing real robots. The VACE is a way to integrate in a standardized way of interaction heterogenous robots from different manufacturers in the same environment, with the same level of abstraction. We intend in fact to integrate robots being shipped with the related drivers and robots internally assembled together with their special-purpose operating system. By providing a unique way of interaction, any robot can be manipulated through standard interfaces and commands, and any communication can be done easily: heterogenous robots are thus *standardized* by the use of a VACE. An example of such an environment is depicted in Figure 1: a team of teleoperators $N_{1:N}$ is able to simultaneously act on a set of robots $M_{1:M}$ through the VACE. This implies that this environment provides a suitable interface for teleoperators, who are able to access a certain number of robots altogether, or also just one robot sensor in function of the task.

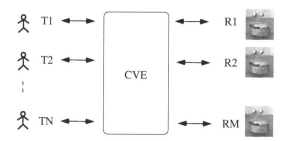

Fig. 1. Basic principle of a Virtual-Augmented Collaborative Environment: N teleoperators can interact with M robots

3.2   Abstraction Layers for Interactions

In the VACE of our framework, several Teleoperators can interact simultaneously with $K = 3$ layers of abstraction, from the lowest to the highest (Figure 2) :

1. the Control Layer
2. the Augmented Virtuality (AV) Layer
3. the Group Manager Interface (GMI) Layer

In this scheme layers concerning ways of teleoperating closer to the human way of acting are closer to the depicted teleoperator. We detail in the following the role of those layers. Note that a more complete description of the VACE and the global system can be found in [20].

   The *Control layer* is the lowest level of abstraction, where a teleoperator can take full and direct control of a robot. The purpose is to provide a precise control of sensors and actuators, including wheel motors, vision and audio system, distance estimators etc... Directly accessing such layer is useful when delicate, new or atypic operations have to be performed with a single component of a

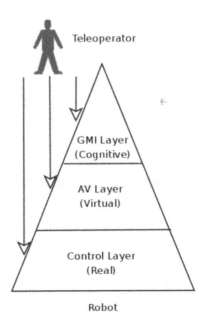

Fig. 2. In our VACE three abstraction layers (GMI, AV, Control) are available for teleoperation

single robot. Operations at this layer are equivalent to using software primitives on top of the robots' hardware, which can be of primary importance when the robot is potentially blocked in certain physical states and no recovering routine is present. Note that directly acting on the Control Layer implies a certain amount of training for the operator: minimizing human adaptation through the layers above is within the targets of a VACE.

The remaining operations, generally classified as simple, repetitive or already learnt by the robots, are executed by the Control Layer without human assistance; whether it is the case to perform them or not it is delegated above to the *Augmented Virtuality Layer*. Such layer offers a medium level of abstraction: teleoperators take advantage of the standardized abstracted level, can manipulate several robots with the same interface, which provides commands close to *what* an operator wants to do instead of *how*. This is achieved by presenting a Human-Machine Interface (HMI) with a purely virtual scene of the environment, where virtual robots move and act. Using that, teleoperators can concentrate on a minimum-information world, where just the essential data (for a given task) is dynamically represented. Peaces of reality (i.e. data from sensors) can be embedded in such world by the operators, thus making the Virtual space Augmented. A typical AV-Layer command is asking to a robot to reach a target, visible in the virtual world through the HMI.

Finally, the highest level of abstraction is offered by the *Groups Manager Interface (GMI)*. Its role is to organize groups of robots according to a set of tasks, given a set of resources. Teleoperators communicate with the GMI, which in turns combines all the requests to adjust priorities and actions on robots. No action is required to teleoperator concerning selection of robots in function of their capabilities or their current availability state: the GMI handles everything. In the example mentioned, the GMI (transparently called via the HMI) would choose the best set of robots able to reach the target, drive the group of robots and report success or failure.

3.3   Overview of Interactions

The figure 3 presents more details about the global interactions system, and the way Teleoperators can interact within groups of robots.

- At the top of the figure, the real world is composed of mobile robots (with wheels, legs, etc.) which have to evolve in their environment, for example a task of surveillance or exploration. By definition, the real world is complex, and can be considered as a *noisy* environment as it can provide many information which are not useful for the task the robots have to realize. For the illustration, we have defined 2 groups of robots: R1, R2, R3, R4 and R6 for the first group, R5 and R7 for the second.
- In the middle the model of the distant environment is depicted. This virtual world includes 3D aspects, and all the necessary informations according to the task the groups of robots have to do. It can be the current state of a 2D or 3D map the robots are building of their environments, or a full 3D map of a known area. It can also be for example particular objects, like doors, or of course the other robots in their current state (position in the space, physical state, etc.). Those virtual robots can contain the definition of the robots behaviors, which can be their autonomy part. Note that this behavior can also be embedded, so the virtual robot is more used as a representation and an interface of control. There's a direct bijection between the real world and the virtual world, as much precise as possible: robots' locations, states, etc.
- At the bottom, 4 human teleoperators are represented. They have to teleoperate the two groups of robots to realize their task. In order to simplify the teleoperation process, we designed the GMI, the role of which is to allow a *cooperation* with the groups of robots. Teleoperators (in the illustrative figure: T1 and T4) can give some basic orders to a *group*, and the GMI will take in charge the virtual robots to realize it. So the real robots. However, the teleoperator can also take a direct control on one precise virtual robot, in the picture the teleoperator T3 directly manipulates the virtual robot VR2. Thus, the precise movements made on the virtual robot are reproduced by the real robot R2. Finally, a teleoperator can have an access on the real robot through its virtual avatar: this is the case of teleoperator T2 which, connected to the virtual robot VR6, has taken a direct control on the robot 6. As presented in section 4.3, the teleoperator can see what the robot see, and act directly on the real robot's head and gaze.

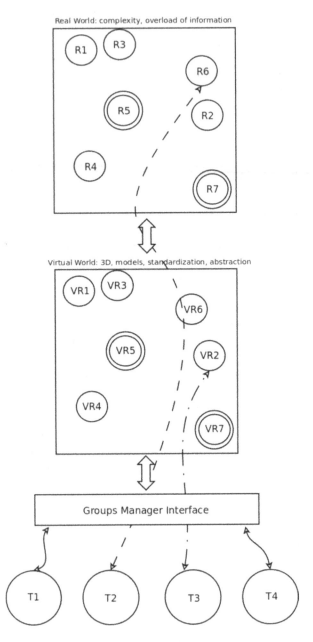

Fig. 3. Overview of the system. Teleoperators Ti can interact with the virtual robots VRi through the Groups Manager Interface (GMI), or can take directly the control on one virtual entity (*ex: T3 and VR2*). Real and virtual robots' states are linked together. It's also possible to access to the distant real robot via the virtual robot (*ex: T2, VR6 and R6*), in particular for the vision in our case.

4   Developments: VR and AR Tools for Abstraction, Standardization and Immersion

This section deals with some of the developments we made in the context of VACE, abstraction, standardization and immersion. We first present the platform we are developing that supports our researches, then the first characteristics and needs of the GMI system through a Scenario Language, and finally our head-tracking system which improves distant immersion for teleoperation.

4.1   The ViRAT Platform as a Collaborative Virtual Environment

We are developing a multi-purposes platform, namely ViRAT (Virtual Reality for Advanced Teleoperation [21][22]), the role of which is to allow several users to control in real time and in a collaborative and efficient way groups of heterogeneous robots from any manufacturer. We presented in the paper [22] different tools and platform, and the choices we made to build this one. The ViRAT platform offers teleoperation tools in several contexts: VR, AR, Cognition, groups management. Virtual Reality, through its Virtual and Augmented Collaborative Environment, is used to abstract robots in a general way, from individual and simple robots to groups of complex and heterogenous ones. Internal ViRAT's VR robots represents exactly the states and positions of the real robots, but VR offers in fact a total control on the interfaces and the representations depending on users, tasks and robots, thus innovative interfaces and metaphors have been developed. Basic group management is provided at the GMI Layer, through a first implementation of a Scenario Language engine. The interaction with robots tends to be natural, while a form of inter-robot collaboration, and behavioral modeling, is implemented. The platform is continuously evolving to include more teleoperation modes and robots.

To explain how ViRAT is built and how it works, we are now presenting the running basic demonstration.

The basic demonstration in detail. We use for this demonstration two real and distant environments. One operator is acting through a PC, equipped with classical physical interfaces (mouse, keyboard, monitor) and more immersive devices (head mounted display, joystick). In ViRAT we find the three Layers of Figure 2. The operator manages the three robots through a Human Machine Interface (HMI): such interface offers a unified virtual world and a menu-based decision console. Figure 4 depicts the data flow and the mutual inference between GMI, scenarios, tasks and resources: orders passed to the HMI are processed by the GMI, at the moment resident on the PC. The GMI is responsible of scheduling and executing scenarios (in function of the current Language) and tasks in function of the available resources; GMI also generates new scenarios, task, and possibly new resources. The AV Layer is represented by the HMI. Note that, though the GMI is conceptually closer to the cognitive level of the operator, it is hidden behind the AV Layer. This complies with the main characteristic of the GMI: it does what the teleoperator would do, but it does not require

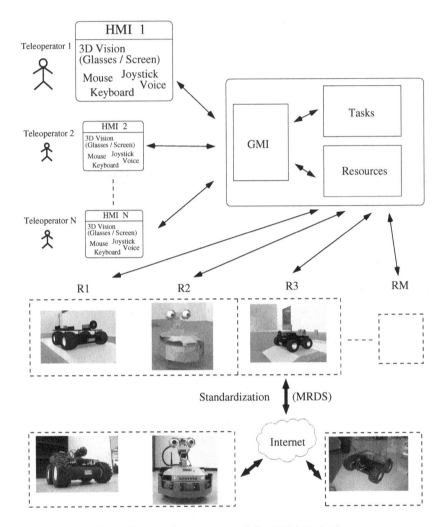

Fig. 4. Interactions scheme of the ViRAT platform

him to think about it. The output from the GMI is then dispatched through the internet to the distant rooms. Robots, each of them hosting an embedded system equipped with Wifi cards, are connected to the internet and receive the orders at the Control Layer. Finally, movements and actions of the robots can be finally followed in the virtual world by the operator. As a result, real, distant robots are connected together with their virtual avatars. More specifically, we recall Figure 1, in ViRAT $N = 1$ and $M = 3$; *Room1* contains two Robots (*R1* and *R2*), while *Room2* contains one robot (*R3*). Figure 5 depicts the virtual world and the decision console in such configuration. In our current prototype, we use Microsoft Robotics Developer Studio (MRDS) as the tool to provide virtual immersion to teleoperators and to encapsulate as services our algorithms which

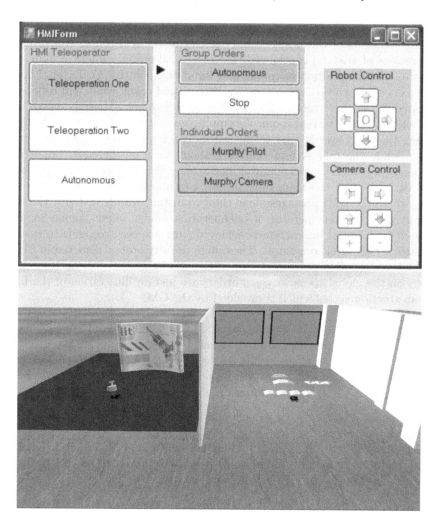

Fig. 5. The HMI console and unified virtual world seen by the teleoperator

handle human-robot and robot-robot communication. In fact MRDS acts as a
server, offers a way to implement and standardize the abstractions of the real
robots, and allows us to integrate synchronization aspects between the virtual
and the real world. The advantage of using such a versatile interface is that
teleoperators can navigate freely in the two rooms, both when robots are moving
or not. Operators can choose the most suitable world for the task: AV Layer or
Control Layer. An example of the two view from these layers is available in
Figure 6, (the two images in the bottom). Note that the operator can include or
exclude some details (such as the plant), which may increase the cognitive load
of the teleoperator, depending on the current task. Note also that a switch from
the real on-board view of the camera to the virtual camera is possible *anytime*,

because the virtual world is constantly re-calibrated to match the real world. The real-time tracking of the position and velocity of the real robots (mirrored by the locations of avatars) is achieved thanks to a calibrated camera system, able to locate the real position of robots and input them in the AV Layer. Finally, note that virtual avatars appear in the same virtual room, while real robots are separated in their real rooms. Thus, a *distributed, complex* space is represented via a *unique, simple* virtual room. We emphasize that one of the big advantaged of using the AV Layer is that teleoperators can freely navigate in the virtual system, while the real system evolves without their interference. Concerning teleoperation modes, the teleoperator interacts by default with the GMI through the HMI. In ViRAT there are substantially two macro-modes : an autonomous mode, where the GMI manages alone the two distant worlds, without the need of input from the teleoperator; a teleoperation mode, where human input is required. Such initial interaction is achieved with a speech recognition system, recognizing high-level commands. These high priority orders, depicted in Figure 5, offer three possible controls: teleoperation of the Room1, of the Room2, or actions on the global scenario. Such orders are just an illustration of the high-level abstraction access which is provided by the GMI.

Autonomous mode. The default scenario in ViRAT is the autonomous mode, which is a session composed by two parallel tasks: R1 and R2 interact in a typical master-slave paradigm, while R3 accomplishes a video-surveillance task. The tasks are independent, thus with no possible conflict.

The interaction in Room1 includes the following events:

- R1 follows a known path, which pairs with a virtual path in the virtual environment.
- R2 follows R1 with its vision tracking system (an onboard digital camera).
- R1 is able to randomly stop himself, stop R2, order R2 to reach R1. Orders are spoken by R1 through an audio system.

In Room2, R3 evolves alone, avoiding obstacles, thanks to an exact replica of the camera system. The role of R3 is to continuously verify that there's nothing abnormal in the room: a new obstacle, or an alert given on an object in particular. Because the virtually unified environment is in fact physically separated, particular metaphors show that robots can not switch between rooms.

Teleoperation : a request of interaction given to the GMI. Teleoperators have the ability, through the speech recognition system, to start/stop the global autonomous mode, or to start/stop the two sub-scenarios (these are the *Group Orders* in Figure 5). This because one may want to interact with a specific room, while in the other room everything is still autonomous.

In *Room 1*, AV Layer-specific commands are: "Go To Target" (includes an automatic obstacles avoidance), commands transmitted to Robot R2 ("Stop to follow" / "Come here"). Control Layer-specific commands come from mouse, keyboard or joystick for fully controlled robot displacements. On-board camera can also be commanded by varying its pan and tilt. Note that directly controlling

R1 will still keep R2 controlled by the GMI, depending on the last orders. Recalibration between real and virtual is always performed.

In *Room 2* the AV Control Layer commands for R3 are similar. Unless otherwise specified, the GMI keeps on handling the tasks assigned to R1 and R2 while the teleoperator manages R3. The system randomly simulates a problem in the room 2 (in ViRAT a simple light switch is turned off). For example, the teleoperator can be alerted in case a problem occurs to an electrical device in Room 2. When using the embedded real camera of the robot, virtual arrows on the HMI indicate the correct direction of the target.

Note that this demo shows a general group organization through the GMI, and a collaboration of this one with a human. This basic demo also allows several teleoperators to act simultaneously: for example it's possible for a human to control R3 displacements while another teleoperator controls R3's embedded camera through the head-tracking system presented in the next sub-section. While the GMI continue to manage R1 and R2.

Goals of ViRAT. The design and tests of ViRAT allows us to claim that this platform achieves a certain number of goals:

- *Unification and Simplification*: there is a unified, simplified CVE accessing two distant rooms, which are potentially rich of details. Distant robots are part of the same environment.
- *Standardization*: we use a unified Virtual Environment to integrate heterogenous robots coming from from different manufacturers): 3D visualization, integration of physics laws into the 3D model, multiple devices for interaction are robot-independent. This framework (achieved with, but not limited to MRDS) is potentially extensible to many other robots.
- *Reusability*: behaviors and algorithms are robot-independent as well and built as services: their implementation is re-usable on other robots.
- *Pertinence via Abstraction*: a robot can be teleoperated on three layers: it can be controlled directly (Control Layer), it can be abstracted for general commands (AV Layer), and groups of robots can be teleoperated through the GMI Layer.
- *Collaboration*: several, distant robots collaborate to achieve several tasks (exploration, video-surveillance, robot following) with one teleoperator in real time. We plan to extend ViRAT to multiple teleoperators.
- *Interactive Prototyping* can be achieved for the robots (conception, behaviors, etc.) and the simulation.
- *Advanced teleoperation interfaces*: we provided interfaces which start considering cognitive aspects (voice commands) and reach a certain degree of efficiency and time control.
- *Time and space navigation* are for the moment limited in the current version of ViRAT, but the platform is open for the next steps, and teleoperators can already navigate freely in the virtual space at runtime.
- *Scenario Languages applicability.* The first tests we made with our first and limited implementation of the Scenario Language for the GMI allow us to organize this whole demonstration which mixes real and virtual actors.

4.2   Scenario Languages Requirements for Robots' Management

Scenario Languages allow simple management of complex actors to achieve complex tasks, according to their skills, behaviors, availability and current states. Scenario Languages are well known in the field of Virtual Reality, and we are applying those technics for robots' management, in the development of the GMI (Note that a complete description of the Scenario Language and its engine is behind the scope of this paper). In fact, common features addressing both virtual environments and multi-robot systems are:

- Synchronization. Particular tasks demand synchronized actions from robots, in order to obtain a precise collaboration for complex manipulations. Low-level synchronizations, which have to be handled by the platform, are not included.
- Multi-threading. Authors of scenarios have to be able to specify parallel tasks.
- Job scheduling. Time-driven decision are necessary for multiple aspects: duration of tasks, synchronization, launch particular actions at a certain time, etc.
- Dynamism. As teleoperators have to interact in real-time with groups of robots, Scenario Languages cannot be static: they must adapt to the current state of the whole system. Being dynamic entails such languages to be editable at runtime. This avoids just *playing* a known pre-compiled scenario. A dynamic language allows teleoperators to make requests of interactions, set priorities, possibly change tasks/goals.
- Tasks/goals. Scenarios have to be organized around tasks to achieve. There are several kind of Scenario Languages: a linear description of a scenario is not enough. An initial state is represented by the notion of task itself, which provides a basis to obtain an automatic organization according to this dynamic context.
- Resources. The Scenario Language has to provide a clear notion of *resources*. Those define entities with set of skills and states. The combinations of resources and tasks allow scenario engines to dynamically generate other scenarios to follow.
- Hierarchy. In order to simplify the organization of scenarios and tasks, the notion of hierarchy has to be proposed.
- Uncertainty. To be very adaptable and to allow dynamic arrangements according to states, problems or modifications on priorities, the Scenario Language has to integrate the ability to define tasks and associated resources through an *uncertain* approach: the full way to proceed has not to be clearly specified, except for goals.

We developed a first version of a Scenario Language and its engine, which is in the heart of the GMI. This first prototype is very limited according to the possibilities that can be offered by Scenario Languages, but it allowed us to validate them through the ViRAT project.

4.3   Head-Tracking System for VR/AR Remote Observations

In ViRAT we make use of advanced immersive interfaces: a helmet equipped with displays, earphones and microphone. Worn by a human, all of his head-movements are transmitted to the robot's webcam, so the teleoperator can feel fully immersed in this distant environment, and can see in a very natural way. Note that the camera view takes advantages of the Virtual environment: tele-operators can directly obtain Augmented Reality features, the virtual additions already accessible in the pure virtual world (Virtual arrows for instance).

Clearly, seeing what the robot see is an important opportunity, and it's fundamental in many cases: direct manipulation on a sensible object, a too complex environment where the robot can not evolve alone, the detection of a problem which require a human attention, etc. In order to offer an efficient capacity of distant vision for the teleoperators, we designed and prototyped a system which uses a VR helmet and a head-tracking system:

– As the teleoperator's vision is limited to what the VR helmet shows, it allows an interesting *immersion* sensation, which makes the operators feeling *in* the distant environment, as far as the resolutions of the helmet and the distant camera(s) is good enough.
– The tracking system is used here to track the movements of the head. Usually, such a system is used to improve the feeling of immersion in a pure 3D world,

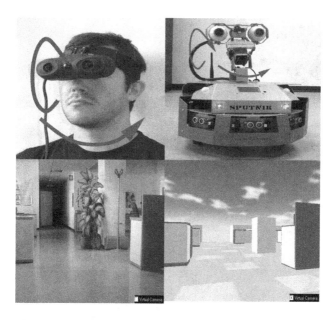

Fig. 6. Relationship between the robot vision system, carried out to the human vision capabilities. Note that the user can switch anytime from the real to the virtual view (both are real-time re-calibrated), driven by his/her quasi real-time head position and orientation.

with any system of visualization. Here, we use the same approach to be fully immersed in the distant world: the movements of the head make the distant camera(s) moving in the same way. The pan-tilt capability is emphasized in figure 6. Though ideally the system would be stereo, currently we use only one of the cameras of this robot. The tracking system has been thus limited to the rotations, so it's not a full head-tracking system. We currently evaluate the possibility of an extension of such a system to allow some small translation movements in the teleoperators area, which would be transformed and adapted to translations on the robots. For the moment, the immersion and its feeling is already enough for facilitating the observation of the distant site; and robots movement can still be control with a joystick for example.

We developed a generic system (figure 7) which allows us to easily deploy vision capacities and remote access on every robots we build or buy. The system is composed of a wired Hi-Res webcam, plugged on a *control module* which offers GPS positions, WiFi and Bluetooth communications capabilities, and inputs/outputs access for controlling small motors and sending the videos. The webcam is articulated with two motors, controlled by the module. We developed a basic remote control program which receives the videos and sends commands to the motors; this program is currently under integration in MSRS as a standard service. The control module has been developed in our team[20].

Fig. 7. A wheeled robot, with an integration of our generic vision system. The webcam moves with two motors, managed by the control module shown on the last photo.

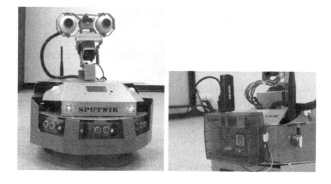

Fig. 8. The integration of the control module on the *Sputnik* robot

Fig. 9. Some Augmented Reality content inserted on what the teleoperators can see: here, the ground analyze and a target to reach (red points)

The figure 7 shows the system in action on one of our simple wheeled robot. We can easily see the camera with the motors, and the control module. The figure 8 presents the current integration of the module with *Sputnik*[1].

In the current version of our prototype, we use a *ARvision-3D* VR helmet (see figure 6, top left image). It shows the videos received by the teleoperator's computer from the distant robot. That's already an interesting way for a better comprehension of the distant environment: the teleoperator is really immersed. As previously introduced, we use a head-tracking system to improve this feeling and the efficiency of the teleoperations. We can use here two systems: a magnetic tracker (*Polhemus* system) or an accelerometer. The tracking, as previously said, is limited on the analysis of the rotations. Those informations are then converted into commands for the motors which are sent in Real-Time to the distant robot (control-module) and to the virtual robot.

In order to help the teleoperator in his task for this usage of the distant vision, we introduced some Augmented Reality (AR) technics. Based on the internal modeling / representation (of the objects, the entities, their behaviors and states,

---

[1] Check for Dr Robot manufacturer.

interactions capabilities, etc.) managed in the VACE, it's easy to add for example the current map of the area, or an indicator on known entities (in particular on other robots). Our system can overlay live vision images by some additional signs to enable to teleoperators to communicate and to achieve a collaborative inspection of an area. The process uses a top view representation of the targeted area as a pointing surface for teleoperators (T1 in the example) in the virtual world. The process calculates then the localization (position and orientation) of the stereo system regarding an absolute framework (well known on the top view map). Using a projective geometry (namely a homographic transformation), we then project on the floor any needed sign (crosses for instance to show the aimed position - see figure 9). This projection become an AR indicator in the vision of the real-world seen by the teleoperator who use the VR helmet.

5 Example of Real Case Application: Improving Immersion in Artwork Perception by Mixing Telerobotics and VR

The ViRAT platform proposes now several demonstrations that are focused on interfaces or human analysis. We are also deploying some real-case projects. One of those is a collaboration with a museum, where the major goal is to offer the ability for distant people to visit a real museum. We'll see in this section that we are interesting in improving the sensation of immersion, of *real visits* for virtual visitors, and that such a system may have different usages such as surveillance when the museum is closed.

The existing VR system for virtual visits of museum, like the excellent *Musée du Louvre*[23], are still limited, with for example the lack any natural light conditions in the Virtual Environment. Another interesting point is that the user is always alone in exploring such virtual worlds. The technologic effort to make an exploration more immersive should also take into account such human factors: should navigation compromise with details when dealing with immersion? We believe this is the case. Does the precise observation of an artwork need the same precise observation during motion? Up to a certain degree, no. We propose a platform able to convey realistic sensation of visiting a room rich of artistic content, while demanding the task of a more precise exploration to a virtual reality-based tool.

5.1 Deployment of the ViRAT Platform

We deployed our platform according to the particularities of this application and the museum needs. Those particularities deal mainly with high-definition textures to acquire for VR, and new interfaces that are integrated to the platform. In this first deployment, consisting in a prototype which is used to test and adapt interfaces, we only had to install two wheeled robots with embedded cameras that we have developed internally (a more complete description of those robots can be found in [20]), and a set of cameras accessible from outside trough

Fig. 10. A robot, controlled by distant users, is *visiting* the museum like other *traditional* visitors

internet (those cameras are used to track the robot, in order to match Virtual Robots' locations and Real Robots' locations). We modeled the 3D scene of the part of the museum where the robots are planned evolve. A computer, where the ViRAT platform is installed, is used to control the local robots and cameras. It runs the platform, so the VR environment. From our lab, on a local computer, we launch the platform which use internet to connect to the distant computer, robots and cameras. Once the system is ready, we can interact with the robots, and visit the museum, virtually or really.

5.2   Usage of Telerobotics and VR for Artwork Perception

As presented in [23], existing works with VR offer the ability to virtually visit a distant museum for example, but suffer from lacks of sensations: first, users are generally alone in the VR environment, and second, the degree and sensation of immersion is highly variable. The success of 3D games like *second life* comes from the ability to really *feel* the virtual world as a real world, where we can have numerous interactions, in particular in meeting other *real* people. Moreover, when we really visit a place, we have a certain atmosphere and ambience, which is in fact fundamental in our perception and feeling. Visiting a very calm temple with people moving delicately, or visiting a noisy and very active market would be totally different without those feedbacks. So, populating the VR environment was one of the first main needs, especially with real humans *behind* those virtual entities. Secondly, even if such VR immersion gives a good sensation of presence, so of a visit, we're not really visiting the reality. Behind *second life*'s virtual characters, we have people sit down, in front of their computer. What about having a bijection between the *reality* and the *virtuality* ? Seeing virtual entities

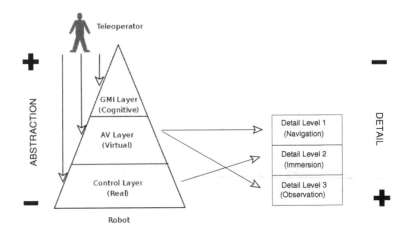

Fig. 11. Different levels of abstraction mapped into different levels of detail

in the VR environment and knowing that behind those entities the reality is hidden, directly increases the feeling of really visiting, being in a place. Especially when we can switch between virtual world and real world.

Following those comments, the proposed system mixes VR and Reality in the same application. The figure 11 represents this mix, its usage, and the adaptation we made of our general framework.

On the left part, we have the degree of immersion, while on the right part, we have the level of details. The degree of immersion is made of the three levels[22]: Group Management Interface, Augmented Virtuality and Control Layer:

- First, the GMI layer, still gives the ability to control several robots. This level could be used by distant visitors, but in the actual design it's mainly used by people from the museum to take a global view on robots when needed, and to supervise what distant visitors are doing in the real museum.
- Second, the AV layer -*Augmented Virtuality*, allows the user to freely navigate in the VR environment. It includes high-definition textures, coming from real high-definition photos of the art-paintings. This level offer different levels of interactions: precise control of the virtual robot and its camera (so as a consequence, the real robot will move in the same way), ability to define targets that the robot will reach autonomously, ability to fly though the 3D camera in the museum, etc.
- Third, the Control layer. At this levels, teleoperators can control directly the robots, in particular the camera previously presented. Users can see directly like if they were located at the robot's location. This level is the *reality* level, the users are immersed in the real distant world where they can act directly. Note that with the current development of large public VR or tracking system like the Nintendo wiimote, the visitors may have an equivalent system as the one we presented in figure 6.

Fig. 12. Detail Level 1 is purely virtual, and is the equivalent of the reality

Fig. 13. Detail Level 3 (high detail) is purely virtual, with high-resolution pictures as textures. This one is used in the scene of the figure 12

On another hand, on the right part of the figure 11, the level of details represent the precision the users perceive of the environment:

- Detail Level 1 represents mainly an overview of the site and robots for navigation. The figure 12 shows the bijection between virtual and real, so the usage that a distant visitor can have of the virtual world as an abstraction of the real word.
- Detail Level 2 represents the reality, seen through the robots' cameras. At this level of details, users are limited by the reality, such as obstacles and cameras' limitations. But they are physically immersed in the real distant world.

Fig. 14. Detail Level 2 is purely real. A user is observing, through his robot and its camera, a art-painting. This screenshot comes from another robot's camera observing the scene: that's what can be seen by another user, so he can see other *distant* visitors like him.

– Detail Level 3 is used when distant visitors want to see very fine details of the art-paintings for example, or any art-objects that have been digitalized in high-definition. We can see in figure 13 a high-definition texture, that a user can observe in the virtual world when he wants to focus his attention on parts of the art-painting of the figure 12, that could not be accessible with the controlled robots.

When distant visitors want to have an overview of the site, and want to move easily inside, or on the opposite when they want to make a very precise observation of one art-painting for example, they use the two Detail Levels 1 and 3, in the Virtual Environment. With this AV level, they can have the feeling of visiting a populated museum, as they can see other distant visitors represented by other virtual robots, but they do not have to fit with real problems like for example occlusions of the art-painting they want to see in details due to the crowd, or displacement problems due to the same reasons.

On another hand, when visitors want to feel themselves more present in the real museum, they can use the Detail level 2. This is the point where we mix Telerobotics with Virtual Reality in order to improve the immersion feeling. In the figure 14, we can first see a robot observing one art-painting. So, a distant visitor is currently observing through the robot's camera the *real* environment, and in particular the *real* art-painting rather than observing it in the virtual world in high-definition. Moreover, this figure comes in fact from another robot's camera: it means that another visitor is actually observing another distant visitor in front of the painting. We offer here the ability for the visitors to be *physically* present in the distant world with this Telepresence system, and to evolve like if they were really present. As a consequence, they can see the real museum and art-work, but also other visitors, local or distant, as we can see in figure 10.

5.3 Same System, Different Usages

While the most interesting aspect for visitors is to feel individually immersed through this system, it is important to note that the use of the GMI allows two separate tasks for the museum. The first one is, as previously introduced, a supervision of the distant visitors: the deployment of the robots, their states and location are directly accessible in the VACE world, and of course control can be taken on those entities. The second one is that the same system can be used as a security system when the museum is closed, or even to prevent security problems during the opening hours. Robots can work alone, easily controlled through the GMI as a global *group entity*, to observe the environment and to detect any kind of problem. And when precise actions or observations are required, exactly in the same way virtual visitors are doing, it is then possible to take a direct control on individual entities.

6   Conclusion

We presented in this paper an innovative system for an efficient teleoperation between several teleoperators and groups of robots. We introduced in this system our vision and usage different levels of interactions: GMI with a scenario language, AV and direct control. We briefly presented the VACE we developed to model the robots activities and states, an environment where teleoperators can have collaboratively an intermediate level of interaction with the real distant robots by using the virtual ones. We illustrated our project through the integration of real heterogeneous robots, and an immersed vision with head-tracking and firsts AR techniques. We finally presented one deployment of this platform for an innovative artwork perception proposed to distant visitors of a museum. Our project is currently very active and new results come frequently. Actual experiments are turned on human's perception evaluation in the case of complex interactions with groups of robots.

We would like to make some special acknowledgments to Delphine Lefebvre, Baizid Khelifa, Laura Taverna, Lorenzo Rossi and Julien Jenvrin for their contributions in the project and the article. The locations for our platform in the museum application are kindly provided by Palazzo Ducale, Genoa.

References

1. Warwick, K., Kelly, I., Goodhew, I., Keating, D.: Behaviour and learning in completely autonomous mobile robots. In: IEE Colloquium on Design and Development of Autonomous Agents, pp. 7/1–7/4 (November 1995)
2. Lidoris, G., Klasing, K., Bauer, A., Xu, T., Kuhnlenz, K., Wollherr, D., Buss, M.: The autonomous city explorer project: aims and system overview. In: IEEE/RSJ International Conference on Intelligent Robots and Systems, 2007. IROS 2007, October 29- November 2, pp. 560–565 (2007)
3. Glasgow, J., Thomas, G., Pudenz, E., Cabrol, N., Wettergreen, D., Coppin, P.: Optimizing information value: Improving rover sensor data collection. IEEE Transactions on Systems, Man and Cybernetics, Part A 38(3), 593–604 (2008)
4. Saffiotti, A., Broxvall, M., Gritti, M., LeBlanc, K., Lundh, R., Rashid, J., Seo, B., Cho, Y.: The peis-ecology project: Vision and results. In: IEEE/RSJ International Conference on Intelligent Robots and Systems. IROS 2008, September 2008, pp. 2329–2335 (2008)
5. Urbancsek, T., Vajda, F.: Internet telerobotics for multi-agent mobile microrobot systems - a new approach (2003)
6. Elfes, A., Dolan, J., Podnar, G., Mau, S., Bergerman, M.: Safe and efficient robotic space exploration with tele-supervised autonomous robots. In: Proceedings of the AAAI Spring Symposium, March 2006, pp. 104–113 (2006) (to appear)
7. Wertheimer, M.: Experimentelle studien über das sehen von bewegung. Zeitschrift für Psychologie 61, 161–265 (1912)
8. Hickey, S., Manninen, T., Pulli, P.: Telereality - the next step for telepresence. In: Proceedings of the World Multiconference on Systemics, Cybernetics and Informatics (SCI 2000), Florida, vol. 3, pp. 65–70 (2000)
9. Kheddar, A., Tzafestas, C., Blazevic, P., Coiffet, P.: Fitting teleoperation and virtual reality technologies towards teleworking (1998)
10. Tachi, S.: Real-time remote robotics-toward networked telexistence. IEEE Computer Graphics and Applications 18(6), 6–9 (1998)
11. Zhai, S., Milgram, P.: A telerobotic virtual control system. In: Proceedings of SPIE, Boston. Cooperative Intelligent Robotics in Space II, vol. 1612, pp. 311–320 (1991)
12. Yang, X., Chen, Q.: Virtual reality tools for internet-based robotic teleoperation. In: DS-RT 2004: Proceedings of the 8th IEEE International Symposium on Distributed Simulation and Real-Time Applications, Washington, DC, USA, pp. 236–239. IEEE Computer Society, Los Alamitos (2004)
13. Monferrer, A., Bonyuet, D.: Cooperative robot teleoperation through virtual reality interfaces, p. 243. IEEE Computer Society, Los Alamitos (2002)
14. Gerbaud, S., Mollet, N., Ganier, F., Arnaldi, B., Tisseau, J.: Gvt: a platform to create virtual environments for procedural training. In: IEEE VR 2008 (2008)
15. Cremer, J., Kearney, J.: Scenario authoring for virtual environments. In: IMAGE VII Conference, pp. 141–149 (1994)
16. Rickel, J., Johnson, W.: Steve: An animated pedagogical agent for procedural training in virtual environments. In: Intelligent virtual agents, Proceedings of Animated Interface Agents: Making Them Intelligent, pp. 71–76 (1997)
17. Querrec, R., Chevaillier, P.: Virtual storytelling for training: An application to fire-fighting in industrial environment. In: Balet, O., Subsol, G., Torguet, P. (eds.) ICVS 2001. LNCS, vol. 2197, pp. 201–204. Springer, Heidelberg (2001)
18. Devillers, F.: Langage de scenario pour des acteurs semi-autonomes. Ph.D thesis, IRISA Université Rennes1 (2001)

19. Mollet, N., Arnaldi, B.: Storytelling in virtual reality for training. In: Pan, Z., Aylett, R.S., Diener, H., Jin, X., Göbel, S., Li, L. (eds.) Edutainment 2006. LNCS, vol. 3942, pp. 334–347. Springer, Heidelberg (2006)
20. Mollet, N., Chellali, R.: Virtual and augmented reality with head-tracking for efficient teleoperation of groups of robots. In: Cyberworlds, Hangzhou, China (2008)
21. Mollet, N., Brayda, L., Chellali, R., Fontaine, J.: Virtual environments and scenario languages for advanced teleoperation of groups of real robots: Real case application. In: IARIA/ACHI 2009, Cancun (2009)
22. Mollet, N., Brayda, L., Chellali, R., Khelifa, B.: Standardization and integration in robotics: case of virtual reality tools. In: Cyberworlds, Hangzhou, China (2008)
23. Brayda, L., Mollet, N., Chellali, R.: Mixing telerobotics and virtual reality for improving immersion in artwork perception. In: Edutainment 2009, Banff, Canada. LNCS, vol. 5670. Springer, Heidelberg (2009)

HES-SPATO: An Online History Educational System Based on SCORM[*]

Jia-Jiunn Lo[1,**], Chuen-Jung Chang[1], Hsiao-Han Tu[1], and Shiou-Wen Yeh[2]

[1] Department of Information Management, Chung-Hua University, Taiwan
jlo@chu.edu.tw, lilina.chang@gmail.com, sheilas@pchome.com.tw
[2] Department of Applied Linguistics and Language Studies, Chung Yuan Christian University, Taiwan
shiouwen@cycu.edu.tw

Abstract. Online learning has become popular in the delivery of history materials. However, not much of the history learning material that is available online has a high level of understandability. Furthermore, not all history course designers and teachers are good at information technologies. To this end, an online history educational system, HES-SPATO, was developed. HES-SPATO is based on SCORM (Sharable Content Object Reference Model) to ensure reusability, durability, accessibility, and interoperability of electronic material. SPATO (Spatio-Person-Attribute-Temporal Object), the backbone of HES-SPATO, is designed to integrate the indispensable elements of historical events such as space, person, action/attribute, and time to increase the understandability of online history learning materials. In HES-SPATO, history SCOs were formed by integrating SPATOs with the associated "Space", "Person", and "Action/Attribute" assets, stored in the Asset Pool. SCOs, then, formed other SCORM components such as lessons and courses accordingly. The authoring module of HES-SPATO can enhance the history teachers' ability for creating online materials in a few guided steps with flexibility. HES-SPATO applies temporal logic to reason the temporal relationships between historical events. By applying the GIS concept of information layers, the learning module of HES-SPATO allow students to select different features with different layers to visualize historical events more clearly according to their own needs, zoom in to see features at closer range, view a variety of supplementary learning material at the same time and view SCOs according to their own progress and learning paths. It can also present specific information directly related to the historical event only, as defined in SPATO, to reduce cognitive load. With these developed functionalities, HES-SPATO can effectively reduce the teacher's burden and increase the understandability of history learning materials. Three teachers, who had taught general college history courses to non-history majors for more than ten years, were invited to evaluate both the authoring and learning modules. After these history teachers using HES-SPATO, semi-structured interviews were conducted to acquire their feedbacks in terms of processes to prepare history learning materials, understandings for students' learning history,

---

[*] This paper is an extended version of the paper, *Developing a Web-Based History Educational System*, which was presented in Cyberworlds 2008, Hanzhou, China (pp. 71-77).
[**] Corresponding author.

Z. Pan et al. (Eds.): Transactions on Edutainment II, LNCS 5660, pp. 160–175, 2009.
© Springer-Verlag Berlin Heidelberg 2009

responses for the map functionalities, and suggestions of the content and the history learning material displaying methods. The results of this interview demonstrated the teachers' acceptance of HES-SPATO and confirmed its helpfulness in teachers' preparation of online learning materials and students' understanding of history learning.

Keywords: history educational system, SCORM, GIS, spatial-temporal model, authoring.

1 Introduction

Traditionally, students acquire history knowledge from hardcopy textbooks. They are usually lost in the geographical space and confused about the relationship between different history events. A history event includes information about "who initiated the event", "what happened", "when it happened", and "where the event happened". If presenting all information about the event in multiple formats at the same time, students will understand the relationships among history events more efficiently and effectively.

Currently, lots of historical materials are delivered on Internet. Since history is highly related to geographical space, some researchers included geographic information into history educational systems and developed their systems based on GIS (Geographic Information System). Applying GIS concepts is useful for spatial information integration. Through the bridging of time and space, and by efficiently gathering, saving, editing, managing, analyzing and displaying every form of spatial information, it can successfully integrate various types of spatial data and digital information management system, and further demonstrate the values of data in different views (Liao et al., 2004; Lo, 2004). Those systems can store, retrieve, map, and analyze geographic information about history, hence, increase the understandability. However, history events happened in sequences. Without presenting related information of history events step by step may cause the problems of information and cognitive overload. Person is the most important element for history events and is indispensable to history. Therefore, not only the spatial and temporal components but also the person component should be included in the history educational system model.

Not all history teachers are good at information technologies so that they cannot easily create electronic history learning materials. The ability of computer operations is a bottleneck of history teachers so that only few products exist nowadays. Design and development of standards need to be put in place to ensure consistency and transferability of skills. Designers and developers of on-line learning materials may have variety of software tools for creating learning resources. These tools range from presenting software packages to more complex authoring environments. They can be very useful in allowing developers the opportunity to create learning resources that might otherwise require extensive programming skills. The Sharable Content Object Reference Model (SCORM), part of the Advanced Distributed Learning (ADL) initiative, promotes efforts to create flexible learning materials with reusability, durability, accessibility, and interoperability. The goal of SCORM is to create flexible learning materials by ensuring content that is reusable, interoperable, durable, and accessible, regardless of the content delivery and management system. SCORM achieves its goal with the use of SCOs (Sharable Content Object) that are composed of assets. In order to identify SCO, assets, or any other kinds of learning materials, ADL proposed "meta-data", which means "data about data", to identify and locate learning materials by managers, learners, designers, programmers and other interested in education and training (Learning Systems Architecture Lab, 2003). Based on SCORM and the GIS concepts, HES-SPATO (History Educational System based on SPATO), a spatial-person-temporal history educational system architecture for both teachers and students was developed in this study.

2 Literature Review

2.1 History Educational Systems

The idea of e-learning brings us the obvious advantage of anywhere-anytime learning. Lots of history materials are delivered through the Internet. However, most online learning materials are developed by simply translating hardcopy textbooks into electronic formats, which does not really facilitate effective online learning.

Since history is highly related to geographical location, researchers tend to include geographic information in history educational systems and develop systems based on GIS (Geographic Information Systems) (Liao et al., 2004; Lo, 2004). A GIS map is composed of many separate, overlapping information layers, each of which has its own meaning (Haag et al., 2004). By applying these information layers, temporal and spatial attributes are integrated in spatial-temporal coordinates. There are several advantages in using GIS to develop history educational systems. Firstly, it is useful for spatial information integration. Then, through the bridging of time and space, and by efficiently gathering, saving, editing, managing, analyzing and displaying all spatial information, it can successfully integrate various types of spatial data and digital information management systems, and further demonstrate the values of data from different perspectives (Academic Sinica, 2005; Liao et al., 2004; Lo, 2004). In addition, these systems can store, retrieve, map, and analyze geographic information about history and, hence, increase the understandability of the learning materials.

Historical events happened in sequences. Though the systems using the GIS technology can present historical data for different times with the concept of information layers of GIS, the dynamics of historical events cannot be clearly presented. Without presenting related information of historical events step by step may make it difficult for students to understand causing information and cognitive overload. Therefore, in this study, a history educational system has been developed to present the dynamics of historical events in sequences with animation which can be controlled by the student.

A historical event includes information about "who initiated it", "what happened", "when it happened", and "where it happened". If presented with all these information components at the same time, students will understand the history event more fully, clearly and effectively. Therefore, not only should the spatial and temporal components be included but also the person component. That is why, in this study, a history educational system integrating "person" into the spatial-temporal data model was developed to more completely illustrate a historical event.

2.2 SCORM

The lack of computer skills is a barrier for most history teachers, and this is one of the reasons why there are a limited number of products available. Therefore, the design and development of standards need to be put in place to ensure consistency and transferability of skills. The Sharable Content Object Reference Model (SCORM), part of the Advanced Distributed Learning (ADL) initiative, promotes efforts to create flexible learning materials which are reusable, durable, accessible, and interoperable (Learning Systems Architecture Lab, 2003). The proposed history educational system therefore is based on SCORM to ensure this. *Reusable*: Content is independent of learning context. It can be used in numerous training situations or for many different learners with any number of development tools or delivery platforms. *Interoperable*: Content functions in multiple applications, environments, and hardware and software configurations regardless of the tools used to create it and the platforms on which it is delivered. *Durable*: Content does not require modification to operate as software systems and platforms are changed or upgraded. *Accessible*: Content can be identified and located when and as needed to meet training and education requirements (Learning Systems Architecture Lab, 2003).

SCORM achieves its goal with the use of SCOs (Sharable Content Objects), which are composed of assets. In order to identify SCOs, assets, or any other types of learning materials, ADL proposes metadata to make it possible for anyone who is interested in education to identify and locate learning materials. Units in SCORM are introduced from the lowest level (asset) to the highest level (course) (Learning Systems Architecture Lab, 2003).

Assets are the smallest physical units in SCORM. They are electronic representations of media, such as texts, audios, Web pages, assessment objects, and other pieces of data, which can be delivered to a Web client. In order to be reused, assets must be described with metadata. Assets may be reusable in many contexts and applications by searching online instructional repositories (ADL, 2001).

SCOs are the smallest logical units of instruction that can be delivered and tracked via a learning management system. They are collections of assets that become independent, defined pieces of learning materials. Each SCO is able to stand alone. Teachers can design the "role" of an SCO. With the usage of metadata described for SCOs, authors can search, discover, reuse, and aggregate SCOs within content repositories (Learning Systems Architecture Lab, 2003).

An *aggregation* is defined as a parent and its children in a tree structure. It is used to group related content so that it can be delivered to the learner in the manner the courseware designer describes (Learning System Architecture Lab, 2003). *Content aggregation* is the process of aggregating resources into a defined structure to build a particular learning experience. In other words, it is composed of one or many SCOs or another aggregation. It is also a course material structure without sequencing rule from both the teacher and student's perspective.

The purpose of *content package* is to provide a standardized way to exchange digital learning resources between different systems or tools. It describes data structures used to provide interoperability of Internet-based content with authoring tools, learning management systems, and run-time environments (ADL, 2004a). A content package contains two components: manifest and physical file. The physical files may be local files that are actually contained within the content package or external files that are referenced by a Universal Resource Locator (URL). A content package may be part of a course, a unit of learning object, or an entire course. It should be able to stand alone. When the content package arrives at its destination, it allows itself to be either disaggregated or aggregated.

A *manifest* is a document that contains a structured inventory of the content of a package (ADL, 2004a). It describes how the content is organized. In addition, a manifest translates source code from content structure to Web files by transferring content structure and behavior, and the list of references to the source in the package (ADL, 2001).

Content structure is a basic tool for course designers to define the course structure. It defines a mechanism that can be used to aggregate learning resources into a cohesive unit of instruction (e.g., course, chapter, etc.), application structure and associate taxonomies (ADL, 2001).

Sequencing and navigation (SN) defines a method for representing the intended behavior of an authored learning experience to sequence discrete learning activities in a consistent way (ADL, 2004b). Based on the concept of activity tree and cluster, the sequences of learning materials are setup by a *sequencing control model*. The sequencing control model allows the content developer to define how navigation requests are applied to a cluster and how the cluster's activities are considered while processing sequencing requests (ADL, 2004b). A course authoring tool not only makes it possible for authors to create course structures but also helps them edit the conditions for moving between learning activities.

In order to ensure that contents are reusable, interoperable, durable, accessible and searchable, unified *metadata* are used to describe the contents. In SCORM, metadata are defined on three levels—assets, SCOs, and content aggregations. Asset metadata provides descriptive information about SCORM assets which are independent of learning content (ADL, 2004a). SCO metadata can be applied to an SCO that provides descriptive information about the learning resource independent of a particular context. Content aggregation level metadata are used to describe the package as a whole (ADL, 2004a).

2.3 Spatial-Temporal Data Model

History happens in a dynamic world in which the time element plays a vital role. A data model can help us understand the dynamic processes of history. The dynamic aspects of the world are described by events, processes, actions, and activities (Allen, 1983). The concept of space-time has been covered extensively. Modeling of space and time, known as spatial-temporal modeling, attempts to define the real life phenomena through objects and their relationships and constraints (Raza, 2001). Different techniques are proposed to describe and model static and dynamic real worlds.

Wachowicz (1999) introduced a conceptual framework called Time Geography for capturing the semantics of space and time. Time Geography represents space and time within a general equilibrium framework; location in space cannot be separated from the flow of time. Time and space are seen as inseparable in this framework. An entity follows a space-time path, starting at the point of birth and ending at the point of death. Such a path can be depicted over space and time by collapsing both spatial and temporal dimensions into a space-time path. A space-time path is a sequential record which includes both spatial and temporal data. It is based on the fact that an observer can move anywhere along the space-time path. There is a starting location, a direction, and a sequence of continuous locations that the observer comes across in following the path.

Raza and Kainz (1999) used cell complexes for representing spatial-temporal objects. The spatial-temporal data are modeled based on cell complex and cell tupple structure. This approach presents space, time, and spatial-temporal data at the same time. In their research, reality is perceived as an object called Spatio-Temporal-Attribute Object (STAO) for modeling purposes. STAO is useful to recode the geographical data through time, for example, the use of land, the popular space data, etc. There are three types of components in STAO, SpatialClass, TemporalClass, and AttributeClass. SpatialClass represents space; TemporalClass deals with modeling of time; AttributeClass captures the thematic mode of reality by defining the characteristics of STAO; and SpatialTemporalAttributeClass encapsulates the objects of the three classes.

Person is the most important element for historical events and is indispensable to history. Though successfully applied to spatial-temporal data models as in urban applications, it is difficult for STAO to model historical events which are centered around persons. Therefore, one of the goals of this study is to extend STAO as introduced by Raza and Kainz (1999) by including "person" for modeling historical events.

It is important to define the temporal relationships between events in history educational systems. Each historical event is indexed by a date. A date is a representation of time so that the temporal ordering between two dates can be computed with a simple operation (Allen, 1983). There are a total of thirteen ways, as proposed by Allen (1983), in which an ordered pair of time intervals can be related. These thirteen relationships can be used to express any relationship that can hold between two intervals. Since these thirteen possible relationships are mutually exclusive, there is no ambiguity in this notation. When a new interval relationship is entered, all consequences can be computed. This is done by computing the transition closure of the temporal relationships. Transitivity rules are used to combine known assertions and deduce new information (Allen, 1983).

Some historical events are represented by time points which can be handled similarly as time intervals. Time points are objects whose interrelations can be described by primitives in logic (Vilain, 1982). The possible relationships for time points can be divided into two groups, relationships between time points and relationships between time points and intervals (Lo, 1995). In fact, time points can be treated as intervals with zero duration. Transitivity rules for time points, similar to those introduced by Allen (1983), can be built as shown in Lo's study (1995). This research applies temporal logic to reason the temporal relationships between historical events so that they can be presented in sequences to increase the understandability of the history learning materials.

3 System Architecture of HES-SPATO

HES-SPATO (History Educational System based on SPATO) is based on SPATO (Spatial, Person, Action/Attribute, and Temporal Object). It has nine components and two interface modules, authoring and learning modules, as illustrated in Fig. 1.

    (1) Asset Pool stores all types of assets developed by learning material designers or imported from other Internet sources. An Asset is the smallest physical unit in SCORM. It can be any electronic format that can be delivered to a Web client (Learning Systems Architecture Lab, 2003).

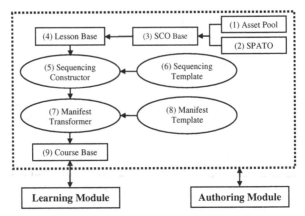

Fig. 1. HES-SPATO System Architecture

(2) SPATO is an object to specify "where", "who/whom", "what", and "when" about history events (Lo et al., 2006). A history event includes space, person, action, and time. A SPATO presents the elements of a history event by integrating assets stored in the Asset Pool. It includes pointers for linking "Space", "Person", and "Action/Attribute" assets to form learning object. It can present history events in animation along the historical timeline when these assets are integrated with the "Time" component specified in SPATO.

(3) SCO Base stores learning objects used in the system. The associated "Space", "Person", and "Action/Attribute" assets, stored in the Asset Pool, are integrated into SPATO to form a history learning object. All learning objects follow the SCORM standard. A SCO can exist alone and is the smallest logical unit in HES-SPATO.

(4) Lesson Base is used to manage lessons combined by SCOs in the SCO Base. A lesson may include one or more SCOs. All lessons belong to SCORM content aggregations. Courseware designers create a lesson by selecting and organizing SCOs in the SCO Base.

(5) A course is composed of two elements, lessons and sequential relationships among lessons. Lessons are defined in Lesson Base and the sequential relationships are defined in Sequencing Constructor. In Sequencing Constructor, courseware designers define the relationships among lessons by sequencing objects (SO) which are provided by Sequencing Template. After defining the relationships among lessons, the layout of a course is defined in Manifest Transformer.

(6) Sequencing Template provides SOs to the Sequencing Constructor for designing the relationships among lessons. In HES-SPATO, two types of sequencing templates, forward and choice, are provided.

(7) A manifest is a document that contains a structured inventory of the content of a package (Learning Systems Architecture Lab, 2003). In Manifest Transformer, the layout of each lesson is defined by using the template provided by Manifest Template. After designing the layout of a lesson, HES-SPATO will translate the course structure into a Web file and store the file in Course Base.

(8) Manifest Template provides manifest templates to Manifest Transformer for designing the layout of a lesson.

(9) Course Base stores and manages course files. Students study history by navigating the course files stored in Course Base through the learning module.

3.1 Authoring Module

Authoring module is designed to be used by courseware designers and teachers. With this module, designers and teachers can develop their own courseware and learning materials in a few guided steps with flexibility.

Asset authoring. The flowchart for asset authoring is illustrated by Fig. 2. A friendly authoring interface is developed to guide designers to create assets (Fig. 3). Different from multimedia assets (image and audio), designers can create text assets by either importing existing electronic documents or inputting texts through the authoring interface. In HES-SPATO, hyperlinks are provided to navigate related Web site outside the system (Web page assets). To develop Web page assets, designers edit metadata of Web page assets, and then input the related data such as "URL".

Unlike image, audio, and text assets, person, space, and action/attribute assets are structured. For example, a person asset may include structured data such as "name", "nationality", "year of birth", "year of death", etc; A space asset may include structured data such as "space name", "location", "year of start", "year of end", "category", etc. An action/attribute may include structured data such as "action name", "number of soldiers in a troop", etc. Fig. 4 shows the flowchart for person asset authoring and Fig. 5 illustrates the sketches of authoring interface for creating person assets.

SPATO authoring. The flowchart for creating SPATO is illustrated in Fig. 6 and Fig. 7 illustrates the authoring interface for creating SPATOs.

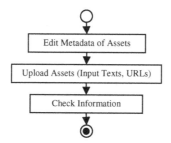

Fig. 2. Flowchart for asset authoring

Fig. 3. Authoring interface for image assets

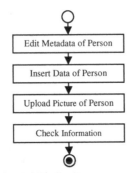

Fig. 4. Flowchart for person asset authoring

Fig. 5. Authoring interface for person assets

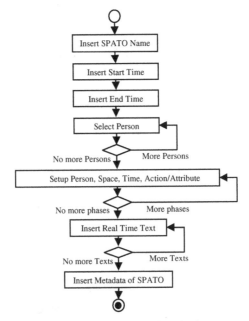

Fig. 6. Flowchart for SPATO authoring

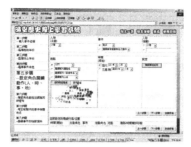

Fig. 7. Authoring interface for SPATO

SCO authoring. The flowchart for SCO authoring is illustrated in Fig. 8. Designers edit metadata of an SCO first. They then select one or more SPATOs for this SCO. After selecting SPATOs, corresponding assets are selected accordingly to form an integrated history SCO.

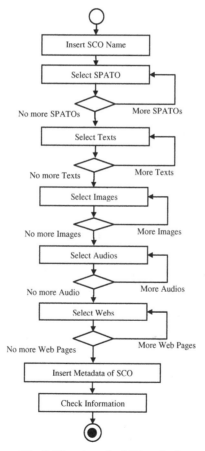

Fig. 8. Flowchart for SCO authoring

Lesson authoring. A lesson Base is a combination of SCOs. It may include one or more SCOs. Courseware designers create a lesson by selecting and organizing SCOs in the SCO Base (Fig. 9).

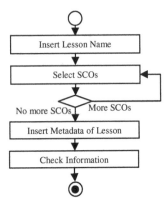

Fig. 9. Flowchart for lesson authoring

Course authoring. A course is composed of lessons and sequential relationships among lessons. The sequential relationships are defined by courseware designers using sequencing objects (SO). Courseware designers' first insert course name and abstract, then create courses by integrating SOs and lessons (Fig. 10). Each node of SOs may be a lesson or another SOs. Courseware designers choose the content of each node by simply clicking and selection. SOs are the objects used to build up the course file structure. It is important that each SO should include lessons and there must be only one lesson at the end of a course. After inserting lesson files to SOs, the course is created.

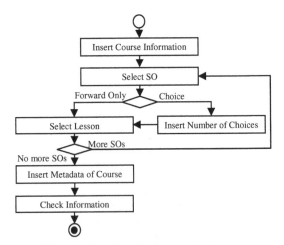

Fig. 10. Flowchart for course authoring

3.2 Learning Module

For a long time, people have studied history with maps. In the last decades, it has become possible to put these models inside computers. These computer models for maps make up a GIS. In a GIS, students can study not just maps, but all possible information related to maps. With the right data, students can see whatever they want, such as land, rivers, political boundaries, and other things, in whatever part of the world interests students (Ormsby et al., 2004). A GIS map is composed of many separate, overlapping information layers, each of which has its own meaning (Haag et al., 2004). Layers may contain features or surfaces. Applying such concept of information layers, temporal and spatial features of people, events, and objects are integrated in spatial-temporal coordinates. How much detail features have depends on the layer the student use (Ormsby et al., 2004). HES-SPATO applied the GIS concepts to develop the learning module so that students can view courses integrated with person, space, and time (Lo et al., 2009). Fig. 11 illustrates the HES-SPATO learning module.

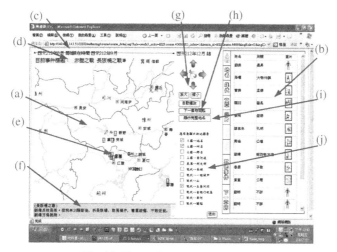

Fig. 11. Illustration of learning module

(a) Main frame: It presents a lesson which includes history SCOs.
(b) Supplementary data: All related supplementary data is showed in this frame.
(c) Time line: It presents the time defined in SPATO.
(d) Event title: It presents the current event title.
(e) Person: participants of the history events.
(f) Real-time information: A piece of text used to specify the key content of the current step of a history event.
(g) Map view controller: Learner can view any part of the map by using zooming and panning tools.
(h) Animation controller: HES-SPATO can present the dynamics of history events in sequences with animation. Students may pause the animation as well as let the system show the animation automatically or step by step by manual control.

(i) Space name display controller: According to the theory of cognitive learning, because humans have limited short-term memory capacity, information should be grouped into meaningful sequences so that the students are not overwhelmed by too much information (Anderson, 2004). In HES-SPATO, courseware designers define the related places to be presented in SPATO. Using the space name display controller, students can freely switch between displaying all place names in a given area or choose to display only the place names directly related to the history event.

(j) Map layer controller: The GIS concepts were applied to develop the learning module. Students can choose any combinations of features from different information layers.

4   Evaluation of HES-SPATO from History Teachers

4.1   The Setting

HES-SPATO provides a new platform not only for students to study history but also for teachers or courseware designers to develop history learning materials. In this study, three teachers, who had taught general college history courses to non-history majors for more than ten years, were invited to evaluate both the authoring and learning modules.

After these history teachers using HES-SPATO, semi-structured interviews were conducted to acquire their feedbacks. The interview consisted of nine open questions which were divided into four parts. The first part was related to the process for the interviewees to prepare history learning materials. The second part was the understandings of the interviewees about students when students learn history by themselves or in class. The third part asked the interviewees' responses for the map functionalities. The fourth part was about suggestions of the content and the history learning material displaying methods.

4.2   The Results

Preparing learning materials. In the term of helping teachers prepare history materials, the interviewees gave positive feedbacks for the authoring module of HES-SPATO. Even though all the interviewees have never developed online learning materials, after using HES-SPATO, they agreed that the authoring module of HES-SPATO can enhance teachers' ability of developing online history learning materials. Though the interviewees did not understand and haven't heard SCORM before, they could easily develop electronic history courses with the authoring module of HES-SPATO. They reported favorably on integrating various types of materials together. In addition to develop electronic courses by themselves, all interviewees expressed positive feedbacks to the sharable property of learning materials of HES-SPATO, which is based on SCORM, and the course content classification functionality in that they can easily find and include the content developed by others in their courses both with the same viewpoint and different perspectives.

Understanding of students' learning. The interviewees were experienced in teaching history. They all agreed that one of the most important things for students in learning history is to show students the corresponding spaces of history events in a map as students read texts about the events. They expressed highly positive feedbacks to HES-SPATO for its integration of textual content and maps. HES-SPATO integrates different asset types, such as texts, images, audios, etc., to present the content. According to the teaching experience of interviewees, in HES-SPATO, they thought textual content is the most popular and clear content for students to study history.

Responses for map functionalities. Based on the responses from the three interviewees, HES-SPATO has got high appraisal in terms of map functionalities such as map layers and space name display control. All the interviewees reported that the data of map are rich and reliable. They pointed out such functionalities were appropriate to solve the problem of the same place with different names. They favorably used the functionality of only displaying key space names. The space information not only can be simply and clearly presented but also can be flexibly modified by teachers. They thought the function of only showing key space names was a good idea in that it was easy, friendly, and helpful for students to study history.

Suggestions for content and displaying methods. Though the interviewees agreed HES-SPATO has effectively presented progresses of history events, they suggested that it is just the basic of history education. What is more important for college history education is to teach students the context of history events and to think historically such as analyses of the background and reasons of wars, factors affect the war, and the after-war situation, etc. They also suggested it would be better if HES-SPATO can include more cultural data. Two of the interviewees also suggested that in addition to present learning materials along history events, HES-SPATO could be improved to present learning materials for specific spaces or persons. In addition, the interviewees suggested that HES-SPATO can be more attractive to students by adding game-based or movie-based learning materials.

5 Conclusions

HES-SPATO, an online history educational system based on SPATO, was developed to integrate the indispensable elements of history events such as person, space, and time for increasing the understandability of history learning materials. It was based on SCORM, to ensure reusability, durability, accessibility, and interoperability of electronic materials. SCORM achieves its goal with the use of SCOs. History SCOs were formed by integrating SPATOs with the associated "Space", "Person", and "Action/Attribute" assets. SPATO specifies "who" initiated the history event, "whom" the event influenced, "what" they did, "when" the event happened, and "where" the event happened. With SPATO, a history educational system with sharable learning objects that are integrated with spatial, person, and temporal history information was implemented.

With the SCORM-based architecture, the authoring module of HES-SPATO can enhance the history courseware designer and teacher's ability for creating online materials in a few guided steps.

By applying the GIS concept of information layers and temporal logic, the learning module of HES-SPATO allowed students to visualize history events more clearly in sequence with different features according to their own needs, zoom in to see features at closer range, view a variety of supplementary learning material at the same time and view SCOs according to their own progress and learning paths. It can also present specific information directly related to the history event only, as defined in SPATO, to reduce cognitive load. With these developed functionalities, HES-SPATO can effectively reduce the teacher's burden and increase the understandability of history learning materials.

Three teachers, who had taught general college history courses to non-history majors for more than ten years, were invited to evaluate both the authoring and learning modules. After these history teachers using HES-SPATO, semi-structured interviews were conducted to acquire their feedbacks in terms of processes to prepare history learning materials, understandings for students' learning history, responses for the map functionalities, and suggestions of the content and the history learning material displaying methods. According to their feedback, several findings were obtained: The authoring module of HES-SPATO can enhance teachers' ability of developing online teaching materials even though they had no experiences in preparing online learning materials and did not understand SCORM before. Teachers can not only develop their own materials in HES-SPATO but also easily find and use the content developed by others. The interviewees agreed the functionalities of HES-SPATO of integrating learning content and maps were helpful for students in studying history. The interviewees gave got high appraisal to HES-SPATO in terms of map functionalities such as map layers and space name display control. They favorably used the functionality of only displaying key space names in that it was easy, friendly, and helpful for students to study history. For the future development, the interviewees suggested that in addition to present progresses of history events, to teach students the context of history events and to think historically is important. They also suggested it would be better if HES-SPATO can include more cultural data and present learning materials for specific spaces or persons. In addition, the interviewees suggested that HES-SPATO can be more attractive to students by adding game-based or movie-based learning materials.

Acknowledgements

This research is supported by National Science Foundation of Taiwan (NSC 95-2520-S-216 -002-MY3) and Chung-Hua University (CHU-95-2520-S-216-002-MY3).

References

1. Academic Sinica: Introduction to Chinese and Taiwan Historical GIS (2005),
   http://ccts.ascc.net/download/presentation_20050128_en.pdf
2. ADL: SCORM version 1.2—The SCORM Content Aggregation Model. USA: Advanced Distributed Learning, 11-134 (2001)
3. ADL: SCORM Sequencing and Navigation Version 1.3.1. USA: Advanced Distributed Learning, 21-48 (2004a)

4. ADL: SCORM Content Aggregation Model Version 1.3.1. USA: Advanced Distributed Learning, 21-200 (2004b)

5. Allen, F.J.: Maintaining Knowledge about Temporal Intervals. Communications of the ACM 26, 832–843 (1983)

6. Anderson, T.: Toward a Theory of Online Learning. In: Anderson, T., Elloumi, F. (eds.) Theory and Practice of Online Learning, Athabasca University, Canada (2004), http://cde.athabascau.ca/online_book/ch2.html

7. Learning Systems Architecture Lab: SCORM Best Practices Guide for Content Developers. Carnegie Mellon University, USA (2003)

8. Liao, H.-M., Yen, E., and Fan, I.-C.: The Construction of the Spatial-Temporal Contents Integrated System Using WebGIS. In: The Second Taipei International Conference on Digital Earth, Taipei (2004) (in Chinese)

9. Haag, S., Cummings, M., McCubbrey, D.J.: Management Information Systems: For the Information Age, 4th edn. McGraw-Hill Irwin Companies, Inc., New York (2004)

10. Lo, F.-J.: Literary and Geographic Space-Time Information System Design and Application: Take Sushi's Poems for Example. In: The Second Taipei International Conference on Digital Earth, Taipei (2004) (in Chinese)

11. Lo, J.-J.: Real-Time and Feedback Control of Flexible Manufacturing Systems. Ph.D. Dissertation, Department of Industrial Engineering, State University of New York at Buffalo, USA (1995)

12. Lo, J.-J., Chang, C.-J., Yeh, S.-W.: A SCORM-Based History Educational System. In: ED-MEDIA 2006, Orlando, Florida, USA, pp. 949–954 (2006)

13. Lo, J.-J., Chang, C.-J., Tu, H.-H., Yen, S.-W.: Applying GIS to Develop a Web-Based Spatial-Person-Temporal History Educational System. Computers and Education 53(1), 155–168 (2009)

14. Ormsby, T., Napoleon, E., Burke, R., Groessl, C., Feaster, L.: Getting to Know ArcGIS Desktop: Basics of ArcView, ArcEditor, and ArcInfo, 2nd edn. ESRI Press, Redlands (2004)

15. Raza, A.: Object-Oriented Temporal GIS for Urban Applications. PhD Thesis, University of Twente and ITC (2001)

16. Raza, A., Kainz, W.: Cell Tuple Based Spatio-Temporal Data Model: An Object Oriented Approach. In: ACM GIS 1999, pp. 20–25 (1999)

17. Wachowicz, M.: Object-Oriented Design for Temporal GIS. Taylor & Francis, U.K. (1999)

18. Vilain, M.B.: A System for Reasoning about Time. In: Proceedings of AAAI 1982, pp. 197–201 (1982)

Pyvox 2: An Audio Game Accessible to Visually Impaired People Playable without Visual Nor Verbal Instructions

Thomas Gaudy[1], Stéphane Natkin[1], and Dominique Archambault[2]

[1] Centre de Recherche en Informatique du Cnam
292, rue St Martin, 75003 Paris, France
tomgody@yahoo.fr, natkin@cnam.fr
[2] Inova/UFR919, University Pierre et Marie Curie-Paris 6
4, place Jussieu, 75252 Paris Cedex 5, France
dominique.archambault@upmc.fr

Abstract. In games, we can discern two approaches to learn how interactivity works: the instructions for use and the interactivity itself. The number of spoken languages is evaluated at more than six thousand eight hundred: for this reason, instructions for use can't make games understandable for all potential users, which is especially true for audio games accessible to visually impaired players, since those games can not count on visual support and have small budgets. Such games don't provide translation, perhaps because of a lack of cost effectiveness. So, if the purpose of a game is to learn in a friendly but challenging way how interactivity can become complex, why not start this process from the very beginning, without the need of textual instructions? Some musical toys have their sighted users accomplish very simple actions in a funny way, without the need of instructions for use. Moreover, video games show us that it is possible to separate the learning process of a complex task in small steps easy to master. We have made a game according to those principles and realized an experiment to test it. All the players managed to progress in the game but not all understood all the principles of the game. For this kind of game, we assume that players do not have to understand the game during the first contact but they have to be encouraged to continue interaction. At last, the increase of the difficulty level has to be very progressive.

Keywords: audio games, accessibility, usability test, interactivity, sound design, interactive music.

1 Introduction: Audio Games without Language for a Greater Accessibility

1.1 Without Visual Support, Languages Are Less Understandable

Accessibility in games is becoming every year a more important preoccupation in the industry and the report published by the IGDA marked a significant step [1]. The purpose of this study is to understand how visually impaired people can easily master new accessible audio games. Recent research and observation gave a good overview of the existing audio games [2], [3], [4], [5]. Actually, there are more than four

Z. Pan et al. (Eds.): Transactions on Edutainment II, LNCS 5660, pp. 176–186, 2009.
© Springer-Verlag Berlin Heidelberg 2009

hundred games which are accessible to visually impaired players. It is possible to adapt mainstream games into accessible ones as it was done for quake adapted into audioquake [6]. It can be easier to think about the accessibility of a game starting from the beginning of its development. For this to be done, research proposed guidelines for a better accessibility in games [7], [8].

However, these studies do not consider accessibility problems related to language aspects: language is an inaccessibility factor for those who can't master it. Moreover, recourse to translation, which implies increasing development costs, doesn't allow us to target all the potential users: there is too much language, even among the most spoken, to operate all the translations. Now, an important part of existing audio games requires good understanding of the principles of interactivity: for this reason, the comfort given by language is tempting but even for those who master the adequate language, it can be an obstacle to amusement. Most of the actual and popular audio games need a lot of reading before players can start to play them efficiently. For players who don't master English, the game is not accessible. This is why it can be advantageous, for accessibility studies or for economical needs for international distribution, to develop games (followed maybe by other kinds of software) without communication via language.

1.2 Some Studies Encourage the Making of Audio Games

Are audio games without language realistic? A. Darvishi confirms that an information technology environment using various sonorities provides support for the understanding of the interactive process [9]. But this study doesn't say if sounds alone could be sufficient for correct interaction. For this reason again, the encounter of experimental research on audio games and the field of non linguistic communication could bring interesting results. This can be a way to orientate the purpose of audio games towards a more musical outcome: interactive music. Even without the help of tactile perception, J.L. Alty points out that music is usable as the main means of communication, with three centres of interest: the communication of musical algorithms, debugging, and communication for blind people [10]. Regarding this third area, A. Darvishi uses sound synthesis in a virtual environment accessible to the blind, each sound being the result of a particular configuration of the environment [9]. One of the problems of this approach could be the difficulty to convey precise information with sound synthesis, because of its very abstract nature, not really suitable for communication. However, there are various ways of arriving at a fuller level of communication. For example, B.N. Walker manages to communicate numerical data via a musical abacus [11]. In addition to scientific studies, other ways of investigation may be very helpful.

2   The Influences of Multimedia Experiments and Video Games

Audio games are not the only interactive enjoyment. We will now study how interactivity works with musical toys and what is the importance of language in them. They could be a good source of inspiration for working on the first contact between an audio game and its users. Then we will consider video games because some of them present interesting learning processes. Both multimedia experiments and video games could provide clues for the design of audio games without language.

2.1 Influences of Multimedia Experiments: Language Is Not Necessary When Simple Actions Must Be Done

Interactive artistic audio experiments provide clues for non linguistic communication. These multimedia experiments are often very abstract audiovisually, with no objectives and with no instructions for use. Users have to discover by themselves how to interact with sounds and their misunderstanding can be considered as a part of these artistic works.

Most of them are unfortunately inaccessible for blind people, due to the importance of the visual interface. This is even truer when these experiments show small interactive buttons on a large non interactive visual surface and when there is no musical information about what is under the cursor. In this case, information is given by language but often in a graphical, inaccessible way. This is the case for "Audiomeister", an experimental musical mixer: it is simple, easy and funny to use but only for the sighted people. This first multimedia experiment suggests that immediate funny audio feedback is essential for the users. In "Snapper 8:8", all the visual zones are interactive. It is thus possible for blind users to use the mouse and click randomly on the screen, but it must be on the zone covered by the experiment. For a sighed user, this musical toy doesn't use instructions: users discover by themselves how to produce music, and it works well with sighted users. They realize two kinds of usual gestures: first, they move the mouse, anywhere on the surface of the experiment and then they click, nothing else. They just have to do these two usual gestures. We have presented these experimentations to some blind people; for them, it is harder: they need to know they must move the mouse and click. Moreover, for a blind user, the purpose of the experiment is not evident and they must be informed that it is a multimedia experiment. Other experiments are linked with movements of the mouse, without the need of clicking, for example to give an attractive musical rendering when the cursor meets specific fields. This kind of interactivity can be done without linguistic instructions for use.

The interaction in this type of experiment depends on exploration of zones. The "Spacializer" is a good example of this kind of musical toy. We can hear interactive sound, when the cursor is on specific zones, just by moving the mouse. This kind of experiment is even more easy to use because it needs the user to do not two but only one kind of gesture: to move the mouse.

However, these multimedia experiments present two problems for visually impaired people: the use of the mouse is not a habit, even if more and more audio games are based on this device and without visual perception, the purpose of these experiments is not evident.

Therefore, we suppose, on a strictly hypothetical way, that multimedia experiments using the keyboard may be more easy to use for blind people. Actual audio games use the keyboard. But this is not sufficient: keyboards have many keys and users must know which keys are useful.

Moreover, without the visual representation of the multimedia experiment, blind people can't represent to themselves the purpose of this activity. "are there any objectives?" Or "what am I supposed to do?" Are things some of them said while they tried these experimentations. One particularity of these experiments is that they usually are toys where users don't have to accomplish objectives. Concerning video games or audio games, they are no longer toys but games. We want to make a study on games rather than on multimedia experiments because we want to understand how users can elaborate a complex way of interaction with an application. Multimedia experiments only present simple ways of interaction with interesting audio feedback. There is no particular challenge to beat. Games, through different objectives, manage to complicate the interaction through a learning process. We think that the starting point of the learning process of audio games needs some characteristics of multimedia experiments in order to make a pleasant first contact. We have considered multimedia experiments and we will now consider video games to know more about the learning process.

2.2 Learning Process of Video Games: Simple Learning Processes May Be Combined for the Understanding of a More Complex Task

Over the last years, video games have been more often analyzed by scientific studies. These new studies allow us to define the nature of games, writing processes, technologies and the cultural impact [12].

It is easier for the player to learn a game with instructions included in the first step of the game. In this way, the player uses less his memory and he can practice without delay the instructions he learnt without risks of forgetting. Moreover, it is only when a lesson is understood by the player that the next instructions are given. A complex task may be divided in a great number of short or funny and easy to understand lessons often called "tutorials". For more complex games, we might fear that the amount of instructions is much greater. This will be more often not true than true. Linguistic communications are sometimes used but not always. The first basic actions are explained with verbal instructions and the player must understand by himself the combination he can make.

The great difference with simpler games is that learning is no longer presented before the game but incorporated in the game itself. Tutorials often have the following characteristics:

• No or very few « game over » situations;
• Players face situations that can only be resolved in one way;
• Clues make the resolution easy. Clues may be audio, visual and / or tactile;
• There are few advantages to the player to go back;
• Players should be very interested in going further.

Approaching each of these characteristics from an auditory rather than a visual point of view may be of great interest. So, there is a paradox. The number of instructions does not depend on the degree of complexity of the game. For complex games, developers are looking for other ways to make players learn and quickly enjoy themselves without being discouraged. Considering, on one hand, that perhaps simple interactions don't need instructions, as suggest to us multimedia experiments, and on the other hand, that the understanding of simple interactivity may be combined, it should be possible to develop audio games without linguistic communication.

2.3 Playing Toy-Games

For an audio game without language to work, the game should also be a toy. The learning process isn't homogeneous. It depends on each user individually and in order to avoid discouraging them, each action should bring enjoyment. This was one of the objectives of a particular game: the phase project [13].

Phase is a game which can be understood in three different ways: in a visual, an audio or a tactile way. Area exploration and gesture have both been integrated, each of these kinds of interactivity provides musical transformations in the game. For this reason, phase is a toy because each action has an amusing outcome. In the same way of the musical experiment we have considered, players can produce music just by moving a haptic joystick. They can produce other sorts of spatialized sound by exploring zones. Phase is also a game and more exactly a race game where players can catch a musical entity running along the horizon of an audio tactile landscape. The rule of the game is also induced by the musical outcome. The faster the players go, the more the music is exciting and interesting. Because of the constraints arising from the context of an exhibition, this game was voluntarily very simple. Phase was used by people of all nationalities, without having to be given instructions, except in a few cases. A lot of blind people successfully played this game as a toy and some of them succeeded in the game. These are very encouraging results for using this type of design in audio games. We have made a game on similar principles, for a more standard configuration: no more tactile feedbacks, but the use of the keyboard, and the audio feedback in stereo only.

3   Experiment

3.1   General Hypothesis

Ideally, a game should be playable as soon as a player has a first contact with it, during the learning phase and without the help of someone else.

3.2   Study Environment

During tests of preliminary projects without verbal instruction, we have noticed that it is better if the player chooses himself the adequate moment for interaction. The making of an action game where timing is important seems harder to do.

This is the reason why we have made two maze games. Players have all the time they want to interact without any consideration of timing. The first one, named "Pyvox, musical maze" uses an included verbal tutorial but it was also tested without these instructions. Results were encouraging: in the non-verbal version, the players did not manage to progress as far as in the verbal one, but almost all the players managed to play the game [14]. The second one, named logically "Pyvox 2, more musical mazes" doesn't use verbal instructions. The beginning of this game also works as a musical toy. For both of these projects, we have used usability tests as often as possible since the beginning of the development. During these tests, we don't present any instructions to the player except that "it is a game and for the purpose of the test, it is better if nothing is told about the rules of this game." Then we consider the progression, the keys the player uses and the problems of understanding he (or she) meets. After each test, we include new modifications to the game.

After this iterative process, we obtained a game with the following features: the player directs a character in a seventy floor labyrinthine tower, seventy floors corresponding to seventy game levels which can be explored one after another in an unchanging order. The character can also be considered as a cursor that can be moved on a grid from one square to the other. The player can move the cursor towards target areas but obstacles block up some access paths. This game is a maze with a square-to-square moving system, divided into game levels, each level presenting an exit and a certain number of walls. The aim of the game is to teach the player to recognize an exit sound just by using non-speech audio. The game also aims at making the player recognize the sounds coming out of the walls in order to avoid them without hitting them; this recognition is obtained with similar non-verbal principles: the walls emit sounds in order to make the player feel where the obstacles lie. This principle is conveyed implicitly: we wanted the sounds to be slightly unpleasant so as to force the player to take his character away from the walls. The link between those sounds and the walls is understood rather quickly. More pleasant sounds can then be heard. As a first contact, the game introduces the character sleeping. The keys of the keyboard almost all trigger alarm sounds. The closer the player gets to the arrow keys, the louder the alarm sounds become. The use of the arrow keys wakes the character up and the exploration of the maze can start.

3.3 Aim of the Study

We want to optimize the handling of audio games by tackling the problems linked to language. We also want the visually impaired player to be able to learn the rules of the games without verbal instruction.

3.4 Studied Population

The testers selected for the experiment are two groups of teenagers who have participated in the international computer camp 2007 (ICC) in the Arla institute from Espoo, Finland. They are all visually impaired. During the first week of the ICC, the teenagers were between fourteen and seventeen years old. During the second week, the first group left and older teenagers aged eighteen to twenty two came instead. The experiment was realized during specific workshops about audio games, so the testers had very little time - about three hours - to try more than a dozen games. Some of the testers wanted to put an end to the tested game in order to try the other ones before the end of the workshop. The other presented games were: "Terraformers", "Shade of Doom", "Sonic Zoom", "Sarah in the Castle of Witchcraft and Wizardry", "Super Egg Hunt", "Mudsplat", "Super Liam", "Pyvox Musical Maze", "Tampokme", "Chrono Mouse", "Descent into Madness" and "Top Speed 2". However, all these games were not always presented at the same time due to computer reconfiguration. Due to the conditions of the workshop, it was not possible to make a preliminary study to know for example if each tester was familiarized with audio games. The players were here to discover audio games and they had very little time; also, during the tests, we had to help players who were trying other games. Unlike with Pyvox 2, we had to explain the rules of those other audio games since they were not meant to be played without prior knowledge of instructions in the manual.

3.5 Variable Independent from the User

We counted the duration of each game and the highest level reached.

3.6 Variable Dependent from the User

We tested a unique version of our game, but we consider separately the two groups of testers, with different ages:

C1: testers from the first week of the ICC07, between fourteen and seventeen years old.

Unfortunately, we only managed to gather seven testers during the first week. Workshops did not occur all the days, and the first attempts were lost due to the preparation of the audio games for the ICC.

C2: testers from the second week of the ICC07, between eighteen and twenty two years old.

We managed to collect sixteen testers during this second week.

3.7 Instructions

In this study, the testers are not faced with the device freely, they are aware of the following details: they are going to try a game, the purpose of which is not given. They can play as much as they want. They can give up the game whenever they want to but they cannot resume it. They can adjust the sound volume with the controls indicated by the experimenter. The controls to adjust the sound volume are tested by the players. The experimenter starts the game and leaves the players to use the device until they want to stop the game by themselves.

Each tester only does a single game without preliminary training.

3.8 Operational Hypothesis

We assume that our game without language but including the learning principles previously suggested could be understood and properly played by players from the two age groups. However, we have noticed from previous tests that there could be very different reactions between players, depending on their ages. Adults without game experience for example may have great difficulty to handle audio games and to understand them. For this reason, we want to compare these two groups, without manipulating any other variables in order to have a better understanding of the different kinds of reactions to a same material.

4 Results

All the testers managed to pass the three first levels. Six testers ended the game at the sixth level. The majority of the testers, sixteen players out of twenty three, have played the game between eight and twenty four minutes. Six players have played more than thirty minutes. The five more persevering players are from the older group and the most persevering has played fifty minutes. The four players who have reached the highest levels are all from the older group too.

Table 1. Main results of the two groups of players

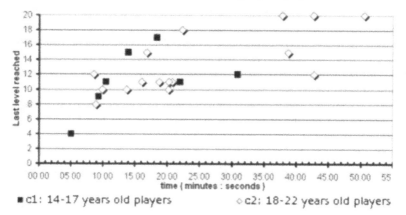

■ c1: 14-17 years old players   ◇ c2: 18-22 years old players

5 Discussion

All the testers managed to pass the three first levels (Fig 1). However, it doesn't mean that all the testers understand the principles of the game. At this point, the majority of the testers did not represent to themselves the game as a maze game. We have noticed during the ICC, that some sighted staff members failed to pass this third level, staying on the left of this audio maze without being able to go to the right side. For this reason, we consider that the level design of the first level should be improved with a lower difficulty level.

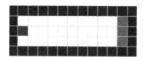

Fig. 1. The third level of Pyvox 3. The starting point is on the left and exits are on the right.

The increase of the difficulty level seems particularly problematic for the level number eleven (Fig 2.). Six testers ended the game on this level. Six others did not manage to reach this level and ended the game before. Eleven testers managed to pass this level.

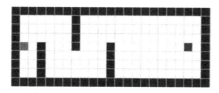

Fig. 2. Level eleven of Pyvox 2. The starting point is on the left and the exit is on the right. The player has to recognize and avoid three walls on the path before he can find the exit.

We think that the testers who managed to pass the level number eleven have understood the main principles of the maze game: players have to find an exit and the exit is indicated by a specific audio rendering using stereo and pitch variation depending on the position of the player's character compared to the position of the exit. However, at this point, we are not sure whether the players know how to identify walls without hitting them and recognizing the related sounds on impact. The maze is still relatively simple.

We have six testers who have played more than half an hour. The five more perseverant testers are from the older group of testers. The four better players who have reached the higher levels are also from the older group.

Three testers of the older group managed to pass the level number eighteen (Fig. 3). For these players, all the rules of the game seem to have been well understood.

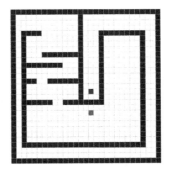

Fig. 3. Level eighteen of Pyvox 2. The starting point is in the center. The exit is near below. The player's character has to take the path on the right and go round the maze.

Despite these observations, there does not seem to be strong difference between the two groups.

We assume that not all the players understood all the rules of the game, but these results are related to their first attempt, without any preliminary training. Other attempts from the players should allow them to progress further in the game.

We consider that the players do not have to understand the game but have to experience enjoyment during the progression. What is important in games is the feeling of enjoyment. This particular sensation in games has been well studied since the works of Csikszentmihalyi about the flow theory [15]: a game is good enough if it strikes a balance between the challenge proposed by the game and the player's abilities. The flow zone, which is the feeling produced by good games, is in the middle of two opposite sensations: anxiety and boredom. It is not directly linked with the concept of understanding. Jenova has worked on the flow theory and used it to give us a very interesting game named "flow", without any verbal explanation [16]. Pyvox 2 is a game, and we consider that the difficulty to understand the principles of the game can be a part of the proposed challenge. However, the learning process could be facilitated and reviewing the level design and the sound design should help to do so.

6 Conclusion

We have envisaged that multimedia experiments allow the players to play with music as if they were playing with a toy: there is no objective. Then, we have seen that there are many ways to interact with these toys: by clicking or just by moving the mouse. Some of these experiments don't need instructions for use for sighted players who understand by themselves how to play. There are no multimedia experiments which are specifically adapted for blind people, we suppose that three factors are important for a good use of these multimedia experiments: usual gestures, funny and immediate audio feedback and finally, a good representation of the purpose of the multimedia experiment. In the next part, we have considered video games and their learning process: a complex task may be divided in many simple lessons that are easy to master, all included as a first part of the game. The first contact between players and audio games without language or other accessible audio software should combine the qualities of toys and games. Toys are fun to manipulate without instructions. Games encourage progression in the manipulation by a pleasant learning process. An audio game without language could imply that first, the player discovers a toy and then, because the audio rewards are not all the same for all the interactions, he is looking for the manipulations which provide the best encouragements. So the sound toy should successfully become an audio game without language. The making of an audio game without language implies that we can't develop a specific type of game without making other games for prerequisite knowledge: how to use the keyboard, which keys are really useful and which keys are not, what are the consequences of their usage. This is a whole chain of minigames that should be linked up in order to understand and play the desired game.

We have tried to implement those principles in a maze game. We are satisfied with the results, considering that they concern the first attempt without any preliminary training and without any explanation. However, we think that the learning process can be facilitated by making a level design with a more progressive increase of the difficulty and by improving the sound design again.

We are currently working on a third audio game named "Pyvox 3", it is also a maze game without verbal instruction and with a multiplayer feature. Thus, we think it can be easier for players to communicate hypotheses about the rules of the games.

Acknowledgements. This work has partially been realized with the support of CECIAA, in the framework of a CIFRE contract.

Our thanks to the ICC organization and to the Arla institute of Espoo, Finland, for giving us the possibility to make this study.

References

1. IGDA: I. G. D. A.. Accessibility in games: Motivations and approaches (2004),
   http://www.igda.org/accessibility/
   IGDA_Accessibility_WhitePaper.pdf
2. Archambault, D., Ossmann, R., Gaudy, T., Miesenberger, K.: Computer games and visually impaired people. Upgrade viii/2 (July 2007)

3. Feir, M.: A decade's accessible gaming: an old editor's anniversary observations. Audyssey 49 (2006)
4. France, M.: Audio game survey results. Audyssey 50 (2007)
5. Gaudy, T., Natkin, S., Archambault, D.: Classification des jeux sonores selon leur type de jouabilité. In: Proceedings of Handicap 2006 conference (2006)
6. Atkinson, M.T., Gucukoglu, S., Machin, C.H.C., Lawrence, A.E.: Making the mainstream accessible: What's in a game? In: Miesenberger, K., Klaus, J., Zagler, W.L., Karshmer, A.I. (eds.) ICCHP 2006. LNCS, vol. 4061, pp. 380–387. Springer, Heidelberg (2006)
7. Ossmann, R., Miesenberger, K.: Guidelines for the development of accessible computer games. In: Miesenberger, K., Klaus, J., Zagler, W.L., Karshmer, A.I. (eds.) ICCHP 2006. LNCS, vol. 4061, pp. 403–406. Springer, Heidelberg (2006)
8. Grammenos, D., Savidis, A., Stephanidis, C.: Unified design of universally accessible games. In: Stephanidis, C. (ed.) HCI 2007. LNCS, vol. 4556, pp. 607–616. Springer, Heidelberg (2007)
9. Darvishi, A., Guggiana, V., Munteanu, E., Shauer, H.: Synthesizing non-speech sound to support blind and visually impaired computer users, computers for handicapped persons (1994)
10. Alty, J.L., Rigas, D., Vickers, P.: Sing music as a communication medium (1996)
11. Walker, B.N., Lindsay, J., Godfrey, J.: The audio abacus: representing numerical values with nonspeech sound for the visually impaired (2002)
12. Natkin, S.: Video games and interactive media: a glimpse at new digital entertainment, ak peters (2006)
13. Rodet, X., Lambert, J.P., Cahen, R., Gaudy, T., Guedy, F., Gosselin, F., Mobuchon, P.: Study of haptic and visual interaction for sound and music control in the phase project. In: Proceedings of the 2005 conference on new interfaces for musical expression, Vancouver, May 2005, pp. 109–114 (2005)
14. Gaudy, T., Natkin, S., Archambault, D.: Playing audiogames without instructions for uses: to do without instruction leaflet or without language itself? In: Proceedings of CGAMES 2006, Dublin, November 21-24 (2006)
15. Csikszentmihalyi, M.: Flow: the psychology of optimal experience (1990)
16. Jenova, C.: Flow in games, mfa thesis, university of southern California (2001)

Design Tools for Online Educational Games: Concept and Application

Louise Sauvé

Tele-university / Center for expertise and research in lifelong learning (SAVIE)
lsauve@teluq.uqam.ca

Abstract. A research and development program initiated under the aegis of the Center for expertise and research of lifelong learning (SAVIE) has developed a series of generic educational game design shells to enable teachers, trainers and community service workers to create educational games that provide effective learning conditions and are adapted to their distance learning needs. These environments were based on the frame game concept and on the essential attributes of games. In this paper, we will first describe the context which deals with the development of generic shells for educational games. Then, we define the concept of educational games and present the indicators for choosing an educational game that is efficient. Then, we define the concepts of generic game shells and describe the interactive pedagogical design model. Finally, we show an example to illustrate how a generic shell such as that of the Parcheesi game can generate quality educational games adapted to the needs of learners studying in distant locations at various levels of schooling.

Keywords: Design, Game, Educational, Online.

1 Introduction

Digital games are seen more and more as effective learning resources (DeMaria, 2007; Gee, 2007; Moline, 2008). Their effectiveness is such that the Federation of American Scientists (FAS) supports the use of these educational games in teaching academic content, in improving critical thinking in students and also in evaluating their learning process (FAS, 2006).

Academic literature often discusses the creative potential of new technologies including educational games, in practice this promise has yet to be realized. What has been found, as it pertains to the learner, is that certain new aptitudes lay dormant when they are susceptible to being developed, such as: cooperation abilities, abilities for structuring knowledge and also problem solving abilities. It seems that schools do not explore the educational potential of these new techniques. In many countries including Canada, the educational potential of digital games have not become reality (Dempsey et al., 2002; J. Piette, personal communication, April 9, 2005; Prensky, 2006). A European Union inquiry into education and the media (Mediappro, 2006) found a major gap between Internet use at home and in the schools; all important learning tools were found outside the schools including those essential for self-directed learning and learning among peers – functions which online educational games can support.

In order to facilitate the use of online educational games in schools, we focused on developing and experimenting with learning environments that evolved from games.

Z. Pan et al. (Eds.): Transactions on Edutainment II, LNCS 5660, pp. 187–202, 2009.

This is done in order to provide teachers with the ability to easily develop online educational games that are adapted to their pedagogical requirements.

In the first section we present the context which deals with the development of generic shells for educational games from the Educational Games Central– EGC (http://egc.savie.ca). In the second section, we define an educational game and the pedagogical needs of teachers who will use these games in their teaching environment. In the third section we describe the concept of generic educational game shells and their creation process. Furthermore, we briefly explain how the framework of the Parcheesi game was adapted to answer the needs of educators. Finally, in the fourth section we illustrate an example of an educational game that was developed with the generic game shell of Parcheesi.

2 Context

Currently, millions of students invest a phenomenal amount of time playing with computers, the internet and with games. These young people, strong on techno, are hooked on games of skill. An investigation in 20 American colleges and universities has shown that "all students play video games and study with the use of their computer and that 65% of the students describe themselves as regular or occasional digital game players (Jenkins, 2005). Other studies have shown that 80% of people 18 years old or younger and more than 70% of adults play video games (ESA, 2005).

In 2007, the video game sector represents a 25 billion Euro turnover (FUTURN, 2007). Forest (2006) estimates that the 2010 video game market will be $1.3 billion in Canada and $46.5 billion in the US. In Canada, 63% of 15-69-year-olds had a mobile phone in 2004 (Ericsson Canada Inc., 2004). In Quebec, the NetAdos poll (Lamy, 2004) found that 60.7% of Quebecois aged 12 – 17 years play online and that 26.5% of young adults (18-24 years) do so regularly. A more recent Quebec poll found that 68% of Quebecois use the Internet and 26% own a fixed or portable game console (Centre francophone d'informatisation des organisations [CEFRIO] and Léger Marketing, 2007). The success of video games now rivals television and the film industry since it has become the most desirable form of entertainment (Hutchison, 2007). Who are these students to whom we teach?

Online games offer to the digital generation (Digital Natives) the opportunity to make use of inductive reasoning, to increase their visual abilities and their capacity for cross-checking information sources (Van Eck, 2006). The game allows the player to resolve cognitive conflicts. "Playing a game demands a constant cycle of hypotheses, tests and revisions".

"The game generation" has developed a new cognitive style characterized by multitasked learning, a relatively short attention span during the learning process, and a way of learning which relies on exploration and discovery[1]. Today's teenagers are "born" communicators, intuitive and visual[2]. They have strong spatial and visual aptitudes which are due most assuredly to their practice of video games. They prefer to learn through experimentation rather than following a teacher; they pass easily from one subject matter to another and also from one activity to the next when the activity does not offer great interest. They respond with promptness and demand a

---

[1] Asakawa and Gilbert (2003), Bain and Newton (2003) and Prensky (2006).
[2] Oblinger and Oblinger (2005).

rapid answer in return. The use of video games has modified the way young people learn from a constructivist approach: the student first plays, then comprehends and finally generalizes to apply what has been learned to new situations[3]. The young internet user wishes the following during the learning process: interactivity, interaction, active visualization, kinesthesis and immediacy.

What happens to the role of the teacher? The role for conveying information of the traditional teacher transforms itself little by little to the context of the digital generation: the student becomes active and participates in the construction of his knowledge base and the teacher collaborates to this learning process. It is more and more clear that the introduction of games into the learning environment of this new generation will favour learning and for some students it will help bring them back into the learning environment. Knowing this, how can teachers integrate digital games into their learning environment?

The task for every teacher is to put into place situations that are susceptible in favouring learning in the students. To carry out this task, the teacher must choose the most appropriate pedagogical formulas for the situation in order to reduce the obstacles for learning. We have noted that even though there are certain advantages for using video games, few teachers and trainers use them because of the lack of material appropriate for their teaching or training situation. To facilitate their use, a developmental research program, started in July 2000 and successively financed by Francommunautés virtuelles (Industry Canada), Office of Learning Technologies (OLT), Inukshuk Wireless funds, The Initiative on the New Economy (SSHRC, Canada) and Standard Research Grants (SSHRC, Canada) have permitted the development and the experimentation of 6 generic educational game shells.

To create these generic shells for educational games, we first defined what we mean by a game, and then we centered on the demands of the teachers and then based ourselves on these demands to create generic shells for educational games from the EGC.

3   Defining and Designing Educational Games to Meet Pedagogical Needs

A game is a fictitious, whimsical or artificial situation in which players are put in a position of conflict. Sometimes players square off against one another and at other times they are on the same side and are pitted against other teams. Games are governed by rules which structure their actions in view of a learning objective or a purpose determined by the game such as to win or to take revenge (Sauvé, Renaud, Kaufman and Marquis, 2007).

In order to add an educational aspect, O'Neil (2004) summarized the demands of teachers in relation to digital devices and to the content offered by these devices:

- The device must be reliable, convenient and complete;
- The device must be flexible so that it can be easily used in different learning situations. This signifies, among other things, that the teachers can adapt these devices to the particularities of their students (knowledge, level of language, age);
- the device must be ready to go, friendly and easily accessible so the teachers can easily find all the necessary elements for a given context or situation;

---

[3] Saethang and Kee (1998) and Shaffer, Squire, Halverson and Gee (2004).

- The content presented must be accurate and directly linked to the teaching programs.

Based on these requirements and the work of Sauvé & Hanca (2007), Table 1 proposes a series of indicators that the teachers can use when choosing a digital educational game.

Table 1. Some Indicators for choosing an Educational Game that is efficient with respect to its Structure

Game play aspect of the game
• Game board format in relation to the visualization
• Presence and well placed display of the scores
• Full time access to the game rules.
• The presence of pawns or elements that permit active participation of the players.
Intuitive dimension of the interface
• Clarity of the directions.
• Clarity of the rules.
• Ease of navigation.
• Ease of game execution.
Pedagogical legibility of the game content
• Vocabulary adapted for the target audience.
• Size and color of the characters.
• Display format for the pictures and video.
• Quality of sound reception.
• Display quality for the pictures and video.
• Presence of feedback messages linked to navigation to permit players to visualize at any moment the results of their actions within the game.
Game Dynamics
• Various types of questions.
• Chance and Misfortune cards.
• Voting system.
• Scoring system.
• Diversified routes (optional).
• Number of levels to reach the end of the game (optional).
• Degree of interactivity (manipulation, rapidity of the actions) in relation of the targeted audience.

4   Developing Design Environments for Educational Games

In view of the difficulties encountered by teachers searching the Internet for pedagogical games adapted to their needs, six generic shells for online educational games were developed at the Center for expertise and research in lifelong learning (SAVIE).

We define a generic shell for educational games to be an online design environment that facilitates the creation of games for teachers or trainers by providing them with the necessary tools for: (1) setting the game parameters; (2) generating the rules governing the movement of the players; (3) creating pedagogical material; (4) defining the criteria dealing with the end of the game and determining the winner, and (5) elaborating the tools necessary for the revision and evaluation of the game. This is done so that the game is continually updated in order to ensure its impact on learning.

The concept of the generic shell is based on the frame game concept elaborated by Stolovitch and Thiagarajan (1980). A frame game is an already existing game, such as Snakes and Ladders, from which the contents are removed, leaving only its basic structure. Any game can be broken down into two main components:

- The structure determines the way in which you play: the rules, the steps for the course of the game, the movements of the players, the challenges the players must face and the strategies they must employ to win. The game's contents have been eliminated so that the underlying structure of the game can be exposed. This structure, once clearly defined and analyzed, becomes a "frame" or a generic game shell once it is programmed and placed online.

- The content refers to the information conveyed during the game: this content is usually found in the game cards or on the game board. In the case of a pedagogical game, it is also the objectives being pursued and the abilities that will be developed by practicing the game. When the game is elaborated, you only need to insert the new content accompanied by the predetermined objectives to generate a new educational game which is adapted for a particular target audience.

Every existing game is potentially a frame game. The game must be carefully analyzed to separate the structure from the contents. A good game can be recognized by the harmony between its structure and content. A frame game would be a good example of this, but what renders it particularly useful is that the contents can be switched to something else while remaining perfectly compatible with its structure. It is this fundamental characteristic, the interchangeability of the contents, which makes the frame game an interesting pedagogical tool.

In general, board games are easier to adapt into a game shell and this for several reasons: (1) they are generally known to the public at large (who has not played Snakes and Ladders, Tic-Tac-Toe or even Parcheesi!); (2) they offer simple structures with few rules which makes them easily adaptable and, more importantly, (3) they correspond to the notion of a game by distinguishing themselves from simulations since board games rely on an imaginary environment rather than a simulated one.

In order to create an online generic educational game shell, an interactive pedagogical design model has been developed by Sauvé (2002) and validated by Sauvé et al. (2002, 2004). It consists of five phases:

- Analysis: analysis of the target learner group(s) and the context in which learning will take place; specification of the shell's pedagogical and technological requirements; review of existing frame-games and selection of the structure of the game to be adapted; and identification of the shell's compositional elements, based on the structure and contents of the existing game.
- Design: identification of the structure and content elements of the game that need to be modified to create the shell; description of the elements of the shell

and its functions; and design of a visual model using screen images of the shell and its variants and scenarios.

- Technical development: drafting of technical specifications that take into account the principles of online construction; graphic and multimedia development of the shell; programming of different elements and their functions in the shell; and functional integration testing of the shell with the contents of an educational game.
- Formative evaluation of the generic game shell: specification of the formative evaluation criteria and process; development of evaluation instruments for the target population; target population trials; and making any necessary revisions.
- Summary evaluation of the games created using the generic game shell: development of an educational game using the shell; specification of the experimental framework; development of measurement instruments to be used by experts and the target population; validation of the game by experts, and revisions if necessary; game trial by the target population, and revision of the game and the shell if necessary.

Examine briefly the modifications made to the original version of Parcheesi (Fig .1) during the design phase.

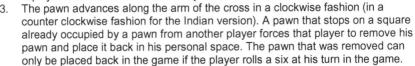

Purpose of the game: be the first player to arrive with all four pawns into the final zone.
Number of players: 2 to 4
Length of game: 30 to 45 minutes
Game play:

1. Four pawns are then automatically placed into each team's personal space.
2. To get to the starting square of your personal square, a player must roll a six.
   A player that rolls a 6 is rewarded by another roll of the die.
3. The pawn advances along the arm of the cross in a clockwise fashion (in a counter clockwise fashion for the Indian version). A pawn that stops on a square already occupied by a pawn from another player forces that player to remove his pawn and place it back in his personal space. The pawn that was removed can only be placed back in the game if the player rolls a six at his turn in the game.
4. A pawn can only enter the end zone of the game by an exact die result. For example, if a pawn is five squares away from the end zone and the player rolls a six, the player must wait for his next turn to try and roll a five. But since the player rolled a 6, the player can move any other pawn or he can also liberate one pawn from the personal space.
5. Different throws of the die can be made to move different pawns. A throw of the die cannot be split in two; for example, a result of 6 cannot be separated to move one pawn forward 4 squares and another pawn moved forward by 2 squares.
6. A pawn that enters the end zone is removed from the board. The first player to remove all his pawns wins the game.

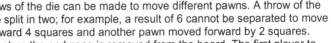

Fig. 1. Original board game and rules of Parcheesi

Structure Adaptation

Concerning the structure of the game, the game board, in general, is rarely modified in a generic shell. In this case, we have taken into account the pedagogical demands and we have added a second route, which is much faster, to the initial route of the game board all while maintaining the number of spaces and the square shape of the board. The materials of the game, the number of pawns for each player or team (4) and the number of dice (2) are maintained.

Three types of game cards have been added (Learning cards, Team cards and Chance cards) and also the use of two dice instead of only one for the movement of the pawns. These additions required us to review the unfolding of the events that constitute the scenario of the game. Seven events have been inserted and this has led to modifications to the presentation of the game board and the original rules.

Mechanisms have also been put into place: (1) to ensure competition between players by integrating a system of points according to the level of difficulty of the learning activity; (2) to ensure cooperation by permitting teams to regroup and offering them Team cards to stimulate both cooperation and competition; (3) to be able to vary the number of players using the game by creating a fictitious player if one is playing alone, and (4) to motivate the players that answer correctly by allowing them access to a faster path to reach the center of the game board.

The rules which govern the movement of players in the game have been improved (Table 2). These rules are accessible Online to the players whether before or during the game. The procedure rules describe the components of the game: the number of participants (players) or the number of teams, the role of each participant, their activities, and the way they move and their possible movements, how the game starts, how the players proceed throughout the game, the scoring and the duration of the game. In our adaptation, we have added the following rules: 5 to 8, 10, 12 and 13 which deal with the actions of the players during learning activities and the movement of the pawns between the normal and rapid route.

The end rules explain how the game can be won and how the game ends. Generally, the end of the game determines a winner; however, there are certain games where there can be a draw. In Parcheesi, the end of the game happens when a player or team have completed the route. We have added a second way to end the game in order to respect the time constraints of a study period and this is shown by rules 2 and 14 of the adapted version. The rules of control describe the consequences for a player who executes an action which does not conform with the rules or a player who does not respect the directives and the preceding rules. In the shell of Parcheesi, we did not have any control rules link to the original structure but we have added movement constraints to the pawns, as shown in rules 5 to 7, when a team does not successfully pass a learning activity.

Table 2. Structure of the Generic Shell of Parcheesi

Goal of the game: there are two ways to win the game:
- Be the first player or team to move your four pawns into the end zone and also succeed in the final challenge.
- After a set time for the length of the game, be the player or team with the most points when the game ends.

Table 2. *(Continued)*

Number of players or teams: the minimum number of players is at least 2 players or two teams of two players and the maximum number of players is 4 or four teams of four players.

Length of the game: When players are creating their teams, they can decide in advance what the length of the game will be. They can also decide not to impose a time limit to the game and simply let the game go on until one team has moved their four pawns into the end zone and have completed the final challenge.

Game Play

1.   The game must be played with a minimum of two players each forming a team or a maximum of 16 players divided into 4 teams. Any other combination is also possible.

2.   Before starting the game, teams have to decide how the game is to be won:
- When all four pawns of a team have reached the end zone and correctly completed the educational activity.
- When the predetermined amount of time has elapsed.

3.   To start a game, the system records the number of teams and their make-up. Four pawns are then automatically placed into each team's personal space.

4.   Who begins the game is purely random. Each team clicks on the dice. Whichever team rolls the highest number begins the game.

5.   A team must obtain a double (1-1, 2-2, 3-3-, 4-4, 5-5, 6-6) for the system to move a pawn to the Start square. The team then clicks on the coloured pawn they want to move to the Start square. When a pawn is placed on the Start square, the team in question must attempt to complete an educational activity which corresponds to the color of their pawn:
- If the team successfully completes the first activity, they can then roll the dice and move the pawn the appropriate number of squares along the fast track.
- If the team does not complete the first activity, the pawn remains on the Start square and the team waits their next turn to try again.
- If, on the next turn, a team completes the second activity, the pawn on the Start square is allowed to move along the regular track.
- If a team does not complete the second activity, the pawn remains on the Start square. The team must then wait another turn to try again until they do complete an activity.

6.   As soon as a team has moved a pawn, turns will happen as follows:
- Players must complete an educational activity corresponding to the colour of the pawn which was moved during the last turn.
- If the team successfully answers the question in the time allotted, the team then clicks the dice and can move a pawn the number of squares corresponding to the result of the dice. A team can also decide to bring a pawn into the game if the result of the dice allows it. Two pawns from the same team cannot occupy the same square. This means that a team cannot bring new pawns into the game if there is already a pawn on the Start square.
- If a team fails an activity, they cannot click the dice. They will have to wait until the next turn to try to answer a question of the same category in order to be able to click the dice.
- Once a team has finished their turn, the next player or team plays.

Table 2. *(Continued)*

7.   When a team moves their pawn (either on the regular or the fast track) and crosses a Start square, the team must successfully complete an educational activity. This has to be done even if, given the results of the roll of the dice, the pawn crosses over the Start square. Successfully completing the educational activity is important since it determines which track the pawn will take, whether in finishing the move in progress or with regard to the next turn. If a team successfully completes an activity, the pawn may continue to move along the fast track. If the team fails, the pawn will move to the regular track. The same rule applies if the team lands on the Start square with an exact roll of the dice. When successful (in completing an activity), the team does not click on the dice but the pawn will go on the fast track at the next turn even if the team decides to move another pawn after having completed the activity. In other words, a pawn retains the ability to move along the fast track if the team has successfully completed an activity.

When a pawn crosses a Start square before embarking on a track that leads to the end zone, the team must yet again complete an educational activity. If the team does not succeed in this, the pawn remains where it is. The team must complete a new activity before being able to take the track that leads to the end zone. If a team completing an activity has a pawn that was interrupted in its movement because it crossed the Start square, the pawn can resume its movement along the track that leads to the end zone.

8.   Each team who successfully completes an activity earns points. The points vary according to the amount of time taken to complete the activity.

9.   If a pawn lands on a square already occupied by another pawn, the latter is sent back to the Start square. If the returning pawn lands on a Start square which is already occupied by another pawn, it is sent back to the team's personal space.

10.   Each pawn can only reach the end zone on the board with an exact throw of the dice. The result of the dice has to be the exact number of spaces needed to reach the end zone (the center counts as one space). When arriving in the end zone, the pawn is removed from the game and the team gets 200 points.

11.   When a team throw the dice and get a higher number than the number of spaces required for a pawn to reach the end zone, they have two options:

- The team can decide not to move the pawn until they obtain an exact result and, instead, move another pawn which can move according to the result obtained by the dice.

- They can move the pawn to the center square and move the pawn back corresponding to the roll of the dice. For example: say the pawn is two spaces away from the end zone and the team rolls a 5, the pawn moves forward 3 spaces and then moves back two.

- The pawn cannot move back further than the first space of the track. If the pawn reaches this first space and still has moves to make, the pawn simply returns in the direction of the end zone with its remaining moves.

12.   Once a team draws a Team card, all of the teams may compete simultaneously. The first team to successfully complete the activity earns additional points.

- If a pawn of the winning team is on the Start square, it immediately accesses the fast track.

Table 2. *(Continued)*

- The team that drew the Team card does not lose their turn. Immediately after having played the Team card, their team may attempt to complete another educational activity.

13. When a team draws a Chance card, the team then performs one of the following actions:

- Win a Free Start. This card allows the team to move one of their pawns to the Start square, which requires that the team immediately attempts an educational activity. If the Start square is already occupied by one of the team's pawns or if all of the team's pawns are currently in play, the team may keep the Chance card and use it later on in the game to position one of its pawns on the Start square.

- Exact Throw. This card allows the team to move one of its pawns (any pawn which is currently in play and not on the Start square) into the end zone. If the team has only one pawn in play and that pawn is on the Start square, the Chance card is kept by the team to be used later on in the game to move one of their pawns directly into the end zone.

- Go back to Start. This card moves a team's pawn back to the Start square. If the square is already occupied by another pawn, the latter returns to the personal space of the pawn's team. If the team has only one pawn currently in play and that pawn is on the Start square, the card is kept by the team and the pawn will have to return to the Start square the next time it is moved. If the pawn associated with the card is removed from play before the card is played, the team puts the card back (it is discarded).

- Fast-tracking. This card allows a team to move the pawn used to pick the card from the regular track to the fast track without having to complete an educational activity, if the pawn is on the Start square or past it.

- A maximum of two Chance cards can be retained at any one time by a team. If a team has two Chance cards in reserve, any new Chance card will replace the first Chance card held.

14. Game over:

- When a team moves all four pawns into the end zone, successfully completing an educational activity, it wins. If a team picks a Team card as the final educational activity, the team wins the game only if they complete the educational activity. If the team does not correctly answer the question, the team must wait till their next turn to try to successfully complete another educational activity and win the game.

- When the allotted time has run out, the team with the most points wins the game.

In traditional board games, there are no distinctions between the rules and the directives as in computer games. In a board game the players themselves move their own pawns on the board. In a computer game, a game engine moves the pawns, identifies which player will start the game and the player who follows, etc. These directives (Table 3), which we distinguish from the rules, only have as a goal to facilitate comprehension for the players on the constraints imposed by a game engine. For example, it indicates the name of the player that must click the dice or the player that must attempt a learning activity in order to obtain points, etc. No other player can act in the game until the identified player has finished their turn.

Table 3. Example of the directives

---

1. Please select a set of pawns for your team.

2. The game is initializing. Please wait untill all teams are ready to play before beginning the game.

3. To determine which team will start the game, each team must click on the dice one after the other. The team with the highest result begins the game.

4. The team **Player`s Name / Team** has obtained the highest result.

5. Player`s Name / Team , you have obtained a double! You can move your pawn to the Starting square.

6.The team **Player`s Name / Team** has successfully passed the Educational activity! The team Player`s Name / Team must click on the dice to move a pawn.

7. Player`s Name / Team , you have picked a Team card: all the teams are in play!

8. Player`s Name / Team , you have picked a Chance card!

9. Player`s Name / Team , click on the pawn you wish to move.

10. Player`s Name / Team , your four pawns have been removed from the game. You must successfully pass the final Educational activity on your next turn to win the game.

11. Player`s Name / Team , you have not successfully passed the final activity. Wait for the next turn to try again.

12. The game is now finished. **Player`s Name / Team** , you have won the game!

13. Player`s Name / Team , you have obtained a result that makes your pawn cross over the centre square. By clicking on it, the pawn will move to the centre then move back the number of moves in surplus.

14. Player`s Name / Team you have won a start! Place the pawn of your choice to the Starting square!

15. Player`s Name / Team , you have won a start but you cannot use this Chance card right now. The card will be placed in your bank to be used later on.

16. Player`s Name / Team , you have won an exact throw of the dice! Move one pawn that is not on your Starting square to the centre square!

Etc.

Content Adaptation

In general, the content of a game can be completely modified. First of all, we have added learning activities to the shell in order to respond to certain demands previously stated. The predetermined formats linked to thirteen types of learning activities have been included in the shell in order to develop simple to complex knowledge and to modify behaviors and attitudes: True or False questions, Yes or No questions, Multiple Choice questions (2, 3 or 4 choices), Missing Segment questions (2 or 3 segments), Logical Sequence questions, Open questions with short answers, Open questions with long answers, Role-playing type questions and Modeling type questions. All of the activities include a correction mechanism as well as a real time mechanism for feedback.

Other tools have also been integrated into the shell. Tools for the conception of pedagogical materials in the form of learning objects have been integrated. This material is available for players either before or after the game. The creator of the game can activate a whiteboard for debriefing and also for feedback from the players. This debriefing is strongly recommended because it is an important step to the integration of the knowledge, emotions and attitudes developed by the game.

Technological options

Several technological options were also integrated in the Parcheesi game shell, such as:

- the option of playing the game on a single or on many computers in order to facilitate its integration in schools;
- an identification mechanism when the game is played on a single computer so that all the players who are playing the game can identify themselves with their password;
- a mechanism that allows for single players to play alone;
- a real time communication tool as well as a team display mode (up to 16 players) when the game is played in multi-player mode in order to favor audio exchanges between the players or the members of a same team that are playing at a distance;
- a real time communication tool as well as a display mode that varies according to the number of players (2 to 6) that allows exchanges (textual, audio or audiovisual) between the players.

In order to achieve a higher level of user-friendliness and usefulness, a first formative evaluation (phase 4) was carried out by nine teacher candidates. The participants considered the generic Parcheesi game shell to be user-friendly, useful and easy to master. They reported that the majority of its templates were easy to use and that their level of pedagogical readability was very high regarding the language quality, the structure of the contents and the ease of navigation. Few recommendations for improvement of this generic educational game shell were made by these teachers (Sauvé & Hanca, 2007).

5 Developing Your Own Educational Games

The adaptations brought to the original structure permits the integration of the learning content needed from elementary schools to universities The Parcheesi game shell works well with simple or complex learning: acquisition, integration, use of knowledge, transfer of learning, evaluation, etc. The game requires that you write down a minimum of 40 educational activities to challenge the players. The ideal number of activities ranges from 48 to 64. You wish for a team game where the level of difficulty is more elevated? If this is the case, choose this shell. This game plays with at least 2 players or 2 teams and with a maximum of 4 players or 4 teams. This game can also be played alone.

In this section, we illustrate how we used the Parcheesi game shell to create an online game offered in a program for asthma prevention, therapeutic monitoring and health promotion that aims to improve the well being and the quality of life of people suffering from asthma (http://asthme.savie.ca).

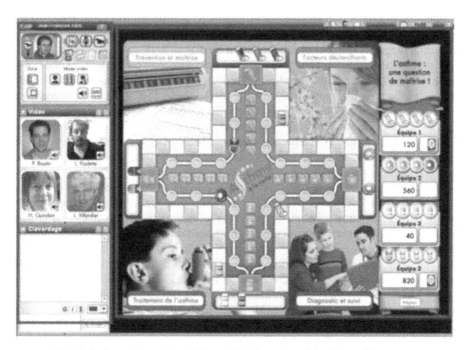

Fig. 2. Asthma: A question of Control! Adaptation of the Game of Parcheesi

Financed by the Inukshuk Wireless Fund, the game Asthma: A Question of Control! has the following objectives: to identify the elements that may trigger an asthma attack and the measures to prevent these attacks; to differentiate the different treatments for asthma; to identify the causes of asthma and finally to identify the ways to diagnose and monitor this condition.

Created in under 4 hours, the creators have created 85 learning activities with varying levels of difficulties. They have completely modified the game board (colors, illustrations and pawns) and also the wording of the rules. Fig.2 shows the four aspects dealt with in the game: (1) control and prevention, (2) triggering factors, (3) asthma treatment and (4) diagnosis and monitoring. Observe also that the screen is divided into two zones. The right zone, common to all users who participate in the game in real time, allows them to consult the rules of the educational game, answer questions or perform activities, display results (scores, successful or failed activities) and consult the help functions online. The left zone permits the coordinator and each player to talk to (voice) and see (video image) the other players of his team (private communication), talk to the players of the other teams (public communication) and write messages in a chat space (private or public).

6 Conclusion

The appearance of the information superhighway and the diversification of learning technologies have resulted in an increased interest in educational games within the learning environment, whether initial or ongoing. According to Livingstone (2002) and Ridley (2004), games have become the principal form of entertainment for learners when compared to books or other types of media.

A systematic analysis of the literature over the last ten years (1998-2008) shows that games provide favorable conditions for learning, such as: competition and challenges, feedback, active participation on the part of the learner, teamwork, interaction, repetition and breaking the learning content down (Sauvé, Renaud, Kaufman & Sibomana, 2008). This analysis also emphasizes that games have a positive impact on cognitive, affective and psychomotor learning. The consensus of the authors is that games motivate the learners, structure and consolidate their knowledge, promote problem solving skills, changing of attitudes, as well as the development of transversal skills (communication, negotiation, decision making, cooperation, etc.).

The generic shell of the game Parcheesi proposes to the creators all the tools necessary to define the game parameters, generate the directions and the rules concerning the movement of players, constructing learning activities and the pedagogical materials, establish the criteria about how the game ends by declaring a winner and the elaboration of debriefing, evaluation instruments so that the game is always revised and also tools to measure its effectiveness on learning. This shell allows for the generation of team games supported by a multiplayer platform (ENJEUX, http://enjeux.savie.ca) and also provides real time communication tools (audio or videoconference) according to the equipment that the players possess (headphones or webcam) at the moment they access the game.

This pioneering work in the development of generic shells for educational games on the Internet, with its varied environments (Snakes and Ladders, Concentration or Memory, Tic-Tac-Toe, Trivia, Mother Goose or Parcheesi), provides an opportunity for teachers, trainers, pedagogical counselors and education specialists to quickly develop educational games. These games can be created in four languages (French, English, Spanish and Greek) and made available to teachers and students all over the world. To know more and to become part of these game creators, register at the Educational Games Central at the following Internet address: http://egc.savie.ca.

References

1. Asakawa, T., Gilbert, N.: Synthesizing Experiences: Lessons To Be Learned from Internet-Mediated Simulation Games. Simulation & Gaming 34(1), 10–22 (2003)
2. Bain, C., Newton, C.: Art Games: Pre-Service Art Educators Construct Learning Experiences for the Elementary Art Classroom. Art Education 56(5), 33–40 (2003)
3. Borduas, F., Boulet, L.P., Blais, J., Rouleau, M., Sauvé, L., Pépin, K., Royer, M.: Asthma: A question of control! Quebec: SAVIE - Educational Games Central (2008),
   http://www.savie.qc.ca/CarrefourJeux2/Site/Jeux/Parchesi/
   infoParchesi.Asp?NoPartie=260
4. Centre Francophone D'Informatisation Des Organisations (CEFRIO), & Léger Marketing, NETendances CEFRIO - Léger Marketing (2007),
   http://www.infometre.cefrio.qc.ca/loupe/omnibus/
   internet_0707.asp (retrieved October 6, 2007)
5. Demaria, R.: Reset: changing the way we look at video games. Berrett-Koehler Publishers, Inc., San Francisco (2007)

6. Dempsey, J.V., Haynes, L.L., Lucassen, B.A., Casey, M.S.: Forty simple computer games and what they could mean to educators. Simulation & Gaming 33(2), 157–168 (2002)
7. Entertainment Software Association – ESA. Facts and Research. Consulté le 12 décembre 2005 de (2005), http://www.theesa.com/facts/index.php
8. Ericsson Canada Inc. Ericsson study: Canadian mobile phone ownership climbs to 63 percent; wireless talk time averaging 49 minutes a day (2004), http://www.ericsson.com/ca/en/press/2004_11_23.shtml (retrieved October 6, 2007)
9. Federation Of American Scientists - FAS. Summit for educational game: Harness the power of games for learning (2006), Consulté le 5 juin 2007 de, http://fas.org/gamesummit/Resources/Summitoneducationalgames.pdf (retrieved October 6, 2007)
10. Forest, C.: Canadian entertainment and media market maturing at a steady pace. Toronto: PriceWaterhouseCoopers (June 22, 2006), http://www.pwc.com/extweb/ncpressrelease.nsf/docid/0EE0753076513A1C852571940070FCCC (retrieved October 30, 2006)
11. Futurn. L'iDate passe au crible l'Industrie française du jeu vidéo! [iDate examines the French Video Game Industry] (March 29, 2007), http://www.futurn.net/article.php?sid=258 (retrieved October 6, 2007)
12. Gee, J.P.: Good video games + good learning: Collected essays on video games, learning and literacy. Peter Lang, New York (2007)
13. Hutchison, D.: Video games and the pedagogy of place. The Social Studies 98(1), 35–40 (2007)
14. Jenkins, H.: Getting into the game. Educational Leadership 62(7), 48–51 (2005)
15. Lamy, C.: NetAdos 2004 - Sondage réalisé auprès des ados québécois & de leurs parents [Poll of Québécois adolescents and their parents]. CEFRIO, Québec (2004), http://www.cefrio.qc.ca/rapports/NetAdos_2004_rapport.pdf (retrieved October 6, 2007)
16. Livingstone, S.: Young people and new media: Childhood and the changing media environment. Sage, London (2002)
17. Mediappro. The appropriation of New Media by Youth (Final Report). Louvain-La-Neuve. Mediappro, Belgium (2006)
18. Moline, T.: I Get Competent Pretty Quickly: How Adolescents Play Their Way To Cognitive Self-efficacy. In: McFerrin, K., Weber, R., Carlsen, R., Et Willis, D.A. (eds.) Proceedings of 19th International Conference Annual of Society for Information Technology & Teacher Education, pp. 1213–1219 (2008)
19. O'Neil, M.: Final Report on Gaps in Resources Available to deliver History and Social Studies Curricula in Canada, Historica, 37 pages (2004)
20. Oblinger, D.G., Oblinger, J.L.: Educating the Net Generation. EDUCAUSE report (2005), Disponible en ligne, http://www.educause.edu/educatingthenetgen/
21. Piette, J.: Conférence de Jacques Piette lors du congrès de la FADBEN à Nice, Médias communication TICE académie de Nice, avril (2005)
22. Prensky, M.: Don't Bother Me Mom – I'm Learning! Paragon House, St. Paul (2006)
23. Ridley, K.: ACNielsen Reports Continued Growth for Video Gaming Industry. ACNielsen (2004, 18 octobre) (Consultée le 15 décembre 2004 de), http://www.acnielsen.ca/News/VideoGamingThirdQtr2004Results.htm
24. Saethang, T., Kee, C.C.: A gaming strategy for teaching the use of critical cardiovascular drugs. Journal of Continuing Education in Nursing 29(2), 61–65 (1998)

25. Sauvé, L., Power, M., Isabelle, C., Samson, D., St-Pierre, C.: Rapport final - Jeux-cadres sur l'inforoute: Multiplicateurs de jeux pédagogiques francophones: Un projet de partenariat. Bureau des technologies d'apprentissage, mai, 105 pages. Savie, Québec (2002)
26. Sauvé, L.: Jeux-cadres en ligne: un outil d'aide pour le concepteur d'environnement d'apprentissage. Nouveau centenaire - nouveaux modèles. Acte du Colloque de l'ACDE/ICDE, 11 pages (2002),
    http://www.cade-aced.ca/icdepapers/sauve.htm
27. Sauvé, L., Samson, D.: Rapport d'évaluation de la coquille générique du Jeu de l'oie du projet. Projet - Jeux génériques : multiplicateurs de contenu multimédia éducatif canadien sur l'inforoute. décembre, 41 pages. Savie and Fonds Inukshuk inc., Québec (2004)
28. Sauvé, L., Renaud, L., Kaufman, D., Marquis, J.-S.: Games and Simulations: the differences. Educational Technology & Society Journal 10(3), 247–256 (2007)
29. Sauvé, L., Hanca, G.: Validation d'une coquille générique de jeu éducatif auprès des enseignants : Parchési [Validation with teachers of a generic educational game shell : Parcheesi] (Research report). Sage and Savie, Québec (2007)
30. Sauvé, L., Renaud, L., Kaufman, D., Sibomana, F.: Revue systématique des écrits (1998-2008) sur les impacts du jeu, de la simulation et du jeu de simulation sur l'apprentissage. Rapport final, avril, 122 pages. Sage and Savie, Québec (2008)
31. Shaffer, D.W., Squire, K.R., Halverson, R., Gee, J.P.: Video games and the future of learning. University of Wisconsin-Madison and Academic Advanced Distributed Learning Co-Laboratory (December 2004) (Consulté le 30 mars 2005 de),
    http://www.academiccolab.org/resources/gappspaper1.pdf
32. Stolovitch, H.D., Thiagarajan, S.: Frame Games. Educational Technology Publications, Englewood Cliffs (1980)
33. Union Européenne En Éducation Des Médias / European Union in Media Education The appropriation of New Media by Youth. A European Research Project, Mediappro (2006)
34. Van Eck, R.: The effect of contextual pedagogical advisement and competition on middle-school students' Attitude toward mathematics and mathematics instruction using a computer-based simulation game. Journal of Computers in Mathematics and Science Teaching 25(1), 165–195 (2006)

Earth and Planetary System Science Game Engine

Gloria J. Brown-Simmons, Falko Kuester, Christopher J.H. Knox,
and So Yamaoka

University of California - Irvine
gbs@uci.edu, fkuester@uci.edu, knoxc@uci.edu,
syamaoka@uci.edu

Abstract. The widespread use of on-line computer games makes the medium a prime vehicle for communicating information and their scalability is especially conducive for facilitating global collaboration focused on developing a better understanding of the underpinnings and complexities of planetary systems beginning with climate change. Game engines generally provide an intuitive interface allowing focus to be shifted to the understanding of scientific elements rather than hiding them between a wealth of menus and other counterintuitive user interface components. Unconventional interaction and visualization techniques are introduced as a method to experience geophysical environments. Players are provided with dynamic visualization "assets," which enable them to discover, interrogate and correlate scientific data in a game space. The spirit of exploration is to give players the impetus to truly understand how complex Earth and planetary systems work and their intrinsic beauty, the impact of humans, and a sense of responsibility to serve as caretakers of those systems.

Keywords: scientific visualization, edutainment, game engines, Earth system science.

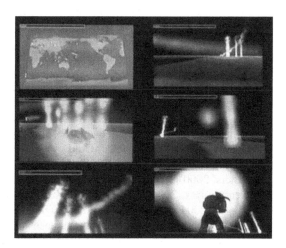

Fig. 1. EPSS-GE

Z. Pan et al. (Eds.): Transactions on Edutainment II, LNCS 5660, pp. 203–218, 2009.
© Springer-Verlag Berlin Heidelberg 2009

1 Motivation

The study of climate change was introduced by the Earth system science (ESS) community and has become a focus of major international Earth observing and modeling campaigns [1, 2]. While ESS data indicates that climate change is heavily influenced by human activity [3, 4], the analysis of climate change data is challenging. Model data sets are time consuming to generate, extremely large, cover long periods of time, and are difficult to interactively examine. Other challenging aspects include communicating the results to students, policy makers and the public in order to support decisions for climate change mitigation and adaptation.

ESS data is not easily accessible to the general public untrained in climate research. Thus, the data and associated Earth processes remain opaque to most people and they are usually not aware of how everyday activities such as their use of natural resources impacts the climate. Therefore, we seek to find ways to engage the public in the pursuit of geophysical and human impact knowledge.

Climate change information is typically disseminated to the public in popular media through newspapers, magazines, radio, television and, with some added artistic freedom, in motion pictures. In his book, Winchester described the global climate change resulting from the massive 1883 Krakatoan volcanic eruption and the technological milestones (communications) which made Krakatoa the first global media event [5]. At least one oral history of the 1883 eruption was passed down through the ages. A Sumatran reported hearing ancestral stories about the eruption and resulting tsunami, which caused him to flee the coastal area upon seeing the ocean recede in anticipation of an ocean born disaster [6]. Popular media has also provided information on global warming and international agreements such as the Kyoto Protocols [7, 8]. Major newspapers often link their on-line news articles to sophisticated model based visualization such as those used to illustrate the 26 December 2004 tsunami [9] with related lesson plans [10].

Scientific visualization techniques for depicting realistic geothermal events, "El Nino," and ozone depletion have been in the public domain since the 1980's when computer graphic techniques were first used to enhance broadcast weather presentations. In 1994, a Washington, DC, NBC subsidiary transformed a segment of their daily weather report into "environmental spots," and the Global Learning and Observations to Benefit the Environment (GLOBE) program produced a weekly "global environmental observation spot" on CNN in 1995. More recently, broadcast news agencies have begun to integrate source material from Google Earth and other on-line GIS ESS portals.

Motion pictures depicting extreme geophysical events are illustrated by such films as Krakatoa (1933); Krakatoa East of Java (Metro- Goldwyn-Mayer, 1969); Twister (Crichton and Martin, Universal and Warner Brothers, 1996); A Perfect Storm (Junger, Warner Brothers, 2000); The Day After Tomorrow (Emmerich and Nachmanoff, 20th Century Fox, 2004); Category 6: Day of Destruction and Category 7: The End of the World (2004 and 2005, CBS). Although the special effects are often pushed past the limits of nature to unsuspecting audiences the hail depicted in The Day After Tomorrow was half the size of the large seven inch hail actually recored in a midwestern U. S. storm [11]. Recent analysis [12] of college students indicate that students have widely varied understandings of ESS and some students base both scientific and non-scientific concepts on information gleaned from diverse sources including prior education in combination with information from popular media and, at times, religion.

Today's students are proficient with several types of interfaces that in many cases govern their lives: cell phone, TV remote controllers, joysticks and game consoles. In a U. S. survey for 2002, 45% of computer households and 30% of non-computer households had a video console; and 22% of computer households and 9% of non-computer households had a hand held computer [13]. The majority of U. S. students are introduced to video, computer and on-line games prior to entering college and most play the games at home [14]. Oblinger [15] calls this generation the "Millennials" and has found that they prefer active learning. Considering that according to the Entertainment Software Association (ESA) surveys, over 50% of Americans play computer and video games, 35% of game players are under 18 [16], and game players are increasingly playing games rather than watching TV [17], this media provides an important and interesting path to disseminate information and stimulate critical thinking. ...

In Canada, Denmark, Japan, Korea, Norway, Sweden, and the U. S., over 50% of the households had access to the Internet by 2003 [18]. Surveys indicate that Korea has the highest percentage of inhabitants with broadband access listed as just under 25% in 2003 which was over twice the approximate percentage of 11% for the U. S. [19]. Combined with the trend towards broadband connectivity users increasingly play games on-line. For example, the massive multiplayer on-line game (MMOG) World of Warcraft enlisted 2M+ U. S. partici- pants, and South Korea's MMOG Lineage enlisted 4M+ subscribers. In addition, the majority of experts in a recent Pew survey estimated that by 2014 90% of all Americans will go online from home [20]. The potential of this home computer/internet and computer/gaming base to engage in planetary system science is enormous, especially considering that "sim" or simulation based games are one of the dominant genres in the game industry. The widespread home technology base and pre-existing knowledge of computer game mechanisms is an advantage when it comes to engaging students and the general public in geophysical play. The potential for on-line simulation games to expand into human environmental impact genres and instill a sense of wonder and excitement towards learning for large collaborating constituencies through immersive game play is a significant motivational factor for our research.

2 Approach

One way of providing game engines with the capability to visualize natural phenomena and climate change data is to create tools for integrating accurate geophysical data. ESS observational data, models and simulations can be used as inputs to game assets to achieve this goal. We categorize ESS games into three major methods: those based on observational data; those based on geophysical models; and those based on integrated assessment models. Observational data is captured by satellites as well as Earth based instruments. In contrast, model data is generated and can be forward looking as in a weather forecast or backward looking to simulate historical patterns. An integrated assessment model is a more complex geophysical model as it provides more control over other parameters impacting climate such as human activity and economics. In addition to observational data being critical for the validation of the developed scientific models, it can be used to enhance simulation data and generate photo-realistic scene effects such as cloud patterns and wind movement. Models and their associated climate change scenarios are useful in constructing mechanisms for complex goal oriented games.

We present a prototype MMOG with an open ended discovery scenario to demonstrate ESS data mapping into multiplayer game space. We provide new types of visualization tools as game assets, called "visualizers," with which to collaboratively explore the data. We address the inability to directly observe the phenomena which Libarkin [12] suggests is a limiting factor to climate change comprehension. Among our overarching goals is for the participants to develop principles of how geophysical models can be "forced" by simply interacting with them; and hopefully, over time see how they can achieve positive environmental results of their collective behavior in the real world. An added benefit is that the ESS integration game tools also provide scientists with a means to rapidly explore large data-sets within a setting that provides a fresh vision. The specifics of the current work focus largely on the first application, however, it should be noted that the tools can be used in alternative interfaces to easily serve the second application.

Our basic assumptions are that the players are in a transient environment in which there are persistent ESS simulations, that the players can all interact with the same simulation, and that the players do not have a deep knowledge of the system's dynamics or a pre-conceived idea of how the data is traditionally visually represented. The research questions we address are how do we best represent data for geophysical systems that are normally not "seen" by players, and how do we provide for interaction with data in such a way as to give the players the direct experience of its' dynamics and spatial configuration.

3 Related Work

There has been much research on the use of simulation and modeling in education. However studying the effectiveness of using ESS scientific visualization in education is a relatively new area of research. There have been a considerable number of studies and materials development for sub-systems (i.e. atmospheres, oceans and land processes), but, there has been very little research in applying these methods to climate change or integrated ESS. Questions related to data representation and visualization interaction have been well researched in traditional scientific visualization and virtual/augmented reality venues, however, they have rarely been addressed for computer games, a medium that has a much greater variance in time and space from the user's point of view. Thus, there is very little research in the area of integrating advanced scientific visualization techniques or ESS modeling into game engines. The background research is drawn from interdisciplinary areas including scientific visualization, visual art, virtual and augmented reality, ESS, modeling and simulation, education and MMOGs; as well as engineering practice for emerging new computational and communication technologies.

Research has been conducted on using models and simulations in ESS learning environments [21, 22, 23]. The majority of the projects are designed for supplemental K-12 curriculum such as EdGCM, Earth System Simulation and the GLOBE program which use ESS models in various ways. EdGCM [24] supports limited parameter boundary manipulation, model runs of the GISS GCM Model II, and interactive analysis of the resulting simulation/visualization; Earth System Simulation [25] focuses on spatial scale by using a series of models including the PSU/NCAR MM5, the NWP, a numerical model for regional atmosphere [26] and a GCM [27]; and GLOBE [28] supports the selection of a number of NOAA NCEP modeling resources that are specifically related to the GLOBE observation suite then presents the simulations as isosurfaced maps. GLOBE is the largest ESS education program with 1M+ participating international students. The public participatory project, Climate Prediction Net [29], with 89K+ registered international participants [30], supports the downloading of APIs to enable processing of HadCM3, HadSM3 and UM model ensembles on globally distributed pc's. The models used by Climate Prediction Net are among the most advanced ESS models disseminated for public processing.

Many exhibits throughout the U. S. now enlist traditional ways to interpret ESS data such as iso-surfaces and pseudo-colored maps. Several natural history museums present pre-computed simulations. The American Museum of Natural History, for example, presents results from models as animation. The Earth mantel model TERRA, the Parallel Ocean Program (POP) model and the Regional Atmospheric Modeling System (RAMS) [31] are included in the Earth Hall exhibition. The AMNH models are among the most scientifically accurate available on public display. For example, the POP model uses 20 non-uniformly spaced depth levels and bathymetry. The resulting visualization includes "hill shading" techniques to depict large surface structures. Particle traces were also used to identify surface circulation patterns.

Computer ESS games available to the public include an early very popular single player climate change game titled SimEarth (Maxis) based on the GAIA model [32]. The game was well received by the gaming community, teachers and the lay public, but, the computational time delay often frustrated the players. The GAIA and geophysical models underlying the game produced various simulations and forecasts including ocean circulation, atmospheric circulation, and mantle tectonic movement. The game remains one of the more sophisticated examples of an environmental literacy game. The technological factors that were detrimental and limiting to SimEarth have, for the most part, been resolved since SimEarth's premier in 1991. Maxis has produced other "sims" including their most recent multiplayer Spore which has implications for disseminating concepts related to ESS including geological time and climate change. Role playing multiplayer interactive games include NCAR's Disaster Dynamics [33]; and NitroGenius based on the Integrated Nitrogen Impact Assessment Model on a Regional Scale (INITIATOR), representing processes in the nitrogen chain [34]. Only a tiny fraction of ESS simulations have been presented to the public due to their vast size and the lack of widely accessible scientific visualization methods.

Educators have proven the effectiveness of using models and simulations in games as they observed methods for soliciting ones ability to understand events using features that are characteristic of games. Winn [35] states that games can "exploit challenge, curiosity and, to some extent, fantasy in order to heighten presence" increasing the players abilities to "observe and reason about what they observe" in order to understand events. Kleiboer [36] has shown that games also provide "occasions for decision, allowing for the enactment of roles and direct experience with the immediacy of simulations." These methods have direct relevance to games focused on environmental behavior since human induced climate change is of the "complex curricular nature" Winn identifies as being the type of learning problem especially well suited for immersive computer games.

Simulation games have demonstrated that the public can gain a sense of ownership and control through the use of interactive environmental simulation. Furthermore, these games are popular because they are fun and challenging, encouraging long term engagement and a significant commitment to learn the simulation model and is properties. Learning theorists studying the use of these mechanisms believe '...microworlds as Papert defines them, claim their autonomy by providing tangible and shareable externalizations of hidden aspects of a "reality." Their purpose is to bring to the fore for exploration, and combine in novel ways some important underlying mechanisms otherwise unnoticed' [37].

One aspect of climate change comprehension through geophysical visualization is the identification of visual constructs that match the geophysical system under study to visually trigger the cognitive processes. Kepes [38], Marr [39] and Zeki [40] provide a continuum of visual theory relevant to visualization with ever increasing accuracy. Common to their theories are the perceptual features of primal vision: motion, contrast, form and perspective (direction). Experimentation in perceptual techniques for ESS visualization [41] illustrates these features as used by biological vision systems to capture visual attention and identify what is being seen. These cognitive functions have been observed to be most active during the preattentive state [42] and are well suited for communicating the properties of geophysical systems in transient spaces where reducing the time it takes to appreciate a construct is critical. ..

Perceptual techniques are useful in addressing questions raised by educational theorists who have focused on the problems associated with "verbal overshadowing" demonstrating the need to allow for deeper use of visual skills during learning processes. Perceptual attributes can be seen in the kinetic visualization described in Lum et al. [43, 44]. Kinetics have been shown to exploit motion while effectively funneling representations through to visual understanding [45]. Particle systems are a type of kinetic visualization. Particle visualization techniques have been described by Bruckschen et al. [46] and Kuester et al. [47] for interactive immersive environments. Particle visualization techniques have been implemented for game engines by Kruger and Westermann [48].

The challenges and advantages of using game engines specifically for scientific visualization have been described by Rhyne [49, 50] and Lewis and Jacobson [51]. Techniques for modeling geophysical phenomena have until recently treated the world as a solid object [52]. Global time stamp based scalable frameworks, an underlying mechanism relevant to ESS data and game engine integration, have been researched by Kim et al. [53]. Research on methods to render natural phenomena using game engines has been described by Fritsch and Kaka [54]; Perbet and Cani [55], Chenney [56] and Shi et al. [57] for wind effects; and Harris [58] and Umenhoffer and Szirmay [59] for impostor clouds. The re-purposing of game engine technologies for other related areas include Zyda [60]; Herwig and Paar [61] and Stang [62] for landscapes; Jacobson [63] for VR; McGrath and Hill [64] and Ryan et al. [65] for simulation; and Laird [66] for artificial intelligence.

4 The EPSS-GE

We have developed a prototype for an Earth and planetary system science game engine (EPSSGE) to provide a means for very large groups of individuals to collectively interact with accurate geophysical simulations informed by the best data available in addition to streaming inputs from modeling resources. The EPSS-GE is designed to support a range of applications built for client side game engines (CGE). The demonstration EPSS-GE CGE is envisioned as an open ended discovery game using Intergovernmental Panel on Climate Change (IPCC) models as the simulation engine with interaction provided through a simple interface. The EPSS-GE CGE supports interaction with ESS data in a nonphotorealistic abstract form by employing data reduction and aesthetically biased symbolic representations designed for a fast paced transient environment (immersive game scene) and subtle player interaction mechanisms. The goal of our closely monitored reciprocal feedback is to give the players a virtual representation of the dynamics of the geophysical system they are exploring.

The use of geophysical data and models in games for scientific visualization has until now been limited by game architecture, the lack of ESS data ingest handlers, and the lack of data visualization techniques appropriate for MMOGs. Thus, the focus of the EPSS-GE work is the reduction, transformation and translation of scientific visualization into CGE technology. The project combines aspects of grid computing, distributed simulation and visualization with scientifically anchored ESS data in order to study real-time computer graphics and multi-modal interaction, in the context of multiplayer gaming frameworks. This also requires a new paradigm for network interaction that fuses CGEs (specifically MMOGs) with complex scientific simulations while dealing with the heterogeneous resources. The latter calls for adaptive technology to automatically scale (reduce in size and complexity) the presented contents to satisfy local processing, networking and interface limitations. At the core of this work are the processing of ESS data by highly responsive systems and the translation of data analysis techniques into new game methodologies.

Real-time game engine scene handling techniques by default support perceptually based image recognition. For example, the low resolution of background elements (terrain detail) deemphasize them so that processing can be devoted to elements that require a higher level-ofdetail which in our example are the scientific visualization constructs. We explored perceptual techniques for scientific visualization and selected kinetic methods as they are especially well suited for the analysis of geophysical systems. Kinetics are supported as particle systems within the EPSS-GE prototype CGE application. The "player" encounters phenomena first by motion, then motion and form, and then color. The normally invisible atmospheric substances are dynamically etched out from space through player interaction.

4.1 Data

The most recent IPCC data for the Fourth Assessment Report (AR4) consists of an ensemble of 20+ model results of 100 year time series simulations, spanning the years 2000-2100, for a range of different scenarios. The data set contains over 100 variables. Among the relevant variables are surface precipitation, surface temperature, air temperature, wind direction, net downward short wave flux in air, net upward longwave flux in air, and cloud area fraction. The variables are calculated on a longitude, latitude, and altitude grid. The models use different surface grid resolutions ranging from 72 x 46 to 360 x 256 with a range of different grid types. Our prototype EPSS-GE uses the IPCC AR4 INM-CM3.0 model from the Institute for Numerical Mathematics in Moscow [67] for rapid prototyping. INM-CM3.0 has a 5 x 4 degree resolution in longitude and latitude and 21 vertical levels. The second model used in the prototype is the National Center for Atmospheric Research's (NCAR) Community Climate System Model (CCSM) [68] for a 720 CO_2 stabilization scenario. CCSM has a 360 x 256 degree resolution in longitude and latitude and 21 vertical levels. The CCSM, with a horizontal resolution at the equator of approximately 1.4 x 1.4 degrees, is the highest resolution model within the IPCC AR4 ensemble and produces data sets that are approximately an order of magnitude larger than those produced by the INM-CM3.0 model.

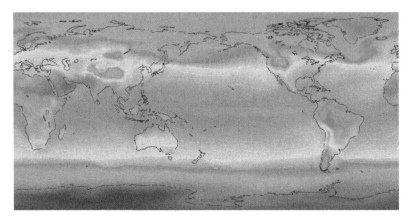

Fig. 2. Average Surface Temperature Jan 2000, NCAR CCSM

Data Reader. In order to ingest the IPCC model data, we implemented an EPSS-GE Networked Common Data Format (NetCDF) reader. NetCDF's widespread adoption by the ESS and space sciences ensures our ability to inquest a wide variety of data and to compare the results of the ESS models. The EPSS-GE NetCDF asset loads the NetCDF data and makes the data available to other game assets (implemented as specific visualization tools) for interactive 3D space exploration. The NetCDF asset is a data-only game asset invisible to players and was built using a publicly available NetCDF library [69].

4.2 Visualization Assets

A set of game assets for visualization of ESS data, called "visualizers," is supported within the CGE application enabling the players to interactively explore the environment. Each visualizer probes the properties of the ESS data in a different way. Conventional visualization strategies for scientific data, are frequently focused on the extraction of iso-contours or surfaces, identification of gradients, interfaces and characterization of vector fields. To provide more flexibility and a means for the intuitive exploration of complex relationships by experts as well as novice users, a set of particle-based approaches for data interrogation is introduced. Global surface temperature data was selected as one of the core parameters and served as the basis for the development of the three visualizers which can be manipulated in multiplayer mode.

RPE - Responsive Particle Emitter. A RPE is a basic particle visualizer, which draws from a combination of color mapping, velocity mapping, and direct time

Fig. 3. Responsive Particle Emitter

Fig. 4. Directional Constant-velocity Particle Emitter

mapping techniques. The RPE responds to the data in two ways. 1) Velocity is mapped such that particles go up in the hotter areas and go down in the colder areas. 2) The hotter the surface temperature is the more reddish, the colder the more bluish. These effects combine such that the RPE emulates a fire or smoke in a hot area and chilled air in a cold area. The velocity mapping is influenced by the behavior of the gaseous matter in the real world to help a player understand the surface temperature data. In addition, time advancement of the data is one parameter of this visualizer.

DCPE - Directional Constant-velocity Particle Emitter. A DCPE is a particle stream visualizer traveling upward at a constant velocity and utilizing time-height mapping. The time axis is set to the vertical axis of the 3D game space extending from the first time step to the end of the series. The player can observe the particles assume the color associated with datum as they pass through levels. Each level corresponds to a single (monthly) time step. The data set contains 1,200 time steps corresponding to one hundred years. The vertical time axis for the DCPE was bound to three years, limiting the time scale, in order to present the data at a resolution that was more accommodating of exploration for the temperature data set. The length of displayable years is a variable which also defines how long the particles stay within the game space.

DFPE - Directional Focus Particle Emitter. A DFPE visualizer emits particles along the player's viewing direction. The particles fill a small deltaic region in front of the player. The DFPE is particularly useful in illuminating areas of the data space in collaboration with other players. The time mapping of this asset can be either time advancement mapping or timeheight mapping.

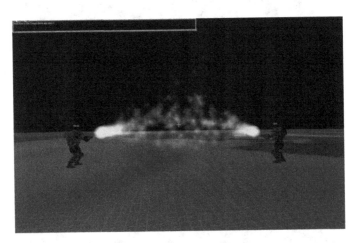

Fig. 5. Directional Focus Particle Emitter

4.3 Game Play

Single Player Mode. A player is randomly placed into the geospatially referenced 3D game space containing surface temperature data and a global reference base map as the "game board." The space also contains the interactive visualizers. The player can freely walk around the game space, and can manipulate the position and function of the visualizer assets. The player can pick a visualizer up and observe its color change as the player walks through the data space. The player can throw the visualizer around data space, for instance, to observe it as it moves about from any distance. The visualizer assets are automatically regenerated at certain locations, providing an infinite supply of assets. Since the visualizers will not disappear from the virtual space while the game is running, the player can propagate visualizers throughout the game space as long as the computational resources are sufficient.

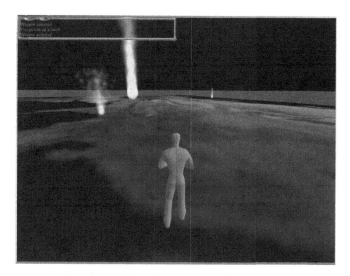

Fig. 6. Single Player Mode

Multiplayer Mode. The Torque Game Engine (TGE) was selected due to its open architecture and networking capability. The number of players is bounded by the bandwidth of the network and computational power of the computer. Multiplayer mode, a collaborative exploration of the data space, is an important aspect of our research in the use of MMOGs to develop climate change concepts. In multiplayer mode, the player sees other players exploring the same data space and can interact with them. Players can exchange visualizers, chat via a chatting window, and collaboratively explore the data space. With increased numbers of players and their particle emitter assets, larger areas of the data are revealed providing the players with more views of the geophysical structures.

5 Observations and Conclusions

EPSS-GE was evaluated on HIPerWall, a massively tiled display aimed at facilitating interaction with, and analysis of, complex scientific information; and utilized Calit2's LambdaRail optical network, the OptIPuter, designed to enable scientists generating terabytes and petabytes of data to interactively analyze data from multiple mass storage sites. EPSS-GE has also been exhibited as a six station installation for the Tenth Biennial Arts and Technology Symposium, Ammerman Center, Connecticut College, USA [70].

Adapting traditional game mechanisms to support collaborative geophysical experiences, in addition to incorporating unconventional visualization techniques, provided a vehicle for the students to transition from game play to geophysical analysis. The game play was very engaging as evidenced by highly focused continuous sessions and meta-game activities using dialogue to develop strategies when the EPSS-GE was presented using side-by-side terminals. We believe that the kinetic environment and the entities within it were extremely important for perception. Since the particles are flowing and changing colors as they pass through datum, the players perceive the geophysical structure as a kinetic structure. This is fundamentally different from deducing the same structure from a more traditional two dimensional representation of the data [71, 72]. This representational technique not only relayed the inherent dynamic quality and beauty of the geophysical system under study but also exploited the transient visual characteristics of fast paced game space and technology of game engines. We plan to further exploit kinetics as this type of motion is one of the important primary vehicles leading to understanding, and thus learning, in addition to exploring a range of other visualization strategies that support specific cognitive processes related to the geosciences. We also plan to test diasporic community use of the system in order to observe game play without close physical proximity and verbal meta-game activity.

Acknowledgments

The EPSS-GE was produced at the University of California - Irvine (UCI), as a collaboration between the Department of Earth System Science, the Department of Electrical Engineering and Computer Science, the Game Culture and Technology Laboratory and the California Institute for Telecommunications and Information Technology (Calit2) UCI Division. This research was supported, in part, by the UCI Council on Research Computing and Library Resources (CoRCLR) under award number MI- 2005-2006-26; the Calit2 Graduate Student Fellowship program, and by an HP Technology for Teaching Grant under award number 15923. The above support is greatly appreciated. The authors acknowledge Professor Charles S. Zender, Director, Earth System Modeling Facility, Department of Earth System Science, UCI, for contributing his expertise and generosity in sharing ESS models and data; Michael Brown, SURF-IT Fellow, UCI, for generating the unified data sets; Daniel Repasky for modeling Bauhaus Man and the terrain features; Albert F. Yee, Calit2 UCI Director, and Larry Smarr, Calit2 Director, for their support; Steve Cutchin, Steve Jenks, Joerg Meyer, Robert F. Nideffer, Celia Pearce, and Walter Scacchi for their discussions on game technology.

References

[1] Molina, M.J., Sherwood Rowland, F.: Stratospheric sink for chlorofluoromethanes: Chlorine atom catalysed destruction of ozone. Nature 249, 810–812 (1974)

[2] Houghton, J.: Global Warming: The Complete Briefing, 3rd edn. Cambridge University Press, Cambridge (2004)

[3] Alley, R., Berntsen, T., Bindoff, N.L., Chen, Z., Chidthaisong, A., Friedlingstein, P., Gregory, J., Hegerl, G., Heimann, M., Hewitson, B., Hoskins, B., Joos, F., Jouzel, J., Kattsov, V., Lohmann, U., Manning, M., Matsuno, T., Molina, M., Nicholls, N., Overpeck, J., Qin, D., Raga, G., Ramaswamy, V., Ren, J., Rusticucci, M., Solomon, S., Somerville, R., Stocker, T.F., Stott, P., Stouffer, R.J., Whetton, P., Wood, R.A., Wratt, D.: Climate Change 2007: The Physical Science Basis, Summary for Policymakers, Working Group I to the Fourth Assessment Report of the Intergovernmental Panel on Climate Change (IPCC). WMO and UNEP, Paris (February 2007)

[4] Sherwood Rowland, F.: Atmospheric changes caused by human activities: From science to regulation. Ecology Law Quarterly 27(4), 1261–1293 (2001)

[5] Winchester, S.: Krakatoa: The Day the World Exploded, August 27, 1883. Harper Collins, New York (2003)

[6] Unidentified Sumatran native. Special coverage of the Sumatran earthquake. CNN cable broadcast (December 2004)

[7] Global warming, bulletins from a warmer world. National Geographic, 206(3) (September 2004)

[8] Kolbert, E.: The climate of man. The New Yorker (2005); Part I April 25 81.10:56-71, Part II May 2 81.11:64-73, Part III May 9 81.12:52-63

[9] Titov, V.V., Murty, T.: Asia's Deadly Waves Simulation. New York Times Interactive Feature,
http://www.nytimes.com/packages/khtml/~2004/12/26/international/~0041227QUAKEFEATURE.html

[10] Bank Street College of Education. Asia's Deadly Waves Lesson Plans. New York Times on the Web Learning Network,
http://nytimes.com/learning/issuesindepth/20050104.html

[11] Zender, C.S.: There's Got To Be A Morning After 'The Day After Tomorrow. The Orange County Weekly 9(35), 24 (2004)

[12] Libarkin, J.C., Anderson, S.W., Science, J.D., Beilfuss, M., Boone, W.: Qualitative analysis of college students' ideas about the Earth: Interviews and open-ended questionnaires. Journal of Geoscience Education 53(1), 17–26 (2005)

[13] Venkatesh, A., Kruse, E., Shih, E.C.-F.: The networked home: An analysis of current developments and future trends. Cognition, Technology and Work 5(1), 23–32 (2003)

[14] Jones, S.: Let the Games Begin, Gaming Technology and Entertainment Among College Students. Pew Internet and American Life Project, Pew Research Center (July 2003)

[15] Oblinger, D.G.: The next generation of educational engagement. Journal of Interactive Media in Education, Special Issue on the Educational Semantic Web 8, 1–18 (2004)

[16] ESA. Entertainment software association facts and research, game player data,
http://www.theesa.com/facts/~gamerdata.php
(downloaded, September 2005)

[17] Lowenstein, D.: State of the industry address (May 18, 2005), Speech Delivered at the 11th Electronic Entertainment Expo. (September 2005),
http://www.theesa.com/archives/2005/05/e32005state01.php

[18] Information and Communications Technologies, OECD Information Technology Outlook. Organization for Economic Co-Operation and Development (OECD) (2004)

[19] Information and Communications Technologies, OECD Communications Outlook. Organization for Economic Co- Operation and Development (OECD) (2005)

[20] Fox, S., Anderson, J.Q., Rainie, L.: The Future of the Internet. Pew Internet and American Life Project, Pew Research Center (January 2005); Chart: How respondents assessed predictions about the impact of the internet in the next decade, page vi

[21] Gobert, J.: Harnessing technology to support on-line model building and peer collaboration. In: Proceedings of the Teaching Geoscience With Visualization: Using Images, Animations, and Models Effectively Conference, on the cutting edge, February 2004, pp. 10–30 (2004)

[22] Jackson, D.F.: Case studies of microcomputer and interactive video simulations in middle school Earth science teaching. Journal of Science Education and Technology 6(2), 127–141 (1997)

[23] Jackson, S.L., Hu, J.T., Soloway, E.: Scienceworks modeler: Scaffolding the doing of science. In: Conference Companion CHI 1994, ACM CHI, pp. 249– 250 (April 1994)

[24] Chandler, M.A., Shopsin, M., Richards, S., Sohl, L.E.: The Basic Guide to EdGCM, Draft v.2.3.4. Columbia University, New York (2005)

[25] Thompson, O.E., Johnson, D., Kalnay, E., Zhang, D., Cai, M., Suarez, M., Yanuk, D., Schaack, T.: Computationally intensive models in the classroom. Journal of Earth System Science Education 1, 1–13 (2001)

[26] Arkin, P.A., Thompson, O.E., Bonner, W.D.: Diurnal variations of the summertime wind and force field at three midwestern locations. Monthly Weather Review 104, 1012–1022 (1976)

[27] Held, I.M., Suarez, M.J.: A two level primitive equation model designed for climatic sensitivity experiments. Journal of Atmospheric Sciences 35, 206–229 (1978)

[28] GLOBE. GLOBE visualization data directory (2005), http://viz.globe.gov (downloaded March 16, 2005)

[29] Stainforth, D., Kettleborough, J., Martin, A., Simpson, A., Gills, R., Akkas, A., Gualt, R., Collins, M., Gavagham, D., Allen, M.: ClimatePrediction.Net: Design principles for public-resource modeling research. In: Proceedings of the 14th IASTED International Conference, Parallel and Distributed Computing and Systems, pp. 32–38. International Association of Science and Technology for Development (IASTED) (November 2002)

[30] ClimatePrediction.Net, http://www.climateprediction.net (downloaded, August 2005)

[31] McPherson, A., Painter, J., McCormick, P., Ahrens, J., Ragsdale, C.: Visualizations of Earth processes for the American Museum of Natural History. Computer Graphics, 11–15 (February 1999)

[32] Wilson, J.L.: The SimEarth bible. Osborne McGraw-Hill, Berkeley (1991)

[33] McGinnis, S.: Disaster Dynamics: Serious Games for Disaster Education. National Center for Atmospheric Research (NCAR), http://swiki.ucar.edu/~dd/

[34] Erisman, J.W., Hensen, A., de Vries, W., Kros, H., van de Wal, T., de Winter, W., Wien, J.E., van Elswijk, M., Maat, M.: The Nitrogen Decision Support System: NitroGenius, ECN-C-02-012. Energy Research Center of the Netherlands (ECN), Petten (2002)

[35] Winn, W., Windschitl, M., Fruland, R., Lee, Y.: When does immersion in a virtual environment help students construct understanding. In: Proceedings of the International Conference of the Learning Sciences, ICLS 2002, October 2002, pp. 497–503. International Society for the Learning Sciences, ISLS (2002)

[36] Kleiboer, M.: Simulation methodology for crisis management support. Journal of Contingencies and Crisis Management 5(4), 198–206 (1997)

[37] Edith Ackermann. (Y. Kafai and M. Resnieck Eds.) Constructionism in Practice: Designing, thinking, and learning in a digital world, chapter 2 Perspectivetaking and object construction: Two keys to learning, pages 25–37. Mahwah, N.J.: Lawrence Erlbaum, Associates, Inc., 1996.

[38] Kepes, G.: The Language of Vision. Paul Theobald, Chicago (1944)

[39] Marr, D.: Vision: a computational investigation into the human representation and processing of visual information. W.H. Freeman, San Francisco (1982)

[40] Zeki, S.: Inner Vision: An Exploration of Art and the Brain. Oxford University Press, Oxford (2000)

[41] Healey, C.G., Enns, J.T.: Perception and painting: A search for effective, engaging visualizations. IEEE Computer Graphics and Applications 22(2), 10–15 (2002)

[42] Healey, C.G., Booth, K.S., Enns, J.T.: High-speed visual estimation using preattentive processing. ACM Transactions on Computer-Human Interaction 3(2), 107–125 (1996)

[43] Lum, E.B., Stompel, A., Ma, K.-L.: Kinetic visualization: A technique for illustrating 3D shape and structure. In: Proceedings of IEEE Visualization 2002, pp. 435–442 (2002)

[44] Lum, E.B., Stompel, A., Ma, K.-L.: Using motion to illustrate static 3D shape - kinetic visualization. IEEE Transactions on Visualization and Computer Graphics 9(2), 115–126 (2003)

[45] Zeki, S., Lamb, M.: The neurology of kinetic art. Brain 117, 607–636 (1994)

[46] Bruckschen, R., Kuester, F., Hamann, B., Joy, K.I.: Real-time out-of-core visualization of particle traces. In: Proceedings of the Parallel and Large Scale Data Visualization and Graphics Symposium, pp. 45–50. IEEE, Los Alamitos (2001)

[47] Kuester, F., Bruckschen, R., Hamann, B., Joy, K.I.: Visualization of particle traces in virtual environments. In: Proceedings of the Virtual Reality Software and Technology Conference, VRST 2001. ACM SIGCHI and SIGGRAPH, pp. 151–157 (November 2001)

[48] Kruger, J., Westermann., R.: GPU simulation and rendering of volumetric effects for computer games and virtual environments. In: Proceedings of Eurographics 2005. European Association for Computer Graphics (August-September 2005)

[49] Rhyne, T.-M.: Computer games' influence on scientific and information visualization. IEEE Computer 33(12), 154–156 (2000)

[50] Rhyne, T.-M.: Computer games and scientific visualization. Communications of the ACM 45(7), 40–44 (2002)

[51] Lewis, M., Jacobson, J.: Game engines in scientific research. Communications of the ACM 45(1), 27–31 (2002)

[52] Johnston, D.: 3D game engines as a new reality. In: Proceedings of the 4th Annual CM316 Conference on Multimedia Systems. Southampton University, UK (January 2004), http://mms.ecs.soton.ac.uk/mms2004.dj301.pdf (downloaded November 2005)

[53] Kim, S.-J., Kuester, F., Kim, K.H(K.): A global timestampbased scalable framework for multi-player online games. In: Proceedings of the Fourth International Symposium on Multimedia Software Engineering (MSE 2002), pp. 2–10. Institute of Electrical and Electronics Engineers. IEEE Computer Society (2002)

[54] Fritsch, D., Kada, M.: Visualization using game engines. In: Proceedings of the XXth Congress, Commission 5, 35.B5, pp. 627–631. International Society of Photogrammetry and Remote Sensing (IAPRS) (July 2004)

[55] Perbet, F., Cani, M.-P.: Animating prairies in real-time. In: Proceedings of the Symposium on Interactive 3D Graphics, I3D 2001, pp. 103–110. ACM, New York (2001)

[56] Chenney, S.: Flow tiles. In: Proceedings of the 2004 ACM SIGGRAPH/Eurographics Symposium on Computer Animation, SCA 2004, August 2004, pp. 233–242. ACM SIGGRAPH/ Eurographics (2004)

[57] Shi, L., Yu, Y., Wojtan, C., Chenney, S.: Contollable motion synthesis in a gaseous medium. The Visual Computer 21(7), 474–487 (2005)

[58] Harris, M.J.: Real-time cloud rendering for games. In: Programming Track, Proceedings of the Game Developers Conference (GDC), March 2002, pp. 1–5 (2002)

[59] Umenhoffer, T., Kalos, L.S.: Real-time rendering of cloudy natural phenomena with hierarchical depth imposters. In: Proceedings of Eurographics 2005. European Association
for Computer Graphics (August-September 2005)

[60] Zyda, M.: From visual simulation to virtual reality to games. IEEE Computer 38(9), 25–
32 (2005)

[61] Herwig, A., Paar, P.: Game Engines: Tools for Landscape Visualization and Planning?
In: Trends in GIS and Virtualization in Environmental Planning and Design, Anhalt University of Applied Sciences, pp. 162–171. Wichmann Verlag, Heidelberg (2002)

[62] Stang, B.: Game Engines: Features and Possibilities. Institute of Information and Mathematical Modeling @ The Technical University of Denmark (IMM DTU) (September
2003)

[63] Jacobson, J.: Using "CaveUT" to build immersive displays with the unreal tournament
engine and a pc cluster. In: Proceedings of the Symposium on Interactive 3D Graphics,
I3D 2003, pp. 221–222. ACM, New York (2003)

[64] McGrath, D., Hill, D.: Unrealtriage: A game-based simulation for emergency response.
In: Proceedings of the 2004 Huntsville Simulation Conference (HSC 2004). The Society
for Modeling and Simulation International (October 2004) CDROM HSC121.pdf

[65] Ryan, M., Hill, D., Mc-Grath, D.: Simulation interoperability with a commercial game
engine. In: Proceedings of the European Simulation Interoperability Workshop. Simulation Interoperability Standards Organization (SISO) (June 2005) CDROM 05E-SIW-
043.pdf

[66] Laird, J.E.: Research in human-level AI using computer games. Communications of the
ACM 45(1), 32–35 (2002)

[67] Dianski, N.A., Volodin, E.M.: Simulation of present-day climate with a coupled atmos-
phere-ocean general circulation model. Izvestiya. Atmospheric and Oceanic Physics
(English Translation) 38(6), 732–747 (2002)

[68] Collins, W.D., Bitz, C.M., Blackmon, M.L., Bonan, G.B., Bretherton, C.S., Carton, J.A.,
Chang, P., Doney, S.C., Hack, J.J., Henderson, T.B., Kiehl, J.T., Large, W.G., McKenna,
D.S., Santer, B.D., Smith, R.D.: The community climate system model: CCSM3. For
Journal of Climate Special Issue on CCSM (2005),
http://www.ccsm.ucar.edu/publications/~jclim04/Papers/
SSC1.pdf

[69] Unidata. Network Common Data Form (NetCDF), NetCDF-3.6.0-p1 library (2005),
http://www.unidata.ucar.edu/software/netcdf/

[70] Brown-Simmons, G.J., Kuester, F., Knox, C.J.H., Yamaoka, S., Repasky, D.G.: Kepesian
visualization: Interacting with Earth data. In: Proceedings of Connectivity, the Tenth Biennial Arts and Technology Symposium at Connecticut College, pp. 25–36. Ammerman
Center, Connecticut College, New London (2006)

[71] Scharl, A.: Environmental online communication. Springer, New York (2004)

[72] Halls, P.J. (ed.): Spatial Information and the Environment. Taylor and Francis Inc.,
London (2001)

A XML Tree Based Leveled Filtering Method and Its Application[*]

Jiming Chen [1,2], Yan Zhuang [2], Shiguang Ju [1], and Jingui Pan [2]

[1] School of Computer Science and Telecommunications Engineering,
Jiangsu University, Zhenjiang, 212013, China
[2] State Key Lab for Novel Software Technology, Nanjing University,
Nanjing, 210093, China
jmchen@ujs.edu.cn, zhuangyan@mes.nju.edu.cn, jushig@ujs.edu.cn,
panjg@mes.nju.edu.cn

Abstract. The system's scalability is an important problem in the research of distributed virtual environment. By combining XML technology with active leveled interest management, a new XML tree based leveled filtering method – LevelFilter is presented in this paper. LevelFilter evaluates the level of interests among objects via the similarity matching of XML trees, and processes leveled packet filtering on active routers. Finally, by applying LevelFilter to the design of motion LOD (Level of Detail) in virtual human simulation system, it can manipulate the content detail of virtual human by the DOCBF (Detail of Content Based Filtering) to reduce traffic load. Therefore, LevelFilter can highly improve the system's scalability.

Keywords: XML, active leveled interest management, LevelFilter, motion LOD.

1 Introduction

Active interest management, which combines active routing techniques and the content-based publish/subscribe model, provides an effective solution to the scalability problem in distributed virtual environments[1,2]. In active interest management system, the relationship between publishers and subscribers is shielded. As a result, it reduces the coupling among participants in the distributed virtual environment and improves the system scalability. On the other hand, active routers have some special computing and executing capacities in processing, forwarding and filtering data packets; therefore, while expressing object interests, participants can also indicate interest levels which can be used to help active routers control the content detail of data packets. Thus, based on the dynamic communication relationship in active interest management, the system can achieve active leveled interest management, which not only reduces the amount of data packets that hosts receive, but also effectively reduces the network traffic, so as to further enhances the scalability of the distributed virtual environment [3,4].

---

[*] This paper was supported by the National Science Foundation of China under Grant Nos. 60533080, 60773049.

Z. Pan et al. (Eds.): Transactions on Edutainment II, LNCS 5660, pp. 219–227, 2009.

Nowadays, there are some problems in applying active leveled interest management to distributed virtual environments. First, because of the large number of the factors affecting interest levels, such as distance, size, eccentricity, speed, aura area, information radiation and so on, it is hard to describe all these factors comprehensively and reasonably. Second, various elements are added as properties into the fixed positions of a packet during the implementation of active leveled interest management. It not only limits the ability in expressing object interests, but also relies on specific applications and needs to define fixed transfer protocol format and apply appropriate leveled filtering algorithms which are not universal.

XML can facilitate the description of conceptual models with pluralistic relationships. It makes the conceptual model more easily to be expressed and understood. Describing interest information in the distributed virtual environment based on XML will not only provide a uniform transfer format, but also improve the ability to express information and extend the information description. Therefore, this paper applies XML technology to active leveled interest management and proposes a new leveled filtering method based on XML tree – LevelFilter. According to the characteristics of distributed virtual environments, this method uses XML to express publications and subscriptions of objects, calculates the interest degree based on similarity of XML trees, determines the interest level and achieves level filtering. Finally, we apply LevelFilter into the design of virtual human movement Level of Detail (LOD) simulation system and demonstrate the feasibility and effectiveness of the technology via the experimental results.

2 LevelFilter

2.1 XML Tree

In distributed event models, the publication and subscription of objects are usually described in predicate expressions composed of a number of attributes. The relationship among these attributes is logic "and", and only the data satisfying all attributes are within the scope of subscription; whereas the relationship between different expressions is logic "or" [5]. In distributed virtual environment systems, using predicate expressions to describe the interest regions of publication and subscription limits the expression ability and is not universal. Moreover, the predicate expression can only be used to calculate whether the publication and subscription match, but unable to calculate the matching degree of interest regions between publication and subscription, which is the interest degree among objects.

In this paper, we use Node-Labeled XML trees to describe the publication and subscription of objects. Each node of the tree corresponds to an attribute of the object, and the weight (from 0 to 1) of each edge indicates the importance of each attribute.

In an n-node XML tree ($N^t = \bigcup_{1 \le i \le n} N_i$), its leaf nodes are called N^l and non-leaf nodes are called N^f , i.e., $N^t = N^l \cap N^f$. For each non-leaf node $N_i^f \in N^f (1 \le i \le n)$, we define:

$$\underset{1\le k\le n\wedge f(N_k)=N_i^f}{U} w(N_k) \;=\; 1 \tag{1}$$

In which, $f(N_k)$ denotes parent nodes of N_k, and $w(N_k)$ is the weight of its corresponding edge.

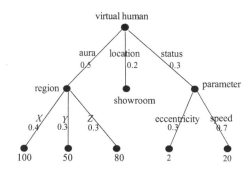

Fig. 1. XML tree of virtual human movement information

Meanwhile, in order to improve the similarity matching efficiency of XML trees, it is necessary to arrange the edges on the same level in a certain order when generating an XML tree. Figure 1 shows an XML tree of virtual human movement information, in which edge labels on the same level are arranged in the alphabetical order: aura, location and status. Moreover, the sum of edge values on the same level is 1(e.g., 0.5+0.2+0.3=1).

2.2 Procedure of Leveled Filtering

In the active interest management system, active routers can not only provide the ability of injecting routing code, but also have memory and executive capabilities to store routing information and compile and execute injected codes. The use of such active routers will facilitate the achievement of active leveled interest management in distributed virtual environment. Figure 2 shows the flow of leveled packet filtering in active routers, and the main functional modules are as follows:

Packet Listener: data monitoring module, receives data from upstream, downstream active routers or hosts which mainly contain publishing and subscribing data (XML information).

Message Pre-processor: information pre-processing module, pre-processes XML information, including decompression, SAX parsing and schema check, in which schema check is mainly used for verifying legitimacy of XML information from users. If the information comes from other routers, this step can be skipped to avoid duplicated check.

Generation Pre-processor: generation pre-processing module, reconstructs XML information and converts it into a Node-Labeled XML tree. In order to make the similarity computation reasonable and comparable, it is necessary to conduct standardization and check for each attribute.

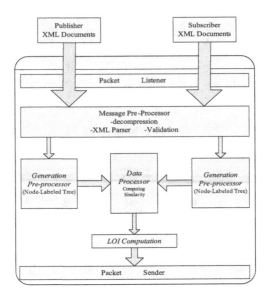

Fig. 2. Flow of leveled packet filtering

Data Process: data processing module, matches Node-Labeled XML trees generated by publishers and subscribers, and calculates their similarity.

LOI Computation: leveled filtering module, determines the matching degree according to the predefined leveled interest formula and filters packets based on the degree. At present, there are two packet filter methods: Detail of Content Based Filtering (DOCBF) and Frequency Based Filtering (FBF). If packets are sorted according to their importance, DOCBF can be used to discard secondary details by levels. If packets are cyclical but interest levels of subscribers are not necessary to update frequently, FBF can be selected.

Packet Sender: Output module, encapsulates the results from the above processes and puts into output pipes before sending them to the corresponding routers or users in UDP protocol.

Based on the above function modules, the processing flow of the leveled filtering method can be described as follows: first, Packet Listener module keeps monitoring and receiving packets from other routers and hosts; second, Message Pre-processor module conducts SAX parsing and effective check for the XML information in received packets, and then deals with it according to the following two situations: ①If packets are subscription message, Generation Pre-processor module will reconstruct the XML data of packets and convert them into Node-Labeled XML trees to create a filter engine that meets the requirements of similarity algorithm module structure; ②If packets are publication message, Generation Pre-processor module will conduct SAX parsing and convert them into XML trees, and then Data Process module will calculate the similarity between the newly generated XML trees and XML trees stored in the routing table; next, LOI Computation module decides their matching degree based on the designed interest levels and achieves leveled filtering via DOCBF or FBF; finally, results are sent to Packet Sender module and further forwarded to appropriate users.

3 LevelFilter in the Movement LOD Simulation

3.1 Movement LOD Design

In 1976, Clark proposed the concept of LOD, claiming that the farther the distance between objects and observers, the fewer details that can be identified; in other words, a lower resolution model can be applied to farther objects. In 1995, researchers from the U.S. Navy Postgraduate School and University of Pennsylvania started the study of the movement LOD technology and applied it to real-time simulation of infantry movement in Distributed Interactive Simulation (DIS) protocol, which mainly provided joint freedom models in different detail levels and selected different joint freedom models according to special metrics for movement entities of joint structure [6]. Researchers from Georgia Institute of Technology proposed the concept of movement LOD simulation, which discussed the simulation of the same object by using different complexity of movement calculating model and in different levels [7]. The calculating model can be simple key frame interpolation, complex kinematics or even dynamics models, and can also be determined based on metrics such as distance and speed. The primary role of movement LOD methods is to reduce computing load of individual movement entities and increase the simulation objects on the basis of certain computing load on hosts, so as to improve the scalability of the system.

3.2 Selection of Movement LOD Criteria

HUMANOID standard proposed a complete joint model with 70+30*2 degrees of freedom, i.e., the body of virtual human has 70 degrees of freedom and 30 degrees of freedom for each hand. This model can be applied to more complex movement LOD simulation, including actions of athletes and so on. Combined with appropriate movement models, it can achieve a relatively high level of realism.

Based on the joint model above, the criteria is the value of interest level, which is between [0, 1]. System determines detail levels of movement for a simulated object at host at this moment and sends data required by movement simulation of this level to the host. [8] discussed a joint model, which is a subset of the standard joint model of HUMANOID and supports 44 freedoms, sorted by the importance. Table 1 shows the detail levels of the joint model.

To reduce the complexity of views and the traffic of virtual environments, our selection rules are very simple, including three levels, and p is the value of the level, as follows:

Level 1 $0.0 < p \le 0.2$, transfer low level data;

Level 2 $0.2 < p \le 0.6$, transfer middle level data;

Level 3 $0.6 < p \le 1.0$, transfer high level data;

Table 1. Detail levels of the joint model

Level / Joint	high	middle	low
Head	3	3	3
Shoulder	3*2	3*2	3*2
Neck	3	0	0
Elbow	1*2	1*2	0
Wrist	3*2	0	0
Waist	3	0	0
Pelvis	3	3	3
Hip	3*2	3*2	3*2
Knee	2*2	2*2	0
Ankle	3*2	0	0
Toe	1*2	0	0
Count	44	24	18

3.3 System Implementation and Performance Evaluation

We design and implement a simple prototype system for movement LOD. The protocol structure, software architecture and rendering engine is similar in [9]. Users only need to log on their closest XML routers and access the system in the form of dimensional avatars. On the active router, LevelFilter is used to compute the similarity of XML trees formed from the XML information of subscription and publication, and determine the levels of interaction between objects. Then, it transfers the data of virtual human joint model based on high, middle or low levels.

The system mainly implements interest management based on spatial regions, that is, users are only interested in and communicate with other users within a certain range from themselves. In distributed virtual environment, the subscribing region of a host is mainly described in a spatial range, which is the coordinate scope in the world coordinate space, so we uses three attributes (x, y, z) to describe it. Users not only input x, y and z as their interest region, but also input relevant parameters impacting their interests (such as size, speed) and assign corresponding importance.

There are three parts of XML packets for publishers: the first part is composed of fragments of XML document describing interest spatial information (x, y and z), in which "range" denotes a range with a pair of upper and lower bounds (as shown in Figure 3a). The second part is the combination of parameters that describes interest degrees between objects. We use "priority" to specify the importance of each element (as shown in Figure 3b) with a range between [0, 1]. The higher the priority values, the more important the XML element is. The third part is the description of the virtual object joint data, mainly includes 44 degrees of freedom of joint model. Figure 3c gives a fragment of XML document for the shoulder of virtual human. Since such data do not need to be operated by the active management, there is no need to format publishing XML data.

In the experiment, we mainly measure the bitrate of packets on the active routers. The packet receiving rates on the active routers before and after the leveled filtering are shown in Figure 4 and Figure 5, respectively. By comparing them, we find that in non-filtering situation, active routers only forward packets based on content and do not change the sizes of packets, so that the packets receiving rate is relatively steady.

However, when leveled filtering methods are applied, active routers pick up and reconstruct packets according to interest levels and transfer different leveled data of human joint body, so the length of each packet is reduced. Therefore, it will reduce the packets receiving rate on active routers, thus effectively reducing the load of the network.

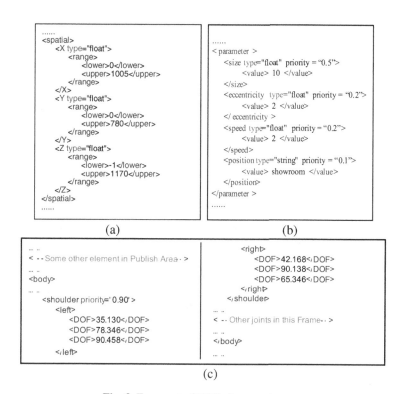

(a)   (b)

(c)

Fig. 3. Fragment of XML document

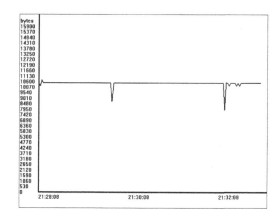

Fig. 4. Packet receiving rate on the active router before leveled filtering

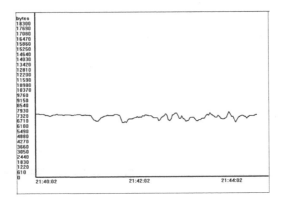

Fig. 5. Packet receiving rate on the active router after the leveled filtering

4 Conclusion

This paper applies XML technology to active leveled interest management and proposes a new XML tree based leveled filtering method. The method takes different importance of each attribute into account and uses Node-Labeled XML trees to describe attributes in the processing of publication and subscription. Through the XML tree similarity matching, it achieves quantitative analysis of interest levels and levered filtering for packets. Finally, it achieves good results by applying it to the virtual human movement simulation system. In addition, combined with multi-agent systems, this approach can also be applied to virtual markets for e-commerce and agent-oriented enterprise information systems with valuable contribution.

References

1. Zabele, S., Dorsch, M., Ge, Z., Ji, P., Keaton, M., Kurose, J., Shapiro, J.: SANDS: Specialized active networking for distributed simulation. In: Proceedings of DARPA Active Networks Conference and Exposition, California, pp. 355–365 (2002)
2. Sun, Y.H., Gong, Z.Y., Li, H., Pan, J.G.: Research on Scalable Active Interest Management. Journal of Image and Graphics 8A(spec), 771–775 (2003)
3. He, L.Y., Li, S.K., Zeng, L.: Hierarchical Interest Management in Large-Scale Distributed Virtual Environment. Journal of Computer Aided Design and Computer Graphics 12(9), 711–714 (2000)
4. Bei, J., Zeng, D.H., Zhai, L., Pan, J.G.: Research on Active Leveled Interest Management. Journal of Software 17(10), 2163–2173 (2006)
5. Gong, Z.Y.: Event Model in Distributed Virtual Environment. Master Thesis, Nanjing University, Nanjing (2003)
6. Granieri, J.P., Crabtree, J., Badler, N.I.: Production and playback of human figure motion for visual simulation. ACM Transactions on Modeling and Computer Simulation 5(3), 222–241 (1995)

7. Carlson, D.A., Hodgins, J.K.: Simulation Levels of Detail for Real-time Animation. In: Proceedings of the conference on Graphics interface, Toronto, pp. 1–8 (1997)
8. Cui, Y.Y.: Research on Active Interest Management with Level of Interest Filtering and Its Application. Master Thesis, Nanjing University, Nanjing (2005)
9. Chen, J.M., Xu, D., Bei, J., Ju, S.G., Pan, J.G.: Research on XML-Based Active Interest Management in Distributed Virtual Environment. In: Proceedings of Computational Science and Its Applications, Malaysia, pp. 315–324 (2007)

Fostering Students' Participation in Face-to-Face Interactions and Deepening Their Understanding by Integrating Personal and Shared Spaces[*]

Etsuji Yamaguchi[1], Shigenori Inagaki[2], Masanori Sugimoto[3], Fusako Kusunoki[4],
Akiko Deguchi[5], Yuichiro Takeuchi[6], Takao Seki[7], Sanae Tachibana[2],
and Tomokazu Yamamoto[8]

[1] Faculty of Education and Culture, University of Miyazaki
etuji@cc.miyazaki-u.ac.jp
[2] Graduate School of Human Science and Environment, Kobe University
inagakis@kobe-u.ac.jp, CZS14613@nifty.ne.jp
[3] Department of Electrical Engineering & Information Systems
Graduate School of Engineering, University of Tokyo
sugi@itl.t.u-tokyo.ac.jp
[4] Department of Information Design, Faculty of Art and Design, Tama Art University
kusunoki@tamabi.ac.jp
[5] Faculty of Education, Utsunomiya University
deguchia@cc.utsunomiya-u.ac.jp
[6] Sony Computer Science Laboratories, Inc.
takeuchi@itl.t.u-tokyo.ac.jp
[7] Fukui Prefectural School for the Deaf
[8] Sumiyoshi Elementary School Attached to Faculty of Human Development,
Kobe University
tyamamoto@people.kobe-u.ac.jp

Abstract. In this research, we introduced *CarettaKids* into the social context of a classroom environment to evaluate whether integration of personal and shared spaces can help promote students' participation in synchronous/co-located interactions in the classroom and deepen their understanding of subject matter. Analysis of videotaped interactions and pre- and posttests clarified the following three points. (1) Students who used *CarettaKids* presented the simulation results and rules for object arrangement they worked out individually in their respective personal space, by using *CarettaKids'* function of projecting object arrangements and simulation results from a personal digital assistant onto a sensing board. (2) Many of the students who used *CarettaKids* examined individually generated ideas collaboratively in the shared space. The patterns of collaborative examination are: (a) Induce a rule for object arrangement from object arrangements devised in personal spaces; (b) Deduce a new object arrangement from the rules discovered in the personal spaces; and (c) Refine the rules discovered in the personal spaces through group discussion. (3) Students

---

[*] An earlier version of this paper was presented at the 5th International Conference for Interaction Design and Children in Tampere, Finland, June 2006, and the International Conferences on Computer-Supported Collaborative Learning in New Brunswick, NJ, USA, July 2007. This research project has been supported by Grant-in-Aid for Scientific Research (B) (No. 16300248) and (A) (No. 18200048).

Z. Pan et al. (Eds.): Transactions on Edutainment II, LNCS 5660, pp. 228–245, 2009.

who used *CarettaKids* not only considered all of the three factors, i.e. residential area, industrial area and forest area, but also understood relations between these factors, thereby deepening their understanding of city planning that takes environmental and financial aspects into consideration. We suggest that the degree to which students deepen their understanding is affected by the presence or absence of collaborative examination of individually generated ideas in the shared space.

Keywords: CSCL, Personal and shared spaces, Face-to-Face collaboration, PDA, RFID.

1 Introduction

Computer-mediated interaction is generally classified into four types in terms of time and space: (1) asynchronous/remote; (2) synchronous/remote; (3) asynchronous/co-location; and (4) synchronous/co-location (McConnell, 2000). In the field of computer supported collaborative learning (CSCL), less research has been conducted on support for synchronous/co-location interaction than on support for other types of interaction (Lonchamp, 2006; Scott, Mandryk, & Inkpen, 2002). However, in the social context of the classroom, students learn not only individually, but also collaboratively while interacting face-to-face with the teacher and other students in the same classroom. Therefore, while amplification of classroom learning is defined as the main agenda of the CSCL research field, working more actively on computer-mediated support for synchronous/co-location interaction is more necessary than ever before.

Regarding computer-mediated support for synchronous/co-location interaction in the classroom, several systems for providing a socially shared space have been developed and evaluated (Suthers, 2006). The shared space allows students to propose their own ideas and discuss them with their peers, thereby facilitating collaborative problem solving. At the same time, through participation in the collaborative problem solving process, students can deepen their own understanding of subject matter.

A system has been developed that allows students to enter characters or pictures by using a mouse and keyboard and displays input results on a computer screen (Moher, Kim, & Haas, 2002; Stanton, Neale, & Bayon, 2002). Another type of system has also been developed, in which students input information by operating three-dimensional physical objects and the input results are superimposed on the physical objects (Arias, Eden, & Fisher, 1997; Arias, Eden, Fischer, Gorman, & Scharff, 2000). The latter type of system not only allows simultaneous input from about six users, but also can integrate the computer-supported shared space seamlessly with the face-to-face interaction in the classroom. Because of these characteristics, this type of system helps increase students' feelings of being immersed in collaborative learning, while promoting shared interaction (Eden, 2002; Fischer & Sugimoto, 2006). Furthermore, this type of system can support a high level of collaborative problem-solving performance by elementary school students (Sugimoto, Kusunoki, & Hashizume, 2002; Sugimoto, Kusunoki, Inagaki, Takatoki, & Yoshikawa, 2003).

However, this type of system has two problems with respect to individual students' interaction in shared space: (1) Some students do not present their own ideas in the shared space; (2) The ideas generated by some individuals are not examined by others in the shared space (Fischer & Sugimoto, 2006). These problems are associated with a lack of feedback on individual ideas from other students, and are considered important causes of inhibition among students that prevent them from deepening their understanding through participation in collaborative problem-solving activities in the shared space. Once these problems are overcome, however, it will be possible to add a new advantage to the existing system (i.e. support for individual cognition), without impairing its existing advantage (i.e. support for group cognition). Therefore, it is considered possible to enhance technologically mediated collaborative leaning in the social context of the classroom, from both aspects of individual cognition and group cognition.

How can we overcome these two problems? By using hand-held devices, we have attempted to create a personal space in which individual students can work without being disturbed by other students, and to integrate individual personal spaces into the existing shared space. The approach to creating a personal space using a hand-held device has been attempted in other CSCL research projects, achieving some positive results (Fraser, Smith, Tallyn, Kirk, Benford, Rowland, Paxton, Price, & Fitzpatrick, 2005; Iles, Glaser, Kam, & Canny, 2002; Roschelle, Rosas, & Nussbaum, 2005; Wessner, Dawabi, & Fernandez, 2003). By applying such an approach to the synchronous/co-location interaction support system, we aimed to achieve three objectives: (1) To enable seamless transfer of problem situations proposed in the shared space to students' respective personal spaces; (2) To ensure that students undergo idea generation and verification in their respective personal spaces, and; (3) To realize seamless transfer of the ideas generated in personal spaces to the shared space. We have developed a system called *CarettaKids*. This system uses a sensing board based on the radio frequency identification (RFID) technology to support collaboration in a shared space, and a personal digital assistant (PDA) device to support activity in personal spaces. This system enables students, in collaboration with one another, to simulate city planning with consideration of environmental and financial aspects.

We have proposed this system in previous works (Sugimoto, Hosoi, & Hashizume, 2004; Sugimoto, Kusunoki, Inagaki, & Yamaguchi, 2005). However, no evaluation has been conducted on the effectiveness of *CarettaKids* in the classroom setting. More specifically, it has not yet been evaluated whether *CarettaKids* is effective in supporting students' generation of ideas and careful examination of others' ideas in the shared spaces and deepening the understanding of individual students. Such an evaluation will give valuable information concerning the computer-mediated support for face-to-face interaction in the social context of the classroom.

In our study, we designed and implemented a curriculum using *CarettaKids* in the classroom environment for elementary school students, and evaluated whether the integration of personal and shared spaces helped promote face-to-face interaction in the classroom environment and deepen understanding. Analysis of videotaped interactions and pre- and posttests clarified the follow-ing three points. (1) Students who used *CarettaKids* presented the simulation results and rules for object arrangement they worked out individually in their respective personal space, by using *CarettaKids'* function of projecting object arrangements and simulation results from a personal digital assistant onto a sensing board. (2) Many of the students who used *CarettaKids* examined indi-vidually generated ideas collaboratively in the shared space. (3)

Students who used *CarettaKids* not only considered all of the three factors, i.e. residential area, industrial area and forest area, but also understood relations between these factors, thereby deepening their understanding of city planning that takes environmental and financial aspects into consideration. We suggest that the degree to which students deepen their understanding is affected by the presence or absence of collaborative examination of individually generated ideas in the shared space.

2 Research Question

Our study aimed to answer three research questions:
(1) Were the students who used *CarettaKids* able to propose ideas in the shared space that they had generated in their personal space?
(2) Did the students who collaboratively used *CarettaKids* examine the individual proposed ideas in the shared space?
(3) Were the students who used *CarettaKids* able to deepen their understanding of city planning that concerns environmental and financial aspects?

3 CarettaKids

Fig. 1 outlines the *CarettaKids*, comprising a sensing board, PDAs, an LCD projector and a PC server. The sensing board supports learning in a shared space. Input devices

Fig. 1. An overview of *CarettaKids*

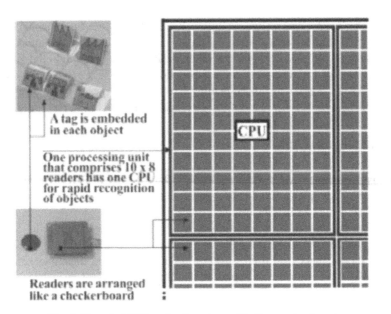

A tag is embedded
in each object

One processing unit
that comprises 10 x 8
readers has one CPU
for rapid recognition
of objects

Readers are arranged
like a checkerboard

Fig. 2. How the RFID technology is used in the sensing board

include physical objects to be placed on the sensing board. The PC server conducts simulation according to information input via these devices. Simulation results calculated by the PC server are superimposed on the physical objects via the LCD projector.

The PDA supports learning in the personal space. Using a stylus, each user can move, on his or her PDA, icons corresponding to physical objects on the sensing board, thus realizing the same simulation as on the sensing board. Inputs on the PDA are transmitted to the PC server on a wireless LAN. Simulation results are in turn transmitted to the PDAs via the LAN and appear on the PDA screens. As explained in a later paragraph, the shared space on the sensing board is linked with the personal spaces on the PDAs via the wireless LAN and RFID technology, allowing users to move seamlessly between the two spaces.

3.1 Shared Space

The sensing board used in the shared space, developed by us (Kusunoki, Sugimoto, & Hashizume, 1999; Sugimoto, Kusunoki, & Hashizume, 2001), is a simultaneous multiple input device capable of high-speed recognition of types and locations of physical objects placed by several users. The RFID technology (V720 series by Omron) is used for object recognition (Fig. 2). The sensing board used in our study has a grid of 20 × 24 squares, each square measuring 3 cm × 3 cm. An RFID reader is buried in each square of the grid, while an RFID tag is buried in each physical object. The RFID reader recognizes tags within an area of up to 10 mm above a square and reads information written on each tag within 0.05 seconds. More detailed technical information about sensing boards may be consulted in (Sugimoto., Kusunoki, & Hashizume, 2002).

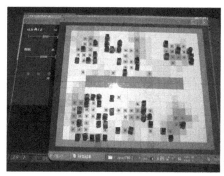

Fig. 3. Shared space in *CarettaKids*

Fig. 3 shows the shared space in *CarettaKids*. The simulation using our system involves designing a city while taking into consideration trade-off between environmental and economic merits, that is, building a city in such a way as to generate as little carbon dioxide and as much financial assets as possible. Physical objects to be placed on the sensing boards represent trees, factories and houses. When these three types of objects are arranged on the sensing board, parameters concerning carbon dioxide and financial assets change according to their arrangements, with simulation results appearing on the squares and on the left end of the sensing board.

For example, when factories and houses are placed on the board, the city's financial assets and carbon dioxide increase. As a result, initially white squares of the sensing board turn dark, in line with the increase in the city's carbon dioxide. Once the city's total amount of carbon dioxide exceeds a prescribed level, the number of blue and brown squares representing the sea and deserts increases. At the same time, the living comfort index, which changes in inverse proportion to the total amount of carbon dioxide in the city, drops, whereas the financial asset index, proportionally reflecting the city's total financial assets, increases. When trees are planted, the city's financial assets and carbon dioxide decrease. As a result, colored squares turn white. At the same time, the living comfort index increases, while the financial asset index decreases. In this manner, the parameters of carbon dioxide and financial assets form a correlation of trade-off. Paying attention to this trade-off, the students participating in the simulation must design a city that generates as little carbon dioxide and as much financial assets as possible.

To accentuate the trade-off in question, in the experiment, the students were given an initial state, with several objects already placed on the board, as well as limits to the number of each type of object that they may use in the simulation: up to 54 houses and 24 factories, both of which the students were required to completely use up in the simulation, and up to 50 trees, whose number to be placed on the board was left to the students' discretion.

3.2 Personal Space

Fig. 4 shows the personal space in *CarettaKids*. On the PDA screen, a 1/6 grid identical to the one on the sensing board is displayed, along with the types and numbers of objects currently placed on the board and the living comfort and financial assets indices. The PDA and sensing board have the equal number of squares on the respective

Fig. 4. Personal space in *CarettaKids*

grid. The user scrolls the PDA screen to display an area to modify, thereby freely "moving about" in his or her personal space.

The user can carry out the same simulation on his or her PDA as in the shared space, without having the individual simulation results appear on the sensing board. In other words, the user can simulate object arrangement in his or her personal space without moving objects on the sensing board in the shared space.

3.3 Space Transition

3.3.1 From the Shared Space to the Personal Space

The user can also copy object arrangements on the sensing board onto his or her respective PDA. By clicking the "Load" button with the stylus while bringing the PDA close to a given area on the sensing board, the user can get the RFID reader to recognize the RFID tag attached at the tip of the PDA carrying user ID information, thereby transmitting object arrangements in the area and simulation results to the PDA via the wireless LAN. In this manner, the user can smoothly shift his or her operation back and forth between the shared and personal spaces with quasi-intuitive moves (Fig. 5). This kind of movement is believed to be helpful for individual attempts to find solutions to problems detected in the shared space, as well as individual reflection on ideas suggested in the shared space.

3.3.2 From the Personal Space to Shared Space

The user can also copy his or her object arrangements and simulation results displayed on the PDA onto the sensing board. By clicking the "Proposal" button on the PDA, the user can superimpose the individual object arrangement on those on the sensing board. Then, the simulation results on the PDA are also sent to the sensing board via the liquid-crystal projector. By clicking the "Finalize" button on the PDA, the object arrangement and simulation results on the sensing board are overwritten on those on the PDA and projected back onto the sensing board via the liquid-crystal projector. Then, once the concerned physical object has been actually moved according to the finalized arrangement, object arrangement can be resumed in the shared space. Thus, seamless, almost intuitive moves are realized between personal and shared spaces. Such moves are believed to be effective when several users discuss individually generated ideas and develop one user's idea in collaboration with others.

4 Curriculum

Our research team comprises teachers, engineering researchers and educational researchers. The *CarettaKids*-supported curriculum was designed through discussion by all members of the research team, in which we took advantage of the specialties of individual members. Table 1 outlines the curriculum. This curriculum was designed for creating the situations that allow students to move seamlessly between the two spaces using *CarettaKids*. So, three types of activity (shared-space, personal-space, and mixed-space learning) were included in the curriculum. And the curriculum was designed for creating the situations that allow students generate ideas and examine others' ideas using *CarettaKids*. So, the learning cycles consisted of three types of activity were repeated several times and the inter-group Interaction activity was included in the curriculum.

Fig. 5. Transition from the shared space to students' pe0072sonal spaces in CarettaKids

4.1 Lesson 1

(a) The Introduction featured a five-minute video presentation explaining that an increase in carbon dioxide released from factories and similar industrial units had caused an environmental problem known as global warming and that tree-planting was being promoted as one solution to this problem. This was followed by the teacher's explanation that city planning in consideration of such environmental problems, in addition to financial matters, could bring about realistic solutions to environmental problems in the future. In the (b) PDA Operation Exercise, the students

Table 1. Outline of the curriculum

Lesson 1 (45 minutes)
(a) The Introduction
(b) PDA Operation Exercise

Lesson 2 (90 minutes)
(c) Shared-space Learning #1 (*sensing board*)
(d) Personal-space Learning #1 (*PDA*)
(e) Mixed-space Learning #1 (*sensing board & PDA*)
(f) Shared-space Learning #2 (*sensing board*)

Lesson 3 (90 minutes)
(g) Inter-group Interaction
(h) Personal-space Learning #2 (*PDA*)
(i) Mixed-space Learning #2 (*sensing board & PDA*)
(j) Shared-space Learning #3 (*sensing board*)
(k) Personal-space Learning #3 (*PDA*)
(l) Mixed-space Learning #3 (*sensing board & PDA*)
(m) Shared-space Learning #4 (*sensing board*)
(n) Summarizing the curriculum

arranged tree, house and factory objects on their PDAs to practice simulation. In this exercise, they learned how to operate the PDA and confirmed the correlations between object arrangements and parameters such as living comfort and financial assets.

4.2 Lesson 2

In (c) Shared-space Learning #1, each group used a sensing board to work on the project of designing a city that is "comfortable for people to live in and financially secure". In (d) Personal-space Learning #1, each group first chose one area on the sensing board that had room for improvement, and the members of each group individually rearranged trees, houses and factories within the area on their respective PDAs. The students were required to identify rules according to which objects should be arranged to realize the target city.

In (e) Mixed-space (integrating shared and personal spaces) Learning #1, object arrangements on the respective PDAs were projected onto the sensing board. The students then took turns explaining rules they had identified on their own, with the entire group discussing the rules presented by each member. In (f) Shared-space Learning #2, object arrangements on one member's PDA were adopted provisionally and superimposed on the sensing board, for the group to rearrange the objects according to the rules discussed in (e).

4.3 Lesson 3

In (g) Inter-group Interaction, the groups examined each other's simulation. The entire class gathered around one group's sensing board and discussed the rules that the group had adopted in arranging objects while studying the objects and simulation re-sults on the sensing board. In (h) Personal-space Learning #2, the students individu-ally examined on their respective PDAs the rules that had been presented in Lesson 2 but had not been recognized as "legitimate" rules for building a city that was comfort-able for people to live in and financially secure. In (i) Mixed-space Learning #2, the students took turns reporting the results of their individual examination of the rules in (h). In (j) Shared-space Learning #3, object arrangement was resumed on the sensing board.

After (k) Personal-space Learning #3, in (l) Mixed-space Learning #3, the students were required to identify new rules for object arrangement yet to be detected. In addi-tion, object arrangement was carried out on the PDAs and the sensing board in paral-lel, simultaneously and in an improvisatory manner. For example, a student worked on the sensing board while the other students used their PDAs, who then took turns working on the sensing board, before immediately returning to their respective PDAs.

In (m) Shared-space Learning #4, objects on the sensing board were rearranged again. Finally, in (n) Summarizing the Curriculum, the rules that each group had adopted for object arrangement were shared by the entire class. The class then dis-cussed the significance of these rules in the real world.

5   Method

5.1   Participants

The curriculum that used *CarettaKids* was implemented in a sixth-grade class (33 students aged 11 to 12 years) in a university-affiliated elementary school in Japan, where two of the authors worked. Students in this school were selected through an admission test. Their financial status was relatively higher than that of students in nearby public elementary schools. The class was divided into six groups (Groups 1–6), each comprising five or six students. Each group was provided with one set of the system. None of the students had used the system before. One of the authors was the teacher. She had more than 10 years teaching experience and had knowledge in sci-ence education and biology at bachelor's degree level participated. All the other au-thors participated in the class for purposes of data collection and technical support.

5.2   Data Sources, Measures, and Analyses

Regarding the evaluation methods for answering the three research questions, for Questions (1) and (2), the Interaction Analysis (Jourdan & Henderson, 1995) was used to analyze videotaped records of the students' classroom activities; and for Question (3), pre- and posttest analyses were conducted.

5.2.1   Interaction Analysis
Students' verbal and nonverbal actions and system operations on the PDA and sens-ing board were video-recorded. One video camera was used per group. The recorded data were transcribed into a written script, which was adopted as analysis data. To an-swer Question (1), we analyzed three Mixed-space Learning sessions and identified

whether in each of the three sessions, students were able to present, in the shared space, "object arrangements" and "rules for object arrangement" that they individually devised in their respective personal spaces, or whether they could not present arrangement results or rules. To answer Question (2), we focused on the arrangement results and rules adopted in each of the three Mixed-space Learning sessions. We identified whether rules were induced from the arrangement results, whether new arrangement results were educed from the rules, or whether rules themselves were refined in the subsequent Shared-space Learning.

5.2.2 Analysis of Pre- and Posttests

Before and after the curriculum, tests were conducted on 32 students, excluding one student who was absent from school, to evaluate their understanding of the environmental and financial aspects of city planning. For the test problem: "Design a city which is comfortable to live in and financially secure", the students were asked to express their opinions and give reasons for them. The following preconditions were provided: regarding the living comfort, "If residential and industrial areas are increased, then the living comfort will decrease", and "If forest area is increased, then the living comfort will increase". Regarding the financial situation, "If residential and industrial areas are increased, then the city's financial security will improve", and "If forest area is increased, then the city's financial security will deteriorate".

The pre- and posttests, which were about 25 minutes, were held simultaneously for all students in the class. The students wrote their answers on an answer sheet. In analyzing the students' answers, the following points were considered. (1) Factors: Of the three factors (residential area, industrial area, and forest area), how many factors was the student able to consider? (2) Relations among factors: Was the student able to consider the relations among factors correctly? (3) Trade-off: Was the student able to consider the relation of trade-off between living comfort and financial assets? For each of these points, the students' answers were rated on a scale of 1 to 4 or 1 to 7. Rating was conducted independently by two researchers, and any discrepancies were resolved through discussion. The rate of agreement in the ratings was high both in the pre- and posttests, with $\kappa = 0.919$ to 0.948 and $\kappa = 0.841$ to 1.00, respectively. For each standpoint, based on this rating, students' answers were scored at a maximum of 12 points. Then, changes in the test scores before and after the *CarettaKids*-supported curriculum were analyzed.

6 Results

6.1 Were the Students Who Used *CarettaKids* Able to Propose Their Own Ideas Generated in a Personal Space in the Shared Space?

Analysis of interactive actions in the three Mixed-space Learning sessions revealed that all students were able to present their "object arrangements" and "rules for object arrangement" in the shared space, in all of the three sessions. As concrete examples of the ideas proposed, Table 2 shows an episode in which a student in Group 6 discovered a rule in her personal space and presented it in the shared space. This student explained that when arranging objects on the PDA in accordance with the rule of placing a factory or house between two trees, the effects of both "living comfort" and "financial situation" parameters were good. The rule of placing a factory or house between trees stated in this explanation had not been discussed in the previous group activities. Therefore, it can be concluded that this rule was discovered by this student in her personal space. In the Mixed-space Learning, this student was able to present the rule that she discovered in her personal space to other group members, by using the function of projecting the object arrangement and simulation results on the PDA onto the sensing board.

Table 2. A student in Group 6 discovered a rule in her personal space and presented it in the shared space

【Timecode: 00:38:50-00:39:30】
(She clicked the "Proposal" button on the PDA to transmit the individual object arrangement onto the sensing board.)
    What I did was to place factories and houses as close as possible to trees, and ... I put a factory between two trees. Or ... to the place beside that tree, I moved a factory sandwiched between two trees. And, beside the tree on the left, I placed a house. I put factories or something, I mean, buildings that increase carbon dioxide, as close as possible to trees. Then I got these values.

6.2 Did the Students Who Used *CarettaKids* Collaboratively Examine Individuals' Proposed Ideas in the Shared Space?

As a result of analyzing interactive actions in the three sessions of Mixed-space Learning and Shared-space Learning, the following three patterns were extracted as representative patterns of collaborative examination of individually generated ideas in the shared space. (Exam1): Induce a rule for object arrangement from object arrangements devised in the personal spaces; (Exam2): Deduce a new object arrangement from the rules discovered in the personal spaces; and (Exam3): Refine the rules discovered in the personal spaces through group discussion. From the pattern of individually generated ideas not being examined in the shared space, the following was extracted: (Unexam): Object arrangement is performed continuously from the arrangement results devised in the personal spaces.

Table 3 shows the patterns of collaborative examination conducted by each group in the three sessions of Mixed-space Learning and Shared-space Learning. Exam1 was found in the first session of Groups 2 and 5. Exam2 was found in the third session of Group 1, in the first and third sessions of the Group 4, and in the first and third sessions of Group 6. Exam3 was found in the first and second sessions of Group 1, in the second and third sessions of Group 2, and in the second session of Group 4. Unexam was found in the first and second sessions of Group 3. From these results, it was learned that, although there were differences in pattern among groups, most groups were able to examine individually generated ideas collaboratively at least once, except Group 3. Group 3 was not able to examine individually generated ideas collaboratively even once.

Table 3. The patterns of collaborative examination conducted by each group in the three sessions of Mixed-space Learning and Shared-space Learning

	Group1	Group2	Group3	Group4	Group5	Group6
1st	exam3	exam1	unexam	exam2	exam1	exam2
2nd	exam3	exam3	unexam	exam3	(none)	(none)
3rd	exam2	exam3	(none)	exam2	(none)	exam2

exam1: Induce a rule for object arrangement from object arrangements devised in the personal spaces.

exam2: Deduce a new object arrangement from the rules discovered in the personal spaces.

exam3: Refine the rules discovered in the personal spaces through group discussion.

unexam: Object arrangement is performed continuously from the arrangement results devised in the personal spaces.

(none): Shared-space Learning is skipped because extension of Mixed-space Learning.

As a concrete example of a pattern of collaborative examination, the episode of exam3 of Group 1 is shown in Table 4. Before the episode began, in this group, the value of "financial situation" parameter was high, whereas that of "living comfort" parameter was low. Therefore, the group needed to work on improving living comfort, while maintaining the current financial situation as much as possible. In the first half of the episode, Student A projected the object arrangement and simulation results on his PDA onto the sensing board and explained the rule he had devised to the other students. Student A explained saying, "If you place a house, you should move a tree placed on the board next to the house. Then, place a factory next to that tree." According to him, with this rule, it is possible to solve the problem on which the group is focusing, that is, improving living comfort, while maximizing financial security as much as possible.

In the subsequent Shared-space Learning, each group member attempted to rearrange objects in the shared space, in accordance with the rule devised by Student A. As a result, both living comfort and financial security parameters achieved high scores. The problem to be tackled by the group was changed to improving financial security, while maintaining the highest possible living comfort level. The latter half of the episode shows interactive actions performed at this stage. Student F suggested to other members a rule of deleting all trees placed on the sensing board. Student B accepted his suggestion and stopped Student C from placing tree objects. At this point, the rule suggested by Student F can be interpreted as the refinement of the rule suggested by Student A in the first half of the episode. Student A's rule involves "arrangement of trees". His rule is to move existing trees on the sensing board to other places. Student F's rule also involves arrangement of trees. However, his rule is to delete all existing trees on the board. Considered from the viewpoint of "how many trees to place and how to place them to design a city which is comfortable to live in and financially secure", Student F's rule is a refined version of Student A's, in that a new condition concerning the number of trees is added to the condition concerning arrangement of trees, which is stated in Student A's rule.

Table 4. An example of a pattern of collaborative examination

【Timecode: 00:32:51-00:33:34 】

(Mixed-space Learning)

01A: Uh, can you place trees, houses and factories alternately?

02F: What? Hey, what do you mean? Well, (pointing at the sensing board) A tree, here? Is this OK? Oh, yes, yes. (Looks convinced, tapping his knee.)

03A: Keep going in that manner. And, delete trees just a little. Uh, although financial situation is a little bad, I aimed to improve living comfort.

(In the Shared-space Learning, objects are rearranged following the rule suggested by Student A.)

【Timecode: 00:52:27-00:53:10】 (Shared-space Learning)

(Both living comfort and financial situation indexes show high values. Students now discuss how to place objects to improve financial security while maintaining good living comfort level.)

05E: Well then, why don't you delete trees a little more?

06C: (Attempting to place a tree object)

07B: No, no. I'm saying, we don't need trees.

08E: Now, take all trees off. Let's try one time. Take all trees off. (Taking all tree objects off the board.)

6.3 Were the Students Who Used *CarettaKids* Able to Deepen Their Understanding of City Planning That Concerns Environmental and Financial Aspects?

Table 5 shows the total scores and the scores for each evaluation standpoint of pre- and posttests. First, the Wilcoxon rank-sum test was conducted for total scores and scores for each evaluation standpoint. The total scores of the posttest were significantly higher than those of the pretest ($Z = -4.81$, $p < 0.01$). Regarding the scores by evaluation standpoint, the scores for "Factors"($Z = -3.81$, $p < 0.01$) and "Relations among factors" ($Z = -4.81$, $p < 0.01$) in the posttest were significantly higher than in the pretest. However, no significant differences were noted in "Trade-off" between both tests. From these results, it can be said that students have deepened their overall understanding of city planning that takes environmental and financial aspects into consideration. It can also be said that these results suggest that students not only considered all three factors (residential area, industrial area and forest area), but also understood the relations between these factors correctly.

Table 5. Average scores and standard deviation of pre- and posttests

	pre	post
Total	17.8 (7.8)	30.6 (4.9)
Each evaluation standpoint		
Factors	9.5 (3.3)	11.8 (1.0)
Relations among factors	3.0 (3.2)	10.6 (2.7)
Trade-off	5.3 (4.2)	8.3 (3.8)

$N = 32$.

Table 6. Average scores and standard deviation of pre- and posttests (Group3 and others)

	Group3		others	
	pre	post	pre	post
Total	22.7 (4.6)	32.8 (2.7)	16.1 (8.7)	28.9 (7.7)
Each evaluation standpoint				
Factors	10.0 (3.3)	12.0 (0.0)	9.0 (3.8)	11.3 (2.5)
Relations among factors	2.7 (3.0)	11.3 (1.6)	3.0 (3.3)	10.0 (3.6)
Trade-off	10.0 (1.5)	9.5 (2.9)	4.1 (4.0)	7.7 (4.3)

$N = 32$.

The analysis of interactive actions revealed that there were groups (Groups 1, 2. 4, 5, 6) that succeeded in examining individual member's ideas collaboratively in the shared space and a group that failed (Group 3). Were there any differences between these groups in the degree of understanding of city planning? To assess this, total scores and averages of scores for each evaluation standpoint were calculated for Group 3 and the others (Table 6). Wilcoxon rank-sum test showed that the groups that succeeded in collaborative examination had significantly higher scores for "Factors" ($Z = -2.80$, $p < 0.01$), "Relations among factors" ($Z = -4.31$, $p < 0.01$), "Trade-off" ($Z = -2.67$, $p < 0.01$) and "Total" ($Z = -4.32$, $p < 0.01$) in the posttest. However, the group that failed in collaborative examination had higher scores only for "Relations among factors" ($Z = -2.21$, $p < 0.05$) and "Total" ($Z = -2.20$, $p < 0.01$) in the posttest than in the pretest, and no significant differences were observed in "Factors" ($Z = -1.34$, $n.s.$) and "Trade-off" ($Z = -0.57$, $n.s.$). These results suggest the possibility that the presence or absence of collaborative examination of individually generated ideas in the shared space affects how much individual students deepen their understanding.

7 Conclusions

In this research, we introduced *CarettaKids* into the social context of classroom environment to evaluate whether integration of personal and shared spaces can help promote students' participation in synchronous/co-located interaction in the classroom and deepen their understanding of a topic.

Analysis of videotaped interactions and pre- and posttests showed three main findings. (1) Students who used *CarettaKids* presented the simulation results and rules for object arrangement they worked out individually in their respective personal space, by using *CarettaKids'* function of projecting object arrangements and simulation results on the PDA onto the sensing board. (2) Many of the students who used *CarettaKids* examined individually generated ideas collaboratively in the shared space. The patterns of collaborative examination are: (a) Induce a rule for object arrangement from object arrangements devised in the personal spaces; (b) Deduce a new object arrangement from the rules discovered in the personal spaces; and (c) Refine the rules discovered in the personal spaces through group discussion. (3) Students who used *CarettaKids* not only considered all of the three factors, i.e. residential area, industrial area and forest area, but also understood relations between these factors, thereby deepening their understanding of city planning by taking environmental and financial aspects into consideration. We suggest that the degree to which students deepen their understanding is affected by the presence or absence of collaborative examination of individually generated ideas.

Our results suggest that integrating shared and personal spaces can be expected to help overcome one of the two problems with respect to support for synchronous/co-located interaction in the classroom, that is, that some students do not present their own ideas in the shared space. It is also suggested that there is a possibility of being able to solve the problem of cases where some individually generated ideas are not examined by others in the shared space to some extent, if not completely.

8 Future Work

In this study, the curriculum was carried out in a short term. Therefore it was difficult to remove the "novelty factor" from the results. In the future, it is necessary to carry out the study in a long term, and to examine whether *CarettaKids* contributes to participation and the understanding of the student.

Other remaining task is to determine how to support collaborative examination of individually generated ideas in the shared space. As suggested in this research, this is also a problem that can affect the relative understanding of individual students. A similar problem is also suggested by the results of the research focusing on correlation between group cognition and individual cognition. For example, Barron (2003) analyzed interactions in collaborative problem solving activities within a group of three students in the sixth grade, and found that students in the group that was able to collaboratively examine reasonable ideas tended to show a relatively high level of performance in the subsequent individual problem solving, whereas the level of problem-solving performance of students in the group that failed to examine reasonable suggestions tended to be low. These results suggest direct intervention in the interaction is required when ideas generated in personal spaces are presented in the shared space.

References

1. Arias, E.G., Eden, H., Fischer, G.: Enhancing Communication, Facilitating Shared Understanding, and Creating Better Artifacts by Integrating Physical and Computational Media for Design. In: Proceedings of Designing Interactive Systems, pp. 1–12. ACM, Amsterdam (1997)
2. Arias, E.G., Eden, H., Fischer, G., Gorman, A., Scharff, E.: Transcending the Individual Human Mind-Creating Shared Understanding through Collaborative Design. ACM Transactions on Computer-Human Interaction 7(1), 84–113 (2000)
3. Barron, B.: When Smart Groups Fail. The Journal of the Learning Sciences 12(3), 307–359 (2003)
4. Eden, H.: Getting in on the (Inter)action: Exploring Affordances for Collaborative Learning in a Context of Informed Participation. In: Proceedings of Computer-Supported Collaborative Learning 2002, pp. 399–407 (2002)
5. Fischer, G., Sugimoto, M.: Supporting Self-Directed Learners and Learning Communities with Sociotechnical Environments. Research and Practice in Technology Enhanced Learning 1(1), 31–64 (2006)
6. Fraser, D.S., Smith, H., Tallyn, E., Kirk, D., Benford, S., Rowland, D., Paxton, M., Price, S., Fitzpatrick, G.: The SENSE Project: A Context-Inclusive Approach to Studying Environmental Science within and across Schools. In: Koschmann, T., Suthers, D., Chan, T.W. (eds.) Computer Supported Collaborative Learning 2005: The next 10 years! Proceedings of the Computer-Supported Collaborative Learning 2005, pp. 155–315. Lawrence Erlbaum Associates, Mahwah (2005)
7. Iles, A., Glaser, D., Kam, M., Canny, J.: Learning via Distributed Dialogue: Livenotes and Handheld Wireless Technology. In: Stahl (ed.) Computer Support for Collaborative Learning: Foundations for a CSCL Community. Proceedings of the Computer-Supported Collaborative Learning 2002, pp. 408–417. Erlbaum, Hillsdale (2002)
8. Jordan, B., Henderson, B.: Interaction Analysis: Foundations and Practice. The Journal of the Learning Sciences 4(1), 39–103 (1995)
9. Kusunoki, F., Sugimoto, M., Hashizume, H.: A System for Supporting Group Learning that Enhances Interactions. In: Hoadley, C.M., Roschelle, J. (eds.) CSCL 1999 Proceedings of Computer Support for Collaborative Learning 1999, pp. 323–327. Lawrence Erlbaum Associates, Mahwah (1999)
10. Lonchamp, J.: Supporting Synchronous Collaborative Learning: A Generic, Multi-Dimensional Model. International Journal of Computer-Supported Collaborative Learning 1(2), 247–276 (2006)
11. McConnell, D.: Implementing Computer Supported Cooperative Learning, 2nd edn. Kogan Page Limited, London (2000)
12. Moher, T., Kim, J., Haas, D.: A Two-Tiered Collaborative Design for Observational Science Activities in Simulated Environments. In: Stahl (ed.) Computer Support for Collaborative Learning: Foundations for a CSCL Community. Proceedings of the Computer-Supported Collaborative Learning 2002, pp. 361–370. Erlbaum, Hillsdale (2002)

13. Roschelle, J., Rosas, R., Nussbaum, M.: Towards a Design Framework for Mobile Computer-Supported Collaborative Learning. In: Koschmann, T., Suthers, D., Chan, T.W. (eds.) Computer-Supported Collaborative Learning 2005: The next 10 years!, pp. 520–524. Lawrence Erlbaum Associates, Mahwah (2005)
14. Scott, S.D., Mandryk, R.L., Inkpen, K.M.: Understanding Children's Interactions in Synchronous Shared Environments. In: Stahl (ed.) Computer Support for Collaborative Learning: Foundations for a CSCL Community. Proceedings of the Computer-Supported Collaborative Learning 2002, pp. 333–341. Erlbaum, Hillsdale (2002)
15. Stanton, D., Neale, H., Bayon, V.: Interfaces to Support Children's Co-Present Collaboration: Multiple Mice and Tangible Technologies. In: Stahl (ed.) Computer Support for Collaborative Learning: Foundations for a CSCL Community. Proceedings of the Computer-Supported Collaborative Learning 2002, pp. 342–351. Erlbaum, Hillsdale (2002)
16. Suthers, D.D.: Technology Affordances for Intersubjective Meaning Making: A Research Agenda for CSCL. International Journal of Computer-Supported Collaborative Learning 1(3), 315–337 (2006)
17. Sugimoto, M., Hosoi, K., Hashizume, H.: Caretta: A System for Supporting Face-to-Face Collaboration by Integrating Personal and Shared Spaces. In: Proceedings of the SIGCHI Conference on Human Factors in Computing Systems, pp. 41–48. ACM, New York (2004)
18. Sugimoto, M., Kusunoki, F., Hashizume, H.: E2board: An Electronically Enhanced Board for Games and Group Activity Support. In: Proceedings of Affective Human Factors Design, Singapore, pp. 227–234 (2001)
19. Sugimoto, M., Kusunoki, F., Hashizume, H.: Design of an Interactive System for Group Learning Support. In: Proceedings of the 4th Conference on Designing Interactive Systems: Processes, Practices, Methods, and Techniques, pp. 50–55. ACM, New York (2002)
20. Sugimoto, M., Kusunoki, F., Inagaki, S., Yamaguchi, E.: Enhancing Externalization and Reflection by Integrating Personal and Shared Workspaces. In: Proceedings of the 9th European Conference on Computer Supported Cooperative Work, pp. 117–119. Springer, Heidelberg (2005)
21. Sugimoto, M., Kusunoki, F., Inagaki, S., Takatoki, K., Yoshikawa, A.: EPRO2: Design of a System and a Curriculum to Support Group Learning for School Children. In: Wasson, B., Ludvigsen, S., Hoppe, U. (eds.) Designing for Change in Networked Learning Environments: Proceedings of the Computer Support for Collaborative Learning 2003, pp. 1–6. Kluwer Academic Press, The Netherlands (2003)
22. Wessner, M., Dawabi, P., Fernandez, A.: Supporting Face-to-Face Learning with Handheld Devices. In: Wasson, B., Ludvigsen, S., Hoppe, U. (eds.) Designing for Change in Networked Learning Environments: Proceedings of the Computer Support for Collaborative Learning 2003, pp. 487–491. Kluwer Academic Press, The Netherlands (2003)

Make Learning Fun with Programming Contests

Gines Garcia-Mateos and Jose Luis Fernandez-Aleman

Department of Informatics and Systems,
University of Murcia, 30100 Espinardo, Murcia, Spain
{ginesgm,aleman}@um.es

Abstract. Usually, higher education teachers have to deal with highly populated classes and low levels of motivation. Making more entertaining courses is a good way to overcome these limitations. But, how can fun and entertainment be introduced in a course which is mainly based on a final exam evaluation? We propose a new methodology based on two key ideas: (i) replacing the final exam with a series of activities in a continuous evaluation context; and (ii) making those activities more appealing to the students. We describe an e-learning experience carried out in a second-year programming course for computing majors. The activities are designed as on-line programming competitions, where all students participate and are able to see their global ranking. Experimental results show the effectiveness of this approach. On average, the dropout rate decreased from 72% to 45% while the pass rate doubled.

Keywords: Learning strategies, programming contests, e-learning, on-line judging.

1 Introduction

Since 1995, the percentage of students who have completed secondary education has increased in OECD countries, on average, a 7%. The number of graduates in higher education has also grown [1]. However, while demand for human resources in science and technology has increased in these countries (it represents between 25% and 35% of the total labour force), the number of university graduates in engineering and science –excluding health and welfare– has declined to one-fifth [2]. Although in absolute terms the number of enrollments has risen, science and engineering degrees are less and less attractive and dropout rates continue to be high. To boost the supply of scientists and engineers, OECD offers some recommendations. One of these suggestions is to make science and engineering more accessible and attractive to young students.

Edutainment is an emerging alternative to traditional education methods. Rapeepisarn *et al* [3] pointed out that "edutainment is the act of learning heavily through any of various media such as television programs, video games, films, music, multimedia, websites and computer software". Entertainment is the media to help students learn. The approach we describe here is in line with this goal: raising interest of the students by *virtually* transforming a computer science course into an on-line programming contest.

Z. Pan et al. (Eds.): Transactions on Edutainment II, LNCS 5660, pp. 246–257, 2009.

In our proposal, a traditional "final exam" methodology is replaced by a series of carefully designed activities, many of them organized as programming assignments. The key element of this e-learning course on programming is a web-based automatic judging system called Mooshak [4], which was originally created to manage on-line programming contests. Preliminary results show the viability of the learning experience, and a high capacity to generate motivation and enthusiasm among students. The approach is highly complementary with other learning techniques and could be applied to other courses, specially in a computer science degree.

The rest of the paper is organized as follows. Section 2 presents a brief review of some related work. Then, we introduce the methodological principles underlying our proposal in section 3. Section 4 describes the main results of the edutainment-based methodology applied to 337 students in a second-year course for computing majors. Section 5 discusses the results obtained by employing this new e-learning method. Finally, in section 6, we present some concluding remarks and outline the efforts to be made in the future.

2   Related Work

Edutainment has been successfully used in robotics, mathematics, language learning and many other areas. Our paper focuses on computer science, particularly programming. Computer programming is in the core knowledge of many science and engineering degrees. In the literature, most authors reach the same conclusion: learning to program is difficult [5].

Therefore, many techniques and methods have been proposed to improve novice students comprehension in teaching programming [5]. E-learning constitutes a viable and promising alternative in programming pedagogy.

A good example is Guerreiro and Georgouli [6,7], who proposed an e-learning educational strategy in first-year programming courses. They adopt Mooshak automatic judging system for grading lab assignments and for self-assessment purposes; some sample views of Mooshak are shown in Figure 1. This automatic evaluation accounts for about 30% of the final mark. The approach provides important benefits in CS1. A well thought out set of test cases prevents wrong programs sent by students from passing test runs. As a consequence, students must be much more rigorous in developing their programs. Likewise, students obtain immediate feedback from Mooshak. Another advantage of the proposal is the objectivity of the evaluation. Moreover, the authors consider that teachers can save time and work if an automatic judging system is used. Nevertheless, important concepts such as robustness and legibility are manually graded by the instructors.

Our novel contribution resides in *how* to apply the on-line judging system: we take Guerreiro and Georgouli's strategy one step further, by completely replacing the traditional "final exam evaluation" with a series of activities, most of them using Mooshak. Thus, two important benefits are obtained: the students are very motivated to take part in the proposed activities, with the hope of avoiding the

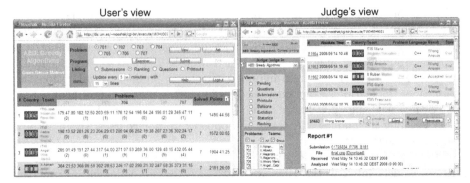

Fig. 1. Two sample views of Mooshak [4]. Left: sample view for a user of the system (the students). The user can access the description of the problems, the list of submissions done by all the users, the ranking of the best students, and the questions done and answered. Right: sample view for a judge (a teacher). The judge is able to see and analyze the submissions done, rejudge submissions, answer questions, and view statistics of system's usage.

final exam; and the work of the students is evaluated along the course, rather than just in a single final exam. To ensure the authorship of the programs, a source code plagiarism detection environment [8] is used. To appraise the quality of the code, the human factor remains to be prominent.

According to some authors, edutainment can be organized in different ways [9,10,11]. Our experience can be classified as follows:

Formal learning: It takes place in an education institution, leading to recognized qualifications and uses organized learning situations.

Interactive and participatory: Students play and participate in the *game*.

Motivation: All students share the same interest: learn to program.

Type of media: The game type is a competition where edutainment is accomplished by a web-based educational system.

3   Methodological Approach

The pioneering experience described here was applied to a second-year course on programming for computing majors; its duration is annual (two consecutive semesters). The main problem observed in this course was a low motivation and participation of the students, that resulted in very high dropout rates. Approximately between 2/3 and 3/4 of the enrolled students dropped out.

With the aim of reversing this trend, we developed a more participatory methodology, based on a continuous evaluation organization, with activities that are appealing and motivating for all students. In this section we describe in detail the key elements of the proposed approach. First, we establish the pedagogical principles that have guided our efforts. Then, the basic aspects of on-line judging systems are presented. Finally, we analyze how to introduce this tool into the learning process.

3.1   Pedagogical Principles

By analyzing our teaching experience in previous years, and also taking into account some recommendations given by other authors [5], we have identified the following pedagogical principles:

Motivation. With a dropout rate around 70%, increasing the motivation of students is essential. By *motivation* we understand the desire to learn new concepts and methods, and to put them into practice.

Active learning. The students have to be involved in, and conscious of, their own learning process. An active methodology, where students are not mere spectators, is necessary to achieve a real and long-lasting learning.

Autonomous work. We believe that the best way to learn computer programming is by programming. A simple memorization of concepts is nearly useless. The students have to reflect on algorithmic problems by themselves and create autonomously their programs.

Feedback of the learning process. This feedback is considered from the point of view of the students. Traditionally, they just obtain a final mark at the end of the course. The method should provide students with a continuous evaluation on how well they are doing.

All of these objectives require more entertaining and participatory activities, both in class and out of class. In these situations is where e-learning tools can produce a great benefit, not by substituting the teachers, but by helping them to control and evaluate the activities.

3.2   On-Line Judging

The key element of our approach is an on-line judging system. This system is an automatic tool which is able to evaluate the correction of computer programs, based on a predefined set of pairs input/output. It has a web-based interface –shown in Figure 1–, which is different for the students, teachers, guest users and the system administrator.

More specifically, we are currently using Mooshak 1.4 [4], which is free and publicly available. This system was originally created by Jose P. Leal to manage programming competitions. However, Mooshak is applied more and more to computer programming learning. It works as follows:

− A set of problem descriptions is available in the students' web interface for each activity that is proposed. These descriptions present problems related with the theoretical concepts studied in class. Each description contains a statement of the problem, a precise specification of the input of the program and the expected output, along with some sample input/output pairs.

− The students can select any problem from the set to solve it. First, they tackle the problem in their own computers, by writing a program which efficiently produces the expected outputs. When they have tested their implementation enough, they submit the solution to the judge using their interface.

- The on-line judge receives the source code, compiles the program, and executes it using the predefined sets of secret input cases. Then, Mooshak analyzes the output of the program (comparing it to the expected output) and sends a response to the student indicating whether the program is correct or not. If the program is not accepted, the judge reports about the rejection cause, such as for example if the program has a syntax error, or it is inefficient in time or memory.
- Statistical information of all the submissions sent to the judge is accessible both for teachers and for students. In particular, a ranking of the students sorted by the number of problems solved is given. The system also includes tools to send comments about the problem, and ask questions to the teachers.

Compared to other disciplines, judging the correction of a program, with a high degree of certain, is relatively simple; that is what makes automatic evaluation feasible. However, there are many aspects of programming that are not so easy to evaluate: computational complexity, design and organization of the code, robustness, legibility, etc. In consequence, the task of human teachers remains to be essential.

3.3   A Judge-Based Methodology

As mentioned in section 2, on-line judging systems have already been applied in computer programming courses. We can distinguish four different kinds of activities using automatic judging:

- **Independent problems.** In this kind of activity, many problems are proposed to the students. The problems are independent of each other, and with different levels of difficulty. The students are expected to select and solve some of them, not necessarily all. Problems can be grouped by category, in such a way that each category illustrates a programming technique discussed in class. Typically, some weeks are given to complete the activity.
- **Dependent problems.** This case is preferable when the objective of an activity is to develop a longer and more complex programming project. The project is divided into small and consecutive subproblems; each of them is described as a problem in the judge. The students have to solve *all* the problems in the given order. In the itinerary, a number of programming techniques can be illustrated. This activity can normally take several months.
- **Contest-style.** Contrary to the other cases, here the presence of the students is required. A set of at most 9 problems is given to the participants. They have to try to solve as many problems as possible, and as fast as they can. The contest can take between 4 and 6 hours.
- **Designing problems.** This is the most creative type of activities. The students have to create a problem with the format of the judge: problem description, source code to solve it, input cases, and expected outputs. The ability of the students to produce original and relevant problems is evaluated.

4   Evaluation of the Method

In this section, we provide detailed information about the course where the experiment was carried out, the application of the methodology, and the obtained results. The study was conducted at the Computer Science Faculty of the University of Murcia (Spain). This Faculty has a long tradition –25 years– in teaching Computer Science degrees.

4.1   Participants and Background

Table 1 summarizes the main information regarding the course and degrees under study. In particular, the new methodology was first applied in the academic year spanning from fall of 2007 to spring of 2008. Considering the enrollments, two of the degrees (TECS and TECM) can be considered as highly populous, while the other (CSE) is a reduced group.

Table 1. Course and degrees where the new methodology was applied. "ECTS": equivalent load in European Credits Transfer System; "Enroll07": enrollment the year before the experience; "Enroll08": enrollment the year of the experience. CSE is a five-years degree, while TECS and TECM are three-years degrees.

Course name	Year	Duration	ECTS
Algorithms and data structures (ADS)	2nd year	Annual	12
Degrees	**Acronym**	**Enroll07**	**Enroll08**
Computer science engineering	CSE	56	44
Technical engineering in computer systems	TECS	162	162
Technical engineering in computer management	TECM	150	131
	Total	368	337

ADS is basically a course in programming, emphasizing issues of algorithms and data representation. This course introduces such topics as data structures –including hash tables, trees and graphs–, objects, abstract data types and formal specifications. The course also includes techniques for performance analysis and design of algorithms. Design techniques such as divide and conquer, the greedy approach, dynamic programming, backtracking, and branch and bound are presented through a variety of algebraic, graph, and optimization problems. The programming languages used to illustrate these concepts are C, C++ and the formal specifications language Maude [12].

ADS was traditionally organized in a *monolithic* form: weekly lectures, laboratory sessions, a final exam and a programming project for each semester. In fall of 2007, the three courses were involved in the new system. Even though the students were also given the possibility to follow the traditional method, more than 2/3 of them actively participated in the proposed activities.

4.2   Instantiation of the Method

Figure 2 shows a global view of the new organization of the course (right), as compared to its traditional design (left). Activities U2, U3 and U5 are partial-exams of the corresponding theory units; P2 is lab assignment involving a theoretical/experimental analysis of efficiency of the project created in P1. The remaining activities are programming contests done in Mooshak.

First Semester: Data Structures

Traditional organization	Continuous evaluation
	U1. Formal specifications
	U2,U3. Hash and trees exam
Programming project + Final exam	U4. Graphs
	P1. Data structures implementation

Second Semester: Algorithms

Traditional organization	Continuous evaluation
	P2. Experimental analysis
	U5. Algorithmic analysis exam
	U6. Divide and conquer
Programming project + Final exam	U7. Greedy algorithms
	U8. Dynamic programming
	U9. Backtracking
	U10. Branch and bound

Fig. 2. Comparison between the traditional methodology based on a "final exam" (FE) evaluation, and the proposed "continuous evaluation" (CE) methodology. The activities that use Mooshak are marked in gray. Activities U1, U2, etc. correspond to units of theory; activities P1 and P2 correspond to practice.

There is a great variety in Mooshak's activities: some of them are to be done in groups, and others individually; sometimes the problems are assigned to the students, other times they can freely choose; they can be dependent or independent problems, etc. Figure 3 provides more information.

When introducing the on-line judge in the course, most work is not done in the presence of the teacher. One of our main concerns was to guarantee the originality and authorship of the programs submitted by the students. Some strategies are applied to reduce the risk of plagiarism and to detect it:

- Some of the activities (P1 and P2) include a compulsory interview of each group with the teachers, where they have to demonstrate their authorship.
- Authorship is guarantied in partial-exam activities (U2, U3 and U5).
- For the activities done in Mooshak, we use a plagiarism detection system developed by Cebrian et al. [8]. Thanks to Mooshak, all the submissions are available in judge's server, so the plagiarism detector can be easily applied.

Finally, we have to note that all the activities have to be documented by the students (written by hand), and they are manually corrected by the teachers.

Activity	Type of problems	# prob. to pass	# prob. to max.	Total # prob.	Indiv./ group	Language	Assigned
U1. Formal specifications	Independent	14	23	26	Group	Maude	No
U4. Graphs	Independent	4	6	15	Indiv.	C/C++	No
P1. Implem. of data struct.	Dependent	13	16	17	Group	C++	No
U6. Divide and conquer	Dependent	1	2	16	Indiv.	C/C++	Yes
U7. Greedy algorithms	Independent	1	4	7	Indiv.	C/C++	Yes/No
U8. Dynamic program.	Independent	1	4	7	Indiv.	C/C++	Yes/No
U9. Backtracking	Independent	1	3	12	Indiv.	C/C++	Yes/No
U10. Branch and bound	Independent	0	2	12	Indiv.	C/C++	No
Local program. contest	Contest	0	3	8	Group	Java/C/C++	No
Total		**35 (8)**	**63**	**120**			

Fig. 3. Description of the activities in the CE method that use Mooshak. "# prob. to pass": minimum number of problems necessary to pass the activity; "# prob. to max.": number of problems to obtain the maximum mark; "Total # prob.": number of problems existing in the judge; "assigned": indicates if the students are assigned different problems or they can select by themselves ("yes/no" means some of them are assigned). Some activities should be done individually, and others in groups of two. All the activities were compulsory, except the last two that were optional.

4.3   Results of the On-line Judge

The overall impact of on-line judging in the teaching of ADS has been dramatic. Up to 273 of the 337 enrolled students (81%) participated in some activity of the judge; 268 of them (79.5%) solved at least one problem. This percentage raises up to 84% in CSE and TECS groups.

In total, the on-line judge received 16054 submissions: 11969 C/C++ programs and 4085 Maude programs in U1. This makes an average of 59 submissions per student: 44 C/C++ programs, and 15 Maude programs. The on-line judge classified around 6427 of these as correct (40.1%), and 4417 as "wrong answer" (27.5%). More information on the classification of the submissions, and the percentages per unit of knowledge is shown in Table 2 and in Figure 4.

Table 2. Detail of the classification of the submissions by activity, as listed in Figure 3. The last column indicates the number of students (or groups) that passed the corresponding activity.

Activity	Total submissions	Correct	Wrong answer	Runtime error	Other errors	Pass the activity
U1	4085 (25%)	1971 (48%)	1511 (37%)	600 (15%)	3 (0.1%)	85 groups
U4	2884 (18%)	1164 (40%)	493 (17%)	366 (13%)	861 (30%)	181 (54%)
P1	3615 (22%)	1229 (34%)	1099 (30%)	273 (8%)	1014 (28%)	41 groups
U6	2032 (12%)	705 (35%)	263 (13%)	161 (8%)	903 (44%)	178 (53%)
U7	1780 (11%)	619 (35%)	688 (39%)	66 (4%)	407 (23%)	182 (54%)
U8	830 (5%)	410 (49%)	189 (23%)	51 (6%)	180 (22%)	170 (50%)
U9	778 (4%)	309 (40%)	171 (22%)	12 (2%)	286 (37%)	162 (48%)
U10	50 (0.3%)	20 (40%)	3 (6%)	3 (6%)	24 (28%)	13 (4%)
Total	16054	6427 (40%)	4417 (28%)	1532 (10%)	3678 (23%)	75 (22%)

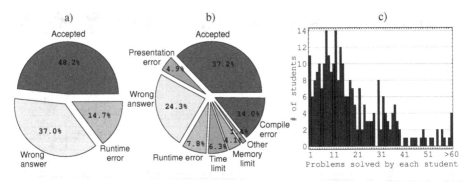

Fig. 4. Some results of the submissions made to the on-line judge. a) Classification of the 4085 Maude programs in U1. b) Classification of the 11969 C/C++ programs in the rest of activities. c) Number of problems solved by each student.

The average number of submissions per student until getting a program accepted is 2.7; anyway, many students found the solution to the problems at the first attempt (mode is 1). As shown in Figure 4, compilation errors, runtime errors, and excessive consumption of time and memory are caught by the system.

There is also a significant difference in the three groups under study. For example, while the average acceptation rate in CSE is 50%, in TECS it is 37% and in TECM 36%; this difference is consistently seen in all the activities.

Figure 4c) shows a histogram of the number of problems solved per student. This value covers a wide range, from 1 to 80, with an average of 18.5, standard deviation of 14.7, and with two modes of 8 and 12. As indicated in Table 2, many students passed individual activities –normally over 50%–, although not all of them passed all the activities.

Finally, it is also interesting to analyze *when* the students work. Figure 5 shows two charts representing the number of submissions per hour and per day of the week. The greatest period of activity takes place at lecture hours and days. However, submissions done by the students *outside* lecture hours represent a total of 48.6%, thus demonstrating the importance of autonomous work. In fact, there is no single hour with 0 submissions.

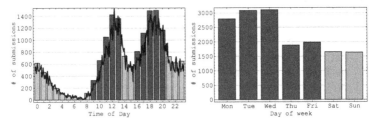

Fig. 5. Left: number of submissions made by the students in each hour of a day. The minimum is at 7 am (18) and the local maxima at 12 pm (1423) and at 7 pm (1499). In thick line, detailed number of submissions per 1/10 of an hour. Right: number of submissions in each day of a week. Darker bars represent lecture hours and days.

Concerning the days of the week, the distribution is quite surprising, with a peak on Wednesdays and a sudden decrease on Thursdays. Working habits also differ from day to day. On Wednesdays, the maximum activity is clearly located at 12 pm. However, in the rest of days the peaks are registered in the interval 6 pm – 7 pm; only on weekends most work is done between 8 pm and 9 pm.

5   Discussion

The results obtained after the application of the edutainment-based methodology are very promising. Considering just the final marks of the students, shown in Table 3, the new approach achieved excellent improvements. The most striking fact is the dramatic decline in the dropout rate, from 72.3% to 44.8%. On the other hand, the increase in the failure rate is due to the high number of students that passed some activities but not all. However, we think they can be better prepared to pass the course in subsequent attempts.

It is also observed that the improvement is far more significant in CSE than in TECS and TECM; the pass rate in CSE degree grows from 19.64% to 61.36%. The reduced size of this group has allowed a better application of the new methodology. It could also be due to a general *higher level* of students in this five-years degree as compared to the students in the "technical engineering".

Analyzing these results, we think the proposed organization of the course successfully meets all the pedagogical principles established in subsection 3.1:

- **Motivation.** In all the ways of using the on-line judge (independent, dependent and contest style problems), the ranking plays a fundamental role in motivating students to solve more problems, faster and more efficiently. If students get an "accepted", a rise in ranking means students get an incentive to continue tackling other algorithmic problems. This is evident in the high number of students who solved more problems than those necessary to obtain the maximum mark: they also wanted to be up in the ranking.
- **Active learning.** When students solve the proposed problems, they play a leading role in their own learning. As an example, it is worth underlining the high number of comments and questions asked by the students in Mooshak. In particular, 1119 questions were answered by the teachers along the course.

Table 3. Pass, failure and dropout rates of the three degrees where the new methodology was applied (in 2008), as compared to the results in the previous year (2007)

Final results	Total		CSE		TECS		TECM	
	2007	2008	2007	2008	2007	2008	2007	2008
Pass rate	10.9%	22.3%	19.6%	61.4%	7.3%	13.0%	11.1%	19.1%
	(40)	(75)	(11)	(27)	(11)	(17)	(18)	(31)
Failure rate	16.8%	32.9%	14.3%	6.8%	22.7%	32.1%	12.3%	40.7%
	(62)	(111)	(8)	(3)	(34)	(42)	(20)	(66)
Dropout rate	72.3%	44.8%	66.1%	31.2%	70.0%	54.9%	76.5%	40.1%
	(266)	(151)	(37)	(14)	(105)	(72)	(124)	(65)

- **Autonomous work.** Students can work in the labs, where they have help from the teachers. However, it is evident that students mostly work at home, and ask questions to the teachers by using Mooshak. Therefore, on-line judging eases to work autonomously.
- **Feedback of the learning process.** The web system provided feedback to help students to correct many errors of the programs, thus avoiding assistants spend much effort figuring out the causes of the failure, as happens in a traditional evaluation. The judge is accessible 24-hours a day and the feedback is instantaneous. From the point of view of the teachers, information is also comprehensive and immediate; they can analyze the difficulty of the problems, the evolution of the students, identify the best students, etc.

To conclude, we have to mention some remarkable results from a survey carried out among the students of the CSE group, regarding their experience in the new methodology. They were asked to indicate a degree of agreement/disagreement with a series of statements. These are some of the items evaluated:

- 77% of the students agree that "they learn better with the new method";
- 68% say that "the public ranking of the judge fosters competitiveness";
- All students disagree with "cheating is easier with the on-line judge";
- 91% say that "if they could choose, they would follow again the CE method".

These ratios have to be considered as subjective *appreciations* made by the students. Nevertheless, we have to observe that 75% of the students enrolled in 2008 were also enrolled in 2007. Thus, they were able to compare the new and the old methodology. Proving that they really *learn better* is difficult, as they were evaluated with different methods. However, considering only the theory units corresponding to U2, U3 and U5 (that were evaluated with a written exam, both in 2008 and 2007), the pass rate went from 18.6% in 2007 to 38.6% in 2008, and the average mark (in range 0-10) went from 4.6 to 5.7.

On the negative side, we can mention two items:

- 86% of the students agree that "the feedback provided by the judge in case of error is insufficient". In order to reduce this problem, we took the strategy of *releasing* one of the secret input/output cases for each problem.
- 60% say that "the total load of work is higher with the new methodology"; only 27% say it is lower. We think this problem can be easily solved by redesigning some of the activities. Nevertheless, the new methodology has a crucial advantage over the traditional one: the students work along the course, and not just some weeks before the final exam.

6   Conclusions and Future Work

In this paper, an innovative experience on computer science education –applying the techniques, concepts and methods of edutainment– has been presented. Entertainment has traditionally been neglected in formal education, and specially in university studies. We have shown that on-line judging systems can be used to make more fun the activities of a programming course.

In general, the results of our experiment are outstanding. The approach improves self-assessment skills and encourages students to work independently. The public ranking and other statistical data provided by Mooshak, promote competitiveness and offer appealing material to the students. The assessment is fair and objective, and students gain additional feedback from the human judges. Obviously, the improvements are also due to the introduction of continuous evaluation and the elimination of the final exam, which constitutes the second key element of the proposed methodology.

Two major aspects remain to be improved in the future: the feedback provided by the judge, and plagiarism detection. We are currently working on extensions of Mooshak to provide detailed feedback in case of "wrong answer", and to integrate the plagiarism detector subsystem into the web interface of Mooshak.

References

1. Education at a Glance: OECD Indicators (2006),
   http://www.oecd.org/edu/eag2006
2. OECD Science, Technology and Industry Scoreboard (2007),
   http://www.oecd.org/sti/scoreboard
3. Rapeepisarn, K., Wong, K.W., Fung, C.C., Depickere, A.: Similarities and Differences Between "Learn Through Play" and "Edutainment". In: Proc. of the 3rd Australasian Conference on interactive Entertainment, pp. 28–32 (2006)
4. Leal, J.P., Silva, F.M.A.: Mooshak: a Web-based, Multi-site, Programming Contest System. Software-Practice, and Experience 33(6), 567–581 (2003)
5. Robins, A., Rountree, J., Rountree, N.: Learning and Teaching Programming: A Review and Discussion. Computer Science Education 13(2), 137–172 (2003)
6. Guerreiro, P., Georgouli, K.: Enhancing Elementary Programming Courses Using E-learning with a Competitive Attitude. Int. Journal of Internet Education (2008)
7. Guerreiro, P., Georgouli, K.: Combating Anonymousness in Populous CS1 and CS2 Courses. In: Proc. ITICSE 2006, pp. 8–12 (2006)
8. Cebrian, M., Alfonseca, M., Ortega, A.: Towards the Validation of Plagiarism Detection Tools by Means of Grammar Evolution. IEEE Trans. on Evolutionary Computation (2008)
9. Khine, M., Suja'ee, M.: Core Attributes of Interactive Computer Games and Adaptive Use for Edutainment. In: Pan, Z., Cheok, D.A.D., Müller, W., El Rhalibi, A. (eds.) Transactions on Edutainment I. LNCS, vol. 5080, pp. 191–205. Springer, Heidelberg (2008)
10. White, R.: That's Edutainment. Hutchinson Leisure & Learning Group (2003),
    http://www.whitehutchinson.com/leisure/articles/edutainment.shtml
11. Martens, A., Diener, H., Malo, S.: Core Attributes of Interactive Computer Games and Adaptive Use for Edutainment. In: Pan, Z., Cheok, D.A.D., Müller, W., El Rhalibi, A. (eds.) Transactions on Edutainment I. LNCS, vol. 5080, pp. 172–190. Springer, Heidelberg (2008)
12. Clavel, M., Duran, F., Eker, S., Lincoln, P., Marti, N., Meseguer, J., Talcott, C.: All About Maude - A High-Performance Logical Framework. In: Clavel, M., Durán, F., Eker, S., Lincoln, P., Martí-Oliet, N., Meseguer, J., Talcott, C. (eds.) All About Maude - A High-Performance Logical Framework. LNCS, vol. 4350. Springer, Heidelberg (2007)

KEI-Time Traveler: A Virtual Time Machine with Mobile Phones for Learning Local History

Hiroyuki Tarumi[1], Keitaro Yamada[1], Takafumi Daikoku[2],
Fusako Kusunoki[3], Shigenori Inagaki[2], Makiko Takenaka[4],
Toshihiro Hayashi[1], and Masahiko Yano[5]

[1] Kagawa University, Takamatsu, Kagawa 761-0396 Japan
tarumi@acm.org
[2] Kobe University, Kobe 657-8501 Japan
[3] Tama Art University, Hachioji, Tokyo 192-0394 Japan
[4] Oita University, Oita 870-1192 Japan
[5] Fujitsu Shikoku Systems, Ltd., Takamatsu, Kagawa 760-0071 Japan

Abstract. KEI-Time Traveler is a kind of "virtual time machine" that requires only commercially available mobile phones with no hardware attachment. In reality, KEI-Time Traveler presents graphical images of a past scene within a given area, viewed from the location measured using GPS and with arbitrary viewing angles. Users can explore a virtual past world using this system. A promising application of KEI-Time Traveler is edutainment. We applied it for learning activities with a group of 34 junior high school students. They virtually visited a world of 1938, when a severe landslide disaster occurred. They were able to compare conditions now and in the past directly at places with which they were familiar. The design approach and evaluation of our edutainment practice are described herein. Technically, the system uses 3D-model-based graphics that can be updated continually. From an educational perspective, students truly enjoyed the experience. It was not merely fun: our system raised their motivation to learn about disaster prevention. We confirmed the edutainment effect based on evidence: user responses and recordings of their experiences.

1 Introduction

Fieldwork gives students experiences with authentic objects, places, situations, and fun. It also enhances students' motivation by allowing them to leave the classroom. However, if one studies history itself, or learns information based on history, one can, at best, merely visit ruins or museums. Ideally, a student should be able to visit a past world to learn about history.

To realize this ideal, we developed *KEI-Time Traveler*, which is a compound word coined from KEITAI and Time Traveler. KEITAI is a Japanese word used to describe a mobile telephone. Of course, it is not a real time machine: it is a kind of browser that enables students to view the past world through the small window of a mobile phone using GPS.

Z. Pan et al. (Eds.): Transactions on Edutainment II, LNCS 5660, pp. 258–282, 2009.

We used KEI-Time Traveler during an educational course for 34 junior high school students. We designed a 3D model of a past world of 1938, at which time a landslide occurred. The past world model contained images of rocks, floods, destroyed houses, and people of the past: victims who needed help. Students visited the past world and learned much about it. We confirmed that they used KEI-Time Traveler and were motivated for learning well. Herein, we present the design of the system and contents, results of its practical use, and its evaluation.

The objectives of this study were the following:

1. Technical aspect: to provide a low-cost interface using only commercially available mobile phones with which students can view, from any desired location or angle, a past world that is designed as a 3D model.
2. Educational Aspect: to evaluate the effect on education of using our system, including evaluation of students' motivation.

2   Related Work

2.1   Mobile Augmented Reality Systems

Augmented reality (AR) (or *mixed reality (MR)*) technologies, which put annotation information to real objects, are studied by many researchers. Using mobile devices such as laptop PCs, tablet PCs, Personal Digital Assistants (PDAs), or mobile phones, outdoor applications of augmented reality systems have been proposed. Location of users must be known by such systems to provide annotation information: location sensors such as GPS, wireless LAN, IrDA, and RFID readers are used.

Some researchers have used heavy devices such as wearable PCs, in some cases with head mounted displays (HMDs), or even larger devices, to make use of their greater available computing power. Some were aimed at guiding services (e.g., [1,2,3,4,5,6]) and some were designed for gaming (e.g., [7,8]). Such approaches would be exciting, but they are inappropriate to our goal, fieldwork by children, because of their weight, bulk, and cost.

The most popular devices for outdoor AR activities are PDAs. Some PDAs provide local area guide services (e.g., [9,10,11]). Some support group activities such as gaming (e.g., [12,13,14]) and sightseeing (e.g., [15]).

A few researchers have attempted to use mobile phones because phones are low-cost and wide-spread [16,17,18].

2.2   Edutainment Applications

Mobile technologies and AR/MR technologies have been regarded as tools for edutainment.

Handheld devices are anticipated for use as powerful tools for education [19]. Roschelle described three application patterns of edutainment with wireless networks that have developed by many researchers: *classroom response systems, participatory simulations*, and *collaborative data gathering*[20]. Among them, our interest is in the second and third categories.

The AR/MR technologies with mobile devices support another category of edutainment applications: *enhanced experiences*. By presenting information of real world's objects to children through mobile devices, their fieldwork would become richer. Guiding applications described in 2.1 were mostly intended to be used by tourists or shoppers, but some might be used for children's fieldwork.

Participatory Simulations. Participatory simulation systems set up a virtual environment in which learners assume some roles and have unusual experiences using mobile devices. Often AR technologies are introduced.

For example, "Outbreak @ The Institute" system [21] simulated a fictional scenario: the outbreak of an emerging disease on campus. Students assumed roles of doctors, medical technicians, or public health experts. Virtual characters appeared in the simulated environment, with whom students were able to have conversations. The PDAs were used as terminals; wireless LANs were used for location-sensing and communications.

Savannah [22] provided a virtual savannah in which children played the roles of lions using PDAs with attached GPS receivers connected to a central server via wireless LAN. The system was used on a football field. Children learned mutual collaboration to hunt animals.

Collaborative Data Gathering. A very early instance of this category was Wireless Coyote [23]. It used pen-based PCs and a wireless LAN. Children measured scientific data in a canyon and input them to the PCs. The data were exchanged via wireless LAN among the PCs.

Ambient Wood [24] was a unique system. Networked devices were set up in a forest, including audio devices called Ambient Horn [25] and large terminals called Periscope [26] that provided students with access to pre-recorded videos. Children visiting the forest took data and learned about nature.

Recent examples of this category took advantage of mobile phones with embedded cameras to capture image data from the real world [27,28].

Enhanced Experiences. Past Viewer [29] was a system used to learn history. It was useful to present a movie of past scenes through see-through type HMD, at pre-defined locations. Learners were able to watch the movie while looking at today's scene. Nevertheless, it did not use so-called ubiquitous technologies such as location sensors or wireless LAN.

DigitalEE II [30] was a system supporting enhanced experiences. Learners in a forest using PDA with GPS, a camera, and wireless LAN were able to communicate with a remote specialist who could support learning about plants.

The BWL system [31] supported bird-watching. It used PDA and wireless LAN. Its design was particularly intended as a learning model with attention devoted to the scaffolding metaphor.

A system by Halloran et al. [32] was produced for primary school children. It supported the study of creative writing during a field trip. Children used PDAs augmented with GPS. They were able to receive location-dependent messages of audio and text from the system.

HyConExplorer [33] used mobile phones with attached GPS receivers and tablet PCs. Children were able to give and take annotation information from and to the system while visiting the field trip destination.

2.3 Our Standpoint

The KEI-Time Traveler is a mobile AR system because it gives past scenes as augmented information of the present world. From an edutainment perspective, it is designed to provide children with enhanced experiences during the field-work. It is not a participatory simulation system because it does not support simulated dynamic behaviors. Instead, its graphical output is richer than that of participatory simulation systems.

As described in section 1, this study has both technical and educational aspects.

Technically, our system uses only commercially available mobile phones with no hardware attachment. Using such phones is appropriate for education for cost and weight reasons. Some systems described in this section also used mobile phones. However, as a unique approach that enables children to visit a virtual past world, we adopted a 3D model-based graphic generation for phones.

From an educational perspective, we have evaluated how children felt and how they were motivated by visiting the past world. Some studies introduced in this section also provided services to watch past worlds. Augurscope [2] presented a past scene, but it was a heavy system and was not evaluated in a educational setting. Past Viewer [29] also enabled people to watch past scenes at the corresponding location, but it presented movie films at only a few pre-defined locations.

3 System Design

Figure 1 depicts the concept of KEI-Time Traveler. Using a mobile phone, a learner can view a virtual world: a reproduction of a past world at that identical location. Some personalities of the past, who can talk to users through short messages, can be viewed in the past world. Actually, KEI-Time Traveler was developed as built-in software running on a phone using the Brew platform. Brew[1] [34] is a software platform designed by Qualcomm Inc. for CDMA-based mobile terminals. Using Brew, it is possible to develop terminal-side software using C or C++ language, which can sense the built-in GPS receiver periodically.

To provide a view of the 3D model of the virtual world from arbitrary locations, KEI-Time Traveler must obtain the user's location parameters and their view angle information. The relevant X and Y location parameters—latitude and longitude—are obtained using the GPS.

The view angle parameters are taken from the user's operations. Some GPS phones have a built-in electronic compass that supports automatic sensing of the

---

[1] http://brew.qualcomm.com/brew/en/

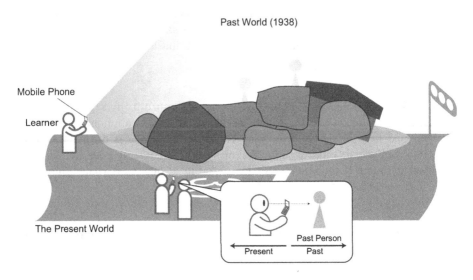

Fig. 1. KEI-Time Traveler Concept

horizontal parameters of the view angle. However, we did not adopt such models because those telephones are not popular and might not be widely available. A depiction of the compass is presented on the telephone's display to indicate the horizontal viewing angle (Fig. 2). The vertical view angle parameter can be controlled by the user's operation. Figure 3 portrays part of the operation manual.

An image on the phone, which is a scene of the past world, is updated constantly within about every 5 s by sensing the GPS receiver, in this case of implementation. It is also updated immediately after any operation is performed by the user.

The graphics are rendered using HI's Mascot Capsule[2] [35] from a 3D world model designed with LightWave 3D [3] [36].

An important technical problem is GPS' inaccuracy. We introduced an error-compensation mechanism using a map of walkable paths. Location parameters obtained by GPS were modified to the closest point on walkable paths. Precisely speaking, a user can view the past world from any location on walkable paths.

A 3D model of the past world and walkable path data are included in the terminal-side software. Therefore, it can be used merely by downloading the package onto the telephone. No special server computer is necessary except for two servers provided by the carrier company: the gpsOne [37] location server and the Brew application distribution server.

---

[2] http://www.hicorp.co.jp/english/product/
[3] http://www.newtek.com/lightwave/

Fig. 2. View Angle Indicator

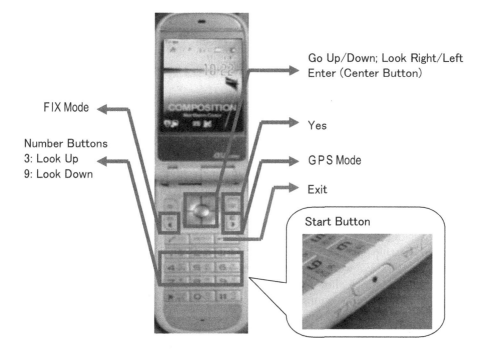

Fig. 3. Part of the KEI-Time Traveler Operation Manual

4   Content Development

4.1   Educational Program

The contents of the program depend heavily on the educational program. The educational program was practiced at a junior high school in Japan. It was applied to an activity with 34 third-year student participants, whose ages were 14–15. The topic of instruction was prevention of mud and sand disasters in local areas. With help from a government office promoting education related to disaster prevention, the program was designed as a series of five sessions (Table 1). We planned two fieldwork activities and applied KEI-Time Traveler for fieldwork 1. Using KEI-Time Traveler, we expected students to visit a past world in which disaster prevention had been insufficient.

Table 1. Session Plan

No.	Date	Session Description
1	Nov. 13, 2007	introduction
2	Nov. 16, 2007	fieldwork 1
3	Nov. 27, 2007	discussion of fieldwork 1
4	Nov. 30, 2007	fieldwork 2
5	Dec. 4, 2007	demonstrative experiment of a landslide by the government office; closing discussion

4.2   Prototyping and Evaluation

For the fieldwork site, we selected a residential area along a river, where a past world presents a scene of the landslide in 1938. We created some virtual characters as victims. A monument of a fallen rock remains in the residential area, which had been crushed by a landslide in 1938 (Fig. 4). The rock is an actual fallen rock of that disaster. The pedestal height marks the flood depth. We expected that the monument would help us to emphasize the magnitude and effects of the past disaster to students and thereby spur their consideration

To create the past world model, we collected photographs taken after the disaster in 1938. We were able to find one photograph taken near the location of the monument, which showed there had been a few two-storied houses. We were also provided with some comments from specialists in mud and sand disasters. As a prototype, we arranged five houses that had been destroyed by the landslide, numerous rocks, and a man and a woman as victims of the disaster. A rock that was identical to that on the monument was embedded in the past world.

Implementation of the 3D model was outsourced to a company that has much experience and excellent techniques for producing graphical game software embedded on mobile phones.

The original design of KEI-Time Traveler did not allow for control of the height of the viewpoint. However, in the virtual world of 1938, the area is covered with mud and sand to a depth of greater than 2 m. The scene viewed by

Fig. 4. Monument of a Fallen Rock

KEI-Time Traveler from the average human height would be mud and sand. Consequently, we introduced a control mechanism for the viewpoint altitude.

Another modification that we introduced into the KEI-Time Traveler prototype software is the FIX mode. The monument is an important object in the

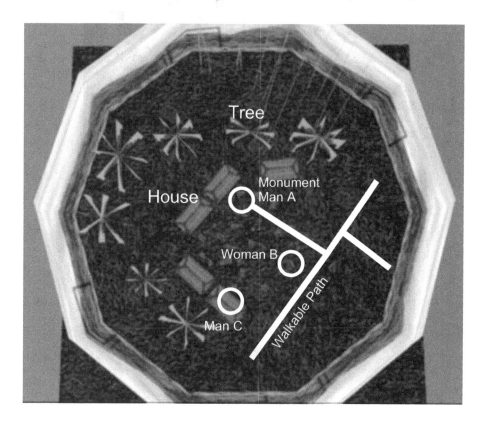

Fig. 5. Past World Map

fieldwork. We intended for students to observe the past world around the monument well. A mechanism that switches off the GPS and fixes the viewpoint to the location in front of the monument was introduced to avoid unstable views around the monument. That mechanism is designated as the FIX mode.

As the error compensation map used for GPS inaccuracy, we defined four paths for students to walk on. These paths are alongside the roads and natural walking paths in the fieldwork area (See Fig. 5).

On Oct. 23, 2007, we evaluated the prototype around the monument. We considered that if students walked freely around the monument without restriction, they might be unable to find people of the past. For that reason, we decided to instruct students to start from the location immediately in front of the monument. We appended a past man on the monument rock who talks to students

Past Man A (FIX Mode)   Past Woman B

Looking Down from the Sky

Fig. 6. Sample Screenshots

first (Past Man A). After hearing from past man A, students would then be allowed to walk freely.

4.3   Final Version

Figure 5 presents the final design of the past world. Walkable paths (white thick lines) were defined based on the present environment. Five houses and three people were prepared. The three people talk to the students as follows (originally in Japanese):

> Past Man A (on the rock): "Such a big rock fell and destroyed my house. Look around you!"
> Past Man A: "Walk around here, but take care."
> Past Man A: "We should preserve this rock as a future monument."
> Past Woman B (in the flood): "Help save me from the flood!"
> Past Man C (on the roof, see Fig. 2): "My house was destroyed by the landslide."

Figure 6 presents some screenshots from a mobile phone.

To evaluate the effect of 3D virtual world, we also developed a 2D version of compatible contents for comparison. The 2D version has four HTML pages, three of which contain typical screenshots from the final version with people of the past as in Fig. 6 and a few lines of descriptive statements.

5   Practice

The fieldwork activity was held on Nov. 16, 2007. For preparation, at the first session on Nov. 13 (see Table 1), we had given a short instruction of KEI-Time Traveler to students, without showing any contents that would be used in the fieldwork.

The participating students were 34 (11 boys (denoted as M1–M11) and 23 girls (F1–F23)). We prepared 19 telephones. Students did the fieldwork in groups of two or three students, with one or two shared phone(s) for each group. The number of groups was 16.

Before starting the fieldwork, we again gave instructions on how to use KEI-Time Traveler, especially about the view angle indicator. We confirmed which direction was north at the fieldwork site.

Around the monument, they were instructed to use KEI-Time Traveler for about 10 min and talk about the disaster with their companions. During the fieldwork for about two hours, they visited four places including the monument area, where KEI-Time Traveler was available.

They were also instructed to view the 2D contents before or after the experience of KEI-Time Traveler. Half of the students (17 students) viewed the 2D contents before KEI-Time Traveler; half viewed 2D after it.

The mobile phones we provided were W31T type "au" [4] telephones. Each had a GPS receiver and QVGA (240 × 320 pixels) display. It does not support an electronic compass. Actually, W31T was released in June 2005. Therefore, it has inferior performance for graphics compared to the latest devices.

Videotapes and still cameras recorded all students' performance at the monument area. After the fieldwork, all students were requested to complete a questionnaire form. In addition, 30 students participated in personal interview sessions after the questionnaire. After finishing the educational program of five sessions described in Table 1, we requested that students write a short essay on the course of five sessions from the viewpoint of their experience, development, and mobile learning with telephone.

6   Results

In this section, quantitative and qualitative analyses related to the questionnaire, interviews, videotaped logs, and written papers are explained. All comments were presented originally in Japanese.

The most noteworthy analyses are those of interviews, conversations, and papers. What students talked and wrote gave us much information related to what and how they learned, and the degree to which KEI-Time Traveler was a good edutainment tool.

6.1   Questionnaire

We asked four questions to compare KEI-Time Traveler's 3D contents and 2D contents with usual HTML. The questions and response summaries are presented in Table 2 (Q1–Q4). For each question, we provided five options (1–5) arranged as a Likert scale, where 5 is the best score for 3D, 1 is the worst, and 3 is neutral. Table 2 shows that students evaluate the 3D model better than 2D.

We asked two questions to evaluate the effects on students of people of the past. Questions (Q5, Q6) and response summaries are presented in Table 2, where 5 is the best score. The people from the past were evaluated positively. The effect of the people of the past characters will be discussed later.

Questions 1–4 might be affected by the order of the two experiences: the 3D model-based expression and the 2D version. Table 3 shows scores comparing them. Group A ($N = 17$) tried the 2D version first, and Group B ($N = 17$) tried them in the reversed order. Group A evaluated the 3D model higher than Group B did, probably because of the fresh impression of their later experiences. However, even Group B evaluated KEI-Time Traveler more highly than the 2D model.

In the questionnaire, we asked students to comment freely about the good and bad aspects of KEI-Time Traveler and any other comments on the fieldwork. Major comments are as follows.

---

[4] "au" is a brand of a mobile phone produced by KDDI Corp. GPS (gpsOne) is provided for au phones of many types.

Table 2. (Questionnaire Results $N = 34$)

	Question	Ave.	S.D.
Q1	Which was better for you to understand the past situation?	4.6	0.60
Q2	Which has presented terrible aspects of the disaster better?	4.4	0.81
Q3	Which has made you feel more empathy with the people living in the past?	4.2	1.00
Q4	Which would you like to use at the next opportunity?	4.5	0.62
Q5	Was it worthwhile for you that people of the past were presented?	4.7	0.52
Q6	Did comments from people of the past help you to learn?	4.1	0.79

Table 3. Comparison related to the order of two experiences

	Group A		Group B	
Question	Ave.	S.D.	Ave.	S.D.
1	4.8	0.39	4.4	0.74
2	4.7	0.59	3.9	0.83
3	4.5	0.71	4.0	1.07
4	4.8	0.39	4.2	0.68

For good aspects, 14 (out of 34) students commented that the 3D model was good. Some examples are:

> "With the 3D model, we can understand the past situation and it was interesting for me to walk in the past world" (M6)
> "It was like a time-slip because the picture was changed as I walked" (F11).

Eight students commented on the comparison between the present and the past. An example is:

> "I was considering what the people of the past experienced and did against the landslide" (F19).

Regarding negative opinions, most comments were related to technical problems: 11 students complained about the speed of graphics or low frequency of updating and 7 complained about the graphics quality. Both criticisms are attributable to the technical limitations of the mobile phones used for the fieldwork. Actually, the W31T is not a state-of-the-art model. Therefore, these problems might be mitigated using the latest model.

For other comments, 13 students commented that using a mobile phone for learning was attractive. The reasons given were its portability, familiarity, and casual feeling.

6.2 Quantitative Analyses of Written Papers

We collected 33 (11 boys and 22 girls) papers written by students after all five sessions. *All students* gave positive comments in relation to KEI-Time Traveler.

Table 4. Topics Mentioned in Papers ($N = 33$)

Topic	Occurrences
Understanding the past situation	22
Merit of 3D	12
Fun, good concentration, or quick understanding resulting from experience-based learning	11
Portability or familiarity of mobile phones	9
Expectation of wide applications of KEI-Time Traveler	6
Past People	4

The quantities of papers that described notable topics are listed in Table 4. The papers were freely written: students did not select topics given by us. A few negative comments related to the usability and graphics quality were given. They will be described later.

6.3   Qualitative Analyses of Interviews, Videos, and Written Papers

Comparison between Past and Present. The most important benefit of KEI-Time Traveler was expected to be the virtual experience of visiting the past world, enabling students to compare the past and present directly. As presented in Table 4 and positive comments in the questionnaire, the benefit is strongly suggested.

Here are some descriptions by participants. First, we present some quotations from the interviews and papers.

> "I visited the monument area without thinking of the enormous damage. However, when I viewed the past with the mobile phone, I found that the debris accumulated very thickly. A telegraph pole suggested the thickness. I was surprised at the damage." (F1, interview)

> "I used a GPS-phone and was able to look into the past world at any location. I felt as if I had time-slipped to 1938, and felt really afraid of the disaster." (F10, paper)

> "Differences between the past and the present were clear to me." (M1, paper)

> "In front of the monument, I felt as if I'd been there in 1938. I think I became able to consider things differently from learning with photographs and pictures." (F17, paper)

Next are excerpts of the students' protocol from the video. They were considering the past situation compared to that of the present world.

> M10: "It's a telegraph pole."
> M11: "I think the debris was so thick because it can be compared with the pole."
> M10: "Yes. This is a roof of a house, isn't it?"
> M11: "Yes."

Left: M10 and M11 checked the height of accumulated debris in 1938, referencing the present world.
Right: F16 (right) began a discussion of the landslide mechanism with her companion.

Fig. 7. Scenes of Fieldwork

> M10: *"A telegraph pole ...."* (looking up)
> M11: *"Then it was so terrible around there..."* (pointing his finger,
> Fig. 7(left)[5]) *"We would have been under water if we had been there."*

By visiting the past world, some students took further consideration.

> *"I gave the exercise more detailed consideration than I had antici-*
> *pated. It was because I was able to look into the world of just several*
> *decades ago."* (F21, paper)
> *"In the mountain, a mountain like this (Fig. 7(right)), there was a big*
> *rock— and—this rock was moved by the water and fell into this house..."*
> (F16, video, talking to her companion)

Effect of 3D Model. To learn history, students usually use textbooks, documents, and photographs (if available). In our sessions, students also had access to a textbook authored by the government office, including some photographs taken after the 1938 disaster. Still, they valued the 3D virtual experiences provided by KEI-Time Traveler.

First, as Table 2 portrays, the 3D contents were more supported than 2D contents that included some HTML pages selected from among the 3D contents.

Second, we acquired much evidence from video recordings showing students using the 3D movement positively. The following are just some examples.

> F15: *"A tree is floating."*
> F14: *"How high do we go?"*
> F15: *"It's enough, maybe."*
> F14: *"What a disaster around here!"*

---

[5] All photographs appear with permission of students and their parents.

F15: "Ye...s..."
F14: "Because the water came just a little below the roofs ..."
F15: "Can we see houses if we enter?"

As this protocol implies, they changed their viewpoint to a higher point; then they were going to enter a house by moving themselves.

Below is another protocol that shows that students enjoyed the 3D movement:

M8: "Go up to the highest."
M9: "9?" ('9' button?)
M8: "Yes."
M9: "Gee! There is a guy. Shall we rotate more?"
M8: "Let's do it."
M9: "In which direction?" (rotating his body synchronizing with the view angle indicator)
M8: "Oh, a woman is floating."

Third, we present some evidence from students' interviews and writings.

"I think it is different between looking at a snapshot from a pinpointed location by PC or anything and visiting the real site with confirmation of the past situation using the phone. So I think it was a very good experience for me." (F13, interview)

"I think 3D is better since I can look up or down. 2D is the same as paper." (F8, interview)

"It was interesting that the picture was updated as I walked." (F12, paper)

"By looking down from the sky, I understood the scale of damage." (F9, paper)

A few students preferred 2D to 3D. Actually, F10, who marked '2' for question 2 in the questionnaire, stated that the graphics of the 2D version were easier to view. However, the graphics for the 2D version were merely copied from the graphics generated from the 3D model; the resolution was the same. Because of this fact, we consider that F10's impression resulted from the instability of the graphics attributable to the technical limitations of GPS sensors.

Empathy with People of the Past. Not so many, but several students were able to consider the disaster from the perspective of people of the past, or were able to feel empathy with them. Table 2 presents that four students wrote something about people of the past in their papers.

"By seeing people of the past in the past scene, I was able to put myself in their place." (F3, interview)

"I felt frightened when I saw people on the roof who needed help." (F6, interview)

"It was a good experience to hear from the people of the past. I would never understand it if I were only to see today's world. I understood how people in the past felt." (F12, paper)

F19, who was not included among the four students described above, made a similar comment in the questionnaire, as already described in 6.1. Including her, five students gave comments on the people of the past in the questionnaire. In all, 8 (one was duplicated) of 34 students commented somehow about the people of the past.

Mobile Phones are Commodities. We used commercially available mobile phones because they are inexpensive and familiar to students. Students did not care about the cost because we provided telephones, but familiarity was important for them. At least 31 of 34 students use their own mobile phones. Portability is another important benefit.

As demonstrated from the free responses in the questionnaire, 13 students offered positive comments especially related to using mobile phones. In the papers, students also gave some comments related to its familiarity and portability.

> *"I was able to learn things by walking around and comparing things of today and the past. Phones gave me strong impressions." (F19, interview)*

> *"I had been thinking that a mobile phone was just for conversations and e-mail, but not for school. However, I have found that it can help us to learn." (F20, paper)*

> *"A familiar thing, mobile phone, has changed my sense of values." (M8, paper)*

> *"Because a mobile phone is portable, I think it is very appropriate for such fieldwork." (F16, paper)*

> *"Phones made it easy for me to learn difficult things." (M7, paper)*

> *"It was fun to use mobile phones for learning. Phones are familiar to us and can give pictures." (F11, paper)*

We were concerned about the small display of mobile phones. Small screens often engender problems when presenting learning objects [38]. However, some students left positive comments in their papers.

> *"Although a mobile phone has a small display, I think it gave us much information." (F7, paper)*

> *"The display is small, but a mobile phone is available anywhere and we can quickly access such pictures." (F10, paper)*

Another student (F23) also gave a positive comment on the display size in the interview. However, only one student gave a negative comment in the questionnaire described in section 6.1.

> *"Because the size of display was very small and its response was bad, I often could not understand it well." (F8, questionnaire)*

Fig. 8. Scenes in the Fieldwork (2)

Enhancement of Motivation for Learning. Students' comments suggested that the motivations were heightened by their visit to the past world using mobile phones.

> *"It was my first experience and fun. I understood the past situation by watching 3D." (F20, interview)*
> *"Using a familiar mobile phone, I think I was able to concentrate on learning more than during usual outdoor learning." (M9, paper)*
> *"Using a mobile phone, I felt that I was able to understand something very smoothly, even though it was a difficult matter." (M7, paper)*
> *"If classes were given with this system, I would like to attend them for tens of hours!" (F19, paper)*
> *"It was not a formal lecture, but I was able to learn things by heart." (F21, paper)*

Figure 8 presents some scenes that prompted the students' concentrated interest during their visits to the past world.

What students learned. It must be confirmed that students learned what the teacher wanted them to learn using KEI-Time Traveler. The objective of this educational program was to make students understand the importance of disaster prevention. By using KEI-Time Traveler, the teacher expected students to notice that the disaster in 1938, which occurred when facilities for disaster prevention were poor, was much severer than what they can imagine.

As we expected, students noted the severity of the disaster. In all 26 students described the disaster in the past world or the difference of disaster prevention system between today and the past. For example:

> "I was so surprised that a terrible disaster occurred in this area that I often visit. I noticed that the flood higher than houses came there, and imagined what would have happened if I had been there." (F19, interview)
>
> "I had never thought of it, but I think it would be terrible if a disaster like that in 1938 occurred here now." (F17, paper)
>
> "I understood the difference of damage between the two cases, with a barrier against landslides and without it." (F5, paper)
>
> "I clearly understood the disaster in 1938. I recognized that today's situation is safer." (F22, paper)
>
> "Past peoples' feelings and past damage made me understand that today we have a system to avoid damage like that which occurred in 1938." (F12, paper)

Technical Problems. We had worried about the usability of KEI-Time Traveler, but only one student complained about it in the papers (F15) [6]. Because they acted in groups of two or three students, students helped each other with usability problems. Two students (F21 and F14, papers) requested more graphics and more realistic ones. As presented in the description of free comments in the questionnaire, 11 students complained about the processing speed.

On the other hand, students' behaviors sometimes show that they understood the technical limitations, as one protocol from the video represents.

> M10: "I think the movement of this map is strange. Is it my misunderstanding?"
>
> M11: "It has a technical limitation!"

Over-influence by Contents. We designed the 3D contents based on documents and photographs as correctly as we were able. Nevertheless, it was impossible to re-create the past world precisely. Houses, people and other objects such as trees were created from our imagination to some extent. Of course, illustrations in typical history books are also often created. However, we found some cases in which students were influenced by details of the 3D contents. For example:

> "I thought that many trees existed in the area. I thought they were cut down to develop residences." (F2, interview)

In reality, the number of trees was not precise because we had no documents or photographs including descriptions or depictions of information.

---

[6] F15 appeared in the protocol in the "Effect of 3D Model" paragraph. She also enjoyed her experiences with KEI-Time Traveler.

Another misunderstanding was highlighted by M10's utterance:

"Roofs of houses are all blue." (M10, video)

The roof color was not correct. It was our mistake. The typical roof of a home of 1938 was dark gray.

7   Discussion

We described two objectives of this study in section 1. Based on the analyses described in the previous section, we can review them. We will also discuss the cost problem in this section.

7.1   Technical Aspects

Our experiences show that KEI-Time Traveler, an inexpensive mobile learning tool using commercially available phones with no hardware attachment, well satisfied students' needs. Although its performance was constrained by some technical limitations such as the processing speed, size of display, and quality of graphics, students enjoyed using the system. Some students complained about these problems, but their evaluations were good.

An expected problem was related to the horizontal viewing angle. We avoided adopting phones that had electronic compasses. Consequently, students had to find a correct direction to watch by referring to the view angle indicator. It was not always easy for all students. However, they formed groups of 2–3 students during the fieldwork. They helped each other to use the system. As a result, all groups used this system successfully.

Students' comments suggest that mobile phone's portability and familiarity were important for them. An important implication is that they would be able to use KEI-Time Traveler anytime and anywhere if contents were supported simply because they have mobile phones available anytime and anywhere.

Overall, our study shows that we can construct an inexpensive system using only commercially available phones that provide a mobile edutainment environment with which learners can visit a virtual past world. That constitutes the most notable advantage compared with other studies [5,22,24,30,32,33].

7.2   Educational Aspects

Students supported the use of the virtual 3D past world for learning. The salient benefits were that students were able to visit the past world and feel something about it, comparing the past and present at the location of the past event. The benefit of 3D was that students were able to view the past world from any location: even from the sky. People of the past were not described by many students in the papers, but some students were moved by their fate.

Their learning motivations were enhanced by the fieldwork with KEI-Time Traveler, as described in the previous section. This fact underscores that learning with KEI-Time Traveler is a good practice of edutainment.

7.3 Cost

Cost is an important consideration. Total costs consist of the hardware cost, the software cost, the communication cost, and the contents cost.

Hardware Cost. We provided mobile phones to all students this time, but it is technically possible to run the software on students' private phones if they are compatible (about 30% of phones in Japan are compatible). The hardware cost is limited.

Software Cost. The viewer software can be reused for other locations, although it might necessitate minor modifications.

Communication Cost. This cost will depend on the contract with the carrier company. Today, most companies offer some kind of flat rate for data communication. With the KEI-Time Traveler's implementation used this time, its data communication needs during the fieldwork were limited to location sensing.

Content Cost. The main cost for KEI-Time Traveler for fieldwork is incurred for the development of 3D models because they must be created for every fieldwork target. The 3D model can be developed with a popular 3D-modeling tool: LightWave 3D. In our case, it took about three person-weeks to develop the 3D model of this location in 1938, including research of the location, prototyping, and revisions until the final model. The 3D model design was ordered to a company that has experience in developing graphical games for mobile phones. They used professional techniques to minimize the data size while maintaining the graphics quality. It is usually difficult for a typical teacher to develop such models because some special techniques are required.

The contents for KEI-Time Traveler are location-dependent. Therefore, the cost for content development is important. We cannot say that contents for KEI-Time Traveler can be developed at many schools. However, the development cost is sufficiently low to allow fieldwork at popular destinations, where many students might be expected to visit, such as UNESCO's World Heritage sites.

Easier development tools for content authoring are considered as an important topic for future work. However, we can say that the cost needed for the current KEI-Time Traveler is lower than that for other related work. At the very least, the content development costs have not been discussed by other researchers.

8 Conclusions

As described herein, we explained the design of KEI-Time Traveler and experiences and evaluation of its use by 34 junior high school students. The evaluation illustrates that the practice was effective. Students had a good learning experience, displayed enhanced motivation, and wholeheartedly supported KEI-Time Traveler.

As future work, we expect to address some remaining technical problems: the processing speed, update frequency, quality of graphics, and location inaccuracies. They are not so easy to improve drastically, but results show that even the current version can support learning. Minor improvements might be sufficient.

A more important development is porting KEI-Time Traveler to PDA-style phones such as iPhone by Apple. Actually, PDA-style phones have not been popular in Japan, but the debut of iPhone in Japan in July 2008 might cause a change in the Japanese market.

Some students requested more various applications of KEI-Time Traveler. Of course, we would also like to try to widen the applications of this system. We would like to create more contents for other fieldwork sites and evaluate learning experiences further. Technically, a function of gradually downloading the 3D world model is necessary to realize wider applications. Such a function is possible and has almost been developed.

Finally, we introduce an encouraging result of our efforts. One student, designated as F11 in this paper, proceeded to a civil engineering course in a college of technology, which is particularly noteworthy in Japan because few women choose to study in such a course. She told us that she had become interested in disaster prevention through her experience with KEI-Time Traveler.

Acknowledgments

We appreciate the support and cooperation received from KDDI Corp., bit-SHIFT Co. Ltd., HI Corp., Sumiyoshi-Gakuen, and Rokko Sabo Office. This research was partially supported by KAKENHI (18300289).

References

1. Feiner, S., MacIntyre, B., Höllerer, T., Webster, A.: A Touring Machine: Prototyping 3D mobile augmented reality systems for exploring the urban environment. In: Proceedings of the first International Symposium on Wearable Computers, pp. 74–83. IEEE Computer Society Press, Los Alamitos (1997)
2. Schnädelbach, H., Koleva, B., Flintham, M., Fraser, M., Izadi, S., Chandler, P., Foster, M., Benford, S., Greenhalgh, C., Rodden, T.: The Augurscope: A mixed reality interface for outdoors. In: Proceedings of CHI 2002, pp. 9–16. ACM Press, New York (2002)
3. Vlahakis, V., Karingiannis, J., Tsotros, M., Ioannidis, N., Strieker, D.: Personalized augmented reality touring of archaeological sites with wearable and mobile computers. In: Proceedings of the sixth IEEE International Symposium on Wearable Computers, pp. 15–22. IEEE Computer Society Press, Los Alamitos (2002)
4. Tenmoku, R., Kanbara, M., Yokoya, N.: A wearable augmented reality system using positioning infrastructures and a pedometer. In: Proceedings of the seventh IEEE International Symposium on Wearable Computers, pp. 110–117. IEEE Computer Society Press, Los Alamitos (2003)
5. Dow, S., Lee, J., Oezbek, C., MacIntyre, B., Bolter, J.D., Gandy, M.: Exploring spatial narratives and mixed reality experiences in Oakland Cemetery. In: Proceedings of the International Conference on Advances in Computer Entertainment 2005, pp. 51–60. ACM Press, New York (2005)
6. Miyamae, M., Terada, T., Kishino, Y., Nishio, S., Tsukamoto, M.: An event-driven navigation platform for wearable computing environments. In: Proceedings of the ninth IEEE International Symposium on Wearable Computers, pp. 100–107. IEEE Computer Society Press, Los Alamitos (2005)

7. Cheok, A.D., Wan, F.S., Yang, X., Weihua, W., Huang, L.M., Billinghurst, M., Kato, H.: Game-city: A ubiquitous large area multi-interface mixed reality game space for wearable computers. In: Proceedings of the sixth IEEE International Symposium on Wearable Computers, pp. 156–157. IEEE Computer Society Press, Los Alamitos (2002)

8. Cheok, A.D., Goh, K.H., Liu, W., Farbiz, F., Fong, S.W., Teo, S.L., Li, Y., Yang, X.: Human Pacman: a mobile, wide-area entertainment system based on physical, social, and ubiquitous computing. Personal and Ubiquitous Computing 8, 71–81 (2004)

9. Cheverst, K., Davies, N., Mitchell, K., Friday, A., Efstratiou, C.: Developing a context-aware electronic tourist guide: Some issues and experiences. In: Proceedings of CHI 2000, pp. 17–24. ACM Press, New York (2000)

10. Izadi, S., Fraser, M., Benford, S., Flintham, M., Greenhalgh, C., Rodden, T., Schnädelbach, H.: Citywide: Supporting interactive digital experiences across physical space. Personal and Ubiquitous Computing 6, 290–298 (2002)

11. Kamisaka, D., Yoshino, T., Munemori, J.: NAMBA Explorer: A participative location-based city area information sharing system. In: Proceedings of the IEEE International Conference on Consumer Electronics, pp. 459–460 (2005)

12. Björk, S., Falk, J., Hansson, R., Ljungstrand, P.: Pirates! - using the physical world as a game board. In: Proceedings of Interact 2001, IFIP TC. 13 Conference on Human-Computer Interaction, pp. 423–430 (2001)

13. Flintham, M., Anastasi, R., Benford, S., Hemmings, T., Crabtree, A., Greenhalgh, C., Rodden, T., Tandavanitj, N., Adams, M., Row-Farr, J.: Where on-line meets on-the-streets: Experiences with mobile mixed reality games. In: Proceedings of CHI 2003, pp. 569–576. ACM Press, New York (2003)

14. Munemori, J., Miyai, S., Itou, J.: Electronic Treasure Hunt: Real-time cooperation type game that uses location information. In: Harper, R., Rauterberg, M., Combetto, M. (eds.) ICEC 2006. LNCS, vol. 4161, pp. 336–339. Springer, Heidelberg (2006)

15. Munemori, J., Tri, T.M., Itou, J.: Forbidden City Explorer: A guide system that gives priority to shared images and chats. In: Harper, R., Rauterberg, M., Combetto, M. (eds.) ICEC 2006. LNCS, vol. 4161, pp. 306–309. Springer, Heidelberg (2006)

16. Tarumi, H., Nishihara, K., Matsubara, K., Mizukubo, Y., Nishimoto, S., Kusunoki, F.: Experiments of entertainment applications of a virtual world system for mobile phones. In: Kishino, F., Kitamura, Y., Kato, H., Nagata, N. (eds.) ICEC 2005. LNCS, vol. 3711, pp. 377–388. Springer, Heidelberg (2005)

17. Tarumi, H., Tsurumi, Y., Matsubara, K., Hayashi, Y., Mizukubo, Y., Yoshida, M., Kusunoki, F.: Kotohiragu Navigator: An open experiment of location-aware service for popular mobile phones. In: Hazas, M., Krumm, J., Strang, T. (eds.) LoCA 2006. LNCS, vol. 3987, pp. 48–63. Springer, Heidelberg (2006)

18. Tarumi, H., Yokoo, K., Nishimoto, S., Matsubara, K., Harada, Y., Kusunoki, F., Kim, S., Mizukubo, Y.: Open experiments of mobile sightseeing support systems with shared virtual worlds. In: Proceeding of the International Conference on Advances in Computer Entertainment Technology 2006. ACM Press, New York (2006)

19. Roschelle, J., Pea, R.: A walk on the WILD side: How wireless handhelds may change computer-supported collaborative learning. International Journal of Cognition and Technology 1, 145–168 (2002)

20. Roschelle, J.: Unlocking the learning value of wireless mobile devices. Journal of Computer Assisted Learning 19(3), 260–272 (2003)
21. Rosenbaum, E., Klopfer, E., Perry, J.: On location learning: Authentic applied science with networked augmented realities. Journal of Science Education and Technology 16(1), 31–45 (2007)
22. Benford, S., Rowland, D., Flintham, M., Drozd, A., Hull, R., Reid, J., Morrison, J., Facer, K.: Life on the edge: Supporting collaboration in location-based experiences. In: Proceedings of CHI 2005, pp. 721–730. ACM Press, New York (2005)
23. Grant, W.C.: Wireless Coyote: A computer-supported field trip. Communications of the ACM 36(5), 57–59 (1993)
24. Rogers, Y., Price, S., Fitzpatrick, G., Fleck, R., Harris, E., Smith, H., Randell, C., Muller, H., O'Malley, C., Stanton, D., Thompson, M., Weal, M.: Ambient Wood: Designing new forms of digital augmentation and learning outdoors. In: Proceedings of the third Conference on Interaction Design for Children, pp. 3–10. ACM Press, New York (2004)
25. Randell, C., Price, S., Rogers, Y., Harris, E., Fitzpatrick, G.: The Ambient Horn: designing a novel audio-based learning experience. Personal and Ubiquitous Computing 8, 177–183 (2004)
26. Wilde, D., Harris, E., Rogers, Y., Randell, C.: The Periscope: supporting a computer enhanced field trip for children. Personal and Ubiquitous Computing 7, 227–233 (2003)
27. Takenaka, M., Inagaki, S., Ohkubo, M., Kuroda, H., Doi., S.: Development of a collaborative learning support system using camera-equipped mobile phones: A demonstrative experiment in a 1st-grade class of a Japanese elementary school. In: Proceedings of the International Conference on Computers in Education, pp. 457–465 (2004)
28. Mitchell, K., Race, N.J.P.: uLearn: Facilitating ubiquitous learning through camera equipped mobile phones. In: Proceedings of IEEE International Workshop on Wireless and Mobile Technologies in Education 2005, pp. 274–281. IEEE Computer Society Press, Los Alamitos (2005)
29. Nakasugi, H., Yamauchi, Y.: Past Viewer: Development of wearable learning system for history education. In: Proceedings of International Conference on Computers in Education, pp. 1311–1312. IEEE Computer Society Press, Los Alamitos (2002)
30. Okada, M., Yamada, A., Tarumi, H., Yoshida, M., Moriya, K.: DigitalEE II: RV-augmented interface design for networked collaborative environmental learning, designing for change in networked learning environment. In: Proceedings of the International Conference on Computer Support for Collaborative Learning 2003, pp. 265–274. Kluwer Academic Publishers, Dordrecht (2003)
31. Chen, Y., Kao, T., Sheu, J.: A mobile learning system for scaffolding bird watching learning. Journal of Computer Assisted Learning 19(3), 347–359 (2003)
32. Halloran, J., Hornecker, E., Fitzpatrick, G., Weal, M., Millard, D., Michaelides, D., Cruickshank, D., De Roure, D.: The literacy fieldtrip: Using ubicomp to support children's creative writing. In: Proceedings of the fifth Conference on Interaction Design and Children, pp. 17–24. ACM Press, New York (2006)
33. Bouvin, N.O., Brodersen, C., Hansen, F.A., Iversen, O.S., Nøøregaard, P.: Tools of contextualization: Extending the classroom to the field. In: Proceedings of the fourth Conference on Interaction Design and Children, pp. 24–31. ACM Press, New York (2005)

34. Leavitt, N.: Will wireless gaming be a winner? IEEE Computer 36(1), 24–27 (2003)
35. Han, Y., Ling, D., Xin, L., Boya, X.: A virtual agent based mobile 3D game with mascot capsule Micro3D API. In: Proceedings of the third international conference on Mobile technology, applications and systems, article number 36. ACM Press, New York (2006)
36. Chen, J.X., Yang, Y.: 3D graphics formats and conversions. Computing in Science and Engineering, 67–73 (September/October 2000)
37. Shimada, S., Tanizaki, M., Maruyama, K.: Ubiquitous spatial-information services using cell phones. IEEE Micro, 25–34 (November 2002)
38. Churchill, D., Hedberg, J.: Learning object design considerations for small-screen handheld devices. Computers and Education 50(3), 881–893 (2008)

A 3D Campus on the Internet – A Networked Mixed Reality Environment

Jiung-yao Huang[1], Ming-Chih Tung[2], Huan-Chao Keh[3],
Ji-jen Wu[3], Kun-Hang Lee[1], and Chung-Hsien Tsai[4]

[1] Dept. of Computer Science and Information Engineering, National Taipei University,
San Shia, Taipei, 237 Taiwan
jyhuang@mail.ntpu.edu.tw, wildjcrt@gmail.com
[2] Department of Computer Science and Information Engineering, Ching Yun University,
229 Chien-Hsin Road, Jung-Li, Taoyuan County 320, Taiwan
mctung@cyu.edu.tw
[3] Department of Computer Science and Information Engineering, Tamkang University
Tamsui 251, Taiwan
keh@cs.tku.edu.tw, wujj5770@yahoo.com.tw
[4] Dept. of Computer Science and Information Engineering, National Central University,
Taoyuan County 32001, Taiwan
chtsai@csie.ncu.edu.tw

Abstract. This paper presents a study of networking the mobile augmented reality system with the conventional networked virtual environment and it is
called the networked mixed reality environment in this study. The 3D virtual
campus is an ongoing project aiming to explore the techniques how to design
such a networked mixed reality environment. This study starts with investigating the temporal and spatial synchronization issues between the mobile computing system and the conventional networked virtual reality system. The proposed
solutions are then followed by a demonstration prototyping system, called Multiplayer Mobile Mixed Reality(M^3R) system. The tips of implementing the
M^3R system are presented in the end. The 3D virtual campus project successfully demonstrates the promise of building a pervasive virtual environment between the live player and the virtual player. Inspired by the preliminary success,
further experiments and application are currently being examined.

Keywords: Networked Virtual Environment (NVE), Mobile Computing,
Mobile Supporting Server, Multiplayer Mobile Mixed Reality.

1 Introduction

Cyber-learning has already become an important and vital part of university education.[1] With the cyber-learning technology, the students do not need to go to the
physical campus to attend lectures, seminars, or access learning materials. Cyber-
learning is successfully used in the education for science[2], for children [3], and for
archeological education.[4] The cyber-learning in virtual campus is to augment traditional lecture-based teaching with online learning materials and communication and
to provide distance learning with all interactivity and materials available online.[5]
Therefore, the function of virtual campus is not only to publish the multimedia

Z. Pan et al. (Eds.): Transactions on Edutainment II, LNCS 5660, pp. 282–298, 2009.

presentations of learning materials[6], but also to provide an environment of a learning community.[5] Meanwhile, Mather proposes virtual lecture and virtual seminar to enhance the effectiveness of virtual campus. Unfortunately, these two approaches still lack for drill practice learning. It will reduce the performance of cyber-learning. With the rapid progress of the computing technologies, using collaborative virtual reality technology to realize a cyber-learning environment becomes a significant trend in the recent years.

The Collaborative Virtual Environment (CVE) is the research of integrating a distributed system, computer communications, and virtual reality technology into a graphical multi-player interactive environment.[7] In this synthetic environment, each player is embodied by a graphical representation called the avatar to convey his identity, presence, location, and activities to others. The cyber-learning by CVE is an approach to replicate a real university to provide a virtual environment for students learn "on-the-fly" in the learning areas. Such a cyber-learning environment is also referred as the 3D virtual campus.[8] Prasolova[9] proposes characterization framework to define the place metaphors in educational cyberworlds by CVEs. The framework utilizes terms of outlook, structure, and role to discuss the learner, artifact, and place of virtual campus.[1] All of the previous researches regarding 3D virtual campus could only allow users to navigate the virtual world from their desktop computers.

This study extends the 3D virtual campus research with the mobile augmented reality(MAR) technology to enrich the cyber-learning within the cyberworld. MAR is the technique of implementing the augmented reality in the mobile computing system. The significance of MAR is to enrich the application of the mobile computing by adding friendly interface from the augmented reality technology.[10] With the help of the mobile computing, MAR frees the conventional augmented reality application from the desktop.[11-12] Mobile augmented reality allows computer-generated virtual objects to overlap with live images when the user is navigating the physical world. Among the researches of the mobile augmented reality, MARS[11] and ARQuake[13] are two well-known systems. Both systems allow users to interact the physical environment with a "pervasive" graphical user interface. That is, the user can see a 3D object on top of, says, any walls within his FOV, without actually installing a video screen on that wall. This capability promotes the augmented reality to a more friendly and daily applications. However, none of the previous MAR researches attempted to integrate CVEs with MARs to enable MAR users to interact with conventional CVE users within a shared mixed reality space. This study presents an experience of designing such a shared mixed reality environment between mobile and desktop users. In the following sections, the issues and proposed solutions to design a virtual world for such a mixed reality system are given first. The architecture of the supported platform is discussed next. The implementation then follows.

2   The NTPU 3D Virtual Campus

The NTPU 3D virtual campus is a networked virtual environment of National Taipei University (NTPU), Taiwan. Compared with existing 3D campus projects [14], this project focuses on allowing mobile players and desktop players to interact within a shared virtual space. That is, there are two types of players within this 3D campus environment: the mobile player and the desktop player. The desktop player is the user who joins the virtual environment through his desktop computer. Whereas, the mobile player, named this way thereafter, refers to the user who uses a wearable computer or a notebook to wirelessly login the virtual environment and to interact with others while he is moving inside the physical NTPU campus. The position of the mobile player is decided by the GPS receiver. The mobile device, i.e. a wearable computer or a notebook, will translate and transmit received GPS data to the server. The server then forwards the received data to other players for them to remote render his avatar. Hence, the 3D campus project allows more vivid interactive experiences when the user is navigating this overlapped virtual and physical world.

To design a 3D virtual world to support real-time interaction between the mobile player and the desktop player, there are several issues to be solved. The main problem is the differences of the coordinate systems individually used by the 3D virtual campus and the physical world. The scaling is another important issue when modeling the 3D virtual campus in the real one. This scaling difference can cause the spatial synchronization problem when the mobile player is navigating the physical campus. That is, the mobile player may approach a building, yet his avatar is remotely rendered as flying through the model of that building inside the 3D virtual campus. The other issue is, since the computing resources of the mobile computer are inferior to the desktop computer, the complexity of the virtual scene also needs to be carefully evaluated. All of these design issues are discussed in the following subsections.

2.1 The Landscape Design

The legacy approach of designing networked virtual worlds, such as Second Life [15] and Virtual Campus by Nanyang Technological University[8], aims to clone physical places to create a familiar atmosphere for the user to interact with the shared environment. However, the previous studies did not consider the scale relationship between the virtual world and the physical world, and only created a limited degree resemblance to the physical place. This type of virtual environments is acceptable only when all the participants are desktop users. In case the mobile player in the physical space wants to join and interact with others within such a shared virtual environment, faulty interactions will occur if care is not taken when designing a virtual world of a physical place. These incorrect interactions are stemmed from the discrepancy of coordinate systems used by the virtual world and the physical world.

The differences in the coordinate systems used individually by the virtual world and the physical world can cause both the spatial and temporal inconsistency problems between the mobile player and the desktop player. For example, a mobile player in front of a building may have his avatar rendered at different locations when viewing from a desktop computer. The position of the mobile player is determined by the GPS receiver which uses World Geodetic system (WGS) 84, called the Geographical coordinate system, to describe its positional information. On the contrary, the virtual world is often designed without any coordinate systems in mind. To solve the spatial inconsistency problem, the coordinate correlation between the physical world and the virtual world needs to be computed beforehand.

However, there is no direct translation from a point in the Geographical coordinate system to its corresponding coordinate in the Cartesian coordinate system. Hence, a third coordinate system, called the Earth-Centered, Earth-Fixed(ECEF) [16] is often used as the mediator. That is, GPS data are first translated from the Geographical coordinate system into data in the ECEF coordinate system, and then the Cartesian coordinate system. This pipeline of translation consists of a sequence of complex matrix manipulation which is not suitable for the computation requirement for CVE. Especially when the client device is mobile device, the complexity of computation may not be acceptable. To solve this coordinate reconciliation problem, a simple yet effective translation is developed. First, the Cartesian coordinate system is manually assigned to the virtual world when the virtual world is designed. Each object within the virtual world is then placed corresponding to this Cartesian coordinate system. Second, fixed positions within the virtual world are carefully chosen as the virtual markers. In the physical world, the geographic markers that are corresponding to those virtual survey markers, respectively, are then computed, as illustrated in Figure 1. In other words, each geographic marker is a physical location that is mapped to the virtual marker. The geometric relationship between the geographic marker and the virtual survey marker is then calculated. This relationship becomes the equation to transfer the geographic position in the physical world to a coordinate data in the virtual world and vice versa.

In addition, the proportional scale between the virtual world and the physical world will cause a temporal inconsistency problem between the mobile player and the desktop player. For example, when a mobile player is walking across the road, his motion may be misinterpreted by a desktop computer as a fly motion due to the scaling difference in the input data. "A shared sense of presence" is one of five common features for the networked virtual environment.[17] This feature is achieved by allowing each player to control the motion of an avatar inside such a shared space. For a desktop player, the mouse and keyboard are two legacy input devices to support navigation and interaction within the virtual environment. On the other hand, since the mobile player uses the GPS data to navigate the virtual world, the GPS receiver becomes an input device to control the motion of his remote avatar. That is, when the mobile player is walking in the physical world, his location is tracked by the location sensor and transmitted to other players through the server. From the viewpoint of the desktop player, the mobile player is navigating the virtual world by his own motion. Hence, the Geographical coordinate from the GPS receiver and the orientation from the electronic compass needs to be correctly mapped to position and direction, respectively, inside the virtual world. This mapping is achieved by first computing the geometrical ratio among received Geographical coordinate and geographic markers that were set when the virtual world was designed. The Cartesian coordinate of this Geographical coordinate is then derived from computed geometrical ratio with respect to the virtual markers. This approach allows fast translation between the Geographical coordinate and Cartesian coordinate with an acceptable spatial inconsistency. This technique also tolerates different moving speeds when the mobile is walking in the real world. Only when the walking speed is under a predefined value, the accurate Cartesian coordinate will be actually computed.

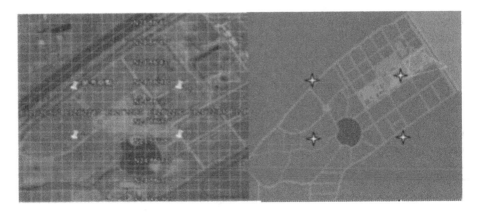

Fig. 1. The geographic markers(left) and its corresponded the virtual makers(right)

2.2 Navigation of the Mobile Player

Similar to human pacman[18], the mobile player uses the GPS data to navigate the virtual world. Given the Geographical coordinate from the GPS receiver and orientation from the electronic compass, these data are mapped to correct position and direction in the 3D virtual campus. As discussed in the previous section, this mapping may cause temporal inconsistency problem between the mobile player and the desktop player. The proportional scale between the 3D virtual campus and the physical campus is part of the reason that causes the temporal inconsistency issue. Further, the temporal inconsistency problem also is induced by the inaccuracy of the GPS data. Based upon the GPS data received from more than three satellites, the GPS receiver uses the tri-laterality technique[19] to compute its position. However, due to various environmental factors, it is difficult to guarantee a precise transmission time on each reception which in turn affects the accuracy of the computed GPS positioning. These factors include time and clock discrepancies, ephemeris uncertainties [19], ionospheric and tropospheric propagation delay, receiver noise, and hardware computation numerical errors. Such imprecision of the GPS data will further impact the temporal synchronization problem. Hence, a context-aware technique based on the GPS data is proposed[20] to improve the computed position information. Furthermore, since the GPS data becomes unreliable when the carrier is standstill, an electronic compass module is added to obtain the orientation information to amend this situation.

Hence, the mapping between two coordinate data is achieved by first computing the geometry relation among given position and geographic markers that were set when the 3D virtual campus was designed. The 3D Cartesian coordinate is then derived from re-evaluating the previously computed geometric result with respect to the virtual markers. To further speed up the calculating process, the map of the 3D virtual campus is further partitioned into fixed-size grids. The corresponding geographic coordinate of each grid point is also pre-computed. That is, the physical campus is also implicitly partitioned into grids that are closely matched with the grids in the 3D virtual campus. Further, the ratio of grids between two coordinates is also derived.

Hence, the translation is then replaced by calculating the grid number when a Geographical coordinate is derived from the GPS data. When a grid number is derived, the position of the avatar denoting the GPS receiver is then computed from the ratio of the grid number. A smooth algorithm is also employed when an avatar is moving between the adjacent grids. This approach allows fast translation between the Geographical coordinate and 3D Cartesian coordinate with an acceptable spatial inconsistency. This technique also tolerates different moving speeds when the mobile is walking in the physical campus. Only when the walking speed is under a predefined value, the accurate 3D Cartesian coordinate will be actually computed.

2.3 The Limitation of the Mobile Device

The computing power of the mobile device is also an important issue when we design a 3D virtual campus. The mobile device is always designed with the constraint of minimal power consumption, and this constraint will significantly affect the computing performance. This result will in turn influence the sense of interaction. To reduce the computing load of the mobile device, the dynamic loading and Level of Detail (LOD)[21-22] mechanisms are designed. The dynamic loading mechanism allows the user to navigate the virtual world without the entire virtual scene being loaded into the system memory. The other benefit of this approach is that the performance increases since the mobile device does not require rendering the entire scene. To further reduce the rendering complexity, the level-of-detail method allows distance objects to be rendered with a simpler geometric shape.

In order to make the most use of the dynamic loading and LOD mechanisms, the objects of the 3D virtual campus are classified into static and dynamic objects. The static objects include all the building, trees and other constructions. The dynamic object only refers to the avatar at this moment. Each static object has at least two levels of details to represent in the virtual campus. Further, each building uses a box as its coarsest shape and each face of this box is texture mapped with a picture of that building. That is, if the player is far away from a building, that building is modeled by a box. Only when the player comes near to the building, the detail representation of that building will be actually loaded into the virtual space. The geometric shape of that building will be switched back to a box when the player moves away from that building. Finally, a hierarchy relationship among buildings has to be set up to ensure the distance relation among them. The dynamic loading is achieved by checking this hierarchy tree.

3 Multiplayer Mobile Mixed Reality System

The platform that supports the 3D virtual campus is called Multiplayer Mobile Mixed Reality(M^3R) system. As implied by its name, M^3R is designed to enable the player of the mobile augmented reality system to join the conventional networked virtual environment. To achieve this goal, the M^3R architecture is composed of two types of servers. One is the multiuser server, called the game server, and the other is the Mobile Support Server.

3.1 The Server Architecture

Similar to the design goal of CVE[7], the M^3R environment aims to provide an illusion to distributed users who all observe the same things and interact with each other within the virtual space. This goal implies that each player has to share his status and event with others within the virtual space for them to realize his existence by a graphic rendering engine. This dynamical state sharing is achieved by message exchange among players in the virtual world. There are three general approaches to implement this message exchange mechanism among hosts of a networked virtual environment. They are centralized repository, frequent state regeneration, and dead reckoning [17]. Due to the instability of the wireless signal, the frequent state regeneration approach can easily flood the wireless bandwidth on the mobile host. Further, the instability of the wireless signal may also cause the dead reckoning method to produce jittering remote avatars on the mobile host. Hence, by considering the computing resource of the mobile player, M^3R adopts the centralized repository approach to design its server system. In addition, the implementation of the centralized repository can be broadly classified into three techniques, including the file repository, the repository in server memory, and the virtual repository[17]. Due to the latency of the instability of the wireless signal, the transmission overhead induced by the server on the mobile host has to be minimized. Hence, the method of repository in server memory is implemented to achieve prompt message exchange between the desktop players and the mobile players.

Figure 2 takes the Use Case diagram of UML to illustrate the M^3R architecture. The M^3R architecture can be roughly divided into the server side and the client side. The server side contains the login server and the game server; whereas the client side includes the login agent, a 3D campus scene file, and the application agent. The user has to register a user name with a password to the login server before being allowed to join the 3D virtual campus. After successful registration, the login server will validate the user information whenever a player wants to enter the 3D virtual campus. The game server is responsible for exchanging dynamic shared states and events between the desktop and the mobile players. On the client side, the login agent provides an interface for the user to register and login to the 3D virtual campus. For each registered player of the 3D virtual campus, the login server will return a validation key to the login agent. This key will then activate the application agent to enter the 3D virtual campus. The application agent then takes over all the interactions while the player exits in the 3D campus.

To reduce the transmission delay between the server host and the client host, the message pushing methodology is realized on the game server. There are two known technologies, i.e. push and pull[23-24], to implement message passing mechanism between the server and the client. The pull approach demands the client to specifically request message from the server; while the push method allows the server periodically and automatically to send message to the client. Another benefit of the push approach is its lower overhead on the client host. Further, this pushing method allows the server to control and filter message flows to each client host.

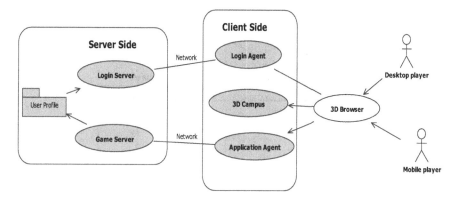

Fig. 2. The use case diagram of the M^3R system

Finally, in order to reduce the bandwidth consumption, a packet aggregation mechanism is implemented on the game server. The packet aggregation is a technique to aggregate several packets into one before messages are transmitted.[25] The goal of the packet aggregation is to reduce the number of headers on each transmission.[25] According to the study from [17], this saving can achieve around 50% of the required bandwidth depending upon different types of networked virtual environments. There are three aggregation policies generally considered: Timeout-based transmission policy, Quorum-based transmission policy and Hybrid transmission policy.[17] Considering the wireless bandwidth and latency, the timeout-based transmission policy was realized on the game server. In summary, to reduce the transmission time and bandwidth consumption at the same time, the game server periodically collects messages from clients and then pushes aggregated packets to each client.

3.2 The Mobile Support Server

The most challenging issue of designing the M^3R system is to enable the mobile player to interact with other players in the same virtual world. Due to the signal instability and the limited bandwidth of the wireless network, messages from the server may easily jam the wireless network bandwidth if the mobile player is directly connected to the game server. Further, if the mobile player is directly receiving message from the game server, the limited computation power of the mobile device will be unable to proceed interactive messages while the number of simultaneous players increases. To solve these problems, a Mobile Support Server (MSS) is designed as a data mediator between the game server and the mobile player as shown in Figure 3.

The major role of MSS is to solve the message flow problems between the game server and the mobile player. In addition to the known research issues of the networked virtual environment [17], there are other issues needed to be solved before the mobile player can interact with a shared virtual space. These issues can be broadly

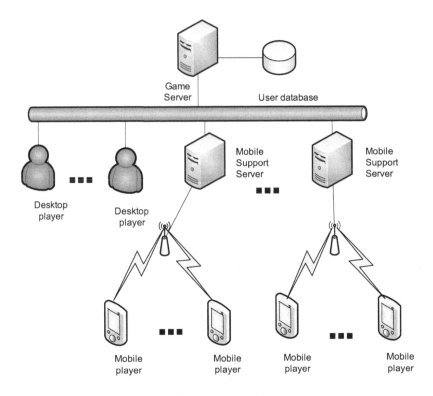

Fig. 3. MSS to support mobile players

classified into three categories. One is the stability and bandwidth problem of the mobile network. The second issue is the limited computation resources of the mobile device. The last one is the data correlation between the Geographical coordinate system and the Cartesian coordinate system.[26] These three problems lead to the further sub-problems as depicted in Figure 4.

a. Mobile Networking (box labeled A): The ultimate goal of M³R is to allow both desktop players and mobile players to interact with each other in the shared space. Since the desktop device is often connected by a fixed-location network, there is not much to be discussed due to signal stability of such a network. On the other hand, the mobile player can only join through the wireless network and interact while he is moving around. The available choices of wireless network include GPRS, 3G, WiMAX and WiFi, etc. Due to the fragility of wireless signal while the user is moving, this issue targets on how to keep logical link between the mobile player and the server alive while the signal strength still within an acceptable threshold. However, the 3D campus project does not focus on the network technologies of any specific wireless network, but only the logical linking problem is explored. The MSS periodically detects the connecting status to re-login the mobile player or dead reckoning missing data.

b. Data Filtration (box labeled B): The mobile player uses a mobile device, such as a notebook or a wearable computer, to navigate the 3D virtual campus. Due to the limitation of power consumption, the mobile computer has inferior computing resource and insufficient network bandwidth. Hence, this issue focuses on how to filter messages to reduce the computing load of the mobile device. To achieve this goal, part of rendering related computing work is shifted to the MSS, such as the visibility of objects, the level of detail of object appearance, and the realism of object animation.

c. Data Mediation (box labeled C): Since the mobile player uses the location sensing device (such as GPS) to navigate the virtual world and animate his remote avatar, this location information has to be converted into the position data recognizable by the virtual world. However, since the data from GPS is expressed in Geographical coordinate system whereas the virtual world uses Cartesian coordinate system, this conversion may cause spatial and temporal inconsistency between the mobile player and the desktop player. Further, since the mobile player is moving in the physical world, the difference of these two coordinate systems may further corrupts the causal order relationships of events within the shared virtual world. Hence, how to harmonize coordinates and events between these two coordinate systems is the last issue. MSS uses the GPS time to synchronize messages between the mobile player and itself. Further, the grid approach to translate data between the two coordinate systems as discussed previously is implemented in MSS.

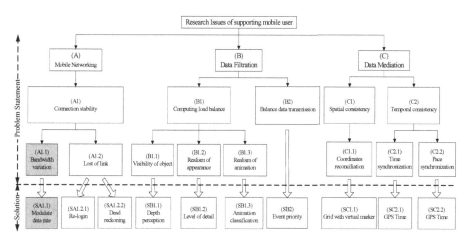

Fig. 4. The MSS research issues

4   Implementation

The components of the M^{3}R environment can be broadly classified into the client device, the servers, and the Mobile Support Server. The implementation approach of each is discussed as below.

4.1   The Servers

The servers include the game server and the login server. Both servers are implemented on the Windows XP platform. The login server uses mySQL database to save the registered user data. The game server employs several techniques to increase the performance in the server site.

First, the multi-thread approach is adopted to design the game server. In addition to the threads to manage user status, the game server assigns a thread, called client thread, for each connected client. Each client thread uses TCP to receive message from its corresponding client and forward the received data to a server thread. The server thread uses the time-based aggregation method to collect data from all client threads. Each client thread then uses UDP to forward aggregated packets back to its corresponding client. Since more than one client thread are simultaneously accessing aggregated packet from the server, a mutual exclusive mechanism is designed to insure data consistency. The game server uses double queues with read/write flip-flop method to solve the mutual exclusive problem. That is, while the server thread is writing aggregated packet into one queue, called the back queue, client threads only allow reading packet from another queue, called the front queue. When the server thread finishes writing, it will then flip the back queue into the front queue. By this way, the server thread and client threads can work parallelly without causing any data inconsistency problem.

4.2 The Mobile Support Server

The Mobile Support Server (MSS) is also implemented on the Windows XP platform. The MSS implements all the solutions for the issues depicted in Figure 4. The logical linking problem of the Mobile Networking issue refers to the disconnection problem. Since the wireless network allows the mobile player to move around the physical space, various environmental factors may influence the signal strength between the mobile player and the wireless access point.[27-28] This situation will also lead to lose the wireless signal. To solve this problem, MSS will periodically detect the connection status of the mobile player. If the duration of disconnection is within a given threshold, MSS uses dead-reckoning [22] algorithm to simulate the position for the mobile player and forwards this computed position to the game server. Otherwise, MSS will automatically logout the mobile player from the game server and require the mobile player to re-login.

The Data Filtration issue attempts to reduce the computing load of the mobile device. Since the mobile device always has inferior computing resource than the desktop device, we can employ the limited human vision to balance their performance disparity. For example, when the human being is moving, his vision to a distant object tends to be less perceptible. Hence, we employ the depth perception[29] technique to reduce the number of the rendered objects when the mobile player is moving. Further, the level-of-detail[21-22] technique, a conventional approach to reduce the computation load, is also implemented. These approaches can effectively reduce the computing load of the mobile device. However, due to the resource limitation of the mobile device, if all of these methods are implemented into the mobile device, which will still be overloaded. Hence, MSS shares parts of these computations before it pushes remote players' data to the mobile player. To further adapt the bandwidth variance during interaction, MSS adopts data priority[30] mechanism to sort transmitted message to the mobile device. That is, MSS will push remote data to the mobile player base upon message priority. Meanwhile, the mobile player will reduce the frequency of transmitted message when the bandwidth is decreased.

Finally, the Data Mediation issue stems from the difference between Geographical coordinate system and Cartesian coordinate system. The affected factors include the difference of motion data, such as distance and speed, and the difference of movement time between two coordinates. For example, due to the difference between two coordinate systems, a mobile player in front of a building can be misinterpreted by the desktop player as inside the building. To solve this problem, the correlation between the physical campus and the virtual campus has to be taken care of first. That is, when the 3D virtual campus was initially designed, the virtual survey markers have to be set up with respect to the given positions, i.e. geographic markers, in the physical campus. The functional relationship between two types of markers is then derived to perform data translation between two coordinate systems. However, considering the power consumption of the mobile device, the translation cost is very high since the mobile device needs to continuously perform such location translation in real-time. To solve this problem, the satellite map with longitude and latitude information of the physical campus is captured from Google Earth first. The map is then partitioned into grids according to longitude and latitude. The survey markers are further chosen from the grid points. The positions in the 3D virtual campus that are corresponding to the survey markers are then pre-calculated. Hence, while the mobile user is navigating the physical campus, the mobile device will extract longitude and latitude values form the received GPS data to compute the grid coordinate value. This grid coordinate value is then passed to the MSS to actually compute the corresponding 3D Cartesian position.

4.3 The Client Device

The client device is also running Windows XP with a 3D browser from a commercial virtual reality toolkit called Virtools.[31] The Virtools package is a component based virtual reality development software. It provides a plugin mechanism called Building Block (BB) to enable the user to control the render and the interaction of a virtual environment. For example, the developer can set up the logical flow of various BBs to animate the walking of an avatar. During the simulation, the core of the Virtools will execute a sequence of BB flow to achieve the designated animation. The flexibility of the Building Block allows the developer to set up special effect in each frame. For instance, to reduce the computing load of entering the 3D campus, a BB is employed to allow dynamical loading in real-time. When the user first enters the 3D campus, each building in the campus is just a box texture mapped with pictures on each side. The detail polygons of a building will be dynamically loaded into the 3D campus depending upon its distance to the player.

Figure 5 is the snapshot of the initial window. When the user logins the 3D campus, the help dialog box is overlapped on the scene of the 3D virtual campus. The user can press F1 button to toggle the display with this help window at any time.

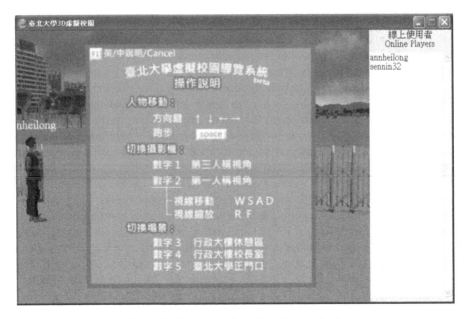

Fig. 5. The initial window when the user login

Fig. 6. Entering the 3D virtual campus and making a voice call

Figure 6 is the snapshot of the third party view of the user "sennin32" after he successfully logs in the 3D virtual campus. The right sub-window is a list of user names that are currently resided in the 3D virtual campus. Further, every avatar has its user name exhibited on top of it.

The 3D virtual campus designs a customized chatting BB to enable live chatting among players. When a user wants to chat with another player on the user list, he can click the name of that player. The chatting BB will be activated to request the Skype account of that player. The chatting BB is then proceeded to launch the Skype software to connect to that specific player. For example, if the user "sennin32" wants to voice chat with, says, "annheilong", he can click the receiver's name on the right sub-window or on top of the avatar. As illustrated in Figure 6, the browser window of the caller will have a "hung-up" shown on the bottom-left corner.

On the other hand, as shown in Figure 7, a calling notification will pop-up on the receiver's browser. The receiver can decide whether to accept or deny this call by clicking buttons on the pop-up window.

The ultimate goal of the mobile device for the 3D virtual campus project is an optical see-through mobile augmented reality system running on a wearable computer. However, due to the availability of the optical see-through head-mounted display, a notebook is tested at this moment. Figure 8 demonstrates the result when the user is using a notebook as the mobile device to navigate the physical campus. There are total three players in this demonstration. Except for the mobile player, the other two avatars in the screen are desktop players.

Fig. 7. Live chatting through Skype software

Fig. 8. The snapshot of the mobile device

5   Conclusion and Future Works

The 3D virtual campus is a networked mixed reality environment that is designed for both conventional desktop player and mobile augmented virtual reality player. It enables the user to wear a mobile device and interact with the conventional desktop player in the shared virtual campus. The main issue of enabling the mobile player to join the networked virtual environment is how to allow the player himself as a navigating device of the mobile device. The solution of this issue is not simply to add a location sensor to the mobile device. The cause of this issue stems from two main sources; one is the difference between the Geographic coordinate system and the 3D Cartesian coordinate system, and the other is the limited computing resource of the mobile device. This study fully discusses various problems to design such a networked mixed reality environment.

Further, an architecture to support a Multiplayer Mobile Mixed Reality(M^3R) environment is presented in this study To fully support the mobile player, M^3R includes a Mobile Support Server(MSS) as the data mediator between the mobile player and CVE. The MSS is designed to reduce the computation load of the mobile device while the mobile player is interacting with the mixed reality environment. This study points out three resource-related issues of MSS; they are mobile networking, data filtration, and data mediation. The discussions and solutions of these issues are presented in this paper.

Although this project has successfully demonstrated the possibility to design a networked mixed reality environment for both of the desktop player and the mobile player, more research issues are exposed for further studies. For example, notebooks are unsuitable for mobile users to operate in moving. The ultimate goal of the mobile device is an optical see-through mobile augmented reality system running on a wearable computer. The rotation of the mobile player and, hence, the corresponding 3D display of the virtual campus is another important issue. In M^3R system, the digital compass is used to detect the rotation of the mobile player. The digital compass has a well-known inaccurate and unstable problem. Consequently, other auxiliary direction sensing devices require further exploration. Currently, the research of using the optical flow technology to detect the mobile player's rotation is under investigation. Finally, the performance of MSS is another important topic that deserves further probing. More experiments to explore this issue are underway presently. According to the implemented prototype system, the future work will concentrate on how to plan the educational experiments like [32] to result in more advanced outcome.

Acknowledgments. The construction of the 3D campus virtual environment is sponsored by National Taipei University, Taiwan, and the study of M^3R technique is funded by Nation Science Council, Taiwan, at Grant No: NSC 97-2221-E-305 -008. The authors would like to acknowledge Miss Rai Liu for her help on editing the 3D virtual scene.

References

1. Prasolova-Førland, E., Sourin, A., Sourina, O.: Place Metaphors in Educational Cyberworlds: a Virtual Campus Case Study. In: Proceedings of the 2005 International Conference on Cyberworlds, CW 2005, Singapore (2005)
2. Shin, Y.-S.: Virtual experiment environments design for science education. In: International conference on cyberworlds, pp. 388–395. IEEE Computer Society Press, Los Alamitos (2003)
3. Gerval, J.-P., Popovici, D.-M., Tisseau, J.: Educative Distributed Virtual Environments for Children. In: 2003 International Conference on Cyberworlds, pp. 382–387. IEEE CS Press, Los Alamitos (2003)
4. Green, D., Cosmas, J., Degeest, R., Waelkens, M.A.: Distributed Universal 3D Cyberworld for archaeological Research and Education. In: 2003 International Conference on Cyberworlds, pp. 458–465. IEEE Computer Society Press, Los Alamitos (2003)
5. Maher, M.: Designing the Virtual Campus as a Virtual World. In: Proceedings of CSCL, Palo Alto, CA (1999)
6. Gero, J.S.: Design Prototypes: a Knowledge Representation Schema for Design. AI Magazine 11(4), 26–36 (1990)
7. Benford, S., Greenhalgh, C., Rodden, T., Pycock, J.: Cooperative Virtual Environment. Communications of the ACM 44(7), 79–85 (2001)
8. Sourin, A.: Nanyang Technological University Virtual Campus. IEEE Computer Graphics and Applications 24(6), 6–8 (2004)
9. Prasolova-Førland, E.: Place Metaphors in Educational CVEs: An Extended Characterisation. In: Proc. WBE, Grindelwald, Switzerland, pp. 349–354 (2005)
10. Schmalstieg, D., Fuhrmann, A., Hesina, G., Szalavari, Z., Encarnação, L.M., Gervautz, M., Purgathofer, W.: The studierstube augmented reality project. Presence: Teleoperators & Virtual Environments 11(1), 33–54 (2002)
11. Feiner, S., MacIntyre, B., Höllerer, T., Webster, T.: A touring machine: Prototyping 3D mobile augmented reality systems for exploring the urban environment. In: Proc. ISWC 1997 (First IEEE Int. Symp. on Wearable Computers), Cambridge, MA, October 13-14 (1997); also in Personal Technologies, pp. 208–217 (1997)

12. Höllerer, T., Feiner, S., Terauchi, T., Rashid, G., Hallaway, D.: Exploring MARS: Developing Indoor and Outdoor User Interfaces to a Mobile Augmented Reality System. Computers and Graphics 23(6), 779–785 (1999)
13. Piekarski, W., Thomas, B.: ARQuake: The Outdoor Augmented Reality Gaming System. Communications of the ACM 45(1), 36–38 (2002)
14. Prasolova-Førland, E., Sourin, A., Sourina, O.: Cybercampuses: Design Issues and Future Directions. The Visual Computer 22(12), 1015–1028 (2006)
15. Second Life, http://secondlife.com/ (Accessed online 03/09/2009)
16. http://www.satsleuth.com/GPS_ECEF_Datum_transformation.htm (Accessed online 12/02/2008)
17. Singhal, S., Zyda, M.: Networked Virtual Environments Design and Implementation. Addison-Wesley, Reading (1999)
18. Cheok, A.D., Goh, K.H., Liu, W., Farbiz, F., Fong, S.W., Teo, S.L., Li, Y., Yang, X.B.: Human pacman: A mobile, wide-area entertainment system based on physical, social, and ubiquitous computing. Personal Ubiquitous Computing 8(2), 71–81 (2004)
19. Bajaj, R., Ranaweera, S.L., Agrawal, D.P.: GPS: Location-Tracking Technology. IEEE Computer 35(4), 92–94 (2002)
20. Huang, J.Y., Tsai, C.H.: Improve GPS Positioning Accuracy with Context Awareness. In: The First IEEE International Conference on Ubi-media Computing, Lanzhou University, China, July 15-16, 2008, pp. 94–99 (2008)
21. Clark, J.: Hierarchical geometric models for visible surface algorithms. Communication of the ACM 19(10), 547–554 (1976)
22. DeHaemer, M.J., Zyda, M.J.: Simplification of objects rendered by polygonal approximations. Computer & Graphics 15(2), 175–184 (1991)
23. Nakamura, N., Nemoto, K., Shinohara, K.: Distributed virtual reality system for cooperative work. NEC Research and Development 35(4), 403–409 (1994)
24. Anupam, V., Bajaj, C., Schikore, D., Schikore, M.: Distributed and collaborative visualization. Computer 27, 37–43 (1994)
25. Singhal, S.K.: Effective remote modeling in large-scale distributed simulation and visualization environments, Stanford University, Stanford, CA, PhD thesis (1996), ftp://reports.stanford.edu/pub/cstr/reports/cs/tr/96/1574/CS-TR-96-1574.pdf (Accessed online 03/09/2009)
26. Huang, J.Y., et al.: Interaction Wearable Computer with Networked Virtual Environment. Accepted by HCI International 2009, July 19-24 2009, San Diego, CA, USA (2009)
27. Forman, G.H., Zahorjan, J.: The Challenges of Mobile Computing. Computer 27(4), 38–47 (1994)
28. Kim, P.J., Noh, Y.J.: Mobile Agent System Architecture for supporting Mobile Market Application Service in Mobile Computing Environment. In: 2003 International Conference on Geometric Modeling and Graphics (GMAG 2003), London, England, UK, July 16-18, 2003. IEEE Computer Society Press, Los Alamitos (2003)
29. Wann, J.P., Rushton, S.K., Mon-Williams, M.: Natural problems for stereoscopic depth perception in virtual environments. Vision Research 35(19), 2731–2736 (1995)
30. Witmer, B.G., Singer, M.J.: Measuring presence in virtual environments: A presence questionnaire. Presence: Teleoperators and Virtual Environments 7, 225–240 (1998)
31. Virtools, A.: Dassault Systèmes Technology, http://www.virtools.com/ (Accessed online 03/09/2009)
32. Šisler, V., Brom, C.: Designing an Educational Game: Case Study of 'Europe 2045'. In: Pan, Z., Cheok, D.A.D., Müller, W., El Rhalibi, A. (eds.) Transactions on Edutainment I. LNCS, vol. 5080, pp. 1–16. Springer, Heidelberg (2008)

Photo Realistic 3D Cartoon Face Modeling Based on Active Shape Model

Zhigeng Pan[1], Huansen Li[1], Mingmin Zhang[1], Yibin Ye[1], Xi Cheng[1],
Alvin Tang[2], and Ruigang Yang[3]

[1] State Key Lab of CAD&CG, Zhejiang University, Hangzhou, 310027, China
[2] Shanghai Research Center, Intel, Shanghai, China
[3] Department of Computer Science, College of Engineering, University of Kentucky, USA

Abstract. We present a novel framework to automatically build 3D carton face model from a single frontal face image. We use the improved ASM algorithm to automatically detect the deformed key feature control points in the face image. The deformation of the control points is compared to that of a standard (average) face, and exaggerated based on face shape and the type of organs and their pitch. RBF-based smooth interpolation is used to generate a 3D model from the exaggerated control points. The resulting 3D human face model not only preserves the identity of the subject in the photo, but also looks cartoonish with exaggerated facial features. Experiments with a large number of real photographs show that our framework is feasible.

Keywords: Feature detection, Cartoon deformation, 3D human face modeling.

1 Introduction

Cartoon portrait is defined to be the strengthening of some characteristics of the human face, so that it looks like that person but has some exaggerations. Psychologists believe that the identification of a specific person is his characteristics. Therefore, the use of cartoon portrait photographs could make a lasting impression on the people. At present, a cartoon portrait is widely used in artistic exaggeration, business software, etc.

MSN Cartoon [1] is an online system published by Microsoft, which can change a face image into a cartoon one. It firstly selects a template cartoon face, allowing the user to adjust the profile and add accessories; then converts the face to a comic cartoon face. The generated face presents more cartoon effect and less similarity to the photo. There are also many other approaches (e.g. [2, 3]) related to 2D image distortion, among which the common problem is the more cartoon effect and less similarity. Since the generated result after the cartoon processing is still a 2D image, little room is left for further processing, for example, it cannot be rotated and deformed later.

Our design goal of the 3D cartoon face is to combine the real face photo with a cartoon one. It can not only reflect the specific characteristics of the subjects, but also exaggerate some facial features (such as eye and nose) to make a lasting impression. The major components of our framework include: (a) automatically positioning of the eyebrows, eyes, nose and mouth according to the specific input picture and (b) smoothly blending of the characteristics points of the facial features with the standard face model to generate a 3D face model.

Z. Pan et al. (Eds.): Transactions on Edutainment II, LNCS 5660, pp. 299–311, 2009.

The further work of the matching and the exaggeration includes: the matching and exaggeration of the distance between the face features, and the matching and exaggeration of the face shape.

The remaining part of this paper is structured as follows: Section 2 presents related research results, Section 3 describes the improvement of the ASM algorithm; Section 4 introduces the integration with the true face photo to achieve 3D face modeling which meets the bound; Section 5 is the match and exaggeration of the facial features; and Section 6 is the analysis of the results; Section 7 concludes the paper.

2 Related Works

At present, the existed synthesis methods of human faces and cartoon expressions can be divided into two categories: image transformation based and on video detection based. Lee [4] used AAM method (active appearance model) to track video training data, and then created a 3D reference model, and finally exaggerated the feature points to create the cartoon face and expression. Tong [5] used 3D scanners to give the point cloud of the face, together with the special face picture to generate realistic 3D face models.

To detect the face and the facial features, the geometric characteristics-based method separates the face region and non-face region according to the similarity of the image color. Then projects the pixels to get a statistical histogram [6, 7, 8], and identifies the various organs [9, 10].

Another well-known algorithm is the ASM algorithm (Active Shape Model) [11-17], which is based on statistics. For a new input image, it first detects the face region, and then in a local area searches for the feature points through the rotation and scaling operation to find out the actual feature points which are closest to the provided points in the template. ASM algorithm can also indicate the edge of the facial features through the feature points.

However, the feature points obtained by the ASM algorithm do not include the characteristics of the forehead. We improved it by finding out the feature points in the forehead based on the facial feature parameters. And due to the possible small angle of the face inclination, we also rotate the face feature points according to the tilt angle of the forehead to improve the accuracy of the feature point location.

It is very important for the facial animation, facial feature analysis and face recognition to reconstruct the 3D face model according to 2D facial features in a photo. According to the face and texture information in a 2D face photo, Blanz [18] adopted the 3D facial deformation tools to reconstruct the 3D face model. Pighin [19] used multiple images and a standard reference model to restore the 3D face model. Liu [20] used the image processing technology to deal with two images in a video sequence, and reconstructing the 3D facial model. Zhao [21] used the 2D and 3D facial deformation technology to reconstruct the 3D facial shape.

The cartoon deformation methods can be divided into two categories: one is the interactive way of geometric distortion, the other is the deformation method based on sample feature extraction. The early methods [21, 22] mainly belong to the first class, and they provided interactive cartoon drawing tools, and exaggerating and artificially distorting the face based on the average human face. The second class methods [23], used template-based cartoon generator, and analyzing the different character faces and the styles of the face organs, and then applied to the new faces of specific people.

Our 3D cartoon face generation method is as follows: inputting a general photo of a frontal face, and outputting a 3D animated face model which can preserve the facial features of the person, and with exaggerated facial expressions (shown in Fig. 1).

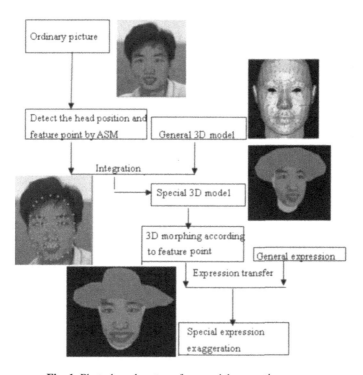

Fig. 1. Photo-based cartoon face model generation process

3   Image-Based Facial Feature Detection and Location

ASM algorithm [12] is based on statistics. At present, the on-line training templates are mostly from Caucasian, which are very different from Asian, for which this framework is designed for. Therefore, we do not use the training template in our algorithm, but directly deform the middle face template. Our algorithm uses 77 feature points, with 5 points corresponding to the eyebrows, 5 points around the eyes, 12 points in the nose, 11 points in the mouth, and 34 points in the outline of the face. The 77 points are listed as the vector:

$$X = (x_1, x_2, \cdots x_n, y_1, y_2, \cdots y_n)^T, \qquad n \in [1, N], \qquad (1)$$

Where $N = 2*77 = 154$.

The feature points in the standard face form the average face template, and by shape alignment with a particular face and through the PCA, we get:

$$X = \overline{X} + Pb , \tag{2}$$

Where X is the feature point vector of a specific face, and $\overline{X}$ is the feature point vector of an average face:

$$\overline{X} = \frac{1}{N}\sum_{i=1}^{N} X_i , \tag{3}$$

P is the main element analysis matrix including t features of the covariance matrix:

$$P = (p_0, p_1, \ldots p_{t-1})^T , \tag{4}$$

$$C_x = \frac{1}{N}\sum_{i=1}^{N}(X_i - \overline{X}_i)(X_i - \overline{X}_i)^T , \tag{5}$$

$$C_x P_i = \lambda_i P_i , \tag{6}$$

Where b is the difference between the particular facial features and the average ones:

$$b = p^T (X - \overline{X}) . \tag{7}$$

After alignment, rotation and translation, X can align with $\overline{X}$ as much as possible:

$$\min(\overline{X} - T(X))^2 , \tag{8}$$

$$\text{s.t. } T(X, X_c, s, \theta) = M(s, \theta)[X] + X_c , \tag{9}$$

$$M(s, \theta)\begin{bmatrix} x_k \\ y_k \end{bmatrix} = \begin{pmatrix} s\cos\theta & -s\sin\theta \\ s\sin\theta & s\cos\theta \end{pmatrix}\begin{bmatrix} x_k \\ y_k \end{bmatrix} , \tag{10}$$

$$X_c = (x_c, y_c, \ldots x_c, y_c)^T . \tag{11}$$

Through the shape alignment, the feature points in the standard face have been located in a specific facial photograph. The next step is the local fine-tuning of the gray-scale image information in the specific face. Searching for image borders can make the feature points align with the gray-scale border of the image.

Let a feature point which corresponds to the point in the image is (x_i, y_i), and its normal vector is (n_x, n_y), and the tangent Vector is (t_x, t_y), so that:

$$(t_x, t_y) = \frac{(d_x, d_y)}{\sqrt{d_x^2 + d_y^2}} .$$

$$\begin{cases} d_x = x_{i+1} - x_{i-1} \\ d_y = y_{i+1} - y_{i-1} \end{cases} \tag{12}$$

$$(n_x, n_y) = (-t_y, t_x) .$$

To search the largest gray gradient value, any feature point along the direction of normal vector is interpolated into several points:

$$(x, y) + i(n_x + n_y), \quad i = 1...N . \tag{13}$$

In order to prevent the noise interferes, the gray value of the pixel is set to the average Gaussian gray in this point:

$$g_i = 0.25g_{i-1} + 0.5g_i + 0.25g_{i+1} . \tag{14}$$

Reach the border of the highest gray-scale gradient by fine-tuning the feature points:

$$\max(\frac{d(g(x))}{dx}) . \tag{15}$$

For the jth feature point in the image, total N migration points should be measured:

$$g_j = [g_{j1}, g_{j2}, ... g_{jN}]^T . \tag{16}$$

The gray differential value of the jth point:

$$dg_j = [g_{j2} - g_{j1}, ... g_{jN} - g_{jN-1}]^T . \tag{17}$$

Among these points, taking the biggest one for feature adjustment points, and after the adjustments of the characteristics points, minimizes equation (18). when $f(b, X_c, s, \theta) < \varepsilon$, the algorithm is finished.

$$f(b, X_c, s, \theta) = |X - T(\overline{X} + Pb, X_c, s, \theta)| . \tag{18}$$

In the forehead part, because of the hair occlusion, the ASM algorithm can not achieve satisfactory results. The training template varies much depending on different hairstyles. Therefore current ASM algorithms do not include feature points in the forehead. We found that most of the human faces had a proportion so that each face could be divided into the upper, middle and lower part in a certain proportion. The additional points can be linear interpolated directly in accordance with the proportion relation and combined with the restriction in the face (as shown in Fig. 2).

Fig. 2. Feature point detection

If the face in the picture is skew, the direct interpolation will be incorrect. In Fig. 3, the blue points through rotation are more accurate than the red points which are directly interpolated to represent the outline of the face.

To determine the skew degree of the face, our method takes the center point of the two eyebrows with the nose point as the Y axis to determine the slope of the face. If the skew angle is greater than a certain value, it is necessary to carry out the spin operation of insertion point on the forehead.

As the outlines of human face and some facial features are curve shapes (the outline of human face can be seen as a cubic curve). Feature points can be quickly obtained by curve fitting based on the feature points which are detected by the ASM (using the least squares curve-fitting method).

Fig. 3. The feature points on the forehead when the face is skew

4 Integration with the Face Image

To meet the above constraints of the face detection, we try to model the face based on the face characteristics: with a standard 3D model as the general model, and through the establishment of the mapping relationship between the standard model and the reconstruction model (especially the characteristic points). By the panning, zooming and key points adjustment of the general model, we eventually obtain a specific model. Finally we do the local deformation and adjustments, including the location, direction, shape based on the standard model.

First of all, we look for a standard 3D general face model, which must be a good neutral model for men and women, middle age, and with a neutral facial expression. The contour of the Asian model generated by the FaceGen software is shown in Fig. 4 and Fig.5. Our method generate a specific 3D human face model through the transformation from the neutral model to a specific face model, and then create a specific 3D face by realistic texture mapping to the specific 3D human face model.

In the amending process from the neutral face model to the particular face model, it is necessary to carry out two transformation operations. The first one is the overall transformation to the neutral face model, which is to complete the amending of the overall face outlines, and make the face model fitting for the location of the specific face shape and the main organs. And then we do the local transformation to the whole neutral face model in order to amend the shape and the size of the brow, eyes, mouth, nose based on a specific person, and marking the specific features in the neutral face model. The current method employs the standard model as a general human face model, and matching the points in the frontal human face photos to adjust a number of key points to obtain a specific face model.

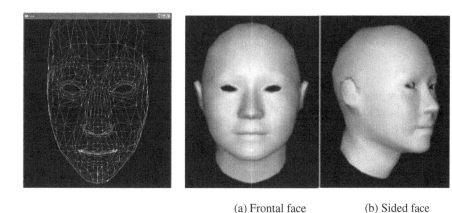

| (a) Frontal face | (b) Sided face |

Fig. 4. The neutral face model   **Fig. 5.** The neutral human face entity model

5 Face Matching and Exaggeration

First of all, we normalize the image and the size of the model. Let the point in the image to be (x,y), and the ratio of the horizontal to the vertical of the face is $r(0 \leq r \leq 1)$, and the region of the face is $D = \{(x,y) \mid 0 < x < r, 0 < y < 1\}$, the point in the standard model is (x_m, y_m, z_m), and the ratio of the horizontal to the vertical of the face is $r_m (0 \leq r_m \leq 1)$, and the face region

$$D_m = \{(x_m, y_m, z_m) \mid 0 < x_m < r_m, 0 < y_m < 1, 0 < z_m < \frac{z_{max}}{y_{max}}\}. \tag{19}$$

The point in the model after the transformation is (x_p, y_p, z_p), which is in

$$D_p = \{(x_p, y_p, z_p) \mid 0 < x_p < 1, 0 < y_p < 1, 0 < z_p < 1\}. \tag{20}$$

Assuming the point in the standard human face model is:

$$X = \begin{pmatrix} x_1 & \cdots & x_n \\ y_1 & \cdots & y_n \\ z_1 & \cdots & z_n \end{pmatrix}, \tag{21}$$

Make them matching with the feature points detected in the photographs:

$$x = \begin{pmatrix} x_1 & \cdots & x_m \\ y_1 & \cdots & y_m \end{pmatrix}. \tag{22}$$

Then the matching problem is the iteration which looks for:

$$c = (r_x, r_y, r_z, t_x, t_y, t_z) .$$ (23)

Let:

$$\min f(c) = \min | P(R(c)X - t(c)) - x |^2 ,$$ (24)

$$R(c) = R_z(r_z)R_x(r_x)R(r_y) ,$$ (25)

$$t(c) = (t_x, t_y, t_z)^T .$$ (26)

The feature matching makes the feature points in the 3D model come as close as possible to those in the 2D image. We deform the feature points in the 3D model to the 2D features points. After pasting texture, the 3D standard model will be a specific 3D model of a person.

We employ the RBF (Radial Basis Function) [24]-based interpolation method to achieve the constraint-based grid deformation. Given a set of constraints: a set of 3D points $X = \{X_1, X_2 \ldots\ldots X_m\} \subset R3$, corresponding to a set of values, $u = \{u_1, u_2 \ldots\ldots u_m\}$, we would like to use these restraints, through interpolation the $S(X)$ function, to get a solid function, and let:

$$S(X_i) = f_i , i = 1, \ldots , m.$$ (27)

Through the experiments, we select the three order tuning function to calculate the values of the other non characteristic grid points:

$$S^*(x) = c_1 + c_2 x + c_3 y + c_4 z + \sum_{i=1}^{N} \lambda_i (x - X_i)^3 .$$ (28)

To ensure the smooth interpolation, we need to meet the following constraints:

$$\sum_{i=1}^{N} \lambda_i = \sum_{i=1}^{N} \lambda_i x_i = \sum_{i=1}^{N} \lambda_i y_i = \sum_{i=1}^{N} \lambda_i z_i = 0 .$$ (29)

Thus a linear solving system is required in getting the specific RBF function:

$$\begin{bmatrix} \Phi_{11} & \Phi_{12} & \cdots & \Phi_{1N} & 1 & x_1 & y_1 & z_1 \\ \Phi_{21} & \Phi_{22} & \cdots & \Phi_{2N} & 1 & x_2 & y_2 & z_2 \\ \vdots & \vdots & & \vdots & \vdots & \vdots & \vdots & \vdots \\ \Phi_{N1} & \Phi_{N2} & \cdots & \Phi_{NN} & 1 & x_N & y_N & z_N \\ 1 & 1 & \cdots & 1 & 0 & 0 & 0 & 0 \\ x_1 & x_2 & \cdots & x_N & 0 & 0 & 0 & 0 \\ y_1 & y_2 & \cdots & y_N & 0 & 0 & 0 & 0 \\ z_1 & z_2 & \cdots & z_N & 0 & 0 & 0 & 0 \end{bmatrix} \begin{bmatrix} \lambda_1 \\ \lambda_2 \\ \vdots \\ \lambda_N \\ c_1 \\ c_2 \\ c_3 \\ c_4 \end{bmatrix} = \begin{bmatrix} u_1 \\ u_2 \\ \vdots \\ u_N \\ 0 \\ 0 \\ 0 \\ 0 \end{bmatrix}$$ (30)

where : $\Phi_{ij} = | x_i - x_j |^3 .$

The interpolation attributes of RBF function well meet the request of constraints-based grid deformation inside and outside without additional demands of border bound, while the energy minimizing properties ensure the continuity and smoothness of the mapping. Meanwhile, the feature points can be non-linear and arbitrary scattered points.

In the following description, we divide the features in the face into three categories to do the cartoon deformation according to specific facial features.

(1) Organ characteristics: the forehead, eyebrows, eyes, nose, mouth and chin
(2) The pitch characteristics of the organs
(3) Characteristics of the face shape

The general characteristics of the organ mainly lie in the changes of the width and height, so we can do the linear variable ratio transformation to all the points in the model. Taking the forehead as an example, let the width of the forehead is W_b, and the width of his forehead in the standard model is $\overline{W_b}$, then for the forehead region:

$$D_b = \{(x_p, y_p, z_p) \mid 0 < x_p < x_{max}, 0 < y_p < W_b, 0 < z_p < z_{max}\} . \tag{31}$$

The model vertex in the region is (x_p, y_p, z_p). Keeping the x, z directions unchanged, y direction makes the linear variable ratio transformation,

$$\begin{cases} x_p = x_m \\ y_p = \dfrac{W_b}{\overline{W_b}} y_m \\ z_p = z_m \end{cases} \tag{32}$$

For the exaggeration of the different organs pitch on the face, we divide the face into several rectangular regions to compare with the standard face, as shown in Fig. 6.

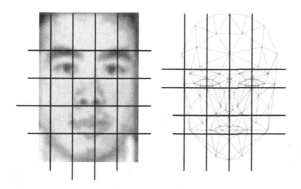

Fig. 6. The characteristics representation of the organ pitches

Fig. 7 is the characteristics representation of the face that the triangle angle is decided as a long face or a round face. The value that the face in the Ω region occupies the background is a decision of a shape face or a square face.

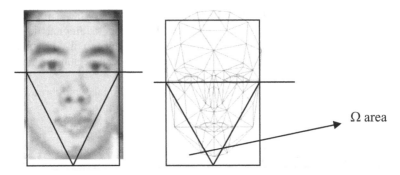

Ω area

Fig. 7. The characteristics representation of the face

The cartoon deformation only selects one or two features to exaggerate, which can reflect the most specific and distinctive characteristics of the person. For the different organs, the different organ pitches and the different face shapes, the feature value is:

$$\frac{(x_i - \tilde{x}_i)}{\tilde{x}_i} * 100\% , \tag{33}$$

Where x_i is the feature point in the specific human face, and $\tilde{x}_i$ is the feature point in the standard human face, and this percentage expresses the difference between the specific face and the standard face. The greater the difference, the more obvious the feature is. However we must also consider the difference of the other people in this feature. That is the coefficient of variation:

$$V_i = \frac{S_i}{A_i} * 100\% , \tag{34}$$

Where S_i is the standard deviation and A_i is the average, then we select the largest value in characteristics to perform the cartoon deformation:

$$F_i = \frac{(x_i - \tilde{x}_i)}{\tilde{x}_i} * \frac{1}{V_i} * 100\% . \tag{35}$$

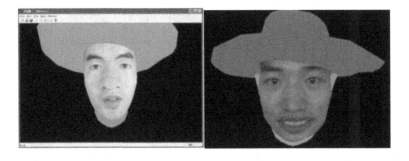

Fig. 8. Nose deformation   **Fig. 9.** Mouth deformation

Fig. 8 is the result after the smooth deformation (nose becomes bigger smoothly), and Fig. 9 is the mouth effect after cartoon deformation.

Fig. 10. Algorithm steps and its results

6   Results Analysis and Conclusions

Fig. 10 shows the 3D human head processed with the synthesis algorithm presented in this paper, and Fig. 11 shows some results generated by our system. After testing a large amount of images, we found that as the impact of the light and the resolution, the images input by a video camera get lower quality effect with comparison to the image taken by a digital camera. However, seeing from the test results, there are small impacts in the detection effect using ASM algorithm in the frontal feature points. The test results of 300 images are as follows:

1) Over 90% of photo detection effect is satisfactory.

2) About 10% of detection in the images appears certain deviations, and the deviations are most concentrated in the jaw region. A preliminary reason analysis indicates that the colors in the chin and neck are very similar, which causes to unclear dividing border, and the algorithm is convergence in a place of the neck, and that leading to the error.

In conclusion, we have developed a photo realistic 3D cartoon face modeling method based on improved active shape model. Our challenge was twofold: the realistic presentation of an ordinary face and the caricature exaggeration of the characterize attributes. Currently, our technique is limited to faces in frontal views. Extending our technique to handle general views is a challenging direction for further research.

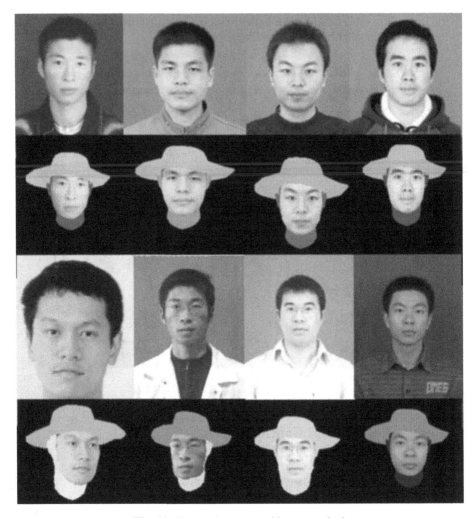

Fig. 11. The results generated by our method

Acknowledgements. This project is co-supported by Intel project, Key NSFC (Grant NO: 60533080) and the On-line Shanghai Expo project: Intelligent Interaction and Navigation in VE (Grant NO: 08dz0580208). And the authors would like to express thanks to Mr. Jing Tong from Hehai University, who has given useful help on the implementation.

References

1. http://cartoon.msn.com.cn/
2. http://www.aniface.com
3. http://www.skycn.com/soft/15444.html

4. Lee, E.-J., Kwon, J.-Y., Lee, I.-K.: Caricature video. Journal of Computer Animation and Virtual Worlds 18(4-5), 279–288 (2007)
5. Tong, J., Guan, H.: Fast Modeling algorithm of 3D face for using in film and animation. Computer Application 27(4), 1013–1016 (2007)
6. Brunelli, R., Poggio, T.: Face recognition: features versus templates. IEEE Transactions on Pattern Analysis and Machine Intelligence 15(10), 1042–1052 (1993)
7. Li, H., Yang, H., Yuan, B.: Feature extraction in human face recognition system. Journal of Beijing Jiaotong University 25(2), 18–21 (2001)
8. Peng, Z., Tao, L., Xu, G., Zhang, H.: Detecting facial features based on color segmentation and KL transform. J. Tsinghua Univ (Sci &Tech) 41(4/5), 218–221 (2001)
9. Wang, X., Shi, Y.: A method of face detection based on eyes Feature. Application Research Of Computers (1), 239–243 (2006)
10. Tang, L., Li, H., Chen, J.: Face Detection and Extraction Based on Part Eigenvalu. Computer Engineering 33(10), 210–211 (2007)
11. Zhou, R., Zhou, J., Chen, Y., Liu, J., Li, L.: Caricature Generation Based on Facial Feature Analysis. Journal of Computer Aided Design & Computer Graphics 18(9), 1362–1366 (2006)
12. Cootes, T., Ed. Baldock, R., Graham, J.: An Introduction to Active Shape Models. In: Image Processing and Analysis, pp. 223–248. Oxford University Press, Oxford (2000)
13. Milborrow, S., Nicolls, F.: Locating facial features with an extended active shape model. In: Forsyth, D., Torr, P., Zisserman, A. (eds.) ECCV 2008, Part IV. LNCS, vol. 5305, pp. 504–513. Springer, Heidelberg (2008)
14. Xu, G.: Gabor Active Shape Model and Its' Application to Face Segmentation. pp. 19–30. Dalian University of Technology (2005)
15. Liu, A., Zhou, Y., Guan, X.: Application of Improved Active Shape Model in Face Positioning. Computer Engineering 33(18), 227–230 (2007)
16. Ge, X., Yang, J., Zhang, T., Du, C.: Application of an Improved Active Shape Model Method in Face Features Location. Journal of Shanghai Jiaotong University 41(8), 1320–1329 (2007)
17. Dong, S., Luo, S.: Two-dimensional grey-level models for an active shape model. Beijing Biomedical Engineering 26(3), 241–244 (2007)
18. Blanz, V., Vetter, T.: Amorphable model for the synthesis of 3D faces. In: Proceedings of the 26th Annual Conference on Computer Gaphics and Interactive Techniques, pp. 187–194. ACM Press/Addison-Wesley (1999)
19. Pighin, F., Hecker, J., Lischinski, D., Szeliski, R., Salesin, D.H.: Synthesizing realistic facial expressions from photographs. Computer Graphics 32, 75–84 (1998)
20. Liu, Z., Zhang, Z., Jacobs, C., Cohen, M.: Rapid modeling of animated faces from video images. In: Proceedings of the 8th ACM International Conference on Multimedia, pp. 475–476. ACM Press, New York (2000)
21. Zhao, M., Chua, T.-S., Sim, T.: Morphable face reconstruction with multiple images. In: Proceedings of 7th International Conference on Automatic Face and Gesture Recognition, pp. 597–602. IEEE Computer Society Press, Los Alamitos (2006)
22. Akleman, E.: Making caricatures with morphing. In: Proceedings of the Art and Interdisciplinary Programs of SIGGRAPH 1997, p. 145. ACM Press, New York (1997)
23. Fujiwara, T., Tominaga, M., Murakami, K., Koshimizu, H.: Web-PICASSO: internet implementation of facial caricatture system PICASSO. In: Proceedings of 3rd International Conference on Advances in Multimodal Interfaces, pp. 151–159. Springer, Berlin (2000)
24. Jin, W.: Study on Video-Based Face Expression Modeling, pp. 32–34. Zhejiang University (2003)

Author Index